CW00557444

Politics and Culture in Wilhelmine Germany

Politics and Culture in Wilhelmine Germany
The Case of Industrial Architecture

Matthew Jefferies

BERG PUBLISHERS
Oxford / Washington D.C., USA

First published in 1995 by
Berg Publishers Limited
Editorial offices:
150 Cowley Road, Oxford, OX4 1JJ, UK
13590 Park Center Road, Herndon, VA 22071, USA

© Matthew Jefferies

Library of Congress Cataloging-in-Publication Data
A catalogue record for this book is available from the Library of Congress.

British Library Cataloguing in Publication Data
A catalogue record for this book is available from the British Library.

ISBN 0 85496 945 4

Printed in the United Kingdom by WBC Bookbinders, Bridgend,
Mid Glamorgan.

Contents

Acknowledgements

This book would not have been possible without the support of a large number of institutions and individuals. Financial assistance was provided by the British Academy, the DAAD and a 'Hanseatic Scholarship' from Hamburg's Stiftung FVS. I am grateful to the numerous archivists and librarians in Great Britain and Germany who helped in the gathering of source material, and to the academic staff of the Universities of Sussex, Oxford, Hamburg and Cologne, who were responsible for fostering and developing my interest in German history. Particular thanks are due to John Röhl, Hermann Hipp, Roland Günter, Michael John, Anthony Nicholls, James Joll and Joan Campbell. Above all I must thank Hartmut Pogge von Strandmann, for a steady stream of perceptive comments and valuable suggestions.

All photographs in this book are by the author unless otherwise stated. They were prepared for publication by the staff of the Photographic Department of Manchester University and published with financial assistance from the University's research support fund. The final manuscript was typed by Liz Brock, whose efforts deserve a special thank you, and copy-edited by Julie Ward. Some of the material included in Chapter Two first appeared in *History* and parts of Chapter Seven were first published in the *Journal of Design History*; I would like to express my gratitude to the editors and publishers concerned. Last but not least, I am indebted to my parents, who have been a source of patience, support and understanding for as long as I can remember. This book is dedicated to them.

List of Abbreviations

AEG	Allgemeine Elektrizitäts-Gesellschaft
BASF	Badische Anilin- und Soda Fabrik AG
BDA	Bund Deutscher Architekten
BdI	Bund der Industriellen
CVDI	Centralverband Deutscher Industrieller
DDP	Deutsche Demokratische Partei
DLBAG	Deutsch-Luxemburgische Bergwerks- und Hütten AG
DNVP	Deutschnationale Volkspartei
DWB	Deutscher Werkbund
FVP	Fortschrittliche Volkspartei
GBAG	Gelsenkirchener Bergwerks-AG
GDK	Gewerkschaft Deutscher Kaiser
GHH	Gutehoffnungshütte AG
HB	Hansabund für Gewerbe, Handel und Industrie
HVV	Handelsvertragsverein
MAN	Maschinenfabrik Augsburg-Nürnberg
NCR	National Cash Register Company
NSV	National-Soziale Verein
NW&K	Norddeutsche Wollkämmerei und Kammgarnspinnerei
RWE	Rheinisch-Westfälische Elektrizitätswerke
RWKS	Rheinisch-Westfälisches Kohlen-Syndikat
SPD	Sozial-Demokratische Partei Deutschlands
VSI	Verein Sächsischer Industrieller

List of Illustrations

(All photographs by the author unless otherwise stated)

Introduction

The English historian David Blackbourn, noting that 'the German bourgeoisie has had a bad press',[1] once claimed: 'we hear much about the Germany of the spiked helmet and too little about top-hatted Germany, much about the feudalisation of the German bourgeoisie and too little about the embourgeoisement of German society'.[2] This book may help to redress the balance, for it is 'top-hatted Germany' which lies at the heart of the following chapters.

Whilst the question 'who ruled in Berlin?' has lost none of its perennial fascination for historians of Wilhelmine Germany, it has to some extent been superseded by another deceptively simple query: 'how modern was the *Kaiserreich*?'. One of the many historians to have wrestled with this theme was the late Thomas Nipperdey: 'was it an authoritarian state, a society of classes and vassals, thoroughly old-fashioned, or was it on the verge of modernity, poised to become the bourgeois society of the present century? Was it up a dead-end street, incapable of further development without war and revolution, or was it on the way to more reasonable, liberal, and democratic forms? Was it a precursor to 1933, or rather more of Weimar and the Federal Republic?'[3]

The alleged failure of Germany to undergo a thorough process of 'modernisation' in the nineteenth and early twentieth centuries has often been cited as the underlying cause of the nation's later misfortunes. It is suggested that the survival in powerful positions of 'pre-industrial élites', and the apparent willingness of bourgeois Germans to embrace 'feudal' values, ensured that Germany did not take the western world's recommended route to modernity, but instead embarked on a *Sonderweg*, with fateful consequences for all concerned. For the generation of 'critical' historians, which first came to prominence in the Federal Republic during the heady days of the late 1960s, the German middle classes appeared to bear a particularly heavy burden of guilt. Not only had they failed to fulfil their historic function in 1848, but had thereafter shown an unhealthy willingness to compromise with the old élites, preferring personal

1. D. Blackbourn, *Populists and Patricians*, Oxford, 1984, p. 67.
2. D. Blackbourn, *ibid.*, p.13.
3. T. Nipperdey, *Wie modern war das Kaiserreich? Das Beispiel der Schule*, Opladen, 1986, p.5.

advancement to progressive reform. This, it is suggested, left a legacy of illiberal attitudes and deep structural flaws in German society for generations to come.[4]

Some of the most pervasive images of the Wilhelmine middle class are indeed far from flattering. The entrepreneur or industrialist, eager to ape *Junker* values and rituals, was, we are told, too concerned with the pursuit of titles, country estates and reserve officer status to grasp the reins of government. He was therefore unable to perform the same function as his counterparts elsewhere in Western Europe. Meanwhile the educated *Bildungsbürger,* unsettled by industrialisation, urbanisation and the 'parvenu' values of a materialist culture, had turned his back on the sordid world of politics altogether, retreating into that dark slough of despond once dubbed by Fritz Stern as 'cultural despair'.[5]

In recent years, however, some of the fundamental assumptions behind such stereotypes have been challenged, most notably in the work of David Blackbourn and Geoff Eley, who have highlighted the gradual but far-reaching bourgeois transformation of German society in the second half of the nineteenth century.[6] Without resurrecting the apologist view of an imperial *belle époque,* they argue that the 'Imperial state between 1871 and 1918' was 'compatible with the adequate realisation of legitimate interests and aspirations of the bourgeoisie'[7] and stress that the 'heroic bourgeois revolution' is as problematic as the existence of a 'normal' or model pattern of development.[8] Whilst acknowledging the disproportionate influence of the *Junker* at some of the highest political levels, in the officer corps and in the Prussian bureaucracy, they list many ways in which the *Bürgertum* increasingly set the tone of life in Wilhelmine Germany, from taste and dress to associational life and professionalisation, and point to such disparate areas of achievement as local government, science, and the law.

The initial reaction in Germany to Blackbourn and Eley's work was critical, even hostile, but the lively debate provoked by their book *Mythen*

---

4. The best known and most complete expression of these views is Hans-Ulrich Wehler's *Das deutsche Kaiserreich, 1871-1918*, Göttingen, 1973 (in English as *The German Empire*, Leamington Spa, 1985). See also R. Dahrendorf, *Society and Democracy in Germany*, London, 1968; V. Berghahn, *Germany and the Approach of War in 1914*, London, 1973.

5. F. Stern, *The Politics of Cultural Despair. A Study in the Rise of the Germanic Ideology*, Berkeley, 1963. See also G. Stark, *Entrepreneurs of Ideology*, Chapel Hill, 1981.

6. See D. Blackbourn & G. Eley, *The Peculiarities of German History*, Oxford, 1984; G. Eley, *From Unification to Nazism. Reinterpreting the German Past*, London, 1986; D. Blackbourn, *Populists and Patricians. Essays in Modern German History*, London, 1987. For Eley's most recent contribution to the debate see G. Eley, 'Putting German Liberalism into Context: Liberalism, Europe, and the Bourgeoisie 1840-1914', Ann Arbor, 1990.

7. G. Eley in D. Blackbourn & G. Eley, *Peculiarities*, p.146.

8. G. Eley, *ibid.*, p.144.

deutscher Geschichtsschreibung,[9] certainly helped to revive academic interest in the *Kaiserreich*'s middle classes. The late 1980s saw the appearance of a large number of volumes on *Bürgerlichkeit* in general and the nineteenth century *Bürgertum* in particular, published under the auspices of historians such as Jürgen Kocka and Werner Conze.[10] At the heart of their investigations was a desire to view the German *Bürgertum* in a wider European context and hence a willingness to reassess the notion of the German *Sonderweg* at an empirical level: in the professions, in the cultural sphere and in the pattern of everyday life. This has prompted Geoff Eley to remark that Kocka's recent work 'seems to have conceded much of the argument in *Peculiarities*'.[11] Even so, Germany's *Defizit an Bürgerlichkeit* and 'incomplete' modernisation look set to remain matters of historical controversy for many years to come.

Since the response of German citizens to 'modernity', in all its guises, is an underlying theme of the seven chapters which follow, it is important we give some consideration to the difficulties in definition which the concepts of 'modernity' and 'modernisation' present. Just as Blackbourn and Eley have questioned the use of the British 'model' as a yardstick for change in Germany, so 'modernisation theory' – developed by American social scientists in the 1950s and 1960s to explain the profound social and cultural transformations which accompany industrialisation – no longer enjoys unreserved acceptance. The theory, which was quickly adopted by the 'critical' school of German historians, seemed to offer a useful method for the comparison of different national experiences, and certainly lent a convenient name to a complex set of structural changes. Its supposed strengths were, however, soon revealed as weaknesses: theorists were accused of ignoring national or regional idiosyncrasies, and of defining 'modernisation' in such broad terms that it became 'almost impossible to

9. For the controversy aroused by D. Blackbourn & G. Eley's *Mythen deutscher Geschichtsschreibung. Die gescheiterte bürgerliche Revolution von 1848* see the long introduction to its revised and expanded English edition, *Peculiarities*.

10. Jürgen Kocka's year-long research project at Bielefeld University's Centre of Inter-Disciplinary Research (1986-87) produced a number of books, including: J. Kocka (ed.), *Bürger und Bürgerlichkeit im 19. Jahrhundert*, Göttingen, 1987; J. Kocka (ed.), *Bürgertum in 19. Jahrhundert* (3 vols.), Göttingen, 1988; H. Siegrist (ed.), *Bürgerliche Berufe. Beiträge zur Sozialgeschichte der Professionen, freien Berufe und Akademiker im internationalen Vergleich*, Göttingen, 1988. In addition, twelve sessions of Werner Conze's 'Arbeitskreis für moderne Sozialgeschichte' were devoted to the theme of the *Bildungsbürgertum* between 1980 and 1987. See W. Conze & J. Kocka (eds), *Bildungsbürgertum in 19. Jahrhundert*, Stuttgart, 1985. Mention should also be made of the 1976 volume, edited by Klaus Vondung and entitled *Das wilhelminische Bildungsbürgertum; Zur Sozialgeschichte seiner Ideen*, Göttingen, 1976. Finally, there is also an English-language volume, David Blackbourn and Richard Evans's *The German Bourgeoisie*, London, 1991.

11. G. Eley, 'Putting German liberalism into context', p.36.

identify precisely the range of phenomena to which the concept [was] intended to apply'.[12]

The tendency, moreover, of modernisation theorists to judge national progress against an idealised Anglo-American model led to charges of ethnocentricity, and their implied equation of modernity with virtue at times seemed dangerously smug. Criticisms were also levelled at the apparent assumption that 'tradition' and 'modernity' were mutually exclusive characteristics, when 'traditional' values and institutions could in fact be found in any number of 'modern' industrial societies. As one critic argued, the dynamics of modernisation did not consist of 'the substitution of one set of attributes for another . . . but rather in their mutual interpenetration and transformation'.[13]

Nevertheless, for those German historians, such as Hans-Ulrich Wehler, who have long attempted to win wider acceptance for the use of social science and its tools in historical research, modernisation theory remains a useful means of highlighting Germany's retarded progress down a well-worn path. Certainly no one can doubt the contribution made to our understanding of Imperial Germany by Wehler's *Das deutsche Kaiserreich 1871–1918*, and the many valuable monographs which have emerged in its wake. Wehler's 'problem-oriented structural analysis' is not, however, well suited to documenting the subtler shifts and changes of history, preferring to paint an impressive, but static, panorama of the Second Empire from a decidedly lofty perspective.

As Thomas Nipperdey noted in a review of Wehler's *Gesellschafts-geschichte,* 'modernisation' is seldom so clear cut: 'The multifariousness of the modernisation process constantly produces partial modernities, disjunctions, different mixtures of tradition and modernity, and conflicts stemming from that'.[14] 'History is grey', he argues, whereas Wehler's appears to be black and white.[15] In Nipperdey's view, any assessment of the strength of 'modernising' elements within Wilhelmine society, or of the relative 'modernity' of Wilhelmine Germany as a whole, should be based on detailed empirical analysis rather than the imposition of a 'straitjacket of interpretation'. This may seem to be little more than common sense, but it is a useful premise nonetheless.

12. D. Tipps, 'Modernization theory and the study of national societies: a critical perspective', in *Comparative Studies in Society and History*, vol. 15 (1973), p.217. See also H. Kaelble (ed.), *Probleme der Modernisierung in Deutschland*, Opladen, 1978; H.-U. Wehler, *Modernisierungstheorie und Geschichte*, Göttingen, 1975; P. Flora, *Modernisierungsforschung. Zur empirischen Analyse der gesellschaftlichen Entwicklung*, Opladen, 1974.
13. D. Tipps, 'Modernization theory', p.214.
14. T. Nipperdey, 'Wehlers Gesellschaftsgeschichte', in *Geschichte und Gesellschaft*, vol. 14 (1988), p.404.
15. T. Nipperdey, *ibid.*, p.415.

One consequence of the historiographical upheavals of the 1960s has been a preoccupation with the question of 'continuity' in German history. Whilst this is undoubtedly a worthwhile and necessary avenue for historians to explore, the ultimate effect of viewing developments between 1871 and 1918 in the context of 1933 is to devalue Imperial Germany as an object of historical interest in its own right. Curiously, the architectural history of the period has suffered a similar fate: whilst much has been written about architecture in the Weimar Republic and the Third Reich, comparatively little research has been carried out on the architectural issues of the Wilhelmine years, and that almost exclusively concerned with the origins of architecture's Modern movement, which made such an impact in Germany after World War One.

Over the years the definition of 'modernism' in the arts has been drawn every bit as widely as 'modernisation' in the social and economic sense, a term with which it shares more than just a semantic affinity. Without a degree of 'modernisation', 'modernism' would have been unthinkable, yet the relationship between the two was always problematic, not least because 'modernism' was in part a reaction to, and a rejection of, the very forces which created and sustained it. There can be no doubt, however, that Wilhelmine Germany did support a nascent modern movement of considerable breadth and influence, thriving alongside the philistinism and cultural conservatism for which the period is often remembered. Indeed, it has been suggested that, from the turn of the century at least, Germany was the 'modernist nation par excellence',[16] as its artists attempted to come to terms with the profound tensions caused by dynamic industrial growth, urbanisation and technological change.

Of course, this in itself does not prove the existence of the other sort of 'modernity', whose absence is so lamented by the likes of Wehler, but it is nevertheless significant. Progressive architects and expressionist dramatists, dance reformers and secessionist painters made their names on the back of patronage from bankers and businessmen, academics and industrialists. Yet despite this, the middle classes of Wilhelmine Germany continue to be chided for a failure to assert their own values on society, an inability to make a deep and distinctive impression on German life. This book investigates the struggle to do just that in the field of industrial architecture; an impeccably *bürgerlich* area of human activity, inextricably linked to the motor of capitalist change itself.

It is sometimes suggested that the Wilhelmine bourgeoisie 'retreated' into areas such as the arts, science and technology as an alternative to, or

---

16. M. Eksteins, 'When death was young..: Germany, Modernism and the Great War' in R. Bullen, H. Pogge von Strandmann, A. Polonsky (eds.), *Ideas into Politics*, London, 1984, p.30.

substitute for, political life, where change proved to be a slow and arduous process. It would be a mistake, however, for political historians to dismiss the socio-cultural sphere as irrelevant. As Richard Evans has noted, the area of human activity located between the dynamic economy and the hidebound – though by no means inert – political system is of crucial importance to any judgement of Wilhelmine Germany's modernity.[17] Of particular interest are those areas in which the economic, political and cultural spheres came into direct contact, extending beyond the exchange of ideas to collaboration on a practical level; where 'modernisation' and 'modernism' rubbed shoulders in the shaping of a new Germany.

It is a commonplace that architecture reflects the ideas and values of a given society. More accurately, perhaps, it is an expression of the distribution of power within society, reflecting the shifting fortunes of individuals and institutions, cities and classes. The appearance, function, layout and location of buildings change as society does, sometimes imperceptibly, sometimes in startling leaps. At the same time, however, it is important to remember that architecture is much more than a 'mirror': it also plays an active role in shaping human behaviour and social practice. Recent attempts by progressive art historians to pursue an anthropocentric or 'subject-oriented' architectural history can be seen as belated recognition of that fact.

In general, however, it must be said that mainstream architectural history has neglected both the context in which the built environment evolves, and the impact of such change on society, preferring to view buildings as isolated aesthetic achievements rather than cultural products. It has largely been left to specialists from other disciplines to investigate architecture in its social and historical context, to ask the sort of important questions posed by Anthony D. King in his *Buildings and Society:* 'what can we understand about a society by examining its buildings and physical environment? What can we understand about buildings and environments by examining the society in which they exist?'[18]

In recent years awareness has grown that historic industrial buildings represent a valuable source of information about the past, to be viewed and used as 'a cipher for social and political change, as a key to the everyday lives of the masses in the industrial age'.[19] The efforts of respected historians to develop approaches to history 'from below' or of

17. R. Evans, 'Liberalism and Society: The Feminist Movement and Social Change' in R. Evans (ed.), *Society and Politics in Wilhelmine Germany*, London, 1978, p.207.

18. A.D. King (ed.), *Buildings and Society. Essays on the Social Development of the Built Environment*, London, 1980, p.1.

19. M. Schumacher, quoted by T. Schleper, 'Kunstwissenschaft und Fabrikbau', PhD thesis, Osnabrück University, 1987, p.37.

'everyday life', together with the popularity of grass roots movements for local history, industrial archaeology and preservation, have led increasing numbers of people to look at old industrial buildings in a new way, even if the number of architectural historians to show an interest has remained small.

A bewildering array of terms, from the 'history of material culture' to 'visual social history', have been employed in an effort to find an appropriate name for the study of historic places of industrial production and distribution, but in general the *Begriffsflut* has succeeded only in highlighting the complex nature of the subject, which can involve not only architectural, social and economic history, but the history of business and technology too. It is significant that the acknowledged pioneers of the field, Kenneth Hudson in Britain, Jan Pazdur in Poland and Roland Günter in Germany, each arrived at the study of historic industrial buildings by a very different route, but have all subsequently stressed the importance of an inter-disciplinary approach.

In Germany, the concept of *Industriekultur*, most notably promoted by Wolfgang Ruppert and Hermann Glaser's *Centrum Industriekultur* in Nuremberg (founded 1979), has gained a particular popularity, even fashionability, over the past decade. The Nuremberg centre, which defines *Industriekultur* simply as 'the cultural forms which develop along with the process of industrialisation',[20] stresses the need for society to be actively engaged in a dialogue with its own history and environment. In an attempt to get away from art history's traditional fetish for façades, *Industriekulturforscher* emphasise the 'subject-oriented' approach; that is to say, their research concentrates on the human dimension, the socio-cultural milieu evoked by old industrial buildings, rather than the objects themselves.

In this way, the utilitarian and anonymous factory is held to offer as much to the historian as the industrial building of striking or innovative design. The value of the term *Industriekultur* is, however, somewhat undermined by its widespread and at times contradictory usage, turning up in the titles of 1960s tracts by Kofler and Marcuse, in works of Catholic social history, and on the cover of Tilmann Buddensieg's 1979 book about the architect-designer Peter Behrens.[21] The last usage is particularly

20. W. Ruppert, quoted by K. Tenfelde, 'Schwierigkeiten mit dem Alltag', in *Geschichte und Gesellschaft*, vol. 10 (1984), p.386 note 41.
21. On the use of the term *Industriekultur* see Klaus Tenfelde, *ibid.*. Also W. Weber, 'Von der "Industriearchäologie" über das "industrielle Erbe" zur "Industriekultur". Überlegungen zum Thema einer handlungsorientierten Technikhistorie', in U. Troitsch & G. Wohlauf (eds.), *Technik-Geschichte*, Frankfurt, 1980; and P. Backes, 'Abenteuerreise in den Alltag? Über den Industrietourismus', in *Tendenzen. Zeitschrift für engagierte Kunst*, no. 159 (1987).

confusing, since Buddensieg's work – which used a much more conventional art history methodology – was fiercely criticised by at least one leading *Industriekulturforscher* for its 'neo-conservative' approach.[22]

The Nuremberg team has itself been responsible for a number of important publications, including a photographic history of the industrial workplace and a collection of essays on Nuremberg's passage through the 'machine age'.[23] The latter formula has been repeated in similar volumes for other German cities, throwing up a wealth of material on a broad spectrum of themes, of which architecture is only one.[24] More specifically, the historic industrial buildings of cities such as Frankfurt, Bielefeld, Augsburg and Erlangen, and the state of Bavaria, have all been the subject of recent studies,[25] whilst detailed inventories of extant industrial and technical monuments have been compiled under the aegis of state preservation departments. In some areas the authorities have promoted further interest in industrial architecture through the publication of illustrated booklets, such as the *Arbeitshefte* produced by the Landeskonservator Rheinland.[26] Other notable contributions to the study of industrial architecture in Germany have come from Bernd and Hilla Becher, prolific photographers of industrial ruins,[27] and the Osnabrück art historian Thomas Schleper, whose 1987 doctoral dissertation

22. T. Schleper, 'Kunstwissenschaft und Fabrikbau', pp.58-81.

23. W. Ruppert, *Die Fabrik. Geschichte von Arbeit und Industrialisierung in Deutschland*, Munich, 1983; H. Glaser, W. Ruppert, N. Neudecker (eds.), *Nürnberg. Eine deutsche Stadt im Maschinenzeitalter*, Munich, 1980; see also H. Glaser, *Maschinenwelt und Alltagsleben. Industriekultur in Deutschland vom Biedermeier bis zur Weimarer Republik*, Munich, 1981.

24. For example, J. Boberg, T. Fichter, E. Gillen (eds.), *Exerzierfeld der Moderne. Industriekultur in Berlin im 19. Jahrhundert*, Munich, 1984; and *Die Metropole. Industriekultur in Berlin im 20. Jahrhundert*, Munich, 1985; also, V. Plagemann (ed.), *Industriekultur in Hamburg*, Munich, 1984.

25. V. Rödel, *Fabrikarchitektur in Frankfurt am Main, 1774-1924*, Frankfurt, 1984; F. Böllhof, J. Bostrom, B. Hey, *Industriearchitektur in Bielefeld. Geschichte und Fotografie*, Bielefeld, 1987; W. Ruckdeschel, K. Luther, *Technische Denkmale in Augsburg. Eine Führung durch die Stadt*, Augsburg, 1984; J. Thamer, 'Industriearchitektur in Erlangen', in J. Sandweg (ed.), *Erlangen. Von der Strumpfer- zur Siemensstadt*, Erlangen, 1982; H. Knauß, *Zweckbau-Architektur zwischen Repräsentation und Nutzen*, Munich, 1983.

26. The Landeskonservator Rheinland has published volumes on *Technische Denkmale in Rheinland* (A. Föhl); *Die Schwebebahn in Wuppertal* (H.-F. Schierk & N.Schmidt); and *Die Entwicklung der optischen Telegrafie in Preußen* (D. Herbarth). The equivalent authority in Hamburg has also published a series of *Arbeitshefte,* including *Die Speicherstadt im Hamburger Freihafen* (K. Maak); *Stadt und Hafen* (J. Ellermeyer & R. Postel); and *Stadtgestalt durch Staatsgewalt? Das Hamburger Baupflegegesetz von 1912* (K. Rauschnabel).

27. See B.& H.Becher, *Die Architektur der Forder- und Wassertürme*, Munich, 1971; and *Zeche Zollern II. Aufbruch zur modernen Industriearchitektur und Technik*, Munich, 1977.

Kunstwissenschaft und Fabrikbau examined the potential role of a 'visual social history'.[28]

It must be said, however, that whilst many authors have drawn up impressive guidelines for a comprehensive approach to the study of historic industrial buildings – to include not only the analysis of the external architecture and internal environment, but the reconstruction of work patterns, safety records, company strategies and public attitudes to the buildings concerned – it has proved much harder to put the suggested lines of enquiry into practice, not least because of the difficulties involved in gathering the necessary source material. The work of Roland Günter in particular has been characterised by a tendency to reach too far, too fast, at times raising more questions than can be adequately answered with the information available.[29]

This book has more realistic ambitions. It takes as its starting point the impact on the built environment of two important movements for architectural reform. In their struggle to win influence both movements – the Bund Heimatschutz and the German Werkbund – were highly active in the publication of programmatic texts and propaganda material, and this body of literature naturally forms one of the principal sources of information for this study. The numerous Heimatschutz journals, the annual Werkbund Yearbooks, essays by prominent *Heimatschützer* and *Werkbundler* are all used extensively, as are unpublished documents such as membership lists, annual reports, press releases and private letters. It must be stressed, however, that the intention is not to offer an organisational history of either reform movement, whose interests were by no means limited to industrial architecture, but rather to use their activities as a framework within which to analyse the wider relationship between culture and politics in Wilhelmine Germany.

The definition of 'industrial architecture' adopted here is a broad one, to include the technical structures of public utilities, railway stations and the administrative buildings of industrial companies, as well as factories, power stations and mines. The fascinating area of company housing in Wilhelmine Germany is not discussed, however, since it has been more

28. T.Schleper's thesis 'Kunstwissenschaft und Fabrikbau' was subtitled 'Über den Beitrag der visuellen Sozialgeschichte zur Industriekulturforschung'.

29. Roland Günter's efforts both to preserve and explain the Ruhr's industrial heritage deserve the greatest acclaim. His work has consistently posed challenging questions and opened up many worthwhile lines of enquiry. He displays a tendency, however, to assume more than the source material will allow, attempting to fit everything into the rather rigid framework of German history drawn up by his colleague at Bielefeld University, Hans-Ulrich Wehler. Moreover, in his desire to ask all the possible questions, he inevitably leaves much unanswered.

fully researched elsewhere.[30] The buildings cited by way of illustration are not limited to any one region or state, but care has been taken wherever possible to choose examples of buildings which still stand today, a task less difficult than one might at first imagine. The main focus falls on the years after 1900, when the movements for architectural reform were at their strongest, but begins with a brief overview of earlier developments.

In addition to the pursuit of visual clues – the buildings themselves, depicted here in photographic form[31] – the book makes use of more conventional historical sources too; from municipal, state and company archives, local and national newspapers and journals, and publications such as company reports and *Festschriften*. Particular mention must be made of the journal *Der Industriebau*, a rare but invaluable source of information, which has until now been largely ignored by historians.

At a time when most industrial buildings have become little more than brightly-coloured corrugated tin sheds, it is perhaps hard to contemplate a period in which the appearance and quality of such structures was an issue guaranteed to excite the passions of architectural practitioners and laymen alike. That this was indeed once the case can perhaps best be illustrated with a reference to a literary 'modernist', whose deeply ambivalent attitude to the world of industry was in many ways similar to that of the architects we shall be meeting in the following chapters. In his famous novel *Women in Love* the author D.H. Lawrence describes an impromptu but memorable speech by a fictional German sculptor, Loerke, on the need to make 'our places of industry our art – our factory area our Parthenon'.[32] Loerke, who was involved in the construction of 'a great granite frieze for a great granite factory in Cologne', proclaims:

30. See for instance R. Günter, 'Arbeitersiedlungen im Ruhrgebiet' in E. Trier & W. Weyres (eds.), *Kunst des 19.Jahrhunderts im Rheinland*, vol. 2, Düsseldorf, 1980; R. Günter, 'Krupp in Essen' in M. Warnke (ed.), *Das Kunstwerk zwischen Wissenschaft und Weltanschauung*, Gütersloh, 1970; N. Bullock & J. Read, *The movement for housing reform in Germany and France, 1840-1914*, Cambridge, 1985; L. Niethammer on workers' estates of Ruhr industrial companies in J.H.Müller (ed.), *Der westdeutsche Impuls. Die Folkwang-Idee des Karl Ernst Osthaus*, Hagen, 1984.

31. In contrast to much of the *Industriekultur* discourse, which dwells on the internal characteristics of the workplace, the emphasis here is on the outward appearance of industrial buildings. This is is not to dismiss the relevance of working conditions and practices as a social and political issue, nor the value of a 'subject-oriented' architectural history, but rather an acknowledgement of the pre-eminence of the factory façade as a medium of corporate expression and identity, both in relation to the workforce and the outside world.

32. D.H.Lawrence, *Women in Love*, Harmondsworth, 1986, p.476. The character of Loerke is treated unsympathetically by Lawrence. Most critics have suggested he is based in part on Mark Gertler, a British painter and acquaintance of Lawrence, but he may well reflect ideas and impressions picked up by the author during his stay in Germany.

There is not only no need for our places of work to be ugly, but their ugliness ruins the work, in the end. Men will not go on submitting to such intolerable ugliness . . . They will think the work itself is ugly: the machines, the very act of labour. Whereas the machinery and the acts of labour are extremely, maddeningly beautiful. But this will be the end of our civilization, when people will not work because work has become so intolerable to their senses, it nauseates them too much, they would rather starve. Then we shall see the hammer used only for smashing, then we shall see it. Yet here we are – we have the opportunity to make beautiful factories, beautiful machine-houses – we have the opportunity.[33]

Loerke's emotional outburst leaves his predominantly English audience in a state of shock, but his conviction that 'art should interpret industry as art once interpreted religion'[34] was by no means uncommon in the later Wilhelmine period. Indeed, Lawrence may well have discovered this for himself, for he spent much of the years 1912–14 in Germany, with his mistress Frieda von Richthofen and with relatives in the Rhineland.

33. D.H. Lawrence *ibid.,* p.477.
34. D.H. Lawrence *ibid.,* p.477.

1

The Rise and Fall of Historicist Industrial Architecture in Germany

As Londoners queued to marvel at the proud products of modern manufacturing on display in the ethereal atmosphere of Paxton's great glass and iron Crystal Palace, the German Commissioners to the 1851 Great Exhibition noted with resignation: 'It is clearly not to be expected that Germany will ever be able to reach the level of production of coal and iron currently attained in England. This is implicit in our far more limited resource endowment.'[1]

By the end of the century, however, Germany had not only overtaken Great Britain in the production of pig iron and steel, but was also competing favourably with British manufactured goods in the markets of the world. The German *Reich*, only unified in 1871, was well on the way to becoming a modern industrial economy, with an increasing proportion of its workforce engaged in industry, mining, and after 1900, in the service sector too.[2] The spectacular industrial advance was most visible around Berlin and in the Ruhr, transformed in the space of a few decades from an insignificant backwater into the heart of Europe's greatest industrial region, but scattered pockets of industry had actually been developing in parts of the Rhineland, Saxony and elsewhere since the late eighteenth century. Germany's first factory, the Cromford cotton mill designed by Rutger Flügel for Johann Brügelmann at Ratingen, was built as early as 1784.

The mid-nineteenth century discovery of large deposits of deep-lying bituminous coal in the Ruhr valley was, nevertheless, a decisive stimulus to German industrialisation. As well as providing a vital source of energy, the coal produced a coke ideally suited for blast furnaces, and iron ore was to be found in some of the measures too. The seams were hard to reach, lying beneath large wet marl deposits, but once they had been tapped coal

---

1. Quoted by D. Landes in *The Unbound Prometheus*, Cambridge, 1969, p.178.
2. In 1875 49% of Germans worked in the primary sector (agriculture, forestry, fishing), 30% in the secondary sector (industry, mining) and 21% in the tertiary sector (services, transport, banking etc.). In 1900 these figures were 38%–37%–25% and by 1914 they were 34%–38%–28%. Figures from F.-W. Henning, *Die Industrialisierung in Deutschland 1800–1914*, Paderborn, 1984, p.20.

output rose dramatically, reaching 11.8 million tons by 1869.[3] Three other factors were crucial for the Ruhr's successful 'take off': the introduction of coke-fired blast furnaces; the early development of rail and water transport links; and the rapid growth in demand for iron and steel, as numerous processing and manufacturing industries sprang up across the *Reich* in the second half of the century. The pace of German industrialisation then gained renewed momentum with the so-called 'Second Industrial Revolution', which saw the rapid expansion of the electrical engineering and chemical industries in the 1890s.

One of the few sectors of the economy able to match the growth rates of German industry throughout this period was the building trade, where the number of employees increased by 208% between 1873 and 1918.[4] The period 1873–93 in particular, witnessed a remarkable expansion of building activity, with the number of building workers as a proportion of the total of German manual workers rising from a stable pre-unification level of around 10% to 14% in just two decades.[5] The reason for this unprecedented building boom is not hard to find, with industry demanding a multitude of buildings to house the new production processes and accommodate an ever-expanding workforce. Profound structural change in the economy and society created a need for other new buildings too: railway stations and department stores, exhibition halls and office buildings, were all symptoms of industrialisation. Indeed, in the second half of the nineteenth century, one could have been forgiven for mistaking Germany's industrial centres for giant construction sites, as industrialisation was accompanied by infrastructural modernisation and rapid urbanisation.

In his influential 1926 work *Der moderne Zweckbau* the leading modernist critic Adolf Behne condemned the industrial buildings of the nineteenth century as the 'roughest and cheapest' of structures, 'put up with insulting disdain'.[6] Behne's judgement, made in a book which celebrated the achievements of post-1900 industrial architecture, was accurate only in part. A vast number of ugly, ill-considered structures were indeed erected in the course of Germany's dynamic industrialisation, but many other factory buildings reflected an exaggerated desire to impress, impose or inspire, often appearing to go far beyond functional necessity to communicate wider meanings to the workforce and the world outside the factory gate.

In fact, remarkably little was known about Germany's early industrial

---

3. D. Landes, *Unbound Prometheus*, p.203.
4. F.-W. Henning, *Die Industrialisierung*, p.218.
5. F.-W. Henning, *ibid.*, p.219.
6. A. Behne, *Der moderne Zweckbau*, Munich, 1926, p.27.

architecture until recent years. The popularisation of industrial archaeology in continental Europe at the end of the 1960s led to a growing awareness within state preservation authorities of the need to document the remaining relics of earlier industrial development, but the first attempts to assess the architecture of historic industrial buildings succeeded only in highlighting the large gaps left by both conventional art history and social history in this area. The pioneering essays of Martin Schumacher, Roland Günter and others[7] showed that in the second half of the nineteenth century, and after 1871 in particular, there was a strong tendency amongst German industrialists and their builders to plunder the styles of bygone ages for the form and façades of their industrial buildings. Where the pioneer generation of industrial innovators had naturally turned to pre-industrial models to find solutions for their new building needs, the industrial barons of Germany's *Gründerzeit* appeared to make a more conscious choice of historic architectural styles, as if to legitimise or disguise the function of their industrial plants.

In recent years many examples of late nineteenth century industrial buildings masquerading as Medieval fortresses, Gothic castles or Baroque palaces have been uncovered amidst the 'rough and cheap' relics of German industrialisation. Moreover it has become clear that the historicist patterns of pre-1900 industrial architecture lived on well into the twentieth century, most notably in the pit-head complexes of Ruhr coal mines and the administrative buildings of heavy industry. This chapter examines the reasons why historical styles remained popular with certain industrial companies long after changing functional requirements and the dictates of fashion had brought such architecture into question.

The stubborn adherence of sections of German industry to historical styles is highly significant, and not only for what it tells us about the values and practices of the companies concerned. The survival (or rather revival) of 'pre-industrial' architecture in an area of German economic life so close to the engine room of modernisation was a prime target for the industrialists, architects and politicians who fought for a reform of architecture and product design in the later Wilhelmine years. Indeed, a true understanding of organisations like the Werkbund and the Heimatschutz movement, whose activities are central to this study, is impossible without first examining the nature of industrial architecture at the time of their inception. The chapter begins with a brief outline of the evolution of German industrial architecture and then considers some of

7. M. Schumacher, 'Zweckbau und Industrieschloss', in *Tradition*, vol.15 (1970); R. Günter, 'Zu einer Geschichte der technischen Architektur im Rheinland', *Die Kunstgeschichte und Denkmalpflege des Rheinlandes*, supplement no. 16 (1970).

the most interesting examples of stylistic historicism from the Wilhelmine years.[8]

The thesis of the British architectural historian J.M. Richards, who wrote on the 'functional tradition' of early industrial buildings in the 1950s,[9] was largely confirmed by the first Germans to investigate the origins of industrial architecture in their country. The early 'functionalism' was not a self-conscious philosophy but the result of a logical transfer of pre-industrial models to the new building tasks. Most of the industrial buildings erected in Germany before the 1850s were based on long-established traditions of utilitarian building; not only of water-mills and workshops, but buildings for agriculture (stables, barns), trade (the large warehouses of the Hanseatic ports), the army (barracks, arsenals) and the Church (cloisters) as well.

Other industrial building-types developed from residential architecture, as production patterns and techniques evolved from the individual and manual to the communal and mechanical. The prevailing architectural ethos of the Biedermeier era, which favoured simplicity, combined with the unpretentious habits of local craftsmen to ensure that the first industrial buildings were usually simple and unassuming. The process of finding a pre-industrial model to match the new methods of production was, however, not always easy. One of the first problems faced by architects and engineers was how to house the giant steam engines which began to appear in Germany around 1800. At the Königsborn salt works at Unna-Afferde, where the Ruhr's first steam engine was installed in 1799, the architect Bückling built a 'church' around the machinery. For a while this practice was repeated in other parts of Germany, but soon it was the tall, slim chimney rather than the church steeple, which became the most potent symbol of industrial progress and prosperity. Even so, as Günter Drebusch points out in his history of industrial architecture,[10] the ecclesiastic solution had a certain logic, since the shape of the first steam engines matched that of the traditional church rather well.

Royal salt works like Königsborn were amongst the largest of the early industrial complexes to be built in Germany, as were other state enterprises, such as iron foundries and munitions factories. These were often much

---

8. 'Historicism' is the English translation of the German word *Historismus*, which came into use in the 1880s as a pejorative term to describe the contemporary practice of building in historical styles. Although historical styles had been revived before, the second half of the 19th century witnessed and unprecedented turnover of past forms, with a host of historical styles in widespread and simultaneous use – often, indeed, on the same building.

9. J.M. Richards, *The Functional Tradition in Early Industrial Buildings*, London, 1958.

10. G. Drebusch, *Industriearchitektur*, Munich, 1976, pp.62–68.

grander in conception than the first buildings of private industry, and frequently reflected the participation of state architectural officials in their symmetrical, monumental designs. The Prussian state iron foundries at Gleiwitz (1794–1806) and the Königshütte near Beuthen in Upper Silesia (1798–1802) were carefully planned complexes, very different in character to their British equivalents. As Eduard Vollhann noted in 1825:

> The English are only concerned with producing a colossal amount of iron, and are constantly on the lookout to show the most profitable side of their blast furnaces, but the German is at the same time eager to pay homage to the genius of art. Therefore [the iron foundries of Upper Silesia] are a fascinating museum not only for the iron experts, but for architects, engineers and painters too. The very different character of the English and the Germans cannot better be demonstrated than by the different ways in which the two nations approach coalmining and iron production.[11]

One of the most remarkable early industrial buildings in Germany was the Royal Prussian iron foundry at Sayn near Coblenz, designed by the state architect Karl Ludwig Althans and built between 1826 and 1830. Unlike the earlier foundries in Upper Silesia, the Sayner Hütte made an architectural feature of the ironwork in its own construction, boasting a cast iron and glass gable at one end of a long basilica-like hall. At the other end of the hall, where one would expect to find an altar, stood the blast furnace. Drebusch writes: 'The Sayn building therefore embodies the claim for power of an enlightened bourgeois class which was orientated towards knowledge and technology rather than the old powers of faith from feudal times.'[12]

Some industrial plants in the private sector later followed the example set by these state iron foundries. The best known case is perhaps the Borsig iron foundry in Berlin (1837), a highly symmetrical building later immortalised in a painting by Biermann (1847). However, the vast majority of nineteenth-century factories were built without the involvement of academically-educated architects, who considered the design of humble *Zweckarchitektur* to be a separate and inferior activity. Those architects with a name to make or a reputation to keep did not take an active interest in the new opportunities presented by the industrial sector until the last years of the century. Their professional journals chose to ignore industrial projects as unworthy or uninteresting, and their theoretical writings seldom touched on the subject either.

It was the engineer, with his expert understanding of the spatial and

---

11. Quoted by H. Friedrich in 'Die bauliche Gestaltung deutscher Eisenhüttenanlagen seit Beginn des 19. Jahrhunderts', *Stahl und Eisen*, vol.80 (1960), p.1634.
12. G. Drebusch, *Industriearchitektur*, p.86.

structural requirements of machinery, who was most closely involved in the design of industrial buildings. The responsibility for the brick or stone walls which then enclosed the machinery usually fell to an artisan master builder or local building contractor, who would also apply any architectural embellishments required for the façades. However, the first German industrialists appear to have been less concerned with the possibilities of self-projection than with maximising output. Most early industrial buildings eschewed ornamentation or direct historical quotation in favour of simplicity and utility.

The architectural form of the first mechanised textile mills was, in Germany as in Britain, a clear illustration of the primacy of function. The system of direct shaft-drive, through which power was transmitted to the machinery, meant that tall buildings of five, six or even seven storeys represented the most economic use of resources. Power – first water-generated, later steam – was transmitted upwards from basement level, with ceiling-mounted shafts branching off to each floor. Visibility and the transport of materials in nineteenth-century factories were thus severely limited by the spider's-web of belts and wheels which linked each machine to the power-shaft, as well as by the large number of internal structural supports. The transmission system also caused considerable vibration problems, as the walls and floors shook to the rhythm of the power shafts.

In order to ensure that some natural light could reach the centre of the shop floor, buildings tended to be narrow. This was particularly the case with early textile factories, which had thick load-bearing walls and a limited amount of window space. Although buildings with iron or steel internal supports, which allowed for thinner walls and greater glazed areas, became more commonplace in the course of the nineteenth century, the shaft-drive system survived into the early years of the twentieth century and the factory environment often remained decidedly gloomy as a result.

The eventual development of small electric motors to power individual machines was a major contribution to improved factory planning after 1900, when the physiognomy of the factory entered a new phase. In North America the availability of cheap land, reinforced concrete and electric power ensured that factories began to look very different from the textile mills of eighteenth and nineteenth century Europe. US manufacturers could at last build plants which mirrored the flow of production, and which permitted the full use of internal transportation devices, such as cranes and conveyor belts, for the first time. These buildings would later inspire a generation of European architects, engineers and industrialists, including many of the men who will feature in this study. For the time being, however, we must return to the factories of nineteenth-century Germany.

In his 1970 essay *Zweckbau und Industrieschloß* Martin Schumacher investigated the buildings of the Rhenish-Westphalian textile industry before 1871, and revealed a series of well-proportioned rectangular box-like structures, with regular fenestration and little ornamentation. If industrialists perceived a representative role for their factory buildings it was communicated through the sheer size of their holdings (printed letter-headings often included a panoramic view of the factory site) or by small touches (the symbolic presence of large clock faces in dominant positions), rather than the extravagance of the overall architectural conception. The first buildings of the Saxon textile industry were in general less austere than those in the Rhineland – often with Mansard roofs and plaster walls – but equally functional. Early textile mills were the basic model for many nineteenth-century factory buildings, and the utilitarian tradition they established has remained a constant characteristic of industrial structures ever since.

From mid-century, however, some textile factories began to receive a more lavish appearance, incorporating the turrets and towers of fortress architecture, or the layout of aristocratic palaces. A textile factory built in the years 1854–5 – the Gladbacher Spinnerei und Weberei in Mönchengladbach – illustrates this trend well. In his first essay on the industrial buildings of the Rhineland, Roland Günter saw the transformation in the architecture of the textile industry as a consequence of political events. In the aftermath of the 1848 Revolution, he argued, the bourgeoisie had lost its self confidence: 'after this attempt at a real emancipation had failed, the bourgeoisie once again orientated itself towards the nobility, and wished to rise to its status by taking over aristocratic forms of building'.[13]

Günter's essay displayed a welcome willingness to consider the political and economic context in which architectural change occurs, which was by no means common in works of art history at that time, but the linkage between political events and architectural change is seldom as clear-cut as the above quote suggests. In the case of the Mönchengladbach factory the prime impulse in its design came not from the buildings of the German aristocracy but from liberal Great Britain, where textile mills were also in the process of becoming more decorative, less utilitarian structures.[14]

Even in their most austere early nineteenth-century form the buildings of the textile industry were generally more substantial than those of coal mining or the nascent metalworking industries, which were often housed in little more than half-timbered barns. The textile industry was of course

---

13. R. Günter, 'Geschichte der technischen Architektur im Rheinland', p.356.
14. See D. Spiegelhauer, 'Fabrikbau', in E. Trier & W. Weyres (eds), *Kunst des 19. Jahrhunderts im Rheinland*, Düsseldorf, 1980, vol.2, pp.318–322.

Figure 1 Gladbacher Spinnerei und Weberei, textile mill, Mönchengladbach 1854–55
Arch. Unknown. Present condition

the leading sector in the early years of industrialisation, and its factories were frequently situated in town centre locations, where the buildings inevitably fulfilled a representative function too. Moreover, as Günter points out, textile factories were often family businesses, owned by inhabitants of the town in which the factory was located, who had little desire to antagonise their local community with shoddy or insubstantial buildings.

Nevertheless, from the 1850s the architecture of heavy industry also became more imposing; a trend well illustrated by the architecture of the Ruhr coal mines. Pit-head buildings began to lose their residential character and compact rural layout, with new pits favouring a more symmetrical, representative form, invariably dominated by tall winding towers. The double-shaft pits, such as the Zeche Oberhausen of 1854, were particularly impressive, even if the rapid expansion of ancillary services meant that carefully planned complexes seldom retained their perfect symmetry for long. The first coal mines had not required winding towers at all, using horizontal tunnels to reach the seams, but as shaft depths and the size of loads increased, so winding towers with higher and stronger equipment were needed.

Early wooden structures were gradually replaced in the first half of the nineteenth century by towers which combined a stout oak frame and thick stone walls. Yet the development of the Ruhr coalfield, with its deep seams and ever-increasing output, required more massive winding towers still. Towards the end of the 1850s the first of the so-called 'Malakow Towers' were built in the Ruhr. These formidable structures, with walls up to 2.5 metres thick and over thirty metres high, were named after a fort in Sevastapol which had provided particularly stubborn resistance in the course of the Crimean War. It is not clear who coined the term 'Malakow Tower' first, but they soon became a familiar sight in the Ruhr, looming above pit complexes from Essen to Dortmund.

The earliest Malakows were virtually free of ornamentation, but subsequently many were built with the complete range of military embellishments. Not surprisingly, the towers became a symbol of the power of the mine owners, but as with much of the historically-influenced industrial architecture of the nineteenth century, it is difficult to ascribe the appearance of the Malakows to the representational desires of industrialists alone. Certainly, Günter's assertion that the towers were a manifestation of the 'increasing feudalisation' of the bourgeoisie,[15] must be treated with some caution. It is true that British coal mines were able to avoid the Malakow phase, jumping straight from wooden winding towers to similar steel structures, but this had as much to do with the

15. R. Günter, 'Geschichte der technischen Architektur im Rheinland', p.364.

Figure 2 Malakow tower at the Zeche Westhausen, Dortmund-Bodelschwingh 1873
Arch. Unknown. Present condition

different mining conditions in the British coalfields as the attitude of employers.

The Malakows were in essence highly practical objects: not only did they owe their existence to the special mining conditions in the Ruhr, but many aspects of their appearance were less fanciful than first appeared. The bricked-in Romanesque or Gothic 'windows' which adorned the walls of many Malakows, for instance, were needed to facilitate the introduction of large spare-parts to the winding and pumping gear, and the small spiral staircase turrets which often formed the four corners of the Malakow were needed as emergency escape routes in case of fire. More importantly, the historicising details which adorned many Malakow towers may have had as much to do with the mid-nineteenth century builders' idea of beauty and aesthetic propriety, as it did with the desire of industrialists to appropriate the Medieval architecture of subjugation and domination.

On the other hand it is clear that Malakows did perform a representative function. They were often the first part of a mine to be built and served as a symbol of credit worthiness to attract new investors. Some of the Malakows built in the boom of the 1850s stood idle for many years when the money for shafting and tunnelling ran out. Few new Malakows were built after the 1880s. The ever increasing demands on the winding machinery – up to 2,000 kilograms of coal to be raised 400 metres – could not be met by even thicker brick walls, and new pits were generally fitted with steel winding towers in the British fashion.

The large watertowers which became such a feature of German towns in the second half of the nineteenth century were subject to the same architectural approach as the Malakows. Although the towers were a direct result of industrialisation – their function being to store water to meet the increasing but fluctuating demand from industry, housing, the railways and the fire service – their architectural models were generally to be found in the towers of Medieval fortresses, or in the palaces of fairy tales. Here the practice of building in historical forms survived well into the twentieth century.

The watertowers of Imperial Germany were frequently situated in highly-visible locations and were therefore seldom left as 'naked' engineering. Indeed it became common practice for municipal authorities to run competitions amongst architects and builders to find designs suitable for such conspicuous objects. The 1905 competition for a watertower at Sternschanze in Hamburg, for instance, specifically referred to the towers of Medieval North German churches as a desirable model. It is debatable however whether the eclectic and at times overbearing structures which were the usual result of such exercises were any less jarring on the townscape.

The trend towards more imposing industrial buildings, which had begun in the 1850s, gained new momentum after 1871. The rash of mergers, take-overs and speculative deals, financed in part by reparations money from the defeated French, and – more importantly – carried along on a wave of euphoria after Germany's belated achievement of nationhood, caused turmoil in the business world. The Essen financier Strousberg wrote: 'The circumstances were such that excesses were encouraged, everything was promoted in unseemly fashion, everything was shoved out of its usual bounds, terms were confused, speculation had become a mania and was becoming a swindle.'[16]

Strousberg's description of the financial markets also serves as an accurate assessment of German architecture during the *Gründerzeit*. Industrial architecture did not develop in a vacuum. The rapid succession of historical styles which were promoted as the true expression of the German nation after 1871 affected all areas of building activity, but it was in the industrial towns that growth was concentrated – Bochum grew by a fifth in the eighteen months between 1871 and 1873 – and it was here that the excesses of the *Gründerzeit* were most apparent.

The architectural styles perhaps best suited to industrial buildings were the round-arched Romanesque style, which had a long tradition in western Germany, and the red-brick Neo-Gothic, with its emphasis on structural 'truth'. The last third of the nineteenth century, however, also witnessed an increased use of Baroque and Renaissance forms, as well as Byzantine, Egyptian and other more exotic languages in German architecture and design. There was nothing novel about the revival of historic styles *per se*: what was remarkable about these years was the rapidity with which the fashions changed, and the eccentric hybrids that were often built as a result. It was this eclecticism which was the key to late nineteenth-century historicism and which marked the main difference with the historically-influenced architecture of previous decades.

Buildings did not cease to function. Behind the façades the achievements of engineering grew ever more remarkable, but industrialists and industrial firms clearly gave increasing importance to questions of representation and display. In an age of joint stock companies and a shareholding public, the desire for worthy – and credit worthy – industrial buildings was growing. Often, however, the imposing façade was little more than a brittle stucco icing, applied to disguise poor materials and sub-standard workmanship. The lifting of guild restrictions in the building trades led to the growth of speculative contracting and developing firms, which cut costs and corners to win commissions.

Two examples of late nineteenth-century architectural historicism are

---

16. Quoted by C. Koschwitz in 'Die Hochbauten auf den Steinkohlenzechen des Ruhrgebiets', PhD thesis, Berlin TH, 1928, p.41.

illustrated below. The Laurenz brothers' textile mill in Ochtrup, Westphalia, was designed by a Dutch architect, Beltmann, in 1893. The lively, colourful façade (red brick, whitewashed stone and green window frames), with its fanlights, pilasters, volutes and other decorative devices, is a good example of the representative 'face' often applied to industrial buildings situated on main transport routes.

The pit-head building of the coal mine Zeche Adolf von Hansemann, which included offices, wash rooms and the wages hall, was erected in Dortmund-Mengede in 1899. Its eclectic use of historical forms is typical of the turn-of-the-century *Zechenburgen*, which attempted to revive the architecture of the Teutonic knights. The construction of new pit-head buildings was part of a six million Mark investment in the previously loss-making mine by its owners, the Gewerkschaft der Mengeder Steinkohlengruben. When the imposing new building failed to secure a loan to cover some of the pit's large debts, the Zeche Adolf von Hansemann was bought up at a favourable price by the Union AG of Dortmund to supply coke to its nearby steelworks.

The formal and iconographical 'signs' displayed by these remarkable buildings were of considerable interest to the first generation of Germans to show an academic interest in historical industrial architecture, who eagerly attempted to place them in a wider social and political context. Joachim Petsch, for instance, wrote:

> If the recourse to historical building types and forms before 1848 occurred primarily for functional reasons . . . so the adoption of feudal building types and forms by the *Großbürgertum* in the second stage of the development of factory architecture, and after 1871 in particular, symbolises the feudalisation of this class.[17]

This interpretation overlooks two key points. Firstly, the late nineteenth century was an age of historicism in architecture and design throughout Europe. Factories and other buildings received historical façades in all countries at this time, not least in America, where social and political conditions were very different. Secondly, the extent to which such architecture was conceived and implemented as a deliberate instrument of company policy has proved hard to ascertain. Such doubts can only be answered conclusively with a detailed analysis of the building process in each specific instance. Unfortunately, however, the documentation of aesthetic and commercial intentions in nineteenth-century industrial building is very patchy: even the names of the architects and builders who

17. J. Petsch, 'Deutsche Farbikarchitektur im 19. Jahrhundert', in B. Korzus (ed.), *Fabrik im Ornament. Ansichten auf Firmenbriefköpfen des 19. Jahrhunderts*, catalogue, Münster, 1980, p.46.

Figure 3 Laurenz brothers' textile mill, Ochtrup 1893
Arch. Beltmann. Present condition

Figure 4 Zeche Adolf von Hansemann pit-head building, Dortmund-Mengede 1899
Arch. Unknown. Present condition

worked on industrial projects are rarely remembered.

Nevertheless it seems clear that for the master-builders who plundered the architectural pattern books, the vagaries of fashion and contemporary notions of beauty were more pressing concerns than the communication of meaning. H.A.N. Brockmann, writing on the British industrial architecture of the High Victorian period, notes that 'with all this confusing stylistic work going on throughout the western world, architects working in the industrial field were swamped with choices and few, if any, were able to detach themselves sufficiently to think of the industrial problem in harness with its architectural expression'.[18]

Historians have tended to underestimate the importance of fashion and convention, but for both industrialists and builders the desire to produce something which looked 'similar but better' than the competition undoubtedly contributed to the rapid spread of historicist architecture after 1871. After all, in the area of product design the prime reason for the success of historicism was the need to provide each mass-marketed product of the rapidly expanding consumer-goods industries with a distinctive, eye-catching appearance, which would at the same time disguise any qualitative shortcomings of the object in question.

One must therefore be wary of confusing the whims of industrialists and their builders with deeply-held convictions. Many of the aesthetic extravagances of the *Gründerzeit* can be taken at face value and nothing more. This is not to deny the political function of such architecture, but rather to highlight the dangers of making glib assertions, which can ultimately only harm the cause of politically-literate architectural history. The new-found economic power of industry was certainly displayed in richer and more expensive façades, its dominance of local communities emphasised by a grandness of scale and conception. On a deeper level, however, the signs displayed by historicist industrial buildings were vague and ambiguous. If German industrialists chose pre-industrial forms of representative architecture to symbolise their new status in society, was it an admission of defeat in the aftermath of 1848 and a symbol of 'feudalisation' or was it rather a case of adopting the rival's language in order to issue a more convincing challenge to his established status? It should not be forgotten that the socialist August Bebel applauded Wallot's monumental and historicist Reichstag building precisely because it appropriated the architecture of privilege in the name of the German people – much to the disgust of the Kaiser.

In a 1978 essay on the social relations of Westphalian industrialists from 1860 to 1914, Hansjoachim Henning investigated the then-fashionable

---

18. H.A.N. Brockmann, *The British Architect in Industry 1841–1940*, London, 1975, p.42.

concept of bourgeois 'feudalisation' and found remarkably little evidence of it, in that province of Prussia at least.[19] His conclusions also provided a possible 'feudalisation-free' explanation for the evident proliferation of post-1850 industrial buildings in pre-industrial guises. He wrote:

> Without doubt the big entrepreneurs, as a new power élite brought about by industrialisation, developed a pattern of behaviour which approached that of the aristocracy. At the same time, however, they resisted personal or social fusion. This apparent contradiction can only be explained in the following manner. The big entrepreneurs . . . believed that the only way [they] could attain and retain power was by adopting the same forms as the existing power élite, whilst at the same time maintaining social independence.[20]

When examined in detail the historicist industrial architecture of late nineteenth century Germany actually appears to confuse rather than communicate. The gatehouse designed by Konrad Reimer and Friedrich Körte for Borsig in Berlin-Tegel (1895–8) is a good example of the way in which historicist buildings could transmit contradictory messages. The works' gate had an important role in the life of any factory. For the workers it was the scene of a daily ritual as they entered the working community; for the products of the factory – in this instance railway locomotives – it formed the backdrop to a company ceremony every time a finished article left for the outside world. The crenellated Borsig gate – at first sight a prime example of 'feudalisation' – certainly echoed Medieval fortress architecture but it also incorporated bourgeois motifs, resembling the main gate of a small German town, with the stepped gables of the proud *Bürgerhäuser* rising in the background. The large reliefs of workmen on either side of the gate only served to confuse the gate's symbolism still further. This ambivalence of meaning was typical of much historicist architecture.

The monumental factory gate was an established part of industry's public face, but it was still rare for respected architects to work on such projects. One of the few exceptions was provided by Fritz Schwechten (1841–1924), architect of Berlin's *Anhalter Bahnhof* and *Gedächtniskirche*, who designed a gate house for the AEG company in the 1890s. Built in 1896, it revealed the tentative beginnings of a search for new architectural forms, to replace the historical styles devalued by indiscriminate use in the last third of the nineteenth century. On the whole, however, the reformist impulse which spelt the beginning of the end for nineteenth-century historicism affected product design before it reached

19. H. Henning, 'Soziale Verflechtungen der Unternehmer in Westfalen 1860–1914', in *Tradition*, vol.23 (1978).
20. H. Henning, *ibid.*, pp.18–19.

Figure 5 Borsig factory gate, Berlin-Tegel 1895–98
Arch. K. Reimer and F. Körte. Present condition

architecture.

For all the efforts of the many museums and colleges of applied art established after unification to improve the quality of the nation's arts and crafts, German products were still widely regarded as 'cheap and nasty' when displayed in the shop-window of international trade fairs. A growing awareness in governmental, creative and commercial circles that the concentration on the historical styles of 'Our Fathers' Works' had not brought increased respect for German products, but merely the dismissive tag 'Made in Germany',[21] led to renewed efforts to find a new form of cultural expression that was both distinctively German and unmistakeably 'of its time'. The campaign against historicism was fought by a disparate collection of cultural activists and became manifest in a wide variety of forms. Ferdinand Avenarius's (1856–1923) journal *Der Kunstwart*, founded in 1887, spawned a host of other publications dedicated to a reform of the applied arts; the writings of Paul de Lagarde (1827–1891), Julius Langbehn (1851–1907) and others attacked historicism as part of a wider critique of contemporary civilisation; the Secession movements in Munich, Vienna and Berlin, rebelled against the 'official' art of the academies; and a growing number of practising designers began to experiment in new and more 'natural' forms of decoration, under the influence of Franco-Belgian Art Nouveau and the British Arts and Crafts movement.

Historicism's hold on product design began to slip with the rise of *Jugendstil* in the mid–1890s. Named after the journal *Jugend*, the German variant of Art Nouveau aimed to integrate ornamentation and utility, and quickly gained popularity with designers and architects at the turn of the century. Some *Jugendstil* artists, such as the Flemish all-rounder Henry van de Velde (1863–1957), professed an admiration for structures of unadorned engineering, like bridges and bicycles, and supported efforts to find functional forms for buildings and objects. Although *Jugendstil* ornamentation was itself comparatively rare on industrial buildings, a historicist factory façade was no longer considered a fashionable option after 1900. *Jugendstil* blossomed only briefly, but with the new century came organisations committed to a fundamental reform of the industrial environment and culture whose members had little time for the 'dishonest' practice of hiding industry's light under a historical bushel. In any case, the changing requirements of industry, and the fresh opportunities presented by new construction materials such as reinforced concrete,

---

21. The 1887 'Merchandise Marks Act', which introduced the stamp 'Made in Germany' for German products on sale in the British Empire, was in part a protectionist measure, but the view that German goods generally lacked quality was widely held; indeed, many Germans were of the same opinion.

suggested that historicist industrial buildings were an extravagant anachronism.

One by one, companies in the chief growth sectors of German industry – the electrical industry, quality manufacturing industries, food and drink producers, the chemical industry – abandoned the styles of the past. Of course, the representative buildings of the state continued to be a defiant bastion of architectural convention, and occasional architectonic fantasies such as the Yenidze cigarette factory in Dresden – designed as a mosque as late as 1909 – could still be found, but in general the commissioning of historicist buildings in the industrial field was left as the distinctive preserve of just one small but powerful grouping. In the decade before the Great War, only the coal mines and the crude iron and steel producers remained hooked on the habits of historicism.

The Architecture of Heavy Industry in the Ruhr

The enormous expansion of the Ruhr coal mining industry in the second half of the nineteenth century brought large profits for some, but also increased competition between the many companies which owned pits in the region. The formation of the Rhenish-Westphalian Coal Syndicate (RWKS) in 1893 marked a concerted effort to regulate prices in the industry, as a means of safeguarding the interests of all participating companies. The syndicate's purpose-built office block, close to the big banks in Essen, was planned in 1893 and opened the following year. Designed by the local architect Lohrmann, it was a strict Neo-Gothic building of generous proportions, and typical of the administrative buildings of heavy industry at this time.

However, such was the economic importance of the RWKS, which covered almost 90% of Ruhr coal production, that it became necessary to enlarge the building just five years later. The extension, which included a large conference room, was designed by an Essen architect Carl Nordmann (1849–1922), who employed the same Neo-Gothic motifs as his predecessor. The extent to which this building reflected the taste of Emil Kirdorf (1847–1938), the man who dominated the RWKS for three decades and who considered its success his 'life's work', cannot be proved conclusively, but his conservative views on artistic matters became well-known in later years. More importantly, a look at the architecture of the Gelsenkirchener Bergwerks-AG (GBAG), the mining company ran by Kirdorf with an iron hand, reveals a consistent and conscious use of ostentatious architecture for its industrial buildings.

After completion of the RWKS extension in Essen, Carl Nordmann teamed up with the young Gelsenkirchen-based architect Paul Knobbe (1867–1956) to design a church at Essen-Altendorf (1900–01). Knobbe,

Figure 6 Yenidze cigarette factory, Dresden 1909
Arch. Unknown. Present condition

an academically-educated architect who had studied in Berlin was then approached by the GBAG to design a new mine complex on a site west of Dortmund to be known as the Zeche Zollern 2, together with further buildings for the nearby Zeche Hansa. Knobbe's work at Zollern 2 involved not only the planning of each individual pit building, but also the overall layout of the complex, and the neighbouring housing estate too. His plans, which repeated details from both the RWKS building and the Essen church, were for a series of red brick Neo-Gothic structures arranged around a formal, tree-lined courtyard, in the manner of a Baroque *cour d'honneur*. The two winding towers were arranged symmetrically to form an imposing backdrop for anyone passing the twin gate houses and entering the main square.

Knobbe's plans were approved at a sitting of the GBAG's Board of Directors on 30 August 1901 and the main buildings were quickly erected in the course of 1901–2.[22] The dominant position at the heart of the complex was taken by the mine's office building, which had a large clock above the main door and a stepped-gable. On the south side of the courtyard stood the wages hall, the bath house and the storeroom buildings. The gable of the wages hall was even more extravagant than that of the office building, and was flanked by two bulbous towers, reminiscent of a south German church. Indeed, the whole building had a sacral air: a large round window above the door of the wages hall was a direct copy of one incorporated into the design of the Essen church a year earlier.[23] When the company put the internal decorating work on this building out to tender it was stressed that 'something really good should be achieved'.[24] It is interesting to note that the rich façades of both the office building and wages hall were the result of a specific intervention by Knobbe's clients, the GBAG directors Kirdorf and Paul Randebrock, who insisted on a more lavish appearance than the architect had originally intended.[25]

22. H. Conrad, 'Zeche Zollern 2. Ein technik- und wirtschaftsgeschichtliches Kulturdenkmal', in B. Becher, H. Conrad, E. Neumann (eds), *Zeche Zollern 2*, Munich, 1977, p.219. The pit has a special place in the short history of German industrial archaeology because it was the fight to save these buildings – and especially the machine hall – which first spurred the nascent industrial preservation movement into action. Although production at Zollern 2 had ceased in 1955, it was not until 1969 that plans were unveiled to finally demolish the complex. As a result of public protests the machine hall was granted a last minute reprieve and was officially 'listed' as a technical monument on 30 December 1969, with the other remaining pit buildings joining it in subsequent years. The site is now earmarked as the headquarters of the Westphalian Industrial Museum.

23. The frequent use of elements from sacral architecture in heavy industrial buildings echoes Alfred Krupp's famous 1873 edict: 'The object of work should be the common good, then work is a godsend, then work is prayer'.

24. H. Conrad, 'Zeche Zollern 2', p.199.

25. H. Conrad, ibid., p.219.

Figure 7 Zeche Zollern 2, gable of office building, Dortmund-Bövinghausen 1901
Arch. P. Knobbe. Present condition

In an article published in the mining journal *Glückauf*, Director Randebrock wrote of his Zollern 2 pit:

> In contrast to the old practice of building works' complexes without paying any attention to their outward appearance, one has here allowed the laws of artistic beauty to come into play. One said to one's self, that the miner, for whom one is trying to create a comfortable new home on the new estates, would surely find it pleasant to have beautiful buildings and large airy rooms at the workplace too. One wanted to exert an influence on the aesthetic sensibility of people, without of course harming the functionality of the complex.[26]

Although Randebrock described the appearance of the Zollern 2 complex as 'friendly', the GBAG's aims in constructing such an imposing mine clearly went beyond a paternalistic concern for the workers' aesthetic feelings. At the time it commissioned the Zollern 2 pit, the GBAG company had no business interests outside coal mining. Its principal competitors were the large mixed concerns, owned by industrial grandees like Thyssen and Stinnes, which were expanding vertically to integrate all aspects of the heavy industrial process, from coal and raw steel production to high-quality finishing industries. The GBAG was therefore a prime target of takeover speculation, and Kirdorf was forced to fight doggedly to maintain the company's independence. It seems that Kirdorf, whose personal relations with the likes of Stinnes and Thyssen were decidedly frosty, took every opportunity to use distinctive architecture to emphasise the GBAG's own character and to help drive up the company's share price. Indeed, as the well-documented genesis of the machine hall at Zollern 2 shows, he was prepared to set aside his own artistic preferences to secure a striking design.

From the beginning the Zollern 2 pit was conceived as a model mining complex. Under the conditions of the RWKS, improvements in the productivity of mines could bring great financial advantage, and Zollern 2 was designed to incorporate the latest mining technology. Most notably, it was to be the first pit in Germany to use only electrically-powered winding and pumping gear. The building in which the new machinery was to be housed was first portrayed in a drawing by Paul Knobbe, dated 22 April 1902. The design reflected the building's importance to the mine's prospects, but was otherwise kept in the same Neo-Gothic form as the rest of the complex. Although the GBAG had been delighted with Knobbe's pit-head buildings, his design for the machine hall was not accepted by the company. Within days of receiving Knobbe's proposals the GBAG had

---

26. P. Randebrock, 'Die Schachtanlage Zollern 2 der GBAG', in *Glückauf*, vol. 41 (1905), p.783.

contacted the Gutehoffnungshütte (GHH) to discuss the possibility of constructing a glass and iron hall instead.[27]

Kirdorf's sudden change of mind was almost certainly influenced by two pavilions built by the GHH for the major Trade, Industry and Art fair taking place in Düsseldorf at this time. The pavilions, which housed the exhibits of the Gasmotorenfabrik Deutz and the GHH itself, were designed by the engineer Reinhold Krohn (1852–1932) and the architect Bruno Möhring (1863–1929), who applied fashionable *Jugendstil* ornamentation to the otherwise 'naked' glass and metal surfaces. Since the other exhibition pavilions, such as the domed halls of the Bergbaulichen Verein and the Krupp AG, were caked in overblown plasterwork, the GHH pavilions caused quite a stir amongst visitors and proved to be effective advertising for the firms concerned.[28] Kirdorf saw the promotional advantages that could be gained by placing the high-tech machinery of his new model pit in such an eye-catching building, and immediately set in motion a correspondence on the subject with the GHH.

As Conrad describes,[29] the process of ordering the machine hall for Zollern 2 did not run as smoothly as the GBAG would have wished – at one point the company considered returning to Knobbe's plan – but the building was eventually constructed in the course of 1903. As with the Düsseldorf pavilions, the machine hall at Zollern 2 was a cooperative effort between the GHH engineer Krohn and the Berlin architect Möhring, who concentrated his decorative efforts on the oval-shaped main doorway area, which resembled one of Guimard's Paris Metro station entrances. The rest of the building, which was nearly 100 metres long, was kept simple, combining large areas of glass with a visible steel-girder framework (painted green) and red-brick infill.

The machine hall shared with the pavilions of the great exhibitions more than just the same architectural team: the complicated Siemens & Halske technology which controlled Germany's first electrically powered pit shaft was hidden from view in the dark cellars of the building, no wires or cables were visible above the brightly-polished tiled floor. Visitors to the machine

27. H. Conrad, 'Zeche Zollern 2', p.240.

28. G.F. Koch, 'Die Bauten der Industrie-, Gewerbe- und Kunst-Ausstellung in Düsseldorf 1902 in der Geschichte der Ausstellungsarchitektur', in E. Mai, H. Pohl, S. Waetzold (eds), *Kunstpolitik und Kunstförderung im Kaiserreich*, Berlin, 1981.

29. H. Conrad, 'Zeche Zollern 2', p.239f. Möhring's *Jugendstil* doorway is portrayed on a current German postage stamp (an accolade it shares with Peter Behrens's AEG turbine factory).

Figure 8 Zeche Zollern 2, machine hall 1903
Arch. B. Möhring and R. Krohn. Present condition

hall – and there were many[30] – were given a sanitised demonstration of the magic of electricity, as white-coated employees paced up and down a nineteen-metre marble pedestal, ritualistically flicking at a mass of brass switches mounted on an altar-like control panel.

It soon became clear that Kirdorf's business instincts were sound, for the building attracted considerable attention, and helped to associate the name of the GBAG with technological innovation and commercial progress. Shortly after the Zollern 2 pit began production,[31] the GBAG was able to launch a massive share issue, which increased its capital reserves from 69 million Marks to 119 million Marks, and enabled the company to begin its own vertical expansion, buying into the iron foundries and iron ore deposits of the Aachener Hüttenverein and the Schalker Gruben-und Hüttenverein in 1904.[32] A year later the trading and transport firm Raab, Kärcher & Co. was added to the concern and at the same time the GBAG became involved in electricity generation with the Essen-based Rhenish-Westphalian Electricity Works (RWE). The RWE's first major power station in Essen, built at the turn of the century, was itself a formidable architectural statement, resembling the town hall of a wealthy nineteenth-century town.

It is ironic, however, that the machine hall at Zollern 2 should today be considered as marking the breakthrough of modern architectural ideas in the Ruhr coal industry,[33] for it was very much a unique response to a particular need, and did not mark a major shift in architectural policy by the mining companies in general or the GBAG in particular. Other GBAG mines continued to use historical forms in the design of their pit-head buildings, and later additions at the Zollern 2 site itself – the ammonia factory and workshops designed by the Dortmund architect Franz Brunck, for instance – returned to more established architectural traditions.

Pit-face miners at Zollern 2 had little experience of the remarkably light and airy atmosphere of the machine hall, which was not visible from the

30. In view of the 'masses' who were trying to gain admittance to the mine, the management was forced to discuss the question of whether the arrangements for visiting the pit should be changed. As a temporary measure, large parties were banned from Zollern 2 in 1905, but within a few months the point had been reached where the number of visitors was adversely affecting production. It was then decided to allow entry only to visitors who had obtained prior permission (Conrad, ibid., p.201). As a response to public interest a scale model of the pit was constructed and displayed at the 1905 World Exhibition in Liège.

31. In 1903 it employed 1,129 men and produced over 230,000 tons of coal. A year later the workforce had risen to 1,353 and production to 300,000 tons. During World War One the pit was producing over 400,000 tons of coal annually (Conrad, ibid., p.203).

32. G. Gebhardt, *Ruhrbergbau. Geschichte, Aufbau und Verflechtungen seiner Gesellschaften und Organisationen*, Essen, 1957, p.212.

33. The Becher, Conrad, Neumann volume was subtitled *Aufbruch zur modernen Industriearchitektur* and suggested that the building of the machine hall represented a significant *Stilwandel*.

pit complex's main courtyard and was out of bounds for the ordinary worker. For them, life at Zollern 2 was confined to the claustrophobic gloom of the deep seams and the imposing gables of Knobbe's Neo-Gothic pit-head buildings. In this respect, Kirdorf's model mine was no different to the many other Ruhr pits in the GBAG empire in the first decade of the twentieth century: by 1904 GBAG owned sixteen coal mines and employed around 25,000 men.[34] The responsibility for building work at these sites, scattered throughout the Ruhr, was spread out between the company's own building department and local master-builders and contractors. The participation of academically-educated architects like Knobbe and Möhring was the exception rather than the rule.

The new pit-head complex for the Zeche Bonifacius in Essen-Kray, erected several years after Zollern 2, was an example of the company's 'anonymous' architecture, but its historicist forms were typical of GBAG pits in the early years of the twentieth century. The Zeche Bonifacius dated back to 1857, producing its first coal some six years later, but the mine was continually dogged by technical and financial difficulties, and was eventually picked up cheaply by the GBAG in November 1899. Massive investment by the Gelsenkirchen concern turned around the mine's fortunes, and by the time the new pit-head buildings were unveiled in 1905 it was employing more than 2,000 men and producing over 550,000 tons of coal per annum.[35] Under the GBAG, horses were replaced by machines, and electricity took the place of steam, but the pit-head buildings looked to the past, rather than the present or the future, for their architectural inspiration.

It was a similar story at the Zeche Westhausen in Bodelschwingh, north of Dortmund, where another loss-making pit – it lost 3.5 million Marks for the Gewerkschaft Westhausen between 1872 and 1897 – passed into the GBAG's hands, on this occasion via the Disconto Gesellschaft bank.[36] This was a good purchase for the company since the Zeche Westhausen lay in an area surrounded by other GBAG pits. In 1898 the GBAG began a programme to renew or replace the bulk of the mine's equipment, and to turn the pit to profit. By 1904 it had 859 employees and was producing nearly 230,000 tons of coal annually. The pit-head buildings were built in 1904–5,[37] with a large basilica-style hall, which housed the showers, wages hall and offices, taking centre-stage. This monumental structure, in red

34. G. Gebhardt, *Ruhrbergbau*, p.212.
35. G. Gebhardt, *ibid.*, pp.209–212. The pit continued in production until the early 1980s. The pit-head building now houses a supermarket and a squash club.
36. G. Gebhardt, *ibid.*, pp.208–212.
37. This is probably correct, although several accounts date the building as late as 1910; for example J. Biecker & W. Buschman (eds), *Bergbauarchitektur*, Bochum, 1986, p.143. It is now used as a car-repair workshop.

Figure 9 Zeche Bonifacius, pit-head building, Essen-Kray 1905
Arch. Unknown. Present condition

brick with white plaster inlays and yellow sandstone trimmings, boasted large Cathedral-like windows, and must have made an enormous impression on all those who came in contact with it.

Many of the other Ruhr mines in the GBAG empire (which included the Alma, Erin, Minister Stein, Rheinelbe and Fürst Hardenburg pits) had imposing historicist buildings, but these examples are sufficient to indicate that the company's use of architecture was both conscious and consistent. The GBAG did not continue to use historical forms because they were the only models available, or because their builders considered them fashionable, but rather because the company's board of directors, and Emil Kirdorf in particular, chose to have the company portrayed in that way. Kirdorf was certainly well aware of the short-term commercial advantage imposing buildings could bring, but the Ruhr pits also demonstrate a longer-term desire to embody the ethos of the company in bricks and mortar.

By utilising the architecture of the Church (wage halls at Zollern 2 and Westhausen), the Army (battlements at Bonifacius) and the Court (layout at Zollern 2) the GBAG emphasised not only its strength, solidity, and hoped-for longevity, but also the authoritarian manner in which the company was run. The GBAG shared with the other major heavy industrial concerns a fondness for regimented work practices and military discipline, and it was surely no coincidence that the three figures who lent their names for roads on the Zollern 2 housing estate were Bismarck, Moltke and Roon. This aggressive approach to industrial organisation was perhaps best summed up by another infamous figure in German heavy industry at the turn of the century, Baron von Stumm-Halberg:

If a factory enterprise is to flourish it must be organised on military and not on parliamentary lines . . . Just as the soldiery includes every member of the army from the field marshall to the youngest recruit, with all pulling together against the enemy when the king calls, so the employees of the Neunkirchen works stand as one, whether it is a question of defeating the competition or of taking on the revolutionary powers of darkness.[38]

The buildings at each of the GBAG pits were arranged in a strict hierarchy of importance and value; a fact quickly apparent to the outside visitor, but probably even more obvious to the miner of the day. Kirdorf was a fierce opponent of any measure which would improve the rights or prospects of ordinary workers. As a key figure in the employers' pressure-group the Centralverband Deutscher Industrieller he had only a '*starres Nein*' for all proposals of *Sozialpolitik* and considered even the Christian

38. Quoted in J. Boberg, T. Fichter, E. Gillen (eds), *Die Metropole. Industriekultur in Berlin im 20. Jahrhundert*, Munich, 1985, p.22.

trade unions to be dangerous revolutionaries. Kirdorf shunned party politics before the First World War, but later joined the DNVP and helped to smooth Hitler's pathway to power. The pit-head buildings which remain as the legacy of his long and active role in the life of the Ruhr are an awe-inspiring yet chilling reminder of a long-lost era in the history of German industrial relations.

The GBAG mines were not unique, however, and some of the pits of rival coal mining operations could also boast eye-catching pit-head structures. In 1903 the Zeche Recklinghausen 1, which belonged to the Harpener Bergbau-AG, received a new pit-head complex designed by the Herne-based master-builder Fuchs. His design, which incorporated the functions of all previous buildings on the site under one roof, was essentially Neo-Gothic in character and included decorative gables and a clock tower, topped by an ornamental spire. The outward appearance of the complex gave no suggestion that this was one of the first coal mine buildings to make extensive use of reinforced concrete in its internal structure.[39] In 1906–7 Fuchs built another large pit-head building for the Harpener Bergbau AG at the Zeche Julia in Herne.

The Zeche Zollern 2 was not the only mine to be conceived as a 'model pit' in the years before World War One. The GHH's Zeche Jacobi, built at Oberhausen between 1912 and 1914, was described by Roland Günter as the 'Versailles of the Ruhr coal industry'.[40] Named after one of the GHH's founders, Hugo Jacobi (1834–1917), the design of the pit and the neighbouring housing estates was subject to a competition, won by the established Stuttgart architect Carl Weigle (1849–1932). As a respected state architectural official – he had built the Finance Ministry in Stuttgart (1904) and three large stately homes – Weigle was an impressive name to attract to the Ruhr, and his work for the GHH reflected the increased importance given to industrial architecture in the later Wilhelmine era.

The Zeche Jacobi's strict Neo-Baroque layout, with a tree lined avenue leading past two 'lodges', through a monumental gate and into the highly-symmetrical *cour d'honneur*, with its well-tended lawns, was largely the result of the company's own specifications, although Weigle's treatment of the buildings also contributed to the pit's aristocratic air. The buildings were designed in a simple classicising style and were all constructed using top-quality Dutch bricks and silver-grey roofing tiles. It is interesting to note the layout of the complex was planned so that underground workers should not have to walk across the central square, which fulfilled a purely

---

39. 'Das Kauen- und Verwaltungsgebäude der Zeche Recklinghausen I', in *Glückauf*, vol.41 (1905), pp.601–7. Today the much-altered building is home to a textile company.

40. R. Günter, *Oberhausen, Die Denkmäler des Rheinlandes* vol.22, Düsseldorf, 1975, p.90. Unfortunately the complex was pulled down in the late 1970s.

Figure 10 Zeche Jacobi, plan of complex, Oberhausen 1912–14
Arch. C. Weigle. Drawing from Bergbau Archiv, Bochum (BBA 30/884)

representative function. The shortage of materials and labour during the war meant that only one shaft was sunk, which somewhat diminished the symmetry of the planned complex. Nevertheless, by June 1917 the pit was producing around 2,500 tons of coal daily.[41]

The Zeche Jacobi provides a good yardstick by which to measure some of the changes which occurred in the architecture of the coal mining industry between 1900 and 1914. Direct comparison with the Zeche Zollern 2 suggests that the desire of industrialists in this sector to 'rule' over imposing architectural ensembles, inspired by the palaces of the Baroque era, had not diminished. At the same time, however, the simple, unadorned façades of the Oberhausen mine show that by 1912 the architectural reform movements were at last beginning to have some influence on the appearance of heavy industrial buildings too. Even so, the death of historicism was a slow and messy process. It was not only in coal mining that historical architectural styles lived on well into the present century: the giant mixed concerns of Ruhr heavy industry, together with their trade associations and pressure groups, were defiant in their defence of historicism too. The interests of Germany's raw iron and steel producers were fiercely defended by the Steel Works Association (Stahlwerks- verband), which became one of the most powerful voices in German industry after it had managed to unite the existing regional steel syndicates in 1904. Such was the economic weight of the Association that many cities showed an interest in attracting its headquarters to their borough. Düsseldorf's offer of a prime building site (worth over 600,000 Marks) and the temporary use of a municipal block during construction, was the option which was finally selected by the Association. The city's Lord Mayor Marx considered the transaction to be in the long term interests of the community. He told a council meeting:

> It is not only a question of the significant amount of tax which will be paid by the large number of officials. Having the headquarters of the Steel Works Association in the city will be most advantageous, for it will promote an increase in the general level of business and will raise the importance of the city in the eyes of the outside world.[42]

The building was designed in the course of 1905 by the Düsseldorf City Architect Johannes Radke – a Prussian architectural official – and the private architect Theo Westbrock. Their plans were unveiled in the

41. H. Kellermann & H. Weigle, 'Die Schachtanlage Jacobi der GHH', in *Glückauf*, vol.58 (1922), p.1. Also Bergbau-Archiv, Bochum; BBA 30/378 (Zeche Jacobi 1912–27), BBA 30/884 (Zeche Jacobi 1911–39).

42. Quoted by F. Wenger in 'Wandlungen architektonischer Vorstellungen..', PhD thesis, Hanover TH, 1967, p.22.

Düsseldorfer General-Anzeiger in the Autumn of 1905, and were warmly reviewed, although the correspondent could not determine its architectural style: 'perhaps it has echoes of the Gothic', he wrote.[43] The Stahlhof, as it became known, was designed to accommodate about 500 employees and was the biggest building yet seen in Düsseldorf. Construction work took over three years to complete and cost in excess of 2.5 million Marks.[44] The structural need for internal supporting walls meant that the arrangement of office space was as rigid and inflexible as the imposing but stiff red sandstone façades. Stone eagles glowered threateningly from every vantage point, as if to protect the building from the passing pedestrians in the busy streets below.

The companies which made up the Steel Works Association also chose foreboding historicist forms and façades for their administrative buildings. The headquarters of the mining and iron company Hoerder Bergwerks- und Hüttenverein AG, built by the local architect Marx at Hörde, south of Dortmund in 1898–9, resembled one of King Ludwig II's Bavarian fantasy castles, employing the full panoply of Medieval military motifs. It was built on the site of the twelfth century 'Burg Hörde' – ironically a simple country manor house – and featured a tall, fortress-like tower that was visible for miles around. The building soon became known and feared by the workforce as *Die Burg*.

The new office block of the Rheinische Stahlwerke, built at Meiderich near Duisburg just five years later, took the eighteenth-century German Baroque palace as its architectural model.[45] The architect, Fritz Niebel, fulfilled his client's desire for an imposing representative structure by giving the symmetrical three-storey building a projecting central block, fronted by a row of eight colossal sandstone columns and a wide flight of steps. The four central columns, which framed the building's main entrance, supported a pediment decorated with garlands, allegorical figures and the symbol of mining and forging, the *Schlägel und Eisen*.

The headquarters of the Krupp concern in Essen (planned 1905–6, built 1908–10), designed by the firm's internal building department under the leadership of the future Werkbund member Robert Schmohl (1855–1944), used historicist motifs more sparingly, and was dominated by an austere sixty-metre corner tower, dubbed the 'hunger tower' by the local populace. The tower was enlivened by some delicate tracery work and cartouches bearing the company symbol – features reminiscent of Gothic churches and subsequently revived in Essen's late nineteenth-century Neo-Gothic

43. F. Wenger, ibid., p.23.
44. F. Wenger, ibid., p.24.
45. Further details on this and other administrative buildings of the Ruhr can be found in Brigitte Schlüter's PhD thesis, 'Verwaltungsbauten der rheinisch-westfälischen Stahlindustrie 1900–1930', Bonn University, 1990.

town hall. Although the eighty-metre long building, with two show façades clad in sombre grey basalt and dark red brick, was brutal and uncompromising in its simple monumentality, it too was not free of historical convention. Gustav Krupp von Bohlen und Halbach's room was distinguished by a tower-shaped bay window, protruding from the façade and decorated with ornamental stone garlands.

The Krupp headquarters, with its steel and reinforced concrete structure, was undoubtedly the most modern heavy industrial office building yet seen in the Ruhr, but the fondness of the large coal and steel concerns for historical prototypes was further demonstrated by new buildings erected in the Dortmund area, for Hoesch in 1912–14 and the Union AG, part of the Stinnes empire, in 1916–21. Both the former, designed by the local architectural practice of Steinbach and Lutter, and the latter, built to the plans of Karl and Dietrich Schulze, were fronted by monumental Classical porticos.

The head office of the Gewerkschaft Deutscher Kaiser (GDK), the mining division of August Thyssen's empire, which was built between 1902–04 at Bruckhausen, north of Duisburg, was less severe in appearance than many of the representative buildings of the Ruhr concerns, but was equally reliant on the architectural styles of the past. The Dortmund-based architect Carl Bern, whose design was probably chosen after a competition, employed north German red-brick Gothic motifs and enlivened the façades with a subtle use of materials and murals, to which further historicising details, including crenellations, were added during construction. The building, which was extended in the 1920s and 'simplified' in the 1960s, stood in great contrast to the GDK's previous headquarters, a two-storey former school house, which had been built without architectural embellishment.

The same pattern was followed with the company's 'works office', where an old, unadorned building was replaced at the turn of the century by a more imposing structure with two stepped-gables. After 1900 even some of the humbler buildings under the concern's control received the historicist treatment. The Beeckerwerth pumping station, built for Thyssen at Mülheim in 1902, revealed a Byzantine influence on Ruhr industrial architecture, whilst the GDK's harbour office at Schwelgern, built in 1906–07, was yet another industrial building to incorporate a fortress tower, with battlements and flagpole. The principal figure in the GDK's building department from 1898 to 1926 was the master-builder Joseph Oest (1873–1951), who joined the company after a bricklaying apprenticeship, four years craft training at the *Baugewerkschule* in Holzminden, and a brief spell working for a building contractor. Although it is not possible to determine his personal role in the design of particular buildings for the GDK it is interesting to note that he was appointed by August Thyssen himself, who was said to have a high regard for his talents. Oest's personal story is probably typical of many of the practical master-builders who worked in the building departments of large industrial companies at the turn of the century. He supervised the design of many industrial buildings at a time of great expansion for the company, but was overlooked in favour of an outside architect for the planning of the major administrative building, and then saw his responsibilities gradually diminish, as architects with degrees began to enter the company in the years immediately before and after the Great War.[46]

By no means all buildings erected for iron foundries and coal mines at this time were historicist in character: the sort of structures which provided Oest with the bulk of his workload were designed to obey the laws of structural engineering and economics rather than aesthetics. The significant fact, however, is surely that the buildings deemed by heavy industrial companies to perform a representative function invariably made a feature of historical styles – notably those styles most closely associated with the Church, the Army and the State – whereas the representative buildings of other sectors of German industry increasingly did not. As we shall see, the reform movements which sprang up in German architecture after 1900 were largely ignored by the big Ruhr concerns. Indeed, the reformers received the bulk of their support from precisely those firms which, for a variety of reasons, most fiercely opposed the economic, social and political views of the Ruhr heavy industrialists.

The Architecture of the State and its Critics

When the big coal and iron concerns employed historic architectural styles for their important representative buildings the immediate inspiration often came not from the past but from the many contemporary historicist buildings designed by state architectural officials. For the heavy industrial companies, which liked to be portrayed as an indispensable pillar of the established order and which identified their activities so closely with the aims and values of the state, such buildings were a most appropriate model. State architecture – which included post offices and railway stations, as well as law courts and government offices – was regularly displayed in the pages of the Prussian Treasury's influential journal *Centralblatt der Bauverwaltung* and rarely risked the new or untried. Their architects were well versed in the intricacies of each of the historic architectural styles and were all-too conscious of the strict parameters in which they worked.

The administration of public building projects in Imperial Germany was highly centralised and rigidly hierarchical. Although the construction of

46. Thyssen Archiv, PA Oest.

public buildings in Prussia was theoretically a matter for the forty-eight government districts (*Regierungsbezirke*), all building plans drawn up by district officials which would cost more than 5,000 Marks to build had to be forwarded to Berlin for scrutiny. Here the experienced building officials of the relevant ministry (usually the Ministry of Public Works, but often the Education Ministry, Agriculture Ministry etc.) would amend or adapt the plans, without direct knowledge of the architect's intentions or the site in which the building was to be erected. Details of many major projects were even passed on to Kaiser Wilhelm II himself, who enjoyed making his own personal 'corrections' and comments. Thus by the time the plans arrived back in the hands of the original district building officials they had often changed beyond recognition. It was hardly surprising, therefore, that the buildings which resulted were often criticised for being cold, impersonal, and formalistic. All signs of individuality, innovation or experimentation had invariably been filtered out by the time construction work began.

If the constant involvement of higher building officials in Berlin ensured that even the most humble railway stations and post offices were condemned to repeat the same hollow historical forms a hundred times over, then at least their efforts were characterised by a high level of professional competence gained over many years of extensive academic training and practical experience. The Kaiser's contributions could hardly be justified in this way; they merely revealed the enthusiasms and prejudices of an individual whose fascination with industry and technology was not matched by an openness to new ideas in architecture. Wilhelm II's role in the artistic life of the *Reich* was an issue which excited the passions of contemporary commentators and continues to fascinate to this day. His pronouncements on aesthetics had a direct impact on the design of stamps, coins, trophies, uniforms and furniture, not to mention fine art, but it was in the area of architecture where Royal interventions were most visible.

In 1904 it was calculated that the Kaiser had 'corrected or influenced in some way' the design of eighty-four public buildings under the jurisdiction of the *Reich*, and a further seventy-nine in Prussia.[47] In a book published by the *Reichsdruckerei* in 1907, entitled *Der Kaiser und die Kunst*, Paul Seidel wrote:

> No important event in the artistic life of the nation escapes the sharp eye of the monarch. All arteries of artistic activity in the various government departments lead to him . . . What an inspiration and awakening of ambition it must be for all concerned, aware that every design of any importance, whether it is for a

47. P. Seidel, *Der Kaiser und die Kunst*, Berlin, 1907, p.38.

church, a station, a post office or a monument, is first laid in front of the Ruler to undergo a thorough examination.[48]

The Kaiser's favourite architectural style was the Romanesque, although he could tolerate Gothic, Classical, and Renaissance forms in the right surroundings. He had no time, however, for buildings which did not employ an acknowledged historic style. As Seidel noted, 'many an architect has seen his design rejected, with the following footnote: "the façade has absolutely no recognisable style"'.[49] The Kaiser had another aversion:

> The Kaiser has often spoken most clearly about his relationship with the so-called 'modern' trends and movements in art. He is against artists who want to ignore the whole evolution of our culture – and the laws of beauty and harmony which have come from it – and who instead claim, or at least give the impression of believing that they have only just rediscovered true art.[50]

At first, the Kaiser's comments on artistic matters seemed to be nothing more than off-the-cuff remarks of a personal nature. After the completion of Berlin's monumental Siegesallee in 1901, however, he invited the sculptors and artists who had worked on the project to Court, where he addressed them with a major speech on the role of art in society. Wilhelm II ordered that the speech to 'his artists' should be published, and his conviction that art 'should help to have an educating effect on the people' was widely reported.[51] Many in the artistic community were perturbed by the Kaiser's comments; not because of the conservative nature of his personal views, or of the Court's commissioning policy, but for the way in which he extended his interest into areas of architectural activity far from the traditional concerns of royalty. The *Kunstwart* was particularly worried by the apparent lack of capable artistic advisors in the Kaiser's entourage, prepared to put alternative views to Wilhelm in person.[52]

A typical example of the monarch's involvement in architectural issues was his intervention in the planning of a new main railway station for the city of Hamburg. A competition to find suitable plans for this major project was announced on 6 May 1900, and by the end of the year sixteen submissions had been received. No entry met the full favour of the jury, but two plans were rewarded with 8,000 Mark prizes and were purchased

48. P. Seidel, *ibid.*, p.10.

49. P. Seidel, *ibid.*, p.31.

50. P. Seidel, *ibid.*, p.14.

51. See, for instance, 'Zur Rede des Kaisers', in *Der Kunstwart*, vol.15 (1902), pp. 361–5.

52. *Der Kunstwart*, ibid. See also 'Hofkunst und andere Kunst', in *Der Kunstwart*, vol.15 (1901), pp.85–90.

for further consideration. The architects Reinhardt and Süssenguth – whose architectural conception was praised – and the railway engineer Möller – who was considered to have proposed the best layout – were commissioned to work on a final design. Once complete, the finished plans were sent to Berlin for consideration, where they met with a mixed response from the Kaiser. Whilst the ground plan and construction of the hall were applauded, he was less happy with the architectural design of the reception buildings, which employed some *Jugendstil* elements: too modern, was his verdict, and he blue-pencilled the offending details. Reinhardt and Süssenguth had little option but to follow Royal advice, and scrapped much of their original plan to accommodate Wilhelm's suggestions. Even then it took several attempts to placate the Kaiser, who was said to have written '*scheußlich*' on one of the drafts.[53] The building was finally opened, amidst much pomp and ceremony, on 6 December 1906, with a neo-Baroque façade. The architects were each rewarded for their patience and flexibility with professorships.

The Kaiser continued to offer his opinions on architectural questions throughout the pre-World War One years. There is little evidence to suggest that the great shifts and movements which occurred in German architecture between 1900 and 1914 made any impression on the tone or content of his contributions. Writing in *Die Tat* shortly before the outbreak of war, Adolf Behne assessed Wilhelm's impact:

> As a patron of the arts, this monarch, who showed such a firm grasp of the political and social problems which faced the modern Germany, remained a defiant reactionary eclecticist and an undistinguished decadent. In this area he did not order the construction of modern battleships, but historical corvettes.[54]

For the critics of historicism the façade of Hamburg's main railway station seemed to provide a good illustration of the way in which contemporary functional buildings were being stifled by façades they called 'dishonest' and 'deceitful'. Writing in *Der Kunstwart* in 1904, the Prussian civil servant and architect Hermann Muthesius (1861–1927) bitterly attacked the ethics of historicism in architecture and design:

> An alarming mania prevails for glossing over real conditions, to over-refine until something is considered 'distinguished', to force one's self to rise into a pseudo-aristocracy. We seem to be ashamed of the very thing which should

53. P. Seidel, *Der Kaiser und die Kunst*, p.44; E. Staisch, *Eisenbahnen rollen durch das 'Tor zur Welt'*, Hamburg, 1956, pp.56–7.; E. Staisch, *Hauptbahnhof Hamburg*, Hamburg, 1981, p.138.
54. A. Behne quoted in B. Bergius, J. Frecot, D. Radicke (eds), *Architektur, Stadt und Politik*, Lahn Gießen, 1979, p.251 note 30.

make us proud, our *Bürgertum*. We want to be aristocrats at the very moment when the *Bürgertum* has become the basis of our economic, social and political life, when it has reached such a height that it is able to determine the culture of our time.[55]

Muthesius's views were shared by a large number of his educated middle class contemporaries, who read journals like *Der Kunstwart* in increasing numbers, and joined in the activities of a bewildering array of cultural reform groups formed around the turn of the century. These societies and associations – which included the Land Reform Movement (1898), the Dürerbund (1901), and the German Garden Cities Association (1902), as well as the two organisations which had a profound effect on industrial architecture in Wilhelmine Germany, the Heimatschutz movement (1904) and the Werkbund (1907) – are sometimes considered under the umbrella term *Lebensreformbewegung*, or movement for the reform of life. The phrase 'reform of life' first appeared in print in 1896, and soon came to encompass everything from vegetarianism and naturism to homeopathy and clothing reform. Indeed, it was the breadth of the *Lebensreform* concept that it was a 'movement' only in the very widest sense: its uses to the historian are therefore strictly limited, and must always be treated with extreme caution.

Several authors have struggled with varying degrees of success to investigate this complex milieu, which combined formal *Vereinstätigkeit* with vague idealism, and to place it at a recognisable point in the political spectrum.[56] It is clear however that the idea of a 'reform of life' attracted all shades of political opinion, from utopian socialists to liberal reformists and conservative nationalists. It would certainly be misleading to portray *Lebensreform* as an expression of the 'unpolitical' bourgeoisie, for although many in the *Bildungsbürgertum* claimed to be 'above' party politics – the *Kunstwart* was aimed at 'the honest people of all parties' and the Dürerbund was to be 'a party of practical people'[57] – the movement attracted a fair proportion of party animals too. The Garden City Association was run by the three Kampffmeyer brothers, each a member of the SPD, whilst the leadership of the Werkbund was, as we shall see, dominated and controlled by activists of the left liberal Freisinnige Vereinigung.

The middle-class reformers of the day had equally divergent views on the pace and value of economic, social and cultural modernisation. The divisions between 'cultural pessimists' and enthusiastic progressives ran

55. H. Muthesius in *Der Kunstwart*, vol.17 (1904), p.469.

56. Most notably G. Kratzsch, *Kunstwart und Dürerbund*, Göttingen, 1969; and W. Krabbe, *Gesellschaftsveränderung durch Lebensreform*, Münster, 1972.

57. G. Kratzsch, *ibid.*, pp.136–8.

through the heart of each and every *Lebensreform* organisation, and often both poles were present in the minds of individual reformers. If there was one theme which united all the disparate elements of the 'movement', however, it was an intense preoccupation with ethics. The word *ethisch* appeared in *Kunstwart* almost as often as *Kultur*, and a more ethical society was championed by everyone from the anti-vivisectionists to the architectural reformers. Indeed, there was an organisation specifically entitled the Society for Ethical Culture.

The charade of historicist architecture was considered to be indicative of the lack of ethical values in contemporary society. Phrases such as 'the unity of appearance and reality' (Avenarius) or 'ethical character is identical with practical character' (Stumpf), were echoed by political reformers and dissident architects alike, but if historicism was irrelevant and dishonest, what was to take its place in the new century? The next two chapters examine the most important responses to architectural historicism after 1900 and assess the impact of reformist ideas and organisations on German industrial buildings. It was only as a consequence of the 'reform of life' movement, in its various guises, that industrial architecture became a topic of general interest, but by the later Wilhelmine years it had become firmly established as a prominent public and political issue. As Adolf Behne was able to write in 1914:

> Today one can say without exaggeration that a new industrial building grabs the attention of the public and the critics to the highest degree. A factory which does not satisfy aesthetic requirements is nowadays judged more harshly than a boring town hall or an unsuccessful monument.[58]

That this was indeed the case, was in no short measure due to members of the Heimatschutz movement, whose activities form the focus of the following chapter.

---

58. A. Behne, 'Heutige Industriebauten', in *Velhagen & Klasings Monatshefte*, vol.28 (1914), p.53.

2

Back to the Future?
The Heimatschutz Movement in
Wilhelmine Germany

Histories of twentieth century architecture have, by and large, chosen to ignore the German Heimatschutz movement. Where the term 'Heimatschutz' – it literally means 'protection of the homeland' – does intrude into the classic texts it is usually in a negative context: as the mouthpiece of organised philistinism; as a misguided body of people who sought to prevent the onward march of modernism. The well-documented campaigns against the Weimar and Dessau Bauhaus in which some Heimatschutz supporters were involved, and their role as 'opposition' in the heroic period of the Modern movement, sealed their fate in the eyes of a generation of art-historians.

Moreover, tragi-comic episodes, such as the touched-up photograph produced by the Swabian Heimatschutz association to portray the flat-roofed and whitewashed houses of Stuttgart's ultra-modernist Weißenhof estate as a 'Suburb of Jerusalem', complete with camels and shadowy Arab figures, are used to illustrate the movement's marriage of convenience with the National Socialists in the late 1920s. The ill-advised flirtation of certain Heimatschutz leaders with racial theory, and the Nazi Party's eager exploitation of the propaganda opportunities which this presented, have inevitably cast a dark shadow on the movement's history. It hardly matters that the Third Reich paid only lip-service to Heimatschutz ideas – Fritz Todt, architect of the *Autobahn* construction programme and from 1940 Hitler's Armaments Minister, described himself as 'Guardian of the Heimatschutz Ideal', as he buried great swathes of the Homeland under concrete and steel – for once the movement had sold its soul to Hitler, there was no way back.

The four decades since World War Two have produced no monograph on the movement in any language, and precious little research into any aspect of its activities.[1] This is unfortunate, because there is more to Heimatschutz than those few well-publicised episodes from the 1920s suggest. Indeed, it is arguable that by the time Hitler came to power, the movement's period of greatest influence had long since passed. The history of Heimatschutz in Wilhelmine Germany has yet to be written, but even the most cursory of glances at the movement's literature reveals a complex and dynamic set of ideas which do not fit neatly into any simplistic 'progressive' / 'reactionary' schema.

If the movement is mentioned at all by historians of Wilhelmine Germany it is usually in the context of the 'cultural pessimists' on the *völkisch* fringe, yet many of its preoccupations would today appear to sit comfortably in the mainstream of progressive thought. From the turn of the century to the Great War numerous Heimatschutz groups throughout Germany campaigned against architectural eyesores and industrial pollution; against the over-development of beauty-spots for tourism and excessive billboard advertising in environmentally sensitive locations; and for the preservation of historic town centres and vernacular building traditions. One of the few examples of research into Heimatschutz activity at a local level, Hans-Günther Andresen's works on Heimatschutz architecture in Schleswig-Holstein and Lübeck,[2] reveal no extremes of 'cultural pessimism', but a movement with a 'pragmatic scepticism about progress'; a highly-modern characteristic.

This chapter examines one aspect of Heimatschutz activity, which well illustrates its Janus-like stance on questions of modernity and tradition; its attitude to industrial architecture in the years 1900–1918. It is divided into four short sections: the first considers the movement's origins, initial aims and membership; the second examines more closely the Heimatschutz attitude to industrial architecture and highlights certain industrial sites which reflect its influence; section three looks at Heimatschutz lobbying and legislation, and the impact of new laws on the character of the built environment; and the final section considers the state of the movement in the aftermath of Heimatschutz legislation.

---

1. Published works which contain sections on Heimatschutz include K. Bergmann, *Agrarromantik und Großstadtfeindschaft*, Meisenheim am Glan, 1970; R.P. Sieferle, *Fortschrittsfeinde? Opposition gegen Technik und Industrie von der Romantik bis zur Gegenwart*, Munich, 1984; J. Hermand & R. Hamann, *Stilkunst um 1900*, East Berlin, 1967; F.-J. Bruggemeier & T. Rommelspacher (eds), *Besiegte Natur: Geschichte der Umwelt im 19. und 20. Jahrhundert*, Munich 1987. For a recent discussion of 'The German Idea of Heimat' see C. Applegate, *A Nation of Provincials. The German Idea of Heimat*, Berkeley, 1990.

2. H.-G. Andresen, *Bauen in Backstein. Schleswig-Holsteinische Heimatschutz-Architektur*, Heide in Holstein, 1989; also 'Heimatschutzarchitektur in Lübeck', in M. Brix (ed.), *Lübeck: die Altstadt als Denkmal*, Munich, 1975.

The Origins of the Heimatschutz Idea

As we have seen the Heimatschutz idea grew out of the wider movement for the 'reform of life', but its particular origins are usually traced back to 1880, when the music professor Ernst Rudorff published an essay on 'The Relationship of Modern Life and Nature'.[3] It was Rudorff who, in 1897, first used the term Heimatschutz (as the title of two short essays in the journal *Grenzboten*). At the same time, the writer and *völkisch* activist Adolf Bartels was promoting the concept of *Heimatkunst*; a form of art and literature that was to take its inspiration from the culture and traditions of Germany's rural regions. From 1900 the movement had its own journal, simply called *Heimat*.

Bartels, and other *Heimat* essayists like Friedrich Lienhard, were often highly political in their writing, echoing the agraro-conservatism and anti-semitism of Germany's nineteenth century anti-urbanites Wilhelm Riehl, Heinrich Sohnrey and Theodor Fritsch, whose 1896 work *Die Stadt der Zukunft* pre-empted the Garden City movement. Bartels was eager to stress that *Heimatkunst* did not exist simply 'to spread aesthetic pleasure', but rather stood 'in the service of a great national movement'[4]; a movement which Sohnrey believed to be 'the strongest and safest barrier to the growing threat of the realisation of the Communist-Socialist state'.[5] Rudorff frequently wrote in a similar vein:

> It is significant that unpatriotic behaviour is reared almost exclusively in the factory districts. What of the Fatherland is indeed worth protecting, worth dying for if every characteristic of the local landscape, every custom and idiosyncracy in tradition and appearance has already been destroyed?[6]

The few existing accounts of the Heimatschutz movement have dwelt for many pages on this shadowy cultural milieu, described by one writer as a form of 'Crypto-Fascism', which 'cast off all intellectual achievements in favour of an irrational attachment to Blood and Soil'.[7] The role of such ideas in the Heimatschutz movement is, however, highly debatable.

---

3. For the origins of the Heimatschutz idea see K. Bergmann *ibid.* and Christian Otto's Summer 1983 *Art Journal* essay 'Modern Environment and Historical Continuity: The Heimatschutz Discourse in Germany'. Also, S. Muthesius, 'The origins of the German conservation movement', in R. Kain (ed.), *Planning for Conservation*, London, 1981.
4. Quoted in K. Bergmann, *Agrarromantik*, p.118.
5. Quoted in K. Bergmann, *ibid.*, p.108.
6. Quoted in K. Bergmann, *ibid.*, p.129.
7. J. Hermand & R. Hamann, *Stilkunst*, p.365. A similar line is pursued by G. Stark in *Entrepreneurs of Ideology. Neoconservative Publishers in Germany, 1890–1933*, Chapel Hill, 1981; and H. Mommsen, 'Die Auflösung des Bürgertums seit dem späten 19. Jahrhundert', in J. Kocka (ed.), *Bürger und Bürgerlichkeit im 19. Jahrhundert*, Göttingen, 1987.

Certainly there is little evidence to suggest that the turn-of-the-century *völkisch* ideologues played anything more than a bit-part in the day-to-day practice of Heimatschutz. As Bergmann points out, even Rudorff's role was limited once an organisational framework for the movement had been established.[8]

Of more immediate impact were the writings of the artist and architect Paul Schultze-Naumburg, whose essays in *Der Kunstwart* were well-received by a growing public. In 1900 Schultze-Naumburg (1869–1949) began work on a series of essays which were to become known as his *Kulturarbeiten*, nine volumes of which appeared over the next seventeen years. Each work employed a simple but effective method combining a concise text with a series of black and white photographs of buildings and landscapes, arranged as 'example' (good) and 'counter example' (bad). These essays introduced questions of architecture, conservation and planning to a large lay-public, and were followed up by some successful pamphlets, with titles like 'The Disfigurement of our Country', which concludes with the warning: 'Yes, we face the terrible danger of losing our homeland and becoming part of a cheerless international set-up, every bit as bleak as the cold, drab abstractions of a future state in which everyone is equal'.[9]

As Christian Otto describes in his 1983 *Art Journal* article,[10] the immediate precursor to the organised Heimatschutz movement was the German Commission for Sound Urban and Rural building which was established at a 1903 congress, held in Erfurt under the aegis of the *Regierungspräsident* von Dewitz to consider the problems of contemporary architecture. The Chairman of the Commission was Schultze-Naumburg, by now a professor and head of a flourishing art school as well as a respected writer. In 1904 it was decided by Schultze-Naumburg and Rudorff, who had continued to write polemical essays on the German environment, to expand the Commission into a popular organisation, which was to be called the Bund Heimatschutz.

The new organisation was founded on 30 March 1904, when some 120 prominent individuals from the arts, politics and public service gathered in Dresden to sign a declaration of intent. It envisaged a body of active citizens, fighting to preserve not only traditional values in architecture, but also to protect wildlife, flora and fauna, country customs and traditional crafts. As the name implies, the Bund Heimatschutz was founded primarily to protect and conserve, rather than to influence the future character of the German environment, but in the course of the next decade the shaping of the new became every bit as important as the preservation of the old.

8. K. Bergmann, *Agrarromantik*, p.129.
9. P. Schultze-Naumburg, *Die Entstellung unseres Landes*, 3rd edn, Munich, 1908, p.78.
10. C.F. Otto, 'Modern Environment', p.148.

Paul Schultze-Naumburg was elected to lead the new organisation, with the Minister of State Freiherr von Feilitzsch-Bückeburg as his deputy.

It was no coincidence that the Bund should be founded in Dresden, for Saxony, along with Thuringia, was widely acknowledged as the spiritual home of the Heimatschutz idea: not only was it the stronghold of Schultze-Naumburg and Ferdinand Avenarius, but it was also home-territory to Karl Schmidt, an architect and civil servant who was to become a key figure in the movement. Schmidt (1853–1922) had joined the civil service in Saxony as an architect in 1882 and advanced to a position as head of the Building and Public Works section of the Treasury by 1902. In addition he was a government representative on the Royal Commission for the Preservation of Historical Monuments and an enthusiastic student of Saxony's rich cultural heritage. Schmidt was the driving force behind the new Saxon Building Code of 1900, which specifically recommended the use of local materials and traditional methods in new buildings, and which marked the start of a whole series of new building and planning laws in the German states. Saxony was to remain the flagship of the Heimatschutz Movement throughout the period and boasted the largest membership of any of the Bund's affiliated regional organisations.[11]

By 1906 the Heimatschutz movement claimed its organisations involved 100,000 people as either individual or corporate members. Between 1900 and 1918 dozens of Heimatschutz groups were founded throughout Germany. By 1911, 29 of these were affiliated to the Bund, although the Rhineland, Bavaria and Baden movements remained independent until after World War One. Individual membership of the Bund stood at around 15,000 in December 1911.[12] In some states and provinces, such as the Rhineland, the Heimatschutz organisation was a semi-official body, closely linked to the preservation authorities, whilst in other areas the organisation was in receipt of state subsidies. This was particularly the case in Saxony where annual state grants had risen to 42,500 Marks by 1914.[13]

11. The strength of Heimatschutz in Saxony was demonstrated once more on 17 February 1990, when the Landesverein Sächsischer Heimatschutz was refounded by around 200 'enthusiastic supporters of the Heimatschutz idea' at a special meeting in Dresden. See *Sächsische Heimatblätter*, vol.36 (1990), pp.145–6.

12. C.F. Otto, 'Modern Environment', p.149.

13. See 'Der Heimatschutz im sächsischen Landtag', in *Deutsche Bauzeitung*, vol. 49 (1915), p.126. The Saxon Ministry of the Interior first contributed to the Heimatschutz movement in 1905 with a 100 Mark donation. In 1907 an annual state subsidy of 15,000 Marks was granted to the Saxon *Heimatschützer* to establish an office with a full-time architect. This figure rose to 42,500 Marks in 1914, before falling to 37,000 Marks per annum for the years 1916–1919. The level of state subsidies for Heimatschutz organisations varied greatly however, with no other state matching the Saxon levels. In the Rhineland, subsidy amounted to 300 Marks per annum (from 1909 to 1914), rising to 500 Marks in 1915. In Schleswig-Holstein the figure was 800 Marks.

Although each region placed a different emphasis on the various aspects of the Heimatschutz concept, and despite disagreements over the suitability of certain architectural forms,[14] there was broad agreement on the standard texts of the movement. Schultze-Naumburg's *Kulturarbeiten* and his pamphlet *Die Entstellung unseres Landes*, Rudorff's republished *Heimatschutz*, Carl Johann Fuchs's *Heimatschutz und Volkswirtschaft* and Karl Henrici's *Über die Pflege des Heimatlichen im ländlichen und städtischen Bauwesen*, formed an ideological backbone to the often modest local campaigns fought by the individual Heimatschutz groups. In addition, journals such as *Kunstwart*, *Heimatschutz* and the Dürerbund pamphlet series, together with numerous local publications, ran regular articles on Heimatschutz activity.

The term Heimatschutz was defined so broadly in the organisation's 1904 founding charter that its supporters could channel their energies in any number of directions. Inevitably, however, certain causes and campaigns emerged to the detriment of others. With governmental agencies gradually assuming responsibility for the preservation of ancient monuments, and autonomous organisations emerging in the fields of animal welfare and the preservation of folk-traditions, the topic which came to dominate Heimatschutz thought was the relationship of the built environment to the natural world. From the Bund's first major campaign – a failed attempt to preserve the spectacular Laufenburg Rapids from becoming part of a hydro-electric power station – to its wartime efforts to rebuild destroyed East Prussian villages in a sympathetic form, this relationship remained a leitmotif of Heimatschutz discourse.

Heimatschutz campaigns attracted support from all sections of society, but certain professions played a predominant role in the movement's day-to-day activity. Analysis of membership of the Hamburg Heimatschutz organisation (Verein Heimatschutz im Hamburger Staatsgebiet – founded in 1911 by the amalgamation of three earlier associations) reveals the following breakdown by profession: of 389 members, 97 were teachers or professors; 40 civil servants (including judges); 39 businessmen or industrialists; 23 architects and 21 pastors.[15] The membership list includes six deputies of the Hamburg parliament, plus the Mayor of the town of Stade.

If the Hamburg organisation could boast a fairly impressive cross-section of middle class society, the membership of the Rhineland's Heimatschutz organisation reveals an even greater array of *Honoratioren*.

---

14. Since there was little tradition of red-brick building in Saxony the movement's early literature attacked its use. This brought a swift and angry response from North German *Heimatschützer*, who viewed brick as the quintessential local material.

15. StA Hamburg A 507/13: Kapsel 1. 'Verein Heimatschutz im Hamburger Staatsgebiet' – 'Verzeichnis der Mitglieder vom 1 Okt. 1911 bis 1 Okt. 1912'.

The Rheinischer Verein für Denkmalpflege und Heimatschutz, which was founded in 1906, had 1600 members by 1910. Its large management committee included the Lord Mayors of Aachen, Cologne, Duisburg and Bonn, the *Landräte* of Erkelenz, Trier, St. Goar, Euskirchen, Ahrweiler and Bernkastel, and many leaders of the business community (no fewer than nineteen *Kommerzienräte* or *Geheime Kommerzienräte*).[16] Meanwhile the Saxony section of the Committee for the Care of Indigenous Art and Building Methods in Saxony and Thuringia, the precursor to the Verein Sächsischer Heimatschutz, included 38 civil servants, 31 state architects or building officials, 27 artists or architects in private practice, and 20 teachers or academics, amongst its 131 members in 1906.[17] The Heimatschutz movement was many things, but it was hardly part of the frivolous fringe.

The important role played by teachers and civil servants in the movement has often been noted and may help to explain the didactic tone of much Heimatschutz literature. It is also a factor of considerable interest to historians searching for the social roots of 'cultural pessimism' in Wilhelmine Germany. Teachers, clerics and civil servants were, after all, some of the alleged 'casualties' of the industrialisation process:

> Instead of honour, money was in demand. Achievement counted rather than bearing, ostentatious wealth rather than inner-values or education. The old middle class, which had defined its place in society through property and education, was particularly affected by this transformation.[18]

According to Rolf Peter Sieferle in his study of 'Enemies of Progress', recently-qualified teachers and professors were particularly eager to defend the old values of culture and learning against the 'parvenu' standards of Wilhelmine society. Whilst employers, workers and even landowners had come to recognise the necessity of the industrialisation process, the *Bildungsbürgertum* remained deeply suspicious of its effects. There may be some truth in this assessment, but we should bear in mind that equivalent organisations in other countries had a very similar social character. The National Trust, founded in Britain in 1894, the American Scenic and Historic Preservation Society of 1895, and the Societé pour la Protection des Paysages de France, were just a few of the environmentalist associations to be established at the turn of the century. Indeed, international conferences on Heimatschutz issues were held in Paris in

---

16. *Mitteilungen des Rheinischen Vereins für Denkmalpflege und Heimatschutz*, vol.1 (1907).

17. StA Dresden MdI 17518. 'Ausschuß zur Pflege heimatlicher Kunst und Bauweise in Sachsen und Thüringen 1903–08'; p.40 -'Mitgliederverzeichnis Abt. Sachsen 1906.'

18. R.P. Sieferle, *Fortschrittsfeinde*, p.206.

1909, and Stuttgart three years later.

One must therefore be careful not to view Heimatschutz as a German 'peculiarity' or assume that industrialisation turned all Germany's teachers, clerics and civil servants into rabid anti-modernists or gloomy 'cultural pessimists'. Furthermore one must differentiate between the opposition to industrialisation and modernisation *per se*, and those who objected only to certain aspects of the process. Geoff Eley is surely correct when he writes on 'cultural pessimism':

> A number of weaknesses reduce the value of the socio-cultural stereotype associated with this idea. On one count, the real anti-modernists – agrarians, artisans and traditional small businessmen with a grievance against progress – were motivated much less by an intellectual cultural pessimism than by the prospects of economic decline. By contrast, the urban middle class with whom the mood of cultural pessimism is normally associated seems readily to have grasped the benefits of the new society with all the buoyancy and self-confidence one could expect in a prosperous and rapidly growing economy. In general they confined their hostility only to certain features of modernity.[19]

In turning now to examine the attitude of the Heimatschutz movement to industrial architecture, it should be possible to assess the mood of a significant section of middle class opinion to questions of tradition and modernity in Wilhelmine Germany.

Heimatschutz and Industrial Architecture

From the beginning, the quality of industrial architecture and technical structures was a prime concern of the Heimatschutz movement. The post-1870 expansion of German industry, and the associated development of the nation's infrastructure, was a major factor in the rapid transformation of the German landscape. Heimatschutz leaders were, however, well aware that they could not halt the industrialisation process – nor indeed did they want to. The Freiburg economics professor and Heimatschutz activist Carl Johann Fuchs wrote:

> What we strive for is in no way regressive, reactionary or romantic – which some people may suggest. We have no intention of jamming the spokes of the 'wheel of time', or indeed of trying to turn it back. But we can and will steer it so that it does not run over the beauties of our homeland, and does not drive us up the creek of affectation and pretentious superficiality, but rather takes us up to the heights of real culture.[20]

19. G. Eley, 'The German Right 1860–1945: How it changed', in *From Unification to Nazism. Reinterpreting the German Past*, London, 1986, pp.235–6.
20. C.J. Fuchs, 'Heimatschutz und Volkswirtschaft', in *Der Kunstwart*, vol.17 (1904), p.212.

Addressing a conference in Mannheim on the relationship between Heimatschutz and technology, the movement's leader Paul Schultze-Naumburg admitted:

> a struggle against it is pointless. The Heimatschutz movement can only hope to extend its influence so far as to persuade the engineer to consider the protection of the landscape as a matter of course, and for it to be a factor from the beginning in the planning of all his creations.[21]

Although the central thrust of Heimatschutz agitation was concentrated on aesthetic issues – the appearance of industrial and technical buildings and their relationship to the environment – the movement's leaders were well aware of the social and ethical questions which surrounded the workplace too. Schultze-Naumburg wrote:

> It must gradually become accepted that the value of our industrial complexes can never be measured in financial terms alone. It is rather a question of recognising what value they can have for the development of harmonious cultural ideals. An awareness of the existence of such ideals has to be reactivated, otherwise we will be ashamed in the future, when we look back to the days when all human activity aimed to create harmony and was carried by the great ideals of mankind.[22]

In a 1908 *Heimatschutz* journal article, the Stuttgart architect Klatte, was more specific:

> It is surely self-evident that factories with a pleasant appearance are good advertisements for the owner. One perceives him to be not just a materialistic money-maker, but a human being with feelings, education and an understanding of the great and the good. Such employers will have an educational effect and in the social conflict will prove that they care for the welfare of their workers as people. It is not irrelevant in which rooms we spend the greater part of our lives. To create a friendly working environment for the workers is an important task for all employers.[23]

At first, however, neither the frequent invocation of a list of qualities desirable in technical and industrial structures, nor the nostalgic evocation of lost 'golden ages' in German architecture, suggested that the movement would make much impact on the practicalities of building or planning.

---

21. P. Schultze-Naumburg quoted in *Deutsche Bauzeitung*, vol.41 (1907), p.571.
22. P. Schultze-Naumburg, 'Kraftanlagen und Talsperren', in *Der Kunstwart* vol.19 (1906), p.136.
23. W. Klatte, 'Zur Umgestaltung des Fabrikbauwesens', in *Heimatschutz*, vol.4 (1908), p.16.

Schultze-Naumburg's pugnacious and direct style made popular points, but evaded questions of detail:

> Whether in the Station Roads of our provincial towns or in the housing estates of our big cities, whether in the west or the east of our nation, on the plains or in the hills – everywhere the same cheerless, enervating view . . . we have grown accustomed to the fact that technical buildings must look cold, boring and indifferent. If someone was to demand that engine-sheds, street crossings, waiting rooms and factories should somehow express to us their worthwhile role in life, we would ask in astonishment, 'can they do that then?' That they can, is indicated by buildings from the early part of the last century.[24]

The emphasis of early Heimatschutz writing about architecture lay on such polemical descriptions of the present, rather than constructive proposals for the future. As so often, it was the Heimatschutz organisation in Saxony which took the debate on a stage further and became involved in the practicalities of building and planning. This occurred in three ways: by influencing the nature of teaching at art schools and technical colleges; by drawing up ideal plans and models for architects and their clients; and by lobbying for legislation at national and local level.

The Heimatschutz association in Saxony (Verein Sächsischer Heimatschutz – 1908) evolved out of the Committee for the Care of Indigenous Art and Building Methods in Saxony and Thuringia, which was founded in 1903 and quickly became an influential body under the chairmanship of Karl Schmidt. As the name suggests, the 'Committee' was not constituted as a club or association, but as a panel of experts, whose tactical approach was clearly designed to win the respect and financial support of local and state authorities. The success of this course was demonstrated by the decision of the Saxon Ministry of the Interior to become a 'corporate member' of the Committee in December 1905.[25] The excellent relations which developed between the government and the Committee over the following months were further illustrated by the decision of the Education Ministry in Dresden to allow the Committee to hold an important meeting in its main seminar room. The meeting, which took place on 2 January 1907, brought together leading *Heimatschützer* with two Ministers and no fewer than thirteen of Saxony's seventeen *Amtshauptmänner* (the equivalent of the Prussian *Landräte*), to discuss a wide range of architectural issues.[26] The Committee was able to persuade the Saxon government to pass a circular around Art- and Technical Colleges recommending the use of simple, indigenous building styles as

24. P. Schultze-Naumburg, *Die Entstellung*, pp.10–12.
25. StA Dresden MdI 17518 'Ausschuß zur Pflege..' p.34.
26. StA Dresden MdI 17518 p.49–53; MdI 17522 p.69.

'models' for students. Moreover, a number of Dresden architects who sympathised with the aims of the Heimatschutz movement were commissioned by the Committee to produce plans for 'model' buildings, or suggest improvements to proposed new developments. The architects, including Ernst Kühn, August Grothe, Kurt Diestel and Karl Schmidt himself, at first concentrated on various projects for small dwellings, such as cottages for Royal forestry workers, and for state schools in rural districts. Soon, however, their attention turned to industrial buildings too, such as factory workshops and electricity sub-stations. The establishment of Building Advisory Committees and the effect of measures introduced under the 1909 Building Code in Saxony, further increased the output of that region's Heimatschutz architects whose work was published in architectural journals and became widely known.

The impact of the 1909 Saxon law, and other Heimatschutz inspired legislation, is discussed later, but the vigorous and well-publicised Heimatschutz agitation also began to exert a direct influence on architects and architectural theorists in all corners of the Reich. The theorists most closely identified with the movement favoured two principal sources for a more healthy architecture: the early nineteenth century Biedermeier period, with its unashamedly *bürgerliche* architecture, and the vernacular traditions of Germany's regions, passed on from father to son over generations. The great variety of the latter – each region could lay claim to a wide range of historical traditions – provided Heimatschutz architects with a rich selection of styles and materials, but at the same time caused the movement many headaches.

It may at first seem paradoxical that a movement which championed the architecture of the 1800–1835 period and which was committed to 'traditional' building should vigorously attack the practice of building in historical styles, but this is exactly what Heimatschutz supporters did. It has already been stated that a deep dislike of historicist architecture – and particularly the application of historical styles on buildings with a modern function – was common to all factions of the turn of the century reform movement. Leading *Heimatschützer* were every bit as scathing in their attacks on architectural historicism as the most avant-garde of the German modernists. In an article on dams and power stations, Schultze-Naumburg referred to a photograph of an electricity power station cloaked in an eclectic historicist façade. He wrote: 'in most cases it is not even the technical part of modern industrial buildings which is such a slap in the face, but the wretchedly stupid "finery" which one puts on the thing'.[27]

At the same time, Heimatschutz polemicists attacked two further trends in contemporary industrial architecture: the blandly utilitarian, functional

---

27. P. Schultze-Naumburg, 'Kraftanlagen..', in *Der Kunstwart*, vol.19 (1906), p.132.

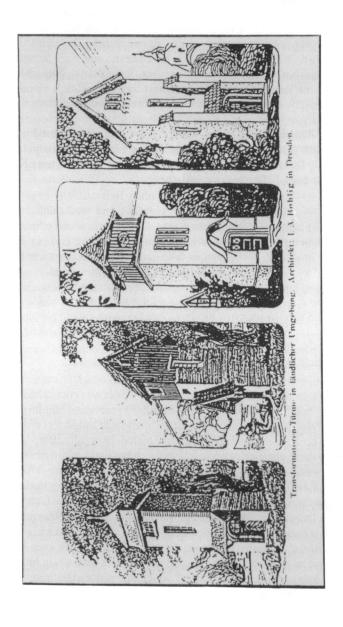

Figure 11 Electricity substations and transformer towers by Heimatschutz architects. From *Deutsche Bauzeitung*, 4 Dec. 1909

building of commercial developers, who used cheap new materials and had no feeling for art or culture, and the fashionable experiments of the architectural avant-garde, who seemed to have no interest in established tradition. The Hamburg Heimatschutz activist Paul Bröcker wrote:

> He who has tradition also has soul . . . He who does not, will not be able to solve even the simplest of tasks: he will build functional buildings with that well-known prison-like appearance, of which there is no shortage today.[28]

Bröcker's Altona-based colleague Oskar Schwindrazheim stressed that while the Heimatschutz movement had no intention of copying past styles, and wished to find a contemporary form of expression, it would not go in for what he called 'the sensational, "never-before-seen" with three exclamation marks' either.[29]

If one were to attempt a brief characterisation of the Heimatschutz view of industrial architecture, three broad areas of concern would emerge. Firstly, that industrial and technical buildings should be built in the established tradition of indigenous architectural forms, using local materials wherever possible. Secondly, that industrial and technical buildings should be 'honest' in reflecting their practical function, without over-emphasising 'naked' engineering. And thirdly, that such buildings should not be sited in sensitive locations, but that where their existence was unavoidable every effort should be made for the building to blend in with the local landscape.

In his article on Heimatschutz architecture in Lübeck, Hans-Günther Andresen offers the following summary:

> Heimatschutz architecture did not wish to quote historical traditions in a formal sense, but aimed rather to interpret the essential character of traditional forms . . . an architecture which did not wish to be sensational, individualistic, exclusive or experimental, but which placed itself in the service of a living tradition.[30]

One of the first industrial buildings to reflect the influence of the Heimatschutz movement was a power station at Bad Nauheim, a small health resort north of Frankfurt-am-Main. In 1904 both houses of the Hesse parliament passed a government Bill to launch a major development of Bad Nauheim's spa facilities, with the aim of turning the town into an international centre for the treatment of heart disease. Nearly 6.5 million Marks were made available for the construction of lavish new bath-houses,

28. P. Bröcker, *Über Hamburgs neue Architektur*, Hamburg, 1908, p.16.
29. O. Schwindrazheim, *Von alter zu neuer Heimatkunst*, Hamburg, 1908, p.33.
30. H.-G. Andresen, in M. Brix (ed.), *Lübeck*, p.51.

medical facilities, administration blocks and a power station to supply both the spa and the town with heat and electricity. The power station complex was also to include a mechanised steam laundry and a redevelopment of the municipal salt-works.

In the event, over 10.5 million Marks were required between 1904 and 1912 to complete the project, but the enthusiastic support of the Grand Duke of Hese, Ernst-Ludwig, ensured that the ambitious development programme was completed.[31] Ernst-Ludwig (1868–1937), a grandson of Queen Victoria, had gained a reputation as a patron of the arts, thanks mainly to his creation of an artists' colony at the Mathildenhöhe in Darmstadt, where architects like Peter Behrens and J.M. Olbrich had been invited to build at the turn of the century. Although the Mathildenhöhe colony was short-lived, it had helped to create a small but thriving community of artists, architects and designers in the Darmstadt area, and many of these were invited to make the one-hour train journey to Bad Nauheim to contribute to the spa development project.

The man in charge of the Bad Nauheim scheme was the architect and building inspector Wilhelm Jost (1874–1944), himself a former student in Darmstadt. His plans for the new spa were essentially Neo-Baroque in character, although the participation of Darmstadt designers such as Albin Müller, Heinrich Jobst and Friedrich Wilhelm Kleukens ensured that the buildings were richly-decorated in *Jugendstil* forms. For the technical complex, however, Jost preferred a different approach.

Plans for the power station complex, drawn up in 1904 by Jost and the architect Albert Marx, revealed a close affinity to the ideas of the Bund Heimatschutz, whose founding earlier that year had been widely reported. In order to avoid problems of noise or smoke pollution, the power station was to be built well away from the spa itself, with underground power-lines linking the two. Although conveniently placed on the main Frankfurt-Gießen railway line, the power station complex was to be built on attractive park land, surrounded by trees and shrubs, and the buildings were to take account of this sensitive location. Building work on the power station began in 1905, taking nine months and costing over 300,000 Marks to complete.[32] The dark red basalt stone of Upper Hesse was chosen by Jost and the architect Kraft, who had replaced Marx, as the most suitable local material with which to clad the iron-framed structure. Further homely touches were provided by the timbered gable on the building's south-east wing and the tiled, pitched roofs, which dominated the building. Rather than hide the complex's practical function, the architects emphasised it:

31. A.H. Murken, *Die neuen Bade- und Kuranlagen in Bad Nauheim zu Beginn des 20. Jahrhunderts*, Göttingen, 1987.

32. *Der Industriebau*, vol.1 (1910), p.266.

Figure 12 Power station, Bad Nauheim 1905–6
Arch. W. Jost, A. Marx & L. Kraft. Present condition

large ventilation cowls rose from the boiler house roof and a fifty-metre chimney was made an architectural feature, visible like an obelisk from all corners of the town.

The correspondent of the journal *Die Rheinlande*, Ebinghaus, wrote:

> If, after this achievement, anyone still claims that our factories cannot be anything but ugly, or that it is necessary to hide their halls behind ornamental mock-façades, one will be able to hold up this model example to shame them.[33]

Upon completion of the power station, work began on the adjacent mechanised steam laundry. This reinforced concrete structure with whitewashed plaster walls was designed by the architect Kraft and well illustrates the Heimatschutz movement's marriage of tradition and modernity. The plainly functional central block, with its large rectangular windows and uncompromising form, contrasted with the more ornamental wings and traditional roofs. The steam-laundry cost 160,000 Marks to build and could cope with 15,000 bed sheets a day.[34]

The Bad Nauheim complex was completed in 1910 with the construction of new buildings for the town's salt works, which were erected opposite the power station at a cost of 208,000 Marks. The nature of the salt production process made it impossible to consider the use of iron, brick or sandstone in the building, so the architect Dr Lipp employed a wooden frame, clad in the local Taunus quartzite stone. The new salt works brought together in one modern plant a number of processes previously scattered throughout the town. The architectural form, however, remained firmly in the tradition of old German salt works, a fact which caused the journal *Der Industriebau* to comment: 'In this way one can learn from the past – not by slavishly copying, but by creating new from the examples of old – thereby giving the new age something of the charm of old buildings'.[35]

Another article in that publication states that the salt works 'show quite clearly that technical buildings can possess a high degree of beauty, as well as pure functionality, without resorting to any architectural decoration.'[36] And *Der Industriebau* concluded its series on the technical buildings at Bad Nauheim with the comment: 'that a state authority has acted in such exemplary fashion in the field of industrial architecture deserves respect and emulation'.[37]

In the years before World War One the Bad Nauheim example was indeed emulated, with many local authorities playing a key role in the

---

33. K. Ebinghaus, 'Bad Nauheim', in *Die Rheinlande*, vol.8 (1908), p.182.
34. *Der Industriebau*, vol.1 (1910), p.266. Also vol.2 (1911), p.97.
35. *Der Industriebau*, vol.3 (1912), p.50.
36. *Der Industriebau*, vol.1 (1910), p.267.
37. *Der Industriebau*, vol.1 (1910), p.267.

Figure 13 Salt works, Bad Nauheim 1910–11
        Arch. W. Jost & Dr Lipp. Present condition

campaign to put Heimatschutz principles into practice. The development of a gas works at the picturesque Rhineland town of Oberwesel is a good example of the sort of building project which attracted the attention of Heimatschutz activists and concerned local planners alike. Situated on the left bank of the Rhine between Coblenz and Bingen, Oberwesel was just the sort of romantic German town *Heimatschützer* held up as a model of harmonious and organic growth, where architectural forms seemed to have evolved over hundreds of years and now 'belonged' to the landscape in a way contemporary architecture seldom did. It was hardly surprising, therefore, that plans by the town council to build a gas works to serve the local community, were greeted with suspicion in Heimatschutz circles.

After putting the project out to tender, the town council duly selected the most economic entry, from an engineering company more interested in the contract to supply technical equipment than the architectural quality of the complex. The responsible authorities in Coblenz, however, refused planning permission on aesthetic grounds, and called for new plans, better suited to such a sensitive location. This decision was hardly surprising, given the close links between the Coblenz planners and the Heimatschutz movement. In 1906 the Rhineland's newly-formed Heimatschutz organisation had been presented with an office and the use of a civil servant in the Coblenz district government headquarters, by the region's *Regierungspräsident* Freiherr von Hövel. Furthermore, Coblenz had been one of the first districts to introduce the assessment of all planning applications on aesthetic as well as technical grounds.[38]

New schemes for the Oberwesel project, camouflaged in a variety of historical styles and including at least one mock castle, complete with turrets and firing slits for gasmen with bows and arrows, were presented and rejected. Then, just when it seemed that Oberwesel would never get its gas works, the Frankfurt-based Heimatschutz architect Stefan Simon submitted a plan that met with everyone's approval.[39]

The gas works were eventually built in 1908, comprising an unpretentious pair of vernacular buildings, and a small gas-holder hidden behind tall trees, located so as to make the iron structure virtually invisible from the Rhine. The buildings were erected using local stone and slate, and special care was taken in the arrangement of the ensemble, so that the actual gas production building, with its steeply sloping roof and cupola, took centre-stage. Simon's most interesting innovation was the way in which he successfully avoided the need for a tall chimney, by placing small

38. See the *Mitteilungen des Rheinischen Vereins für Denkmalpflege und Heimatschutz*, vol.1 (1907), p.14.

39. S. Simon described his building plans in *Der Industriebau*, vol.1 (1910), p.241. Also see *Mitteilungen des Rheinischen Vereins für Denkmalpflege und Heimatschutz*, vol.4 (1910), pp.47–49.

Figure 14 Gas works, Oberwesel 1908
Arch. S. Simon. Drawing by E. Beutinger, from *Der Industriebau*, vol.1 (1910)

chimneys for each of the three gas ovens at the back of the production building. Ultimately, however, the significance of Oberwesel gas works lies not in its architecture but in what it tells us of Heimatschutz influence on the planning process: by 1907, the aesthetics of industrial architecture had become a contentious issue for planners and public alike.

The Rhine did not only pose problems for planners in the small-town environment of Oberwesel. The rapid development of commercial shipping on the river also set a challenge for officials in the major trading centres, who were faced with an ever-increasing demand for quayside facilities. The city of Cologne had opened an extensive dock and warehouse development in 1898, but in the space of less than a decade von Below's Neo-Gothic warehouses had become unable to cope with demand. So, in 1907, the city council decided to construct a new warehouse complex on the Agrippinaufer, a few miles south of the city centre. The 207 metre-long warehouse block was built in 1908–9 at a cost of 1.5 million Marks.[40] It was designed by a municipal architect, Hans Verbeek, in conjunction with the city's technical *Beigeordnete*, Carl Rehorst (1866–1919) – vice-chairman of the Bund Heimatschutz.

The Agrippinaufer development represented the first large-scale use of reinforced concrete in Cologne, but the complex became better known for its rhythmic and highly-distinctive outline, which led to the block being known locally as the 'Danzig warehouses': a reference to the towering gables of that historic Baltic port. The architect Verbeek later wrote:

> The 200 metre-long building was divided up by gables not in an attempt to feign an 'Old Danzig', but rather to prepare Rhine river travellers for the scale of the city, emerging in the distance. At the same time, however, it was important not to dominate the nearby university building, and desirable that an impression of a single, unified building was retained.[41]

The response of architectural critics to the Cologne warehouses mirrors the fortunes of the Heimatschutz movement itself. Until 1918, the complex attracted much praise, not just in Heimatschutz publications, but also from the nascent modern movement and more traditional critics too. It was significant that a print of Verbeek's building adorned the front of the special Cologne edition of the journal *Moderne Bauformen* in 1914. A decade later, however, it attracted only scorn from architectural circles, as an example of Wilhelmine romanticism at its worst.

Cologne's Carl Rehorst, who had been in charge of the city's architecture and planning since 1907, was not the only *Heimatschützer* in

40. *Deutsche Bauzeitung*, vol.44 (1910), pp.71–72.
41. H. Verbeek, 'Die Hochbautätigkeit in der Alt-und Neustadt von 1888 bis 1918' in *Köln. Bauliche Entwicklung 1888–1927*, Berlin, 1927, pp.32–33.

Figure 15 Municipal warehouses, Cologne-Agrippinaufer 1908–9
Arch. H. Verbeek. Present condition

a position of influence. The City Architect of Dresden, Hans Erlwein (1872–1914), was an active member of the Verein Sächsischer Heimatschutz and his buildings for the City Corporation were often admired in Heimatschutz literature. Indeed, one of the Dürerbund's influential pamphlets was devoted entirely to 'Simple Municipal Buildings in Dresden by Hans Erlwein' (1913). One of Erlwein's first major projects for the city was for a new water works at Hosterwitz, a few miles upstream from Dresden in the scenic Elbe valley.[42] Built in 1907–8 on the site of a former royal tobacco plantation, and surrounded by peach trees and vineyards, the Hosterwitz waterworks had whitewashed walls and red tiled roofs, but Erlwein's efforts to harmonise technology and landscape were hampered by the works' towering chimney. A small chimney would have blended more easily with the surroundings, but a tall one offered a better discharge of smoke pollution – the dilemmas faced by architects and planners in attempting to conserve the natural environment had already acquired a very modern complexity.

The Hosterwitz water works was only one of numerous projects for major improvements to Dresden's municipal infrastructure in the decade before World War One. Between 1906 and his death in a road accident in 1914, Erlwein was responsible for a monumental gas holder at Dresden-Reick, an extensive abattoir complex, a fire station in the Schlüterstraße, a sewage works at Dresden-Kaditz, an eleven-storey tobacco warehouse in the Devrientstraße and dozens of individually-designed public conveniences, tram stops and kiosks, in addition to the many schools, hospitals, offices and houses the city council was involved in building.

The Dresden example, which is by no means atypical, indicates the opportunities open to municipal architects at this time. The building boom of the later Wilhelmine years made it possible for an ambitious and hard-working architect to write his own distinctive signature on the face of a large city in the space of a few short years. Fritz Schumacher's Hamburg and Ludwig Hoffmann's Berlin are perfect illustrations of this fact. At the same time, however, the considerable power of City Architects and the intense activity of their municipal building and planning departments, suggests the sphere in which organisations eager to put forward a particular view on the appearance of the built environment were able to operate most effectively.

It is surely no coincidence that the industrial and technical buildings to be considered thus far were all erected by public authorities. A natural affinity appeared to exist between the concept of Heimatschutz and the ethos of public sector officials, at a time when municipal architects,

42. *Der Industriebau*, vol.1 (1910), pp.49–51.

Figure 16 Municipal gasworks, Dresden–Reick 1908–9
Arch. H. Erlwein. Present condition

Figure 17 Municipal abattoir, power house, Dresden 1906–10
Arch. H. Erlwein. Present condition

Figure 18 Municipal tobacco warehouse, Dresden 1913
Arch. H. Erlwein. Present condition

planners and engineers were all seeking wider recognition for their distinctive professional status and responsibilities.[43] In general, architects in private practice proved significantly less willing to embrace the Heimatschutz cause. Similarly, few private companies, small businessmen or commercial developers chose to employ architects associated with the movement on their new industrial building projects. At the same time, however, many individuals from the world of commerce and industry took an active part in Heimatschutz organisations.[44] Reasons for this apparent contradiction are discussed in later chapters, when we turn to consider the motivation of German industrial companies in choosing particular architects or architectural styles during the 1900–1918 period.

There were, of course, exceptions to the general rule, and a few of the private industrial buildings to be constructed along Heimatschutz lines merit some attention. In a special edition of the Rhineland Heimatschutz association's journal, dedicated to past and present industrial architecture,[45] one of the modern buildings singled out for special praise was an extension to the Zanders paper factory in Bergisch-Gladbach, east of Cologne. The managing director of this long-established family firm, Hans Zanders, was himself a member of the Heimatschutz association in his native Rhineland, and an enthusiastic patron of the arts, so the careful consideration given by the company to the appearance of a planned factory extension in 1908 was not totally unexpected. Rather than select a leading architect to create a new work of art on the site, however, Zanders commissioned a local master-builder, L. Bopp, to build in the vernacular tradition of some neighbouring cottages, which had themselves once served as places of production. The modest three-storey extension was built in a coarse grey limestone, quarried just three minutes away from the Zanders factory, and was designed to 'take account of its dominant position' in an attractive valley.

One of the best-known architects to be associated with the Heimatschutz movement was Fritz Höger (1877–1949), who is remembered for the vast and expressionistic 'Chilehaus' in Hamburg, but actually spent most of his life working in the more modest tradition of north German brick architecture. Höger set up his own architectural practice in 1907 and later recalled:

43. See V. Clark's 1983 University of California PhD thesis 'A Social History of German Architects'.

44. For instance, Gustav Krupp von Bohlen und Halbach who was not only a member of the Rhineland Heimatschutz organisation, but paid a 100 Mark annual donation to the national Bund Heimatschutz (HA Krupp FAH 21/876).

45. 'Industriebauten', in *Mitteilungen des Rheinischen Vereins für Denkmalpflege und Heimatschutz*, vol.4 (1910).

It was the time in which the ideas of the Heimatschutz movement were becoming popular, even in my part of the world. Our – that is to say, the Heimatschutz association, to which I belonged from the beginning – resistance against 'pseudo-architecture' was growing ever stronger amongst the masses.[46]

When Höger was asked to design a factory for the North German Net Company in Itzehoe, a small town in Holstein, he produced a building with local red-brick walls, an unusual orthogonal chimney and steep, tiled roofs, under which were housed the drying rooms. Höger was later to expound on his use of brickwork:

> For me, every building in brick or clinker expresses something sacred and religious if it comes from the hand of a good master-builder. This applies even to the most profane cathedral of work, to an industrial building or warehouse. By the way, it is actually from these sort of buildings that the evolution of architectural style comes from. A factory can be unbelievably monumental.[47]

Certainly the journal *Der Industriebau* was impressed with the Itzehoe factory. In January 1914 its correspondent wrote: 'In this instance a small firm has brought about a new artistic creation, which consciously employs the good old ways of building.'[48]

However, the industrial building which received most acclaim in Heimatschutz circles was located hundreds of miles away from Höger's windswept North German Plain. The factory, built by the Munich architect Richard Riemerschmid (1868–1957) for the 'Deutsche Werkstätten für Handwerkskunst' in the Dresden garden-city suburb of Hellerau, was a symbol for many in the 'reform of life' movement of how modern industrial work could and should be. As the focal point of an ideal community, the Hellerau factory – which was built in 1909 – was hardly typical of industrial installations in Wilhelmine Germany, yet it was the workplace of around 600 wood- and metal-workers, and was a 'workshop' in name alone. The rural feel to the factory, arranged around two courtyards and with many whimsical touches, was dismissed by Walter Gropius as 'impractical peasant-romanticism',[49] but Riemerschmid's creation had many admirers in more progressive architectural circles too.

46. C. Westphal, *Fritz Höger. Der niederdeutsche Backstein-Baumeister*, Wolfshagen, 1938, p.67.

47. C. Westphal, *ibid.*, p.67.

48. *Der Industriebau*, vol.5 (1914), p.2.

49. In a letter from Gropius to Karl Ernst Osthaus (23 March 1912), quoted by S. Müller in H. Hesse-Frielinghaus (ed.), *Karl Ernst Osthaus. Leben und Werk*, Recklinghausen, 1971, p.289.

Figure 19 Deutsche Werkstätten furniture factory, Dresden-Hellerau 1909
Arch. R. Riemerschmid. Present condition

The Deutsche Werkstätten, under the leadership of Karl Schmidt-Hellerau (1873–1948), began in 1898 as an idealistic attempt to establish a just working environment, free of the battles between capital and labour which were raging elsewhere in the *Reich*. It shared many of the illusions and experienced many of the failures of the wider Wilhelmine reform movement, but ironically was also a great business success. Indeed, the solid and reasonably-priced furniture produced by the Hellerau workshops could be found in the bedrooms and studies of Heimatschutz activists across the land.

At the heart of the Hellerau experiment lay the belief that an harmonious environment could help to establish harmonious social relations, and this is surely a key to a better understanding of Heimatschutz too. Schultze-Naumburg and the other ideologues of the movement saw buildings as characteristic expressions of a culture – in the case of Wilhelmine Germany, more often than not a symbol of a lack of culture – but they also perceived a more positive role for architecture in society. If buildings could be erected as symbols of harmony – not only architectural harmony, but harmony with the landscape and with the past as well – then could they not help to (re-)create social harmony too? It was not by chance that the architectural characteristics most loudly championed by the *Heimatschützer* – honesty, simplicity, solidity – were ethical qualities above all else.

It would be wrong of course to imply that such weighty matters were on the mind of every conservationist, planner and architect, who became involved in Heimatschutz activities: one of the major weaknesses in the 'cultural history' method is a desire to attach the intellectual flights of fancy of a few, onto the day-by-day actions of the many. Yet the desire for 'harmony' was real enough, and it was widely-accepted within the movement that industrial architecture could make an important contribution to re-creating a more harmonious society. After all, factories were not only an obvious factor in the declining quality of the natural environment, but they appeared to be the prime source of social disharmony too.

Once the Heimatschutz movement had become established, however, its dilemma was clear. How could it ever hope to create enough 'symbols of harmony' to make any real impact on the environment or society as a whole? In its first few years, the Heimatschutz agitation had achieved some notable successes in the field of industrial architecture, but the movement's leadership was well aware that for every model factory and sympathetic architect, there were hundreds of 'money-minded' men doing irreparable damage to the *Heimat*. It would take more than harsh words from an army of schoolmasters if Germany was to be saved: legislation was needed, and that would require political action.

Heimatschutz Legislation

The Altona Heimatschutz activist Oskar Schwindrazheim once claimed, 'we have never thought about laying down draconian laws to prevent this or that, just because something is not strictly *Heimatstil*'.[50] By 1914, however, there were many architects and manufacturers who were prepared to claim that just such measures were already in existence. Even some Heimatschutz supporters had begun to question the direction the movement was taking: 'Should we impose Heimatschutz?', asked the movement's Schleswig-Holstein leader in the title of a 1910 essay, before answering his own question with a clear negative.[51] The chairman of the movement in Westphalia, Freiherr von Kerckerink, was equally adamant when he told a meeting in 1910: 'In the long run, the police truncheon will not be able to protect the *Heimat*; only public opinion [can]'.[52]

Nevertheless, the Heimatschutz-inspired legislation enacted in most German states between 1900 and 1914 was the movement's single greatest achievement, and serves as a testament to the willingness of Heimatschutz activists to become involved in the practicalities of political action; a characteristic not usually considered to have been much in evidence amongst turn-of-the-century 'cultural pessimists'. The legislation has since been largely forgotten, but at the time it aroused heated discussion and sowed the seeds of many of the architectural controversies which were later to enter the political arena in the Weimar Republic.

Heimatschutz organisations and governmental bodies had enjoyed a close relationship since the movement's earliest days.[53] The particularly strong ties in Saxony have already been mentioned, and whilst no other part of Germany could quite match the quality of those connections, Heimatschutz had its supporters in most legislative and executive bureaucracies. The movement had contact with national and local government on various levels, ranging from direct financial subsidy or the use of government offices, to participation in the annual 'Conferences for Preservation and Heimatschutz' and in official competitions to find 'model' buildings. Schools and colleges were encouraged by government to use Heimatschutz publications in their teaching, and the movement

50. O. Schwindrazheim, *Heimatkunst*, p.66.
51. P. von Hedemann-Heespen, 'Sollen wir Heimatschutz erzwingen? Zur Philosophie und Taktik des Heimatschutzes', in *Heimatschutz*, vol.6/3 (1910).
52. Freiherr von Kerckerinck-Borg, 'Heimatschutz in Westfalen' speech 5 Jan. 1910 reprinted in *Der deutsche Heimatschutz. Ein Rückblick und Ausblick*, Munich, 1930, p.221.
53. Heimatschutz was essentially a grass-roots movement which came 'from below', but it clearly also received considerable help 'from above'. The extent to which Heimatschutz was fostered by government, and the reasons for this support, are important issues which merit closer attention.

responded by making thousands of copies available to 'opinion formers', such as teachers and councillors. In 1914 the Saxon Education Ministry went as far as to send every school a questionnaire, enquiring 'What has the school done for Heimatschutz and what can it do in the future?'[54]

Paul Schultze-Naumburg's pamphlet 'The Disfigurement of our Country' appeared to be particularly popular with the authorities. The Bund Heimatschutz, which published the pamphlet, was delighted to receive an order in late 1907 for 500 copies from the Prussian Minister of Public Works, who intended to distribute them to leading civil servants in the building department.[55] The Preface to its third impression noted proudly:

> The second impression of 20,000 copies appeared in April 1908 and was almost completely sold out by October. To a large degree we have to thank the vigorous support of the authorities for this success. The publication was recommended in many of the official gazettes and by special decree, amongst others from the Prussian Ministries of Public Works, the Interior and Education, from the Austrian Ministers of Public Works and Education, and from Ministries in Bavaria, Württemberg, Saxony ... In a number of parishes and districts the publication has been purchased out of public funds to circulate to authorities, craftsmen, teachers and priests.[56]

The civil servants in the Prussian Ministry of Public Works seem to have done their homework. The 1908 Bund Heimatschutz conference was told by one of the Ministry's top officials that the movement's motives were 'fully understood' and that the Ministry's buildings would attempt to reflect their aims.[57] In 1911 the equivalent Ministry in Baden went one stage further and sent out special decrees to the railway and water authorities, stressing the need to consider aesthetic factors in all industrial and technical structures built by the state.[58]

It appears that the movement enjoyed a certain amount of royal backing too: upon the formation of the Rhineland Heimatschutz association in 1906, a telegram of support was received from the Kaiser.[59] Thereafter, the patriotic Rhinelanders sent copies of their publications to Berlin at every opportunity, and always received a message of thanks from the Chief

54. J.K. Niedlich, *Deutscher Heimatschutz als Erziehung zu deutscher Kultur*, Leipzig, 1920, p.8.

55. 'Maßnahmen gegen bauliche Verunstaltungen in Stadt und Land in Preußen', in *Heimatschutz*, vol.4 (1908), p.7.

56. P. Schultze-Naumburg, *Die Entstellung* – Preface.

57. 'Jahresversammlung des Bundes Heimatschutz in Lübeck am 23. Sept. 1908', in *Heimatschutz*, vol.4 (1908), p.90.

58. 'Badische Erlasse über Ingenieurbauten', in *Heimatschutz*, vol.8 (1912), p.45.

59. 'Bericht über die Gründung des Vereins', in *Mitteilungen des Rheinischen Vereins für Denkmalpflege und Heimatschutz*, vol.1 (1907).

of the Kaiser's Civil Cabinet. Prince Friedrich Wilhelm of Prussia was the Honorary President of the Silesian Heimatschutz movement and spoke at its annual meetings[60] and a similar role was played by Prince Johann Georg in Saxony.[61] In 1915 the Saxon Interior Minister, Count Vitzthum von Eckstädt, told Parliament.

> Heimatschutz is no game, but rather a far-reaching cultural movement, whose influence pervades every corner of the nation. The Law against the Disfigurement of Town and Country, of 10 March 1909, is an expression of this, and its implementation means no more and no less than the preservation and re-creation of the basis of all culture: the raising of the feeling of *Heimat*, the protection of beauty and of historical uniqueness, the artistic education of our people to good taste, and thereby also the raising of the economic power of our people on the world market.[62]

Despite such glowing testimonies, the Bund Heimatschutz was always anxious to stress its independence from government. Schultze-Naumburg told a 1909 conference in Trier: 'The Bund Heimatschutz considers it an essential prerequisite for its effectiveness that it should be fully independent of any state authority'.[63] Although he went on to add: 'On the other hand, it should be quite clear to anyone who has ever had the slightest contact with Heimatschutz activity how absolutely essential state support and the co-operation with the authorities is'.[64]

Official support for the concept of Heimatschutz did not mean, however, that the passage of Heimatschutz legislation was a mere formality. On the contrary, wherever such measures were discussed they aroused fierce controversy, both in- and outside the parliamentary chamber. Heimatschutz legislation in Wilhelmine Germany came in two stages. Initial laws, such as the General Building Code for the Kingdom of Saxony (1900) or the Prussian Law against the Disfigurement of Areas of Outstanding Natural Beauty (1902), were significant in introducing an aesthetic component into German planning law: nineteenth century building codes, as administered by the *Baupolizei*, had been concerned only with hygiene and public safety. Paragraph ninety of the 1900 Saxon Code stated: 'Architectural structures which would clearly blight an area

---

60. *Schlesische Zeitung*, 25 Feb. 1913 in StA Dresden MdI 17528. 'Heimatschutz; heimatliche Bauweise 1912–1919' p.103.

61. StA Dresden MdI 17531. 'Heimatschutz..' p.75.

62. Count Vitzthum von Eckstädt, quoted in *Deutsche Bauzeitung*, vol.9 (1915), p.141. Full text of debate (II. Kammer 77. Sitzung 24 April 1914) in StA Dresden MdI 17531. 'Heimatschutz. Interpellation des Abgeordneten Brodauf in der II. Kammer der Ständeversammlung 1913–1914.'

63. P. Schultze-Naumburg quoted by F. Koch, 'Kurzer Überblick über den Stand der Heimatschutzbewegung', in *Heimatschutz*, vol.8 (1912), p.70.

64. F. Koch, *ibid.*, p.70.

can be forbidden. For particular streets, or parts of streets, by-laws can be passed which insist on higher architectural demands being met by the proposed buildings'.[65]

The second wave of Heimatschutz legislation was ushered in by a new, and much tougher, Prussian 'Disfigurement Law' (1907), and continued with specific new laws in Bremen (1907), Munich (1908), Saxony (1909), Oldenburg (1910), Hamburg (1912) and expanded General Building Codes in other parts of Germany (such as Baden and Württemberg) before World War One. The political and geographical structure of the *Reich* ensured that it was the legislation introduced in Prussia which attracted most attention.

The Law against the Disfigurement of Places and outstanding Landscapes (*Verunstaltungsgesetz*) came into effect on 15 July 1907, and contained three main measures. Paragraph one enabled the *Baupolizei* to refuse planning permission for any new building, or extension to an existing building, which 'grossly disfigured' the place or landscape in which it was to be sited. This measure applied to the whole of Prussia. Paragraphs two to seven were concerned with establishing the basis of a system to protect and conserve valuable buildings and the character of historic townscapes, but required the passing of local by-laws (*Ortsstatute*) and could only protect certain streets or buildings designated by name. 'Commissions of Experts' were to help in the drawing up of by-laws suited to local conditions, and to aid the *Baupolizei* in the assessment of planning applications. The 'Building Advisory Committees', as these commissions generally became known, could make alterations to plans submitted to them, provided that these did not cause the client unreasonable extra costs. The law contained no provision for the payment of damages. The eighth paragraph was aimed at protecting landscapes of outstanding natural beauty from development, with the areas in question to be chosen by each region's *Regierungspräsident*, in conjunction with the district council.

The passage of the Disfigurement Law through the Lower House of the Prussian Parliament had not been smooth. In the course of its first two readings deputies of the Centre Party, in particular, were critical of the extensive powers the proposed legislation granted to the *Baupolizei*. Although Centre deputies did not question the Bill's good intentions, many felt it intruded too far into the rights of the individual, and some felt it contradicted article nine of the Prussian Constitution (which provided for the payment of full compensation in cases of state intervention against private property).

The member for Elberfeld, Schmitz (Freisinnige Volkspartei), was also

---

65. F.W. Bredt, 'Die neue Gesetzgebung auf dem Gebiete der Denkmalpflege und des Heimatschutzes', *Dürerbund Flugschriften* no.53 (1909), p.9.

perturbed by the Bill's powers. He told the House that although it was desirable to prevent the construction of ugly buildings, 'we have very serious reservations about the way in which it extends planning powers into the area of aesthetics', and turns the planners 'into judges of good taste in the arts'. The Minister of Public Works, Breitenbach, defended the proposed legislation, claiming it took into consideration 'the aesthetic needs of a culturally advanced time'. The legislation was passed – the size of the majority is not recorded – despite a last-minute point of order by the Centre member Schmidt (Warburg), who tried to invoke Article 107 of the Constitution to ensure a statutory re-vote after twenty-one days.[66]

The 1907 law was welcomed in principle by Heimatschutz campaigners, but criticised on various counts, not least for its ambiguous language and reliance on subjective terms such as 'grossly disfigure'.[67] Clearly, the law's success or failure would depend to a large extent on how it was to be implemented in practice. Thus, for the next three years, much Heimatschutz effort was spent on lobbying local authorities to act in the spirit of the new legislation. *Heimatschützer* helped to find the most effective wording for local by-laws, and were closely involved in the setting up of the Building Advisory Committees – whose size and form had been left unclear by the law-makers.

As if aware of the Disfigurement Law's shortcomings, the Prussian Ministries of Public Works and the Interior issued a supplementary decree on 10 January 1908. The decree outlined how the powers given by the 1907 law should best be used, and stressed the desirability of voluntary co-operation with the planning authorities. The decree, couched in classic Heimatschutz terms, specifically recommended the use of publications by Schultze-Naumburg, Rudorff and Karl Schmidt to 'enthuse, enlighten and explain' the context of the new law to all those involved in the building process.[68] A week later, a further decree went out from Berlin to Prussia's *Regierungspräsidenten*, asking them to ensure that state building and planning officials in their areas supported the development of a 'sound, indigenous building-style', both in- and outside office hours.[69]

By the end of August 1908, nine communities had passed by-laws under the provisions of the 1907 law, and thirty-three towns and villages were

---

66. 'Stenographische Berichte über die Verhandlungen des Preußischen Hauses der Abgeordneten' (3. Session 1907).
67. The Prussian government defined 'gross disfigurement' as 'the creation of a positively ugly and therefore painful condition for any pair of eyes sensitive to the aesthetics of design'.
68. 'Maßnahmen gegen bauliche Verunstaltungen in Stadt und Land in Preußen', in *Heimatschutz* vol.4 (1908), pp.1–5. Also, *Deutsche Bauzeitung*, vol.42 (1908), pp.74–76.
69. 'Zur praktischen Durchführung der preußischen Maßnahmen gegen bauliche Verunstaltungen', in *Heimatschutz*, vol.4 (1908), p.5.

in the process of doing so. A further 112 communities had declared an intention to act.[70] General agreement was lacking, however, as to the wording of local legislation. Even within the Heimatschutz movement there was controversy over certain aspects of the by-law packages. The Dresden architect Fritz Schumacher (1869–1947), shortly to become the City Architect in Hamburg, was one of many to realise the potential dangers of such by-laws. In an article in the journal *Heimatschutz*[71] he attacked the recently-passed by-laws in Magdeburg, which listed 'suitable' architectural styles for buildings in sensitive areas of the city. Although the list gave the historicist architect plenty of choice, it was exactly what creative architects had feared from Heimatschutz legislation. The Heimatschutz expert on legislative matters, F.W.Bredt, was quick to condemn the inclusion of restrictions on 'style' in legislation[72] but the fear of private architects – and particularly the nascent modern movement – of an 'architectural dictatorship' or a 'style police' would not go away.

The number of communities passing Heimatschutz by-laws increased rapidly in 1909 (including Berlin in June), as did the number of Building Advisory Committees, with Heimatschutz activists playing a major role in the shaping of both. Amongst the first communities to receive Heimatschutz by-laws in the Prussian Rhineland province were Mayen, Zons, Bergisch-Gladbach, Zülpich, Königswinter and Barmen, and on each occasion members of the Rhineland Heimatschutz movement were on hand to help with the drafting. A characteristic feature of such by-laws was the designation of zones for particular use. If buildings with an industrial use were to be erected in close proximity to residential areas, they would have to reflect the character of the surroundings in their appearance. A good example is provided by the H.W. Kemna Ribbon Factory in Barmen, where the authorities used the new by-laws to insist on a 'villa style' appearance for the factory, using the 'form, colour and materials' of neighbouring buildings. The result, built in 1908 by the architect Rudolf Schnell, was praised by the local Heimatschutz leader F.W. Bredt.[73]

By 1912 the Rhineland province could boast around seventy Building Advisory Committees, with a central committee based in Düsseldorf (Rheinische Bauberatungsstelle, founded 1911). The Committees varied greatly in size and in the frequency of their meetings, but all were run on

---

70. By November 1909, 101 sets of by-laws were in place. See *Heimatschutz*, vol.5 (1909), p.22.
71. F. Schumacher, 'Gefahren der Ortstatute', in *Heimatschutz*, vol.4 (1908), pp.29–32.
72. F.W. Bredt, 'Ortsvorschriften', in *Heimatschutz*, vol.5 (1909), p.15.
73. F.W. Bredt, 'Fabrikbauten unter Berücksichtigung des bergischen Landes', in *Der Industriebau*, vol.1 (1910), pp.69–70.

voluntary lines. The Düsseldorf committee was funded jointly by state and Heimatschutz subsidies, and numbered up to fifteen members. It consisted of delegates from the Rhineland Heimatschutz association (two), the Rhineland Association for Workers' Housing (two), the provincial authorities (one), the architects' professional body, the BDA (one), the engineers' association, the AIV (one), and up to eight elected members – invariably from the ranks of the Heimatschutz movement. The Building Advisory Committee received building plans both as referrals from the *Baupolizei*, and sent in voluntarily by clients. The plans were discussed, and then either approved or passed on to the Committee's resident architect for 'improvement'. Since the architect concerned, Ernst Stahl, was a devoted supporter of *Heimatstil*, the results were very much in line with the Heimatschutz ideal.[74]

The impact of the Building Advisory Committees on industrial architecture is difficult to assess. The Rhineland committee appeared to deal mostly with house-building plans; just one factory was amongst the first two dozen cases it considered, and only two of the 120 projects to be assessed by the committee in the twelve months from September 1913 were factories. In Saxony, where an architect was employed full-time by the Heimatschutz organisation to aid the committees, 449 building plans were amended in 1909, 760 in 1911 and 631 in 1912.[75] Here the proportion of industrial schemes to be dealt with appears to have been higher, but detailed statistical information is not available.

Since industrial buildings were quite rare in the sort of town centre streets generally protected by the new by-laws, one should not be surprised that such projects formed only a small part of the Building Advisory Committees' activity. Of more importance to architects and builders in the industrial field were undoubtedly the powers granted to the *Baupolizei* under Paragraph One of the 1907 Prussian law, which applied to all areas and did not require local by-laws. Paragraph Two of the 1909 Saxon law was equally wide-ranging, and indeed stricter than the Prussian legislation in stating that a building only had to 'disfigure' (rather than 'grossly disfigure') the environment to attract the planners' attention. Such powers may not seem unusual or unreasonable, but the nature of the *Baupolizei* in Wilhelmine Germany ensured that this was to become the most controversial aspect of the Heimatschutz legislation.

Although in larger towns and cities *Baupolizei* functions had been incorporated into the planning departments of the municipal bureaucracy, the *Baupolizei* was in fact an arm of the state police force, which meant that outside the cities responsibility for planning issues lay with the *Landrat*

74. *Mitteilungen.*. vol.5 (1911), p.143. Also vol.8 (1914), p.177.
75. StA Dresden MdI 17522; MdI 17523; MdI 17524.

Fabrikbau für das sächsische Erzgebirge.
Oben: eingereichter Entwurf; unten: Abänderungsvorschlag
von Brt. A. Grothe †.

Figure 20 An example from the Heimatschutz group in Saxony of how to improve the quality of industrial architecture, at little extra cost to the client. The top drawing illustrates the plan initially submitted to the authorities, and the bottom drawing shows the Heimatschutz architect's alternative proposal. From *Deutsche Bauzeitung*, 4 Dec. 1909 (in Prussia) or *Amtshauptmann* (in Saxony and elsewhere). The *Landrat* was vitally important in the Prussian administrative system, and these unelected 'county sheriffs' already wielded considerable personal power. One potential effect of the new legislation was thus to give a small band of individuals – often conservative and authoritarian in outlook – a powerful weapon with which to impose a personal view of architecture on an unwilling community.

Between 1907 and the outbreak of war, tales of *Landrat* excess abounded, as opponents of the Heimatschutz movement – modern architects, developers and manufacturers of synthetic building materials – seized on stories of *Landräte* forbidding the use of flat roofs, concrete and corrugated iron. The industrialists' pressure-group Bund der Industriellen, set up a commission in 1911 to deal with the 'excesses of the Heimatschutz agitation', whilst manufacturers of tar-paper and roofing-felt saw themselves compelled to spend large sums of money to uphold the reputation of the flat roof.[76] Even the Heimatschutz movement's own F.W. Bredt conceded that the Saxon law gave such extensive powers 'that an unskilled and indiscreet administrative official could inflict damage with it'.[77] Such was the furore stirred up in the aftermath of the Heimatschutz legislation that it is difficult to assess the real impact of the new laws on industrial architecture, but the role of the *Landrat* in Heimatschutz activity certainly merits closer investigation.

Landräte were well-represented in all Heimatschutz associations. Of the six *Landräte* to sit on the Management Committee of the Rhineland association, three were also chairmen of local Heimatschutz groups. In Schleswig-Holstein, where the provincial *Oberpräsident* was a keen Heimatschutz supporter, the *Landräte* played a major part in the success of the movement. A representative of the Schleswig-Holstein *Heimatschützer* wrote: 'It is of great importance for the success of our efforts, that the *Landräte*, who are very influential in their districts, are almost all well-disposed to Heimatschutz ideas, and some are enthusiastic supporters.'[78]

---

76. One of the fiercest critics of Heimatschutz was Wilhelm Wendlandt, general secretary of the Bund der Industriellen and founder of the Verband Deutscher Dachpappenfabrikanten: see his article 'Ein wenig Ästhetik und Statistik', in *Der Industriebau*, vol.1 (1910), p.271. Wendlandt was involved in the setting up of the 'Commission to Remove the Excesses of the Heimatschutz Agitation' which paid for the publication of a pamphlet in the form of a 'submission' to the Upper House of the Prussian Parliament. The manufacturers of roofing felt and other 'threatened' materials also supported competitions to find new and aesthetically-pleasing architectural forms which utilised their products.

77. F.W. Bredt, 'Die neue Gesetzgebung', p.13.

78. G. Rischawy, 'Von der Arbeit des Schleswig-Holsteinischen Landesvereins für Heimatschutz', in *Hamburgische Zeitschrift für Heimatkultur*, April 1913, p.5.

This picture was repeated in many parts of the Reich. By 1906, for instance, no fewer than seven *Amtshauptmänner* (the officials for Auerbach, Chemnitz, Dippoldiswalde, Döbeln, Großenhain, Löbau and Meißen) were members of the Committee for the Care of Indigenous Art and Building Methods in Saxony. One of these, Dr Hartmann from Döbeln, was chosen to speak on the 1909 Saxon law at that year's annual conference on conservation in Trier. Furthermore, it was a *Landrat*, Freiherr von Wilmowski, who was elected to replace Schultze-Naumburg as Chairman of the Bund Heimatschutz in 1914.

Unlike the *Baupolizei* departments of big cities, the *Landrat* or *Amtshauptmann* was not aided by a large staff of planning officials. Indeed, many rural districts did not employ any at all. This had two consequences: firstly, the *Landräte* carried considerable personal responsibility; secondly, they relied greatly on the advice of voluntary bodies such as the Heimatschutz movement, to assist them in decision-making. Some *Landräte*, like Adolf Lucas, *Landrat* of the industrial Solingen district, were instrumental in the establishment of Building Advisory Committees, to help cope with the increasing number of planning applications in their area. Lucas's committee, set up in 1908, included the Heimatschutz activist F.W. Bredt, Peter Klotzbach – a lecturer from the local arts and crafts school – and the Mayor of Solingen.[79]

Other *Landräte* preferred a more 'hands-on' approach. The *Landrat* of Niederbarmin, Count von Rödern, presented three self-drawn 'model façades' to the community, to replace the 'bad taste' designs of local architects and builders. But, as the journal *Kunstgewerbeblatt* pointed out, 'who was to vouch for the "good taste" of the Count?'[80] In another instance, the *Landrat* of Limburg issued a decree to the local population strongly recommending the introduction of ivy and other creepers on to the walls of their buildings, as part of the efforts to 'give our towns and villages a more cosy appearance'.[81] In a 1911 article, *Kunstwart*'s Ferdinand Avenarius noted that since the introduction of the 1907 law, the cases of *Landräte* taking up the cudgels on behalf of the Heimatschutz ideal had steadily increased. Avenarius bemoaned the fact, however, that the press often reacted unfavourably to such interventions, and he was particularly critical of left-wing papers for portraying these cases as a further example of official authoritarianism: 'Surely in the area of building, the *Landrat* is actually the progressive fighting against the philistines and speculators?'[82]

But it was not only the militant Left who were concerned by over-

79. A. Lucas, *Erinnerungen aus meinem Leben*, Opladen, 1959, p.80.
80. 'Falscher Heimatschutz', in *Kunstgewerbeblatt*, vol.19 (1907), pp.59–60.
81. *Deutsche Bauzeitung*, vol.44 (1910), p.116.
82. F. Avenarius, 'Landräte als Heimatschützer', in *Der Kunstwart*, vol.24 (1911), p.281.

zealous *Heimatschützer*: in a 1914 debate in the lower house of the Saxon Landtag (on state subsidies for Heimatschutz), a deputy of the liberal Fortschrittliche Volkspartei launched into a fierce attack on the 'imposition' of Heimatschutz ideas.[83] He claimed to have a bulging postbag of constituents' letters, complaining about the behaviour of *Amtshauptleute* and their 'quite extraordinary treatment of the population with regard to building'. Although he had no quarrel with the general aim of the Heimatschutz legislation, it had been exploited by the 'Heimatschutz hotheads'. In particular, too much power had been given to the subjective opinions of individual *Amtshauptleute*.

The deputy, named Brodauf, went on to describe the situation in one district of the Erzgebirge, where the *Amtshauptmann* had insisted that all buildings must have pitched, slate roofs, artificial materials were not allowed, and only one style was promoted – *Heimatstil*. To make matters worse, the whole planning procedure had been drawn out by the need for building plans to be vetted by bureaucratic committees. After giving further examples of 'Heimatschutz fanaticism', he claimed the call was growing louder in the community for '*Schutz gegen den Heimatschutz*', and argued that values of artistic taste should not be considered absolute and unchanging. Whatever the truth of Brodauf's allegations, a number of districts in Saxony and the Thuringian duchies, including Meiningen, Coburg and Weimar, certainly did pass by-laws insisting on the use of pitched roofs. Hard-line *Heimatschützer* dismissed criticisms of over-zealous officials by pointing out that 'the police are simply an instrument with which to carry out the declared wishes of the people'[84] – a stance which hardly reassured those who felt threatened by the new legislation.

Ultimately, however, this threat was to remain psychological rather than practical. Progressive architects, including those working in the industrial field, did not experience the kind of *Berufsverbot* handed out to many modernists under Hitler. For all the colourful stories of Heimatschutz excess, there are remarkably few documented cases of modern industrial buildings falling victim to a *Landrat*'s whim, and, whilst new planning laws were often a cause of irritation, they were seldom the barrier to fresh ideas and freedom of expression, which some suggested. In fact, the most negative result of Heimatschutz agitation was not a block on the development of new architectural forms – which, as we shall see, continued apace in the later Wilhelmine years – but rather, the creation of a great many second-rate buildings, in the mistaken name of tradition.

83. 'Der Heimatschutz im sächsischen Landtag', in *Deutsche Bauzeitung*, vol.49 (1915), pp.126–188. See also StA Dresden MdI 17531 'Heimatschutz. Interpellation des Abgeordneten Brodauf in der II. Kammer der Ständeversammlung 1913–14'.
84. C. Gurlitt in *Deutsche Bauzeitung*, vol.45 (1911), p.212.

The Development of the Movement after 1910

Even if the threat of Heimatschutz to cultural progress was exaggerated, the impact of the movement's agitation and legislation should not be underestimated. By 1910, Heimatschutz ideas had filtered down to those engaged in the humblest of building tasks, to the local master-builders and commercial contractors responsible for the vast majority of building work in Wilhelmine Germany. The influence was first felt in the area of domestic architecture, but industrial buildings were not far behind, for Heimatschutz had become fashionable, and a new style had entered the architectural vocabulary. *Heimatstil* took its place alongside the Classical, Gothic, Renaissance, Baroque and Rococo, in the repertoire of builders from Bremen to Breslau. This was not, however, cause for great rejoicing in Heimatschutz circles, for, while certain superficial motifs had been appropriated from the best-known Heimatschutz buildings, there was little evidence to suggest that this had been accompanied by a deeper understanding of the movement's aspirations.

The vulgarisation of the Heimatschutz message was a largely self-inflicted wound. The widespread distribution of Heimatschutz propaganda had been tremendously effective in alerting middle-class opinion to the dangers faced by the German landscape, but the layout of their pamphlets was not suited to transmitting complex ideas. It was hardly surprising that the public view of Heimatschutz was superficial, or that local builders appropriated only simple motifs from photographs of 'approved' buildings.

In 1908 Oskar Schwindrazheim had spoken optimistically on why Heimatschutz was not just another fashion:

> Fashionable moods come overnight, and our movement also appeared to spring up from nowhere, but if one looks more closely, one can see that the Heimatschutz idea is the culmination of thoughts which stretch back to the seventeenth century . . . In contrast [to trends in architectural fashion], the Heimatschutz movement comes from below . . .[85]

It was not long, however, before the movement's leaders were bemoaning the 'misunderstood Heimatschutz' of certain builders and developers, who began to erect some rather ridiculous architectural fantasies in their name. Perhaps the most absurd of all was reported in a 1909 edition of *Der Kunstwart*. A tall, reinforced concrete chimney on a picturesque country estate had been designed to look like one of the area's many towering trees. The correspondent described how the concrete 'trunk' came complete with

---

85. O. Schwindrazheim, *Heimatkunst*, p.36–37.

'broken branches', 'so that it would take a skilled eye to recognise that this is not a natural tree'![86]

Whilst seldom as absurd as the 'concrete tree', many examples of pre-war *Heimatstil* amounted to little more than predictable pastiche. The application of pitched, tiled 'roofs' on the canal lock-gates at Machnow, or a proliferation of half-timbered watertowers and signal boxes, can hardly have helped the Heimatschutz cause. The critic Paul Klopfer, a noted opponent of the movement, attacked such buildings:

> [Industry is] something completely new. If Heimatschutz wants to stride in there, with its Mansard- and hipped roofs, its plaster mouldings and little windows . . . it would be laughable . . . A factory, if it has to be built, should not worry about whether it is located in Switzerland or Pomerania, but must be the spatial expression of what the machines and the boilers require . . . Every attempt to 'evoke' a local area makes an industrial building laughable.[87]

Railway stations appear to have been frequent victims of excessive *Heimatstil*, as state and municipal transport authorities half-heartedly attempted to satisfy vigorous Heimatschutz campaigns for more 'local feeling' in railway architecture. A good illustration is provided by three Berlin suburban railway stations built in 1912–13 on the Wilmersdorf-Dahlem line, by three different architects.

The project's client, the Royal Commission on the Division of the Dahlem Domains specified in its brief that the stations should be designed in keeping with the semi-rural character of the wealthy Dahlem suburb.[88] Not surprisingly, therefore, all three architects opted for a variation of the *Heimatstil* theme. The very different solutions they came up with indicate the variety of approaches possible in the name of Heimatschutz. Heinrich Schweitzer's station at Podbielskiallee attempted to interpret the tradition of Brandenburg brick Gothic, with its stepped gable and plaster façade. The station at Dahlem-Dorf, designed by Friedrich and Wilhelm Hennings, was altogether different, utilising a rural vernacular of thatched roofs and half-timbered walls. Inside the booking hall, thick oak beams and tiles decorated with farming motifs, completed the scene. The red-brick station built by Heinrich Straumer at Thielplatz, was a more thoughtful attempt to interpret tradition in a modern context, though it too failed to announce its function in the way suggested by Heimatschutz theory. Whilst all three stations reflected a move away from the fairyland architecture of earlier

86. *Der Kunstwart*, vol.23 (1910), p.409.

87. P. Klopfer, 'Der Heimatschutz und die Neuzeit', in *Der Industriebau*, vol.6 (1915), p.361.

88. *Berlin und seine Bauten*, Teil X, Band B, Berlin, 1971. Also S. Bohle, 'Die Architektur der Berliner Hoch- und Untergrundbahn bis 1930', PhD theis, Berlin FU, 1978, p.130.

Figure 21   Podbielskiallee railway station, Berlin 1912–13
Arch. H. Schweitzer. Present condition

Figure 22 Dahlem-Dorf railway station, Berlin 1912–13
Arch. F. & W. Hennings. Present condition

Figure 23 Thielplatz railway station, Berlin 1912–13
Arch. H. Straumer. Present condition

Berlin suburban stations, none could claim to meet Heimatschutz demands fully.

On a more positive note, the immediate pre-war years did witness an improvement in architectural education, partly as a result of Heimatschutz influence. The craft schools (*Baugewerkschulen*), in which most German master builders received a practical training, had long been a target of Heimatschutz activists. Reformist writers criticised the schools' method of teaching architecture through historic styles, and their concentration on the sort of building project few master-builders could expect to meet in the outside world. The Charlottenburg academic Professor Franz wrote in the *Heimatschutz* journal:

> In the last few decades Germany has become an industrial nation. The last census of occupations revealed a large majority of people employed in trade, industry and transport. This transformation is naturally expressed in the buildings which are erected for these occupations. Not only has the total number of buildings grown rapidly, but the variety has too. Industry, in particular, has produced an almost bewildering number of different building-types. The education of our architects, artists and technicians has almost completely ignored these developments.[89]

So, when some colleges began to offer courses on industrial architecture, it was a source of great satisfaction to the *Heimatschützer*. In 1912, for instance, *Heimatschutz* carried a story on the Stuttgart *Baugewerkschule*, where the architect Paul Schmohl was encouraging his students to plan factories and grain silos rather than museums or farms.[90] Similar courses were offered by Professor Jummerspach at the Technical College in Munich, and other colleges soon followed.

The experience gained during the first decade of Heimatschutz lobbying was reflected in a more sophisticated level of debate in the movement's journals, which reached a qualitative peak around 1910–14. The *völkisch* mysticism and anti-urban rhetoric of the turn-of-the-century prophets of doom had been largely replaced by a more practical, pragmatic tone. The essays and lectures on the theme of 'Heimatschutz and industrial architecture', written by the architect German Bestelmeyer (1874–1942), revealed much common sense:

> All that Heimatschutz requests from industrial architecture is that it expresses its function clearly from the beginning and, wherever possible, takes account of its environment, in its layout, scale and materials. The validity of

89. W. Franz, 'Die Vernachläßigung der Industriebauten auf den technischen Schulen', in *Heimatschutz*, vol.8 (1909), p.23.

90. P. Schmohl, 'Entwerfen von technischen Bauten in der Baugewerkschule', in *Heimatschutz*, vol.8 (1912), pp.24–33.

Heimatschutz has already been recognised in industrialist circles, where one has seen the great advantages to come out of co-operation with artists over product design and the layout of buildings. For the manufacturer, a factory which fits well into the landscape and which possesses a memorable silhouette, is certainly a more effective form of advertising than an obtrusive placard on an ugly building.[91]

Bestelmeyer concludes one *Kunstwart* essay with a then-novel call for the creation of special industrial estates, either by local authority intervention or by means of co-operatives, so that transport facilities and technical services could be provided without too much damage to the environment.[92] The appointment of the engineer and writer Werner Lindner to the post of Executive Secretary in 1914 was a further indication of the Bund's desire to become a reformist pressure group, involved in the day-to-day problems of planning and architecture. In a 1915 *Deutsche Bauzeitung* article Lindner stressed:

A healthy and serious Heimatschutz has absolutely no time for an enslavement of new and creative architects in the service of the old ways of building. The movement has found its own, correct path, attacking sentimentality, such as the idea of building a suburban railway station with a thatched roof and calling it 'Lower Saxon' . This also explains why the movement accepts new phenomena like the flat roof, so long as such jobs are tackled in an artistic manner, which we believe is perfectly possible.[93]

Tragically, Lindner was not able to rid the movement of the preoccupations which were later to bring Heimatschutz into disrepute. Contact established in the early 1920s between Schultze-Naumburg and 'Blood and Soil' theorists like Günther and Darré helped to develop the racial theories of architecture, for which the Heimatschutz idea is now best remembered. Of course, there had been a *völkisch* streak in the movement from the beginning, but, as we have seen, this was only one side of the story. Any conclusions on the relative 'modernity' of the movement must take into account both faces of Heimatschutz, which were revealed in the years 1900–1918.

The wealth of pre-1918 Heimatschutz writing provides a rich and largely untapped source of material for the historian of Wilhelmine Germany. At the same time however, it throws up many problems of selection and interpretation. The pitfalls are clear: by concentrating solely

91. G. Bestelmeyer, 'Industriebauten und Industrieland', in *Der Kunstwart*, vol.27 (1914), pp.194–196.

92. G. Bestelmeyer, ibid., p.196.

93. W. Lindner, 'Ist der Heimatschutz kulturfördernd?', in *Deutsche Bauzeitung*, vol.40 (1915), p.268.

on the movement's own small world of minor battles and petty victories, one risks losing a sense of proportion. By the usual standards of cultural pressure-groups the Heimatschutz movement was highly-influential, but for the majority of Germans it remained an irrelevance. Moreover, neither the concerns which it articulated, nor the solutions which it proposed, were unique to that particular time and place. So what conclusions can one draw about Heimatschutz in Wilhelmine Germany?

From the perspective of the early 1990s, the Heimatschutz movement appears pragmatic rather than idealistic, active rather than passive, optimistic rather than pessimistic. The movement, faced by the dramatic environmental consequences of rapid industrialisation, attempted to find practical solutions and genuine answers. In this, it was more successful than one could have expected, less successful than it would have wished.

Of course, the Heimatschutz activists spent too much time fighting the symptoms, and too little effort in searching for the cause; shoddy industrial architecture, which devalued both the workplace and the landscape, was an inevitable consequence of a productive system in which the quality of life came low in the scale of priorities. But at heart the Wilhelmine *Heimatschützer* had no more desire to sacrifice the undoubted benefits of industrialisation than any generation since. Indeed, the compromises and contradictions displayed by the Heimatschutz movement as it attempted to reconcile the positive and negative aspects of the modernisation process, are strikingly typical of much twentieth century thought.

Ultimately, it is this complexity of Heimatschutz discourse, in which deep insight combined with wishful thinking, which makes the movement so fascinating. With its close links to local and national government, the Heimatschutz movement could hardly be ignored by anyone involved in the design, planning or construction of industrial architecture in Wilhelmine Germany. In the last years before World War One, however, the Heimatschutz movement found itself increasingly overshadowed by a new organisation, the German Werkbund, whose ideas are assessed in Chapter Three.

-3-

'From Sofa Cushions to Town Planning': The German Werkbund

1907 was a significant year for all Germans committed to the cause of improving the built environment. Just three months after the introduction of the Disfigurement Law, over a hundred artists, academics and politicians met in Munich to establish the German Werkbund (DWB); an organisation whose impact on German industrial architecture was later to eclipse even that of the Heimatschutz movement.

The DWB was not set up in opposition to Heimatschutz. It too had its roots in the 'reform of life' movement and many prominent Heimatschutz campaigners – including Schultze-Naumburg and Bestelmeyer – also became members of the new organisation, but the DWB pursued its own distinctive agenda and ultimately found its own solutions. The relationship between the two organisations was always close but never easy. In the words of the Heimatschutz theorist C.J. Fuchs it was a question of 'marching separately, striking together'.[1]

As a catalyst which brought together architects and politicians, artists and industrialists, the DWB must lie at the heart of any investigation into culture and politics in Wilhelmine Germany. This chapter outlines the organisation's attitude to industrial architecture in general and then takes a more detailed look at some of the buildings it produced. Unlike the Heimatschutz movement, the DWB has been reasonably well served by historians[2] and anything but the briefest repetition of its organisational

1. C.J. Fuchs quoted in O. Hoffmann (ed.) *Der Deutsche Werkbund – 1907, 1947, 1987*, catalogue, Frankfurt, 1987, p.26.
2. J. Campbell, *The German Werkbund. The Politics of Reform in the Applied Arts*, Princeton, 1978; E. Haase, 'Die Ideologiefunktion des ästhetischen Produkt- und Umweltgestaltung, dargestellt an der Arbeit und Wirkung des Deutschen Werkbundes', PhD thesis, East Berlin, Humboldt University, 1970; G. Pollak, 'Die ideologische, wirtschaftliche und gesellschaftspolitische Funktion des Deutschen Werkbundes, 1907–1918', PhD thesis, Weimar, 1971; S. Müller, *Kunst und Industrie. Ideologie und Organisation des Funktionalismus in der Architektur*, Munich, 1974; G. von Hartmann and W. Fischer (eds), *Zwischen Kunst und Industrie. Der Deutsche Werkbund*, Munich, 1975; K. Junghanns, *Der Deutsche Werkbund. Das erste Jahrzehnt*, East Berlin, 1982; L. Burckhardt (ed.), *The Werkbund. Studies in the History and Ideology of the Deutscher Werkbund, 1907–33*, London, 1986; P. Kallen, *Unter dem Banner der Sachlichkeit*, Cologne, 1987.

history would be unproductive. However, since Werkbund concerns ranged 'from sofa cushions to town planning',[3] it is perhaps inevitable that certain aspects of its activities have not been investigated in sufficient depth: industrial architecture is one.

The personalities invited to gather at the Hotel Vierjahreszeiten in Munich over the weekend of the 5–6 October 1907 represented the cream of German cultural life. They included the progressive architects Peter Behrens (1868–1940), Josef Hoffmann (1870–1956) and J.M. Olbrich (1867–1908), the left-liberal politician Friedrich Naumann (1860–1919), the educational reformer Georg Kerschensteiner (1854–1932) and the publisher Eugen Diederichs (1867–1930). The focal point of their discussions was the establishment of an organisation to attempt a reconciliation between the conflicting worlds of art and commerce, to improve both the quality of German manufactured goods and the lives of those who produced them. Symbolically, the declaration which had preceded the foundation of the DWB had been signed by twelve 'artists' and twelve 'producers'.

The Munich gathering approved a constitution for the new organisation, in which its purpose was defined as 'the ennobling of commercial work through the co-operation of art, craft and industry, by means of education [and] propaganda'.[4] The members were united in the conviction that the manufacture of poor quality goods made little sense economically, ethically or socially. In place of the 'cheap and nasty' surrogates for which German exporters had become known, the DWB wished to see a greater emphasis on high-quality manufacturing; not only would *Qualitätsarbeit* provide a boost to Germany's long term economic prospects in the world market, but it could also increase the self-respect of industrial workers, and thereby help to restore social harmony to the German people.

The influence of Friedrich Naumann on the DWB's programme was clear from the start. As well as devising the organisation's structure and constitution, he wrote its first publication (*Deutsche Gewerbekunst*, 1908) and filled key posts with his supporters. The vital job of Executive Secretary, responsible for the day-to-day running of the DWB, was permanently in the hands of Naumann acolytes.[5] His idiosyncratic political vision – a synthesis of New Liberalism, Christian Socialism and aggressive nationalism – was the driving force behind the DWB, and will be examined

3. The phrase was attributed to Hermann Muthesius.
4. Paragraph two of the DWB Constitution. See Werkbund Yearbook, 1912.
5. W. Dohrn (1907–10), A. Paquet (1910–11), E. Jäckh (1912–22). Both Dohrn and Paquet had studied with Naumann's friend and 'teacher' Lujo Brentano (1844–1931) in Munich, as indeed had Theodor Heuss, who joined the DWB's management in 1917. E. Jäckh was editor of the *Neckar-Zeitung* in Heilbronn and had helped Naumann's successful 1907 Reichstag election campaign.

at length later.

It was a Naumannite, the architect Fritz Schumacher, who delivered the keynote speech at Munich. His theme was the 'reconquest of a harmonious culture':

> If art becomes more closely connected with the work of the people, then the consequences are not just aesthetic in nature. We are working not only for the sensitive aesthetes who are pained by outward disharmony. No, the effect goes well beyond the small circle of art patrons. Most importantly, it extends to the producers, to the worker himself, who actually makes the product. If art's kiss of life can be introduced into his work, his feeling for life will grow and with it will grow his productivity . . . We must win back the joy of work, which means in effect we must increase the quality of work. In this way art is not only an aesthetic force but an ethical one too, and together these forces will eventually lead to the most important power of all; economic power.[6]

The new organisation's initial interest was focused on the quality of product design in the art and craft industries. Thus when Schumacher and other DWB leaders referred to industrial 'producers' and 'workers' they had in mind the sort of medium-sized craft-based companies which were the first to sign up under the Werkbund banner: Peter Bruckmann's silverware factory in Heilbronn, the printers Klingspor, the publisher Diederichs and several furniture manufacturers, including the Deutsche Werkstätten in Hellerau.

However, even at this early stage the DWB's discussions went well beyond the predictable preoccupations of the Arts and Crafts movement. There was explicit agreement in Munich on the need to acknowledge the reality of machine-led mass-production, and recognition too of the benefits of working with, rather than against, industry. Above all, there was unanimous acceptance of the capitalist system, even if many members admitted to being pained by the excesses of 'materialism'.

It was not long before larger firms, many from outside the world of arts and crafts, began applying for Werkbund membership, and the proportion of industrial and commercial companies amongst the organisation's membership increased swiftly over the next six years.[7] Firms to join the DWB between 1908 and 1910 included AEG, BASF, Bahlsen, Bayer,

6. F. Schumacher's speech printed in *Der Kunstwart*, vol.21 (1908), pp.135–8.

7. Industry became involved in the DWB in three 'waves'. Firstly, in 1907–8, high-quality art and craft manufacturers joined. Then, between 1909–12, companies from the rapidly growing electrical and chemical sectors, the automobile industry, producers in the food and wine trade, and many light manufacturing firms signed up. Finally, the first of the giant 'heavy' industrial companies to join the DWB, the Friedrich Krupp AG, applied for membership in January 1913. After World War One heavy industrial concerns (GHH, Stumm) were just as likely to commission DWB architects as companies from other sectors of industry, although they continued to be wary of the DWB as an organisation.

Degussa, Norddeutscher Lloyd, Pelikan and Zanders,[8] and each in its own way attempted to harness the creative talents assembled under the Werkbund umbrella. In practical terms this meant that the DWB became an agency, mediating between the needs of industry and the desires of artists. Whether in the area of product design, advertising or architecture, the mark of the DWB signet proved good for business. Peter Behrens's seven year reign as 'artistic advisor' to the electrical concern AEG, where he was responsible for everything from the design of kettles to the factories themselves, is the best known example of the Werkbund idea in action.

The character of the DWB was very different from that of the Heimatschutz movement. The DWB boasted an exclusive, professional membership and a centralised structure covering the whole of the *Reich* (with the exception of Bavaria).[9] The DWB had no interest in developing a mass membership. It was the view of the DWB's Executive Secretary Wolf Dohrn (1878–1914) that 'all existing associations suffer from too many members',[10] so the Werkbund maintained strict entrance qualifications, vetting all prospective members for their 'suitability'. Even so, DWB membership rose steadily: from 492 in 1908; 843 in 1910; 971 in 1912; to 1,870 in 1914,[11] with each new individual or corporate member determining the size of his own subscription fee.[12]

In accordance with its constitution, the DWB sought to influence 'education' at every level. It supported lectures on the value of 'good taste' for tradesmen (*Vorträge zur Geschmacksbildung*), it attempted to educate consumers to buy approved 'quality' products (via the *Deutsches Warenbuch*), and it tried to improve the standards of training for apprentices in both the handicrafts and mechanised industry. In addition, DWB members were involved in academic investigations into the economic value of 'quality' production, the science of advertising, and

---

8. DWB Mitgliederverzeichnis 1910 (K.E.O. Archiv DWB 1/331-1).

9. Werkbund supporters in Bavaria were organised in the 'Münchner Bund', which worked closely with the DWB.

10. W. Dohrn, 'Denkschrift über die Organisation und die Arbeit des DWB' (1907) reprinted in K. Junghanns, *Der Deutsche Werkbund.*, p.144.

11. Figures from DWB Jahresberichte (K.E.O. Archiv DWB 1/330).

12. In 1913 the DWB Executive Secretary Ernst Jäckh wrote that individual members of the organisation paid an annual membership of between 10 and 1,000 Marks, and that firms and corporations contributed between 100 and 1,000 Marks per annum (in a letter to the Fried. Krupp AG – HA Krupp WA IV 1541 V.3361 p.183). The DWB's income from members grew only slowly in its first years: in the business year 1908–9 it amounted to just over 17,181 Marks, rising to 18,857 Marks in 1910–11, before slipping back to 17,900 Marks in 1911–12. (K.E.O. Archiv DWB 1/330, DWB 1/94, DWB 1/324). The financial fortunes of the organisation changed in 1913–14, when membership contributions jumped to over 41,000 Marks, due in no small measure to the support of the industrialist Robert Bosch. By 1917 Bosch's annual donation to the DWB had risen to 60,000 Marks (K.E.O. Archiv DWB 1/243).

the art of shop window-dressing.

The DWB preferred to concentrate its publicity efforts on established large-circulation daily newspapers, rather than risk the production of a Werkbund journal. With so many high-profile public figures in its ranks the DWB was able to command space in such influential publications as the *Frankfurter Zeitung, Kölner Zeitung* and *Vossische Zeitung*, as well as the numerous art and architectural journals of the day. The organisation's own publishing efforts centred on the Werkbund Yearbooks, which first appeared in 1912 and contained numerous photographs and articles on all aspects of DWB activity. The Yearbooks proved a great success, selling out increasing print runs each year (in 1912 10,000; 1913 12,000; 1914 20,000)[13] and enjoying the accolade of being used as school prizes in Prussia, where the Ministry of Trade purchased 700 copies of the first edition.[14]

Industrial architecture had not figured prominently amongst the DWB's early concerns, but the presence of politicians like Naumann and Kerschensteiner ensured that the ethics of the workplace were always an issue in Werkbund debates. As Kerschensteiner told the DWB's first Annual Conference in Munich:

> We cannot hold on to able people in commerce and industry if we have nothing more to offer than a lifetime of mechanical work, from early in the morning to late at night. Such a prospect is hardly likely to attract intelligent young people.[15]

At the same time, architecture gradually began to play a more central role in DWB activity. In the last days of 1907 Wolf Dohrn wrote in an internal memorandum 'influence on architecture is absolutely vital, because the development of all Werkbund work depends on it'.[16] Dohrn himself later elaborated the point:

> Manpower, like machinery, is something whose maximum performance depends on how one treats it. So areas which at first seem to be of secondary importance, such as the external appearance of the workplace, become highly significant.[17]

13. Figures from J. Campbell, *The German Werkbund*, p.37.

14. J. Campbell, *ibid.*, p.37.

15. G. Kerschensteiner's speech printed in 'Die Veredelung der gewerblichen Arbeit im Zusammenhang von Kunst, Industrie und Handwerk – Verhandlung des DWBs zu München am 11–12 Juli 1908', p.141.

16. W. Dohrn, 'Denkschrift..' (1907) reprinted in K. Junghanns, *Der Deutsche Werkbund*, p.147.

17. W. Dohrn, 'Eine Ausstellung architektonisch guter Fabrikbauten', in *Der Industriebau*, vol.1 (1910), p.2.

If the quality of manufactured goods was to be improved, then – so the argument ran – the workplace would have to change too. Three factors therefore combined to push industrial architecture into the forefront of Werkbund campaigns: the growth of the 'industrial faction' within the organisation; the agitation of the DWB's political wing for a reform of the workplace; and the increasing importance attached to architecture by the movement as a whole.

By early 1909 industrial architecture was recognised by the DWB leadership as a front-line issue. Meeting at Würzburg in February, the organisation's management committee decided to collect photographic material for a major exhibition on exemplary factory buildings, which was to be shown in conjunction with the DWB's second annual conference in Frankfurt, before touring the *Reich*. Members were called on to supply good examples of industrial architecture from their home areas, and a commission was established to assess the quality of entries submitted.[18] The delegates who assembled in Frankfurt heard a paper on industrial architecture, written by the architect Hans Poelzig (1869–1936), who claimed:

> The most recent period in the history of factory building stands in part under the influence of a misunderstood Heimatschutz. In an effort to make buildings blend in with the landscape the industrial building is being robbed of all its own character, even though it is obvious that the factory demands new solutions. The factory gives us hope of finding such new solutions, because it has no stylistic pre-requirements.[19]

Despite this, there were actually many similarities between the architectural theories of Werkbund and Heimatschutz. Members of both organisations rejected architectural historicism and energetically promoted the values of 'honesty' and 'simplicity'. Both believed that industrial and technical structures should reflect their function in architectural form, and both stressed the social benefits of an attractive working environment. Werkbund activists called for architects and engineers to co-operate on the design of functional buildings, to avoid the crass contradiction between outer facings and inner workings which so typified historicist industrial buildings, and which was most clearly displayed in the architectural schizophrenia of the great nineteenth century railway stations.

Where opinions diverged was on the main source of inspiration for

18. The commission first comprised of the architects Poelzig, Riemerschmid and Wagner, the engineer Urbahn and the DWB's Wolf Dohrn. In 1910 it was reconstituted to include Osthaus, Muthesius, Franz and Paquet.
19. H. Poelzig's paper reported in the *Verhandlungsbericht* of the second annual conference, Frankfurt 1909, p.26 (DWB-Archiv).

contemporary architectural tasks: *Heimatschützer* saw established vernacular traditions as the only legitimate basis for a healthy new architecture, whereas the architects organised in the DWB were more interested in finding novel solutions, and exercising their own artistic vision. For this reason, the DWB shied away from issuing guidelines on architectural style for its members[20] and while certain characteristics were common to many buildings designed by DWB activists, there was never a distinctive 'Werkbund Style'. All attempts by architectural historians to divide the DWB architects into stylistic sub-groupings founder on this variety of individual approaches. In view of the wide spectrum of creative personalities active in the organisation it is perhaps not surprising that Wolf Dohrn once described the Werkbund as an 'association of the most intimate enemies'. Certainly it did not take long for the divisions within the organisation to rise to the surface.

Poelzig's paper sparked off five years of fevered writing on factory design by the DWB's leading lights. It was largely in response to this growing interest in all aspects of industrial architecture that the journal *Der Industriebau* was started, under the editorship of the Heilbronn architect and DWB member Emil Beutinger (1875–1957). The first edition appeared in January 1910 – for some, the birth year of modern architecture[21] – and opened with a major essay by Wolf Dohrn, in which he analysed the changed character of the German industrialist:

> It is not as if the factory owners of today have become sensitive aesthetes, but they calculate more sharply, more subtly, and consider the imponderables too; i.e. they take into account the psychological conditions of work. In fact one could say that the art of the great organiser of our time consists to a large extent of this ability to grasp and develop the moral values of a community, so that they can organise, discipline and form an enterprise.[22]

Dohrn believed the 'great organisers' of industry were coming to realise the value not only of cleanliness, hygiene, order and light, but the benefits of well-proportioned buildings too. For industrialists the prospect was opening up of having factories that were no longer a 'necessary evil', but a 'concentrated expression of the best powers of the age'.[23]

20. Whenever it looked as if a DWB leader was suggesting the desirability of artistic guidelines for the future development of German architecture or design, such as Muthesius's call for a certain amount of standardisation (*Typisierung*) at the 1914 Cologne conference, he was promptly met by howls of disapproval. Any programme which implied a restriction of free artistic expression, was anathema to most Werkbund architects. For the Cologne debates see J. Campbell, *The German Werkbund*.

21. See for example Joachim Petsch's book *Architektur und Gesellschaft. Zur Geschichte der deutschen Architektur im 19. und 20. Jahrhundert*, Cologne, 1977.

22. W. Dohrn, 'Eine Ausstellung architektonisch guter Fabrikbauten', p.1.

23. W. Dohrn, ibid., p.2.

The DWB architects were quick to recognise the potential opportunities this 'prospect' opened up for their profession too. The organisation's principal programmatic essays on architecture had been written by Muthesius, with valuable contributions from Schumacher, Poelzig and Behrens. In the field of industrial architecture, however, no one was swifter to sense the mood of the day than the young Walter Gropius (1883–1969), whose lectures and articles on the ethics and aesthetics of industrial architecture helped turn the rather prosaic task of building factories into a fashionable vocation.

The highly-ambitious Gropius, who worked in Behrens's studio until 1910, was fortunate enough to be invited to play an important role in the new German Museum of Art in Trade and Commerce. The Museum, based in the Westphalian industrial town of Hagen, had been established by the DWB in the summer of 1909, at the behest of the millionaire benefactor Karl Ernst Osthaus (1874–1921).[24] Its collections included samples of exemplary packaging and publicity material, well-designed products and the photographic archive of the DWB, which contained some 40,000 prints. These treasures formed the basis of a series of exhibitions which travelled at home and abroad, spreading the fame of good German design: the Museum staged twenty different exhibitions in fifty locations between 1911 and 1912.[25] The DWB's exhibition of factory buildings was part of the archive which passed into the hands of the Museum in the course of 1910–11, and it was the co-ordination of this material which gave Gropius his big break.

Gropius's first lecture at Hagen, entitled 'Monumental Art and Industrial Building', was given on 10 April 1911[26] and aroused considerable interest. It is a key text and must be quoted at some length:

> The ideas of the age are pressing for architectural expression. The gigantic need for labour requires buildings which can demonstrate with suitable pathos and dignity their inner value; buildings which can successfully characterise the method of modern work in architectural form. Palaces must be erected for labour, to give the factory worker – the slave of modern industry – not only light, air and cleanliness, but also some sense of the value of the great common idea which drives the whole enterprise . . . If awoken in each worker, this awareness could perhaps stave off the social catastrophe, which appears to threaten daily in the ferment of our current economic life.[27]

24. S. Müller, 'Deutsches Museum für Kunst in Handel und Gewerbe', in H. Hesse-Frielinghaus (ed.), *Karl Ernst Osthaus. Leben und Werk*, Recklinghausen, 1971.
25. S. Müller, *Kunst und Industrie*, p.122.
26. The text was dated 29 January 1911.
27. W. Gropius's speech is reprinted in full in K. Wilhelm's book *Walter Gropius, Industriearchitekt*, Brunswick, 1983.

Shortly after this speech Gropius began work on the German Museum of Art in Trade and Commerce's 'touring exhibition eighteen', entitled simply *Industriebauten*. Gropius was responsible for both the selection of exhibits and the accompanying pamphlet which reiterated many of the themes expressed at Hagen. The exhibition was shown in Chambers of Commerce, museums and colleges throughout the country. Many of the exhibits were also sent on a tour of Scandinavia in 1913, with Osthaus supplying the catalogue text:

> The modern factory is no longer a place of horror. The only thing which makes it different from the representative buildings of aristocracy is the cost; the breeding is now the same. The human rights of the worker are clearly recognised, the dignity of labour is the factory's actual expression. This has however only been possible because of the renewal of German architecture. Socialism could never have brought forth such culture.[28]

The photographic collection of exemplary industrial architecture grew steadily. Gropius eagerly added prints of North American factories and monumental grain silos – which he compared to the pyramids of ancient Egypt – but he was also able to call on an increasing number of German industrial buildings, as the DWB's influence spread. The DWB Yearbooks for 1913, (dedicated to 'Art in Industry and Trade') and 1914 ('Transport'), both featured photographs of industrial buildings from the Hagen collection, as well as further essays by Gropius on modern industrial architecture.[29] As Karin Wilhelm points out in her monograph on Gropius,[30] these essays were aimed at both industrialists and fellow architects. For the benefit of the former, Gropius highlighted the improvements in productivity, industrial relations, and advertising that better factory buildings could bring. To his professional colleagues Gropius stressed the need for architecture to break with established practices, and to find fresh forms which could perform a vital function, but which were also able to 'interpret' the world of industry with spirit and dignity.

Gropius's essays also regularly referred to the 'social dimension' of architectural reform, albeit viewed from the employer's standpoint:

> From the social perspective it is not a matter of indifference whether the modern factory worker performs his work in dull, ugly industrial barracks or in well-proportioned rooms. He will work more joyously in the creation of great common goals in a workplace constructed by the hand of an artist, where his

---

28. K.E. Osthaus, 'Industriebauten und Reklamewesen in Deutschland', (K.E.O. Archiv A 1088/4).

29. W. Gropius, 'Die Entwicklung moderner Industriebaukunst' (1913); 'Der stilbildende Wert industrieller Bauformen' (1914).

30. K. Wilhelm, *Walter Gropius*, p.25.

inherent sense of beauty is recognised, and where he can be revived from the monotony of mechanical work. In this way, increasing contentment will boost the working spirit and therefore the productivity of the whole enterprise.[31]

Many of the ideas expressed by Gropius in his pre-war writing on the reform of industrial architecture were not original. As we have seen, Heimatschutz campaigners had been using similar phrases for several years, but it was Gropius who caught the imagination of both his profession and the public: not least, because he could back up his fine words with deeds (building work on his first factory project had begun in early 1911). Gropius later remarked that he was something of an *enfant terrible* in the early years of the Werkbund, as he grabbed the limelight from more established architectural theorists. Certainly he was not the only DWB member to have a view on the reform of industrial architecture at this time, as the pages of the architectural journals reveal.

The tone of other DWB architects was not, however, vastly different. Much of their writing was characterised by a naive faith in the ability of engineers to solve problems, and an equally optimistic belief in the power of art to find answers to political questions. Above all, they reflected the profession's understandable desire to find an area of building which could compare to the great architectural tasks of bygone ages. Writing in *Der Industriebau* Hans Poelzig claimed:

> Many of the nuisances of factories which still exist – the production of smoke, soot and foul smells – will become avoidable with the perfection of technology . . . Our age finds its perfect expression in the great productive buildings of the economy: in fact they are the monumental buildings of today's architecture.[32]

Another DWB member, Otto Schultze, Director of the School of Arts and Crafts in Elberfeld, was equally optimistic:

> Our big business can hold its head high in every corner of the globe. The products of German good-taste are starting to oust those of the old nations. It appears as if culture is beginning to enter our businesses and factories. The number of model businesses is growing all the time, and these healthy, first-rate kernels are increasingly being placed in dignified shells, as the architects and engineers at last start to create buildings which are worthy of their contents.[33]

---

31. W. Gropius, 'Sind beim Bau von Industriegebäuden künstlerische Gesichtspunkte mit praktischen und wirtschaftlichen vereinbar', in *Der Industriebau*, vol.3 (1912), p.6.
32. H. Poelzig, 'Der neuzeitliche Fabrikbau', in *Der Industriebau*, vol.2 (1911), p.101.
33. O. Schulze, 'Die Bauten für Technik und Industrie', in *Der Industriebau*, vol.1 (1910), p.36.

According to the DWB activist J.A. Lux, factory districts should become 'praised places of beauty and fertility, visited with pleasure', because factories 'can also bear the stamp of modern beauty'.[34] For the Dresden architect Mackowsky, industrial buildings were vital for the development of architecture as a whole: 'industrial architecture will be called upon to mark the transition to modern architecture, and will play a leading role in it'.[35] The editor of *Der Industriebau*, Emil Beutinger, wrote a three-part series on contemporary factory design, in which he too stressed the importance of this area of architectural activity:

> The creation of sound and dignified places for technology is extremely important, because in an industrial nation the style of the factories and technical structures has considerable influence on the future development of all other building types. The mighty industries and the thumping rhythm of the machines must be capable of cultural expression.[36]

Alongside Gropius's essay on 'The Development of Modern Industrial Architecture' in the 1913 DWB Yearbook was an article by Hermann Muthesius entitled 'The Problem of Form in Engineering Structures'. Muthesius was a more conservative architect than Gropius, but their two essays had much in common. Muthesius was anxious to bridge the gulf which had opened up between the world of the artist-architect and the engineer, pointing out that Leonardo da Vinci had been responsible for the construction of fortifications and canals as well as the creation of artistic masterpieces. Although he dismissed the notion that all functional structures were automatically beautiful, Muthesius saw 'the actual purpose of architecture' as the 'fusion of the beautiful with the functional'. Thus it would be 'meaningless' to make a distinction between the work of architects and engineers: 'a large number of engineering structures – bridges, railway station halls, lighthouse towers and grain silos – have an aesthetically-pleasing effect'.[37]

The Werkbund's new-found interest in industrial architecture was due in no small measure to the work of Peter Behrens, whose AEG turbine factory of 1909 inspired many pages of positive comment in both newspapers and specialist journals. It was hardly surprising then, that Behrens's views were influential and well-respected amongst his DWB colleagues. In general, he was a good deal less sanguine than Gropius and

---

34. J.A. Lux, 'Der moderne Fabrikbau', in *Der Industiebau*, vol.1 (1910), p.83.
35. Dr Mackowsky, 'Der Industriebau und die moderne Baukunst', in *Der Industriebau*, vol.4 (1913), p.177.
36. E. Beutinger, 'Fabrikbau', in *Der Industriebau*, vol.6 (1915), p.268.
37. H. Muthesius, 'Das Formproblem im Ingenieurbau', in Werkbund Yearbook, 1913, p.30.

the Werkbund's young guns, and was deeply disturbed by the 'materialist' values of modern life. One of his favourite themes was the need for industry to recognise its wider cultural responsibilities. Behrens believed industry had frequently fallen victim to a 'dilettante tendency towards romanticism and ostentation',[38] but he was nevertheless convinced of its vital role in society. As he told an impressive gathering of businessmen, politicians and civil servants at the opening of the new Mannesmann headquarters in Düsseldorf:

> Modern development, which, far beyond the well-ordered world of small town life, threatens to lead our great cities into disorganised confusion, sets new tasks for architecture, and these can only be tackled in the spirit of industry and big-business. The evolution of monumental art has always been an expression of the concentration of power: if one can speak of the art of the Church in the Middle Ages; in the Baroque era of the art of Kings; of bourgeois art in the styles around 1800; then I believe that today our flourishing industry again forms a concentration of power which cannot remain without influence on the development of culture.[39]

His view on the importance of industrial architecture is perhaps best summed up in the text of a lecture he gave 'On the relationship of artistic and technical problems' at the Central Institute of Education in Berlin. Behrens considered that 'the most impressive achievements of our time are the products of modern technology'. However, whilst he acknowledged that these had contributed to the creation of an unprecedented standard of living, he believed such achievements had not been accompanied by a similar raising of cultural or spiritual values: 'It is in industry's hands', he argued, whether a true culture is to be established through the 'bringing together of art and technology'.[40]

A prime opportunity for DWB architects to present their ideas to industry and the general public came through the organisation's participation in national and international trade fairs and expositions, which occurred with great frequency in the years before World War One. Building on the experience gained from the third National Exhibition of the Applied Arts (Dresden 1906), which had been organised by Schumacher and was regarded by many as the first manifestation of the Werkbund idea (railway wagons were exhibited alongside porcelain vases), the DWB was approached by both commercial and governmental bodies to help in the

---

38. P. Behrens speech 10 Dec. 1912 printed in the album 'Zur Erinnerung an die Einweihung des Verwaltungsgebäudes der Mannesmannröhren-Werke in Düsseldorf', p.85. (Mannesmann-Archiv).

39. P. Behrens, ibid., p.85.

40. *Technische Abende im Zentralinstitut für Erziehung und Unterricht*, (1917), pp.3–22.

setting up of many large-scale events. These included the second 'Clay, Cement and Concrete' trade fair (Berlin 1910), where the pavilions were designed by Behrens, and the co-ordination of the German contribution to the 1910 World Fair in Brussels, where the DWB responded to a request for help from *Regierungsrat* Heinrich Albert (1874–1938) of the Ministry of the Interior.[41] The DWB's own major exhibition, held in Cologne in 1914, was a massive affair, involving the construction of a temporary 'new town' on the right bank of the Rhine.[42] One of the most talked about attractions was the life-size model factory, designed by Gropius to house the ubiquitous exhibition of exemplary industrial buildings, as well as many fine products of German precision engineering.

Ultimately, however, the best advertisements for Werkbund ideas were not the plaster-board palaces of the exhibition grounds, but the real buildings its architects erected throughout the country. The dozen or so industrial buildings to be discussed over the following pages were all designed by DWB activists. They range from the famous – Behrens's AEG factories and Gropius's 'Fagus-Werk' are a fixture in all respected histories of twentieth century architecture – to the unknown and forgotten, but most still stand and many continue to fulfil their original function.

The buildings are not united by stylistic ingenuity or technical innovation, nor are they all the work of creative genius. That fateful mixture of luck and judgement, chance and skill, ensured that same Werkbund architects found fame and fortune in architectural beauty contests around the globe, whilst others were left on the shelf of history. What all these buildings do share is their value as historical documents; documents which can tell us not only about the men who designed them, but the men who commissioned them and used them too.

Industrial Buildings by Werkbund Architects

The basis of all DWB exhibitions and articles on industrial architecture before the Great War was the photographic collection of exemplary factory buildings, begun in 1909 by the DWB itself and later continued by the German Museum for Art in Trade and Industry. Since the same sites were displayed with such regularity, it seems reasonable to assume that these buildings were accepted as the best available illustration of the

41. Albert addressed the DWB's first annual conference in Munich (1908). His speech, printed in 'Die Veredelung der gewerblichen Arbeit', closed with the rallying call: 'In Brussels it will be a case of opening up new markets for the quality products of German craft, in the long-running battle for the world market. I can only hope that the members of the Werkbund will not be missing there.'
42. For the Cologne exhibition see W. Herzogenrath (ed.), *Der westdeutsche Impuls. Die DWB Ausstellung Cöln 1914*, Cologne, 1984.

organisation's ideas in practical form. There does not appear to have been any great dissent on matters of selection, and the ever-expanding collection had no obvious omissions. The industrial buildings featured over the following pages are therefore all examples taken from the DWB Yearbooks of 1912 and 1913, where they were displayed as full- or half-page plates, without editorial comment.

Understandably, the emphasis of the DWB's publicity material was very much on the new: the oldest industrial building illustrated in the 1913 Yearbook was Theodor Fischer's warehouse for ironware products in Ostheim, which had been constructed in 1905. Nevertheless the DWB concept of 'ennobling' industry through art had existed for some years before the organisation's 1907 foundation, and several firms had experimented with the commissioning of leading artists to provide posters, packaging or product design at the turn of the century. The collaboration between the businessman Eberhard von Bodenhausen-Degener (1868–1918) and the *Jugendstil* artist Henry van de Velde on the launch of the health product 'Tropon' in 1897–8 is a prime example. Companies with experience of working with artists in other areas were amongst the first to consider the use of artist-architects on the design of their production buildings, as an alternative to the established practice of leaving such work in the hands of local construction firms or master builders. The Bremen-based Kaffee Handels-AG provides a good illustration of a company which chose this route.

Kaffee Hag was the brainchild of the Bremen coffee importer Ludwig Roselius (1874–1943), a wealthy but cultured man who was later to invest much of his fortune in the artists' colony at Worpswede and the creation of Bremen's bizarrely expressionistic Böttcherstraße. As an inventor of labour saving gadgets, including a patented process to de-caffeinate coffee beans, Roselius was fascinated by the mechanics of manufacturing, but at the same time he enjoyed close links with the city's progressive art circles, and was eager to make his own mark on Bremen's cultural life. So, when Roselius made the potentially-risky decision in 1906 to set up a company dedicated solely to the production of caffeine-free coffee, he envisaged an enterprise which would utilise both state-of-the-art production processes and the talents of leading artists, such as the publicity skills of the Berlin poster-design specialist Lucian Bernhard (b.1883). As a result the Kaffee Hag brand name quickly became established as a permanent fixture on German pantry shelves.

The man chosen to build the new company's factory was the respected Bremen architect Hugo Wagner, best remembered for a monumental watertower (built 1904–06) which dominated the city's skyline until 1958. The Kaffee Hag complex was built in the northern dockland area of Bremen in late 1906 and production began in 1907. It consisted of six separate buildings, each constructed in reinforced concrete, and linked by corridors at ground floor and basement level to ease the flow of production. The complex was designed so that the whole production process could be concentrated on one site, from the unloading of raw coffee beans at the quayside to the distribution of the finished, packaged article at the factory gate. The functionality of the layout attracted much praise and, according to the *Bremische Biographie*, 'soon became a model for many industrial enterprises'.[43] The same verdict came from Emil Beutinger in *Der Industriebau*:

> The complete factory complex may be considered as exemplary and technically perfect, and it meets the highest standards in sanitary terms too, since human activity is confined to the supervision of the automatic machines.[44]

The need for six separate buildings, each with a very different function (including a warehouse, offices, and a boiler house) made Wagner's task of giving the complex a convincing architectural form very difficult, but the uniform use of materials (white reinforced concrete and red tiled roofs) at least gave the disparate elements of the factory a common tone. In clear contrast to the timeless functionality of the factory façades, the pitched roofs employed by Wagner now appear rather comical, placing the building firmly in the age of *Heimatstil*, but Beutinger's 1910 article was quick to praise the appearance of the buildings too:

> The architectural solution provided by the reinforced concrete construction must be considered absolutely first-rate, both in detail and in the overall context of the whole complex. It brings together the individual buildings to make a grandiose group, so that the factory does not fail to make a monumental impact. Such achievements require a high degree of artistic ability.[45]

The initial collaboration between Roselius, Wagner and Bernhard predated the founding of the DWB by nearly a year, but each later went on to play an active role in the organisation. Time convinced Roselius that the marriage of art and industry could bring considerable financial rewards and he ensured that Kaffee Hag was always in evidence when the Werkbund was staging an exhibition.

If Wagner's buildings for Kaffee Hag were commended for their functional layout and matter-of-fact appearance, there was another, more extravagant side to the early collaborations between DWB architects and

---

43. *Bremische Biographie 1912–1962*, Bremen, 1962, p.421.

44. E. Beutinger, 'Die Fabrikanlage der Kaffee Handels AG Bremen', in *Der Industriebau*, vol.1 (1910), p.75.

45. E. Beutinger, *ibid.*, p.75.

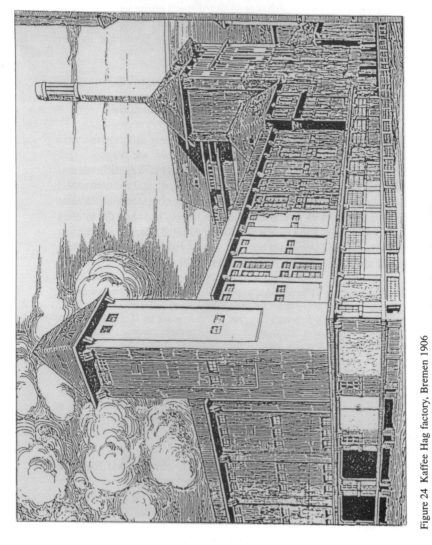

Figure 24 Kaffee Hag factory, Bremen 1906
Arch. H. Wagner. Drawing from *Der Industriebau*, vol. 1 (1910)

Figure 25 Henkell champagne company headquarters, Wiesbaden-Biebrich 1907–9
Arch. P. Bonatz. Present condition

German commercial companies. A good illustration is provided by the work of Paul Bonatz (1877–1956) for the Henkell champagne company, which used expensive materials and a traditional architectural vocabulary, but which was also widely acclaimed in Werkbund circles before World War One.

In the summer of 1907 the company director Otto Henkell announced details of a limited competition amongst seven top architects to produce plans for this established family firm's new headquarters. It was to include offices, production areas and cellar space, and was to be built on a prominent site alongside the main Wiesbaden to Biebrich road. Henkell's uncle, himself an architect, had recently become aware of the young Stuttgart architect Bonatz and suggested that he too should be invited to participate in the competition, to which Henkell readily agreed. When the architects submitted their entries it was Bonatz's proposal which caught Henkell's imagination. In fact, the Bonatz plan was approved by Henkell even before the expert jury assembled to judge the competition had met. Building work on Bonatz's first big project – he was later to gain fame for the design of Stuttgart's main railway station – began in 1908.[46]

The external focal point of the complex, which opened in 1909, was a large administrative block, with three internal courtyards and marble galleries, but the most important provision actually lay underground. From the main reception hall a one-hundred step staircase descended through five levels of reinforced concrete cellars, which provided a storage capacity of over two hectares. The technical side of the operation, including the boiler house, was skilfully placed out of view of the main road. This was a result of functional as well as aesthetic considerations, since Bonatz's solution enabled the bottling and packaging departments to be situated alongside the railway line, the *Lebensnerv* of the complex and its main link with the outside world.

A key feature of the whole plant was the use of technological innovations to ease the flow of production, including conveyor belts, lifts and communication tubes. The staff welfare and dining facilities, of which the company was particularly proud, were located to the rear of the main building, in a series of well-lit, one-storey halls. The use of expensive materials throughout – walls of German travertine stone and copper-clad roofs – were described by Bonatz as 'justified for a luxury industry'. The architect concluded that the building was 'advertising in the good sense',[47] and the company agreed, sending the architect a case of fifty bottles of 'Henkell Trocken' every Christmas until 1939.

---

46. P. Bonatz, *Leben und Bauen*, Stuttgart, 1950, pp.54–55.
47. 'Neuzeitliche Industriebauten', in *Mitteilungen des Rheinischen Vereins für Denkmalpflege und Heimatschutz*, vol.4 (1910), p.31.

The gradual but real increase in living standards in Wilhelmine Germany did not just boost the prospects of coffee and champagne producers. It was also a time of expansion for manufacturers of chocolate, cakes and biscuits. One of the most successful biscuit companies of the day, the Keksfabrik H. Bahlsen in Hanover, was an early member of the DWB, and participated in all aspects of Werkbund activity. Founded by Hermann Bahlsen (1859–1919) in 1889, this was in many ways the model DWB enterprise, combining enlightened industrial relations with a flair for technological innovation and a conviction that the world of art should 'spiritualise' commercial life. On the occasion of the 1914 DWB exhibition in Cologne, Bahlsen even produced special Werkbund packets of biscuits, with a wrapper designed by Peter Behrens. The company newspaper, the *Leibniz Blätter*, wrote:

> This link between our work and that of the Werkbund is not coincidental. In fact we can credit ourselves for having been one of the first and most enthusiastic ambassadors of the ideas which the Werkbund has set as its targets . . . The whole Werkbund and its exhibition is recognition for the correctness of our efforts.[48]

In fact, as the firm never tired in pointing out, Bahlsen had been co-operating with independent artists for nearly a decade before the formation of the DWB, and had achieved some remarkable results in the field of packaging and poster publicity; most notably with the attractive designs of Heinrich Mittag (1859–1920), himself later to become a DWB member. The company had shown itself to be sensitive to the wishes of the Heimatschutz movement too, for its advertising policy pre-empted the Disfigurement Law by restricting billboard advertising in environmentally sensitive locations.[49] This, together with business and technical advances, such as the launching of a company health insurance scheme in 1899, the successful development of the registered trade mark 'TET' in 1900, the implementation of patented air-tight packaging for 'Leibniz-Keks' in 1903, and the introduction of conveyor-belt production in 1905, helped the company to create a progressive, modern image and stay ahead of the competition.

Once it became apparent that the rapidly-expanding firm – it was exporting to thirty-one countries by 1908 – required more space for both production and administration, Hermann Bahlsen approached the DWB architect Karl Siebrecht (1875–1952) to draw up plans for a major new factory and office complex. Bahlsen's choice of architect was an obvious one. Siebrecht was not only a *Werkbündler*, but a Hanoverian and a

48. 'Wir und der Werkbund', in *Leibniz-Blätter*, 21 March 1914, p.3.
49. 'Außen-Reklame' in *Leibniz-Blätter*, 29 June 1912, p.1. (Bahlsen-Archiv).

personal acquaintance of Bahlsen too. Planning permission was applied for and granted in late 1909, and the buildings were erected in 1910–11. The factory, facing Lister Straße, and the office block, on Podbielskistraße, backed on to each other and skilfully utilised all available space in a difficult inner-city site. The character of the two buildings was different, befitting their contrasting functions, but both radiated the desire to introduce art into the industrial environment.

The factory building was a steel-framed construction clad in exquisite violet-red clinker bricks, and enlivened by depictions of fairy tale scenes, sculpted in colourful ceramics by another DWB artist Georg Herting (1872–1951). The factory's towering gable recalled the tradition of North German brick Gothic, but the building made no pretence of its modern purpose. The interiors were just as carefully designed, meeting the most sophisticated standards of ventilation – it was to be a 'breathing house' – and hygiene. The surfaces of walls and floors in the work areas were lined with easily-cleaned tiles, some decorated with imaginative motifs.

The office block was a more conventional building, performing its representative function with appropriate dignity, but it too revealed some unexpected touches. Herting's contribution here was a gilded bronze embodiment of one of the company's trade marks, the *Brezelmänner*, which protruded from the travertine façade above the heads of passing shoppers. Whilst the architectonic emphasis of the factory was very much on the vertical, the administrative building was characterised by long parallel lines of windows, indicating the extended open-plan offices which ran the length of the building. At its eastern end the façade was interrupted by the tall bow windows of the company's banqueting hall, which hosted concerts and readings by visiting artists. Situated underneath the banqueting hall was a 'model' company shop, where sales and design specialists could experiment with the latest theories of advertising and window-dressing, and where customers could look through a large window directly into the main production area, as if to 'control' the quality of workmanship.

The new buildings provided room for a number of welfare services including a roof garden, medical surgery, music room and library, as well as dining and shower facilities for all workers. Above all, however, there was space for art, including paintings by Paula Modersohn, Hodler and Heckel, sculptures by Barlach and Hoetger, and monumental frescoes, wall-hangings and stained-glass windows by the leading craftsmen of the day. For the 1,700 Bahlsen employees art was an inescapable facet of working-life, as were the parties of visitors who trooped around the new buildings to see the Werkbund idea in action. A year after the completion of the new buildings the *Leibniz Blätter* wrote: 'the buildings have become one of the sights of the city . . . There is such interest in our buildings that

Figure 26 H. Bahlsen biscuit factory, administrative building, Hanover 1911
Arch. K. Siebrecht. Present condition

the tourist coaches stop at our factory gate.'[50] One senses, however, that not all were happy about this union of art and commerce. In 1912 the *Leibniz Blätter* wrote:

> One occasionally hears the view expressed that the way in which our business fosters the arts and crafts (e.g. through our new buildings etc.) is unnecessary and that we should instead reduce our prices. This view is completely misguided and only reveals a total misunderstanding of the principles on which our business is based.[51]

The reasoning behind the new buildings was explained in another edition of this weekly paper:

> The idea which led us in the construction of our new buildings was the desire to create something of lasting worth. The decision was not easy, since something like that requires extraordinary financial sacrifices. We were not put off by this because we were convinced . . . that the new buildings could have a great influence on the development of the business. Amongst other things they should be a recommendation for our products, because impeccably designed buildings generally suggest the encouragement of high-quality wares.[52]

The public interest shown in Bahlsen's efforts was manifested in a plethora of magazine articles, each eagerly quoted by the *Leibniz Blätter* as a vindication of company policy. The Leipzig-based *Illustrierte Zeitung* of 11 July 1912, for instance, carried a big article on Bahlsen's new buildings ('excellent propaganda for us' was the verdict of the *Leibniz Blätter*) and in April 1912 all Bahlsen salesmen received a copy of a magazine article on *Moderne Fabrikbauten*.[53] The company kept up the 'art offensive' with pavilions at the DWB exhibitions at Cologne (1914) and Basel (1917), and frequent *Leibniz Blätter* essays by DWB activists like Robert Breuer and Christian Spengemann on the aims of the organisation. At the same time the company's annual turnover rose steadily, reaching eight million Marks by 1914.

Hermann Bahlsen's most ambitious plan for his company was, however, never realised. In the darkest days of the Great War Bahlsen had purchased land on the outskirts of Hanover, on which he proposed to build a new town, which would include Bahlsen factories, offices, and warehouses adjoining the Mittelland Canal, together with housing, a theatre, cinema,

50. 'Beweggründe, Taten und Wirkungen' in *Leibniz-Blätter*, 7 Sept. 1912, p.1. (Bahlsen-Archiv).

51. 'Kunst und Kunstgewerbe in unserem Fabrik-Betriebe' in *Leibniz-Blätter*, 12 Oct. 1912, p.3. (Bahlsen-Archiv).

52. 'Beweggründe, Taten und Wirkungen' in *Leibniz-Blätter*, 7 Sept. 1912, p.1. (Bahlsen-Archiv).

53. *Leibniz-Blätter*, 18 May 1912, p.3. (Bahlsen-Archiv).

church and schools. The "TET-Stadt' was to be a true *Gesamtkunstwerk*, designed by the north German sculptor Bernhard Hoetger (1874–1949), a DWB member who was later to work closely with Kaffee Hag's Roselius on buildings in Worpswede. The dominant material was to be maroon clinker, the architecture monumental and expressionistic. A giant model of the plans was displayed in Hanover's Kunstverein in February 1917, but the financial and material restrictions of wartime put a stop to what Bahlsen himself called a 'beautiful dream'.[54] It is perhaps just as well that the life of Hermann Bahlsen, who died in 1919, is commemorated in Siebrecht's buildings – which, despite considerable wartime damage to the top floors of the factory, are still recognisable today, rather than in the megalomaniacal plans for the TET-Stadt, which had painfully little to do with the realities of 1917.

It was not only companies in the food and drink sector which showed an interest in working with DWB architects. In 1907 the large Berlin engineering company Ludw. Loewe & Co. AG commissioned one of Berlin's leading progressive architects and Werkbund members Alfred Grenander (1863–1931) to design a new administration and warehouse block. Some six years later Grenander also built an imposing new factory complex for the firm. Loewe had actually been involved in the introduction of new ideas into industrial architecture as far back as 1897–8, when the company first moved its headquarters from the cramped inner-city Hollmannstraße site to Huttenstraße in the suburb of Moabit.

The company's strongpoint was the manufacture of precision machine tools; a field in which the market was dominated by the products of the more accurate and efficient American industry. Aware of the Americans' lead, a party of engineers from Loewe left for the United States in 1896 to study their rivals' production methods. The design of the new Huttenstraße factory in 1897–8 was a direct result of their findings. The architect Arnold Vogt and the engineer Franz Holzapfel erected not only the most modern factory yet seen in Berlin, but also one of the first bastions of the 'American System' of manufacturing in Europe.[55]

The buildings boasted flat roofs and façades free of historicist ornamentation, with three-quarters of the wall area filled by windows. Significantly, the complex abandoned the Berlin tradition of courtyard building in favour of three-storey pavilions, surrounded by flower-beds and park benches. Although they were not visible to the passing public – a factor which no doubt played a role in their unusually sober appearance

54. B. Grubert, 'Hermann Bahlsen und das Projekt der TET-Stadt', typewritten manuscript in Bahlsen-Archiv.

55. H. Kreidt 'Industriebauten', in K. Weber (ed.), *Berlin und seine Bauten*, vol.9, Berlin, 1971, p.46–7.

Figure 27 L. Loewe & Co. AG, office and warehouse, Berlin-Moabit 1913
Arch. A. Grenander. Present condition

Figure 28 L. Loewe & Co. AG, machine tool factory, Berlin-Moabit 1913
Arch. A. Grenander. Present condition

– the Loewe buildings had a great impact at home and abroad. The journal *American Machinist*, for instance, published a four-part feature on the factory, which claimed: 'the best American tool shop is now in Germany, and the American or English visitor feels very much like the Queen of Sheba after going around the works of King Solomon.'[56]

The construction of the new factory proved a turning-point in the fortunes of the company. After a period of consolidation, Loewe enjoyed many years of success and expansion under Walter Waldschmidt, General Director from 1902 to 1928. It was probably Waldschmidt who commissioned Alfred Grenander, a Swedish born architect who made his name in the building of underground railway stations, to design a new office and warehouse complex in the Huttenstraße. The result, completed in 1907, was an attractive if idiosyncratic building, which certainly maintained the company's reputation for architectural innovation.

The company's factory for the manufacture of milling and drilling machines, built on the corner of Wiebestraße and Huttenstraße between 1913 and 1917, was also designed by Grenander. The differences between the two buildings highlight some of the changes in architectural fashion in the first six years of the DWB. The earlier building retains to this day a rather self-conscious Arts and Crafts feel, whilst the Wiebestraße factory stands under the clear influence of Peter Behrens's Small Motors Factory for the AEG.

In fact, the Ludw. Loewe & Co. A.G. enjoyed close links with the AEG, its near neighbour in north Berlin. The two firms had co-operated in the Union electrical company, which was taken over by the AEG in 1904, and since then AEG's Walther Rathenau had sat on the Loewe Supervisory Board. In 1907 AEG went one stage further than Loewe by employing a leading architect and designer, Peter Behrens, as a full-time artistic advisor. The first result of this partnership in the field of architecture was erected just a hundred metres from the Loewe headquarters, on the former Union site in Berlin-Moabit. However, whilst Grenander's buildings soon fell into obscurity, the AEG Turbine Factory of 1909 came to be viewed as one of the seminal buildings of twentieth century architecture, and has been 'listed' as an historic monument since 1956.

In sharp contrast to many of the partnerships between DWB architects and industrial companies in Wilhelmine Germany, the AEG-Behrens relationship has often been investigated.[57] Although we are unlikely to ever

56. Quoted in *Ludw. Loewe & Co. AG Berlin 1869–1929*, Berlin, 1930, p.42.

57. S. Anderson, 'Peter Behrens and the New Architecture of Germany', PhD thesis, Columbia University, 1968; H-J. Kadatz, *Peter Behrens. Architekt, Maler, Grafiker*, Leipzig, 1977; A. Windsor, *Peter Behrens: Architect and Designer*, London, 1981; T. Buddensieg with H. Rogge, *Industriekultur. Peter Behrens and the AEG, 1907–1914*, Cambridge Mass., 1984.

learn the precise sequence of events which led to the initial engagement of Behrens,[58] the buildings and products he worked on for the company between 1907 and 1914 have assumed iconical status in the history of industrial design. This fame rests partly on the crucial role Behrens played in the formative years of the modern movement's three great masters – Gropius, Mies van der Rohe and Le Corbusier – who each served spells in Behrens's Neubabelsberg studio before World War One.[59] However, the historic significance of this fact should not obscure the tremendous impact Behrens's own work had on contemporary public and professional opinion. The start of Behrens's contract with the AEG coincided to the month with the foundation of the DWB, and the success of that organisation would have been unthinkable without the shining example being set at the same time in Berlin.

As one of Germany's largest industrial concerns the AEG manufactured a wide range of products, from arc lamps and light bulbs to generators and cables, but little in its output could match the giant steam turbines it constructed for power stations and the ships of the German navy. Such was the size of these extraordinary objects that the AEG's existing factory halls were simply unable to cope, and the company decided a new factory, specifically for the construction of turbines, should be opened as soon as possible. This was to be Behrens's first major architectural task for the company. In his initial year in Berlin he had done much to improve the aesthetic quality of various small household products, revolutionised the company's advertising and designed an AEG pavilion for the German Shipbuilding Exhibition (Berlin 1908), as well as making small alterations to existing factory blocks, but the new turbine factory was on a different scale altogether. It is easily forgotten that Behrens had received no formal architectural training – like many of the progressive architects of this era Behrens had stumbled into architecture from the world of arts and crafts – and he was fortunate to be aided on the turbine factory project by the

58. Most accounts accept the view expressed by Behrens's 1928 biographer Paul Cremers that the man directly responsible for Behrens's employment was Paul Jordan (1854–1937), himself an engineer, manager of the Humboldthain complex and later an elected member of the DWB's management committee. It is likely, however, that Behrens's work for the company was also encouraged by Walther Rathenau (1867–1922), the son of AEG's founder and Managing Director Emil Rathenau. Behrens had lunch with Walther Rathenau on a number of occasions, for instance in March 1911 and January 1912. See *Walther Rathenau. Notes and Diaries 1907–1922*, H. Pogge von Strandmann (ed.), Oxford, 1985, p.116 and p.145. Alan Windsor points out that Behrens mentions 'Freund Rathenau' in a letter to Maximilian Harden as early as December 1905 and by 1909 Rathenau was writing to Behrens as 'Lieber Freund'. See A. Windsor, *Peter Behrens*, p.77.

59. Gropius worked for Behrens between late 1907 and Spring 1910. Mies van der Rohe entered Behrens's studio in October 1908 and remained until Spring 1912. Le Corbusier, then under his real name Jeanneret, spent five months at Neubabelsberg in the summer of 1910.

experienced engineer Karl Bernhard.

Late in 1908 Behrens and Bernhard began planning the Turbine Factory, which was to be the largest steel and glass factory hall yet seen in Berlin. The building, consisting of a main assembly hall and a smaller two-storey side hall, was erected in 1909 and started production in 1910. Building work lasted only five months, during which time over 2000 tons of steel were used. The dimensions of the building were dictated by the requirements of the two giant fifty-ton crane gantries which ran the full length of the main hall (initially 123 metres, it was later increased to 207 metres). The enclosed volume of the building was around 150,000 cubic metres, uninterrupted by internal supports, providing a workplace for some 4,400 people.[60] Of course, such impressive feats of engineering had been seen at German factory sites before – one thinks of the massive workshops for Krupp in Essen – but Behrens used the language of art to make this building a cultural statement too.

It had long been a problem for architects to give structures of steel and glass a solid architectonic form. Behrens's solution was to incline the window panels inwards, so that the roof overhangs the side 'wall' by nearly two metres. This created a form of steel cornice, which gave the roof an imposing heaviness. At the same time he replaced the usual criss-cross lattice-work of steel structures with twenty-two elegant and tapered girder frames, which inevitably echoed the columns of classical architecture. Much of the roof was taken up by a skylight that ran the entire length of the building, and this combined with the glass walls to give a particularly light and airy working environment.

The most talked about aspect of the building was not, however, the long glass and steel elevation on Berlichingenstraße, but the concrete 'temple front' which faced onto the Huttenstraße, a busy main road leading to the city centre. Although neither the pediment – bearing the simple inscription 'AEG Turbinenfabrik' – nor the concrete corner pillars were necessary from a structural point of view, it was undoubtedly these classicising touches which helped to create the impression of monumental power which so inspired Behrens's contemporaries, and presumably delighted his industrial paymasters too. Indeed it is ironic that Behrens has attracted the reputation as a pioneer of Functionalism, since much of his industrial architecture was specifically intended to take factory buildings beyond the purely functional. For Behrens, the structural achievements of engineers alone could never be considered as an expression of *Kultur*.

One of the first responses to the building came in a *Frankfurter Zeitung* article written by Behrens's old friend Karl Ernst Osthaus:

---

60. The Turbine Factory employed 4,400 workers at the end of the business year 1913–14. A. Fürst, *Emil Rathenau. Der Mann und sein Werk*, Berlin, 1915, p.88.

Figure 29 AEG turbine factory, Berlin-Moabit 1909
Arch. P. Behrens. Present condition

The building's expression is one of power and magnificence. The strong and sober modernity is not spoilt by any trifling with ornament. We sense the strong rhythm of an energy harnessed by intelligence. On the inside we may get a premonition of the superiority of future creations. The exterior is perfect, definitive like a Doric temple.[61]

Osthaus was so impressed by the building's power that in 1916 he made the bizarre suggestion of hanging photographs of it in military hospitals, to inspire the recovery process in wounded soldiers.[62] The impact of the Turbine Factory on Berlin's educated middle classes is also hinted at in an obituary for Behrens, written by Edmund Schüler (1873–1952), the Foreign Office *Legationsrat* who was instrumental in securing the AEG's architect to build the German Embassy in St.Petersburg (1911–12):

We used to make pilgrimages to the giant AEG buildings in the Brunnenstraße and to the Turbine Factory. When somebody remarked on the close affinity between the new industrial buildings and the classical architecture of ancient Greece, the door seemed for us to open to a new Heaven, the long sought after Heaven of our own.[63]

Another obituary for Behrens, who died in 1940, had a rather different tone. The Swiss architect Peter Meyer, writing in *Werk* magazine under the title 'Architecture as an Expression of Violence', claimed:

In its time, the AEG Turbine Factory was felt to be epoch-making. One saw in it the epitome of a modern functional architecture of the Machine Age. With our fingers burned, today we have sharper ears for slogans; we feel the false pathos of the ponderous Egyptian-like stylisation, even in the apparent 'simplicity' of this machine shop.[64]

Back in 1912 however, another Swiss, the young C.E. Jeanneret – later to gain great fame under the name Le Corbusier – was more impressed, terming the building 'a veritable Cathedral of Work'.[65] For the architectural critic Franz Mannheimer, writing in the 1913 DWB Yearbook, the Turbine Factory was nothing less than 'the manifesto of the new industrial architecture',[66] and another leading critic of the time, Karl Scheffler, noted:

61. K.E. Osthaus, 'Ein Fabrikbau von Peter Behrens', in *Frankfurter Zeitung*, 10 Feb. 1910.

62. F. Neumeyer, 'Das Pathos des Monumentalen', in B. Bergius, J. Frecot, D. Radicke (eds), *Architektur, Stadt und Politik*, Lahn-Gießen, 1979, p.248.

63. E. Schüler quoted by F. Neumeyer, ibid., p.249.

64. P. Meyer quoted by S. Anderson, 'Peter Behrens', p.44.

65. C.E. Jeanneret (1912) quoted in A. Windsor, *Peter Behrens*, p.102.

66. F. Mannheimer, 'AEG-Bauten', in Werkbund Yearbook, 1913, p.37.

When visiting artists or enthusiasts wander through the new Berlin of today they write home unimpressed by the buildings of the Kaiser Friedrich Museum or the new cathedral, but they speak with great respect about Messel's Wertheim department store or Behrens's factory architecture for the AEG. It will not be long before Baedecker will be marking with stars a form of architecture that until recently was considered insignificant.[67]

A comment made in a letter from the architect Eric Mendelsohn to his future wife Luise in March 1914 was in the same vein. 'Should you be in Berlin before we travel to Florence', he wrote, 'then don't forget to take a look at the AEG Turbine Factory by Peter Behrens. It's something you simply have to see.'[68]

The next stop on any tourist itinerary, then as now, would have to be the AEG complex on the Humboldthain in Berlin-Wedding (a few miles east of the Turbine Factory) for it was here that the bulk of Behrens's architectural work for the company was located. The site, adjoining Brunnenstraße, had been in AEG's hands since the 1890s and was already well-developed before Behrens's arrival at the company. Between 1909 and 1913 he added three more major buildings: the 'Hochspannungsfabrik' (for the manufacture of high-tension components such as resistors and transformers); the 'Kleinmotorenfabrik' (for the manufacture of small motors); and the 'Montagehalle' (an assembly hall for large machinery). All three were essentially steel-framed buildings, clad in a variety of subtly-coloured bricks and clinkers, and each boasted large window areas. The Assembly Hall, in particular, was notable for its glass roof, which turned the shop-floor into a 'sea of light'.

The classicising tendencies which had been so apparent in the turbine factory were also present in the Humboldthain factories. As Behrens searched for an architectural form which was both modern and timeless – which would 'ennoble' industry yet at the same time function efficiently – he developed an architecture of symmetry, simple geometric forms and clear proportions, which owed much to Classicism, but at the same time remained largely free of direct historical quotation. Behrens, like most of the *Gymnasium* – educated *Bildungsbürgertum*, viewed Classical architecture as the ultimate expression of the values of culture, humanism, beauty and permanence, the values he wished to see enter the world of industry. At the same time, he consciously evoked the Prussian Neo-Classical tradition of Gilly and Schinkel, whose austere and dignified buildings in Berlin and beyond were believed to have embodied an age of enlightened reform and civic responsibility.

67. K. Scheffler quoted in H-J. Kadatz, *Peter Behrens*, p.213.
68. E. Mendelsohn quoted in M. Hamm, *Berlin. Denkmäler einer Industrielandschaft*, Berlin, 1978, p.17.

Another key element in Behrens's architecture was repetition. Both the Berlichingenstraße side of the turbine factory and the stunning 196 metre-long Voltastraße façade of the Small Motors Factory, depended on the rhythmic reiteration of a simple pattern for their impact. This was intended in part to reflect the nature of the industrial processes the buildings housed, but it also illustrates one of Behrens's principal concerns of the time. In an essay in the DWB Yearbook for 1914, Behrens examined the changes brought about in man's perception of architecture in an era of ever-faster transport:

> As we shoot at great speed through the streets of our big cities we can no longer make out the details of buildings. Similarly, as we gaze from the windows of an express train, the townscapes that flash past can only be appreciated in silhouette. Individual buildings no longer speak for themselves. The only architecture which can come to terms with this way of seeing . . . is one of compact, unfussy surfaces . . . the regular repetition of important details is necessary.[69]

It was the Voltastraße façade of the Small Motors Factory which most impressed Franz Mannheimer in his 1913 DWB Yearbook essay on Behrens's AEG work. He believed the building came close to finding a true expression for the 'meaning of industrial labour, the pride of the workshops, the forward march of the buzzing machines':

> . . . in this row of pillars, which rise to the height of the roof in steel-blue clinker-brick, there once again lives something of the will of humble, burdened beings lifting themselves up, the same will which created Paestum, Stonehenge or the vaulting of Gothic cathedrals.[70]

Significantly, the Small Motors Factory – like all Behrens's major AEG projects – was built right up to the street line, and no attempt was made to hide production areas from public view. Indeed, as Buddensieg points out, it was these workshops rather than palatial administrative buildings or company residences which became the 'dominant spatial and visual element' of the firm's Berlin complex.[71] In this way the AEG broke with the established industrial practice of using the seat of management as the main focus of a company's representative needs.

Each of the Humboldthain buildings has been described in detail

---

69. P. Behrens, 'Einfluß von Zeit- und Raumausnutzung auf moderne Formentwicklung', in Werkbund Yearbook, 1914, p.8.

70. F. Mannheimer, 'AEG-Bauten', in Werkbund Yearbook, 1913, p.40.

71. T. Buddensieg, *Industriekultur*, p.36.

Figure 30 AEG small motors factory, Berlin-Wedding 1910–13
Arch. P. Behrens. Present condition

elsewhere[72] but the monumental impression made by the AEG site on all who visited it depended to a large degree on the scale and arrangement of the complex as a whole. Artur Fürst, in a 1915 biography of the AEG's founding father Emil Rathenau, gave some idea of the magnitude of the operation: over 14,000 blue- and white collar workers were employed at the site (out of a total AEG workforce of around 70,000), it was illuminated by over 10,000 lightbulbs and was powered by over 7,200 individual electric motors. On average, a machine was produced here every two minutes of the day and night, and the value of a year's output from the Humboldthain site topped 100 million Marks in 1913/14.[73] Moreover, Behrens's Assembly Hall housed the largest operational machine tool in Europe – a giant lathe for dynamo casings. Fürst described the unity of 'tenderness and strength' which he believed typified AEG's combination of 'military' organisation and 'artistic' sensitivity. He continued:

> Since AEG's products have been successful in carrying the name of the industrial nation of Germany around the whole world, one can safely assume that at the places of production you will find superb and exemplary establishments. For an eagle is never born in a sparrow's nest . . . a skilled eye can tell by the appearance of factories, whether quality goods are . . . produced there.[74]

Behrens's work for the AEG did not stop there. Between 1910 and 1915 he designed a series of industrial buildings for the company on a new 'green field' site alongside the Hohenzollern Canal at Hennigsdorf, about ten miles north-west of Berlin. These included a large factory for the manufacture of porcelain insulators, and smaller factories for the production of varnish and oil cloths, all needed for the electrical industry. Such was the wide range of the AEG industrial interests that Behrens also built factories at Hennigsdorf for the construction of railway locomotives and aircraft, together with some workers' housing, in what was still a predominantly rural area. The Hennigsdorf site, far from the public gaze, did not receive the same careful architectural treatment as the Turbine Factory or Humboldthain complex, but the factories were solid enough and remained in use after 1945.

Although Behrens's contract with AEG came to an end in 1914, he continued to do occasional work for the company. In 1915–16, for instance, he designed an automobile factory in the south-east Berlin district of Oberschöneweide for an AEG sister company, the Nationale

---

72. T. Buddensieg, *Industriekultur*; A. Windsor, *Peter Behrens*; S.Anderson, *Peter Behrens* etc.

73. A. Fürst, *Emil Rathenau*, p.95.

74. A. Fürst, *ibid.*, p.82.

Automobilgesellschaft (NAG). The dominant feature of this complex, which became a television factory after World War Two, was a seventy-metre tower rising above the works entrance.

The AEG's great rivals in the German electro-technical industry, Siemens, had no similar tradition of working with outside architects, but in 1915 it too appointed a Werkbund architect, Hans Hertlein (1881–1963), to be director of its internal building department. Hertlein had joined Siemens from government service in Bavaria three years earlier and advanced rapidly through the company hierarchy, where his talents were championed by the 'coming man' of the company, Carl Friedrich von Siemens. Their partnership – Carl Friedrich was for Hertlein the perfect patron and a man with a 'personal desire to build'[75] – was to flourish in the 1920s when the Siemensstadt in Berlin replaced the AEG complex as the focus of German architectural journals, but Hertlein's main pre-1918 project for the company was the massive 'Wernerwerk M', with its monumental eighty-metre tower, built in 1916–17. The tower served a functional purpose, incorporating a chimney and water tanks, but was primarily conceived by Hertlein for aesthetic and representative reasons.

In the meantime Peter Behrens's architectural output showed no signs of flagging. The details of his contract with the AEG have been lost, but it is known to have included a clause which allowed him to work on commissions from outside the AEG group of companies. In view of his heavy workload in Berlin it is perhaps hard to believe Behrens had much time to devote to extra-curricular activities, but between 1910 and 1914 he in fact worked on a whole range of significant commissions, including the German Embassy in St. Petersburg and a number of buildings for other industrial enterprises. It must be remembered, however, that Behrens had the help of a large and talented staff at his Neubabelsberg studio. The extent to which the master himself was involved in some of the schemes must therefore be open to conjecture. Certainly the famous architects who spent brief spells under Behrens before 1914 were each quick to claim the credit for significant technical or stylistic innovations.

The large office buildings Behrens designed for Mannesmann in Düsseldorf (1911–12) and the Continental Rubber Company in Hanover (begun 1912) – both DWB member companies – shared with the AEG factories a desire to raise the world of commerce and industry to a level of culture commensurate with its economic importance. Both in their internal layout, and external appearance, the Mannesmann and Continental buildings marked an important advance from the ostentatious and impractical palaces of profit, which had typified turn-of-the-century

---

75. W. Ribbe and W. Schäche, *Die Siemensstadt. Geschichte und Architektur eines Industriestandortes*, Berlin, 1985, p.179.

corporate architecture. Behrens's talent to combine a worthy, representative exterior with a fully functional interior, was clearly a major factor in his popularity with commercial clients at this time. No other architect could quite capture the same mix of conservatism and progression, dignity and practicality, which so appealed to a section of German industry in the later Wilhelmine years.

Behrens's first office building, a five-storey rectangular block for the Mannesmann tubing company on the banks of the Rhine in Düsseldorf, was a steel-framed structure clad in smooth ashlar on a rusticated limestone base. Despite the obvious influence of the Italian Renaissance, and particularly of Florentine palazzo architecture, the building was refreshingly free of historicist ornamentation. The only decoration was a stone relief by the sculptor Eberhard Encke, above the building's main entrance. The Mannesmann headquarters was described by Behrens as one of the brightest and best-lit office buildings in existence. The unusual fenestration – large numbers of narrow windows were arranged in broad bands around the building – was specifically designed to produce a better distribution of light, whilst not reducing the building's impression of great compactness and solidity. Another innovation lay in the internal structural arrangements, which Behrens claimed had been devised from 'the desk up'. Open floors without structural cross walls allowed for a good deal of flexibility in the division of the office space. In a 1967 dissertation the art historian Fritz Wenger contrasted the Mannesmann office building with that of the nearby 'Stahlhof' and found Behrens's layout to be both more practical and less rigidly hierarchical than that of the historicist headquarters of the Steel Works Association.[76]

For some Düsseldorf cynics the building's façade resembled nothing more than a 'pitted skin',[77] but the General Director of Mannesmann, Nicolaus Eich, saw in his new headquarters, a 'place for the successful cultivation of industrial, commercial, cultural and social progress'.[78] A poem dedicated to 'Our House', gives some indication of how the company saw its new home. The third verse proclaims: 'Away with the little towers, bays and balconies – this building shows to the nations of the world, the high aims of German work. In its cubic compactness it announces for all time the power of industry'.[79]

The Continental building in Hanover was an even more massive affair,

76. F. Wenger, 'Wandlungen architektonischer Vorstellungen', PhD thesis, Hanover TH, 1967.
77. Referred to by N. Eich in his 10 Dec. 1912 speech, printed in 'Zur Erinnerung an die Einweihung des Verwaltunggebäudes', p.55.
78. N. Eich, ibid., p.58.
79. 'Unser Haus' in *MW-Rundschau*, May 1920, p.41 ('Aus der Festschrift zur Einweihung des Mannesmannhauses').

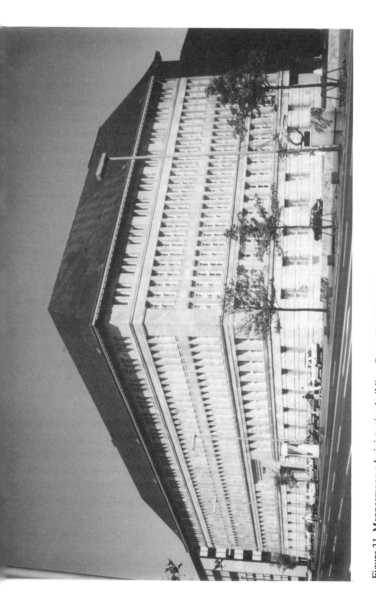

Figure 31 Mannesmann administrative building, Düsseldorf 1911–12
Arch. P. Behrens. Present condition

with a hundred metre façade on the busy Vahrenwalder Straße, and a series of spacious internal courtyards. The company, which specialised in tyres for the motor industry, had seen its workforce grow from 2,200 in 1903 to 12,000 in 1913,[80] and Behrens's headquarters building reflected this new-found importance. An album produced to mark the company's fiftieth anniversary in 1921 stated: 'Whoever visits Continental in Hanover takes with them the best possible impression of this powerful, functional building.'[81]

Both Behrens's major administrative buildings of the pre-1914 era continue to serve their original purpose today, but a third planned office development for a DWB member, the Daimler automobile company's Vienna branch (1914), never went beyond the drawing board. A further office block, for Frank and Lehmann in Cologne, was built in 1914. One other pre-war project contributed to Behrens's formidable reputation in the field of industrial architecture: a large gasworks scheme in Frankfurt's East Docks, consisting of a watertower, tar and ammonia holders, a machine hall, workshops, offices and accommodation for employees, provided the architect with another chance to 'ennoble' the realities of industrial life.

Another architect who attempted to use the classical verities to 'spiritualise' the manufacturing process was the DWB founder-member and leading theorist Hermann Muthesius. Although best known for his country houses, a building type he had grown to admire during his time as a Prussian 'technical attaché' to Britain at the turn of the century, Muthesius also tried his hand at industrial projects. His only factory building before World War One was the Michels silk mill in Nowawes, near Potsdam, built in 1913, where he too was aided by the engineer Karl Bernhard. The Seidenweberei Michels was a DWB member company and its Managing Director Fritz Gugenheim played an active part in the Werkbund's organisational affairs.

Unlike his domestic architecture, which combined a strong Arts and Crafts influence with elements of *Heimatstil*, Muthesius's Michels factory was a fairly conventional Neo-Classical structure. The highly-symmetrical building, which housed production, administration and recreation functions under one roof, was surrounded by well-tended gardens and an ornamental lake, designed by the DWB's leading landscape gardener Leberecht Migge (1881–1935). A quarter of the project's total costs went on the marble encrusted entrance hall,[82] housed in a basilica-like central

---

80. *Gedenkbuch zum 50. jährigen Bestehen der Continental, 1871–1921*, Hanover, 1921.

81. *Continental. Ein Jahrhundert Fortschritt und Leistung*, Hanover, 1971, p.42.

82. S. Müller, *Ideologie und Organisation*, p.39.

Figure 32 Continental rubber company administrative building, Hanover 1912–20
Arch. P. Behrens. Present condition

projection, which dominated the rest of a low façade of pilasters and sparred-windows. A large window at the back of the entrance hall gave a panoramic and 'unforgettable' view of the shop-floor, the carefully arranged weaving machinery and the uniformed workers.

The Michels building used the vocabulary of Classical architecture more blatantly than Behrens's most successful buildings of the period, and was a less convincing portrayal of industry as a result. Indeed, were it not for the large lettering which proudly proclaimed 'Mechanische Seidenweberei Michels', the building's function would have been hard to determine. As if aware of the apparent contradictions between his theoretical writings – which stressed the need for industrial buildings to express in clear terms their function and flow of production – and his personal building practice, Muthesius pointed out that the exclusiveness of silk demanded a more dignified treatment.[83] Above all, however, he stressed the important contribution a representative building such as the Michels factory could make to a company's self-projection, especially when placed near a major transport artery; in this case the main Berlin-Potsdam railway, which skirted the site.

The Michels factory was one of the most written about of its day.[84] The journalist Fritz Hellwag – editor of the influential *Kunstgewerbeblatt* – described the building as the first of a new type, the *Qualitätsfabrik*. The Michels worker, Hellwag believed, 'will be spared the fatal feeling, that he is condemned to spend the rest of his life in a shocking labour camp'.[85] The Michels management also appear to have been pleased with the building, because Muthesius was approached to build another factory for the company, at Kerken in the Lower Rhineland in 1921–22. Carl Kubart's lace, ribbon and braid factory for Ed. Molineus and Sons in Klausen, south of Barmen, is a further DWB factory in this tradition.

It was characteristic of the DWB that its leading architectural theorists were prepared to become involved in the practical aspects of industrial architecture too. Emil Beutinger, the editor of *Der Industriebau*, built a succession of simple but well proportioned buildings in the Heilbronn area, in partnership with Adolf Steiner. These included the J.Bauer celluloid factory (1909), Nettel camera factory (1909–10), Fr. Barth car body workshop (pre-1913), and various buildings for the Portland cement plant at Lauffen a.N. (1909–1913). A good example of Beutinger's unpretentious industrial architecture, a long way from the monumental

83. H. Muthesius, 'Die Baukunst im Dienste der kaufmännischen Werbetätigkeit', in *Das Plakat*, vol.11 (1920), p.259.

84. For example, in *Baumeister*, vol.12 (1914); *Dekorative Kunst*, vol.19 (1916); *Kunstgewerbeblatt*, vol.25 (1914); *Neudeutsche Bauzeitung*, vol.18 (1922).

85. F. Hellwag, 'Der Fabrik-Neubau der mechanischen Seidenweberei Michels & Cie. in Nowawes bei Potsdam', in *Kunstgewerbeblatt*, vol.25 (194), p.123.

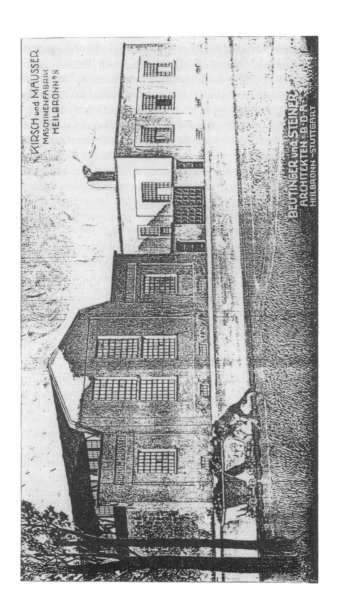

Figure 33 Kirsch & Mausser coffee machine factory, Heilbronn 1909
Arch. E. Beutinger. Drawing by E. Beutinger, from *Der Industriebau*, vol.1 (1910)

pathos of Behrens or Muthesius, but very much in the Werkbund spirit, was the works he built in Heilbronn for Kirsch & Mausser – manufacturers of coffee roasters – in 1909.

The Breslau architect Hans Poelzig, whose paper on industrial architecture at the DWB's 1909 Annual Conference in Frankfurt had been so important, gained respect for his own industrial projects too, such as the uncompromisingly modern 'Werdermühle' on an island in the River Oder near Breslau (1906), which remained unbuilt due to the opposition of the local mayor. His most important pre-war industrial commissions were a large water tower in Posen (1911–12), and a chemical plant at Luban near Posen for the Chemische AG vorm. Moritz Milch & Co. (1911–12). Poelzig's idiosyncratic factory buildings were outside the mainstream of DWB industrial architecture. They impressed through their logic and sobriety rather than any self-conscious desire to be 'monumental' or 'artistic'. As T. Effenberger wrote in an article on the Luban factory site in *Der Industriebau*:

> The harmony which rules the whole complex seems so natural. The thought that 'someone has tried to create art here' simply does not arise. This is a very rare characteristic in modern factory buildings.[86]

The chemical factory complex required a series of large, functional buildings – production centres for super-phosphates and sulphuric acid, a boiler house, warehouses and offices – which presented little room for conventional 'artistic' expression. Although the client Piorkowski had left the architect a free hand on aesthetic matters, Poelzig's solution was to leave the orthogonal brick buildings as plain as possible. The façades were enlivened only by the inventive fenestration and some simple brickwork patterns. In view of the exceptional quality of this early industrial work, it is perhaps surprising that Poelzig's profile in the DWB was not higher – he was not one of the twelve 'apostles' of the Werkbund given his own room at the 1914 Cologne exhibition – but, as his biographer Theodor Heuss later remarked, 'Breslau was not the place to be a front runner of national cultural importance.'[87]

While Poelzig was content to beaver away in the relative obscurity of Breslau, his much younger DWB colleague Walter Gropius was back in Berlin, looking for a client prepared to invest time and money in an imaginative but inexperienced architect. Despite his excellent connections, Gropius had found work hard to find since leaving Behrens's studio in the

86. T. Effenberger, 'Chemische Fabrik AG vorm. Moritz Milch & Co.', in *Der Industriebau*, vol.7 (1916), p.97.

87. T. Heuss, *Hans Poelzig. Bauten und Entwürfe. Das Lebensbild eines deutschen Baumeisters*, Tübingen, 1948, p.26.

spring of 1910. In a desperate attempt to secure a worthwhile commission he began writing 'hundreds' of speculative letters to manufacturers, outlining his credentials and eagerness to work in the industrial sector. One of these 'begging letters', dated 10 December 1910, landed on the door mat of the Hanoverian businessman Carl Benscheidt.

Some time before, Benscheidt had purchased a 'green field' site on the outskirts of Alfeld an der Leine, a small town in the Weser hills, and commissioned an experienced local architect Eduard Werner, to design a factory for the production of shoe-lasts. Gropius had heard about the new factory plan from his brother-in-law Max Burchard, who was *Landrat* in Alfeld. Indeed, Gropius used Burchard's name as a character reference in his initial letter to Benscheidt.[88]

When Gropius's letter arrived Benscheidt was in the USA, finalising a large investment in his new factory by the United Shoe Machinery Company of Beverly, Massachusetts. On his return Benscheidt appears to have been greatly impressed by Gropius's letter, and wrote back on 12 January 1911 with an offer the young architect could hardly refuse. Although building was about to commence along the traditional lines suggested by Werner, Benscheidt offered Gropius the chance to give the whole plant a different, more 'tasteful' external appearance. Gropius and his partner Adolf Meyer responded quickly, and the 'Fagus-Werk' was born. The building Gropius and Meyer built for Benscheidt at Alfeld, has long since entered the mythology of modernism, as one of the key buildings of the twentieth century and has been 'listed' since 1948.

The Fagus-Werk was built alongside the Hanover-Göttingen railway line in two main phases (from June 1911 to early 1912 and from Autumn 1913 to August 1914), and consisted of separate buildings for each stage of the production process. These buildings – for sawing, steaming, drying and storing, and the actual production areas, where patented machinery shaped the locally-grown woods into finished shoe-lasts – were arranged to ensure the most efficient flow of production. The layout of the site remained unaltered from Werner's plans: Gropius's contribution lay in the modern styling of the façades. The main building, a flat-roofed steel structure clad in yellow bricks, standardised iron plates and glass – the ratio of glass to the other materials was about 2:1 – housed the packaging department on the ground floor with offices on the upper two storeys. It was this building, with its startling omission of corner piers in favour of a glass 'curtain wall', which immediately attracted the attention of

---

88. H. Weber, *Walter Gropius und das Faguswerk*, Munich, 1961. See also Reyner Banham's *A Concrete Atlantis*, Cambridge Mass., 1986. Karin Wilhelm suggests, on the basis of a conversation with Gropius's former colleague Ernst Neufert, that *Landrat* Burchard also made a direct personal appeal to Benscheidt to give warm consideration to Gropius's offer. See K. Wilhelm, *Walter Gropius*, note 283.

Figure 34 Fagus shoe-last factory, Alfeld a.d. Leine 1911–14
Arch. W. Gropius. Present condition

contemporaries and which helped to establish Gropius's name as an important innovator in twentieth century architecture.

Carl Benscheidt's swift acceptance of the inexperienced Gropius and dismissal of the perfectly adequate, if uninspired, Werner, is typical of the sort of managerial decision-making later chapters will attempt to explain. Of course, not all companies who joined the Werkbund or chose to work with DWB architects, made such an instant and dramatic leap to architectural modernity, but such decisions were seldom taken lightly, and always involved more than purely aesthetic considerations. The commercial advantages to be gained from a collaboration with the leading progressive architects and designers of the day have already been implied. A later chapter will examine the concept of 'architecture as advertisement' and the creation of 'corporate identity' in more depth. We shall also look at the important role a carefully designed factory could play in rationalising production and increasing output. Invariably, however, industrialists who employed DWB architects were moved by something greater than a pecuniary desire to secure a competitive edge over their business rivals.

By choosing to work with a DWB architect – a small minority within an architectural profession itself outnumbered by a vast number of master builders and 'design and build' developers – a company was endorsing much more than a particular view of the built environment. With its ideas on economic priorities (*Qualitätsarbeit*), the reform of the workplace, and the role of commerce and industry in society, the Werkbund took political positions and attracted political people. In effect, the selection of a DWB architect often became a political act. The next chapter looks more closely at the politics of the DWB. In particular, it examines the role of Friedrich Naumann and his followers in shaping and guiding the organisation in the years before 1918. This aspect of the DWB's history has generally been neglected in favour of the organisation's more photogenic side, but a true understanding of the Werkbund's industrial architecture is impossible without consideration of the context in which it was created.

−4−

Friedrich Naumann and the 'Heilbronn Connection': The Politics of the Werkbund

In the late summer of 1906 the young journalist and political activist Theodor Heuss (1884–1963) was a busy man. By day he was writing perceptive articles on politics, economics and architecture for the Berlin journal *Die Hilfe*, and fighting to arrest the long-term decline of organised liberalism in Wilhelmine Germany, whilst by night he composed self-conscious but affectionate letters to his future wife Elly Knapp in far-distant Strasbourg. At the same time, however, his mind was wrestling with two weighty problems posed by his publisher and mentor Friedrich Naumann. The first concerned the formation of an association of progressive artists and manufacturers, which Naumann had proposed in conjunction with the third National Exhibition of the Applied Arts, on display in Dresden from May to October 1906.

Naumann's initial inclination, expressed casually in conversation at Berlin's Café Unterberg one August evening, was to entrust the organisation of such an undertaking to Heuss himself. To the considerable relief of the 22 year old, Naumann had then reconsidered, asking him instead for suggestions of more suitable candidates. Heuss's response was to recommend a fellow former student of Lujo Brentano's economics seminar in Munich, Wolf Dohrn, who had campaigned for Naumann's short-lived Nationalsoziale Verein (NSV) in the 1903 General Election. Naumann must have been impressed by Heuss's choice, for, as we have seen, Dohrn indeed became the first Executive Secretary of the Werkbund, when it was finally constituted a year later.

The second problem exercising Heuss's young mind in the summer of 1906 appeared more intractable. Reichstag elections were due in 1908, and Friedrich Naumann – a national political figure for a decade, but yet to taste electoral success – was looking for a seat. The Freisinnige Vereinigung, the small left liberal party Naumann and most of his followers had joined on the demise of the NSV in 1903, had no 'safe' seats and no regional strongholds. For all Heuss's powers of imagination and coercion, the outlook seemed bleak. Sentimentality and a healthy dose of *Lokalpatriotismus*, rather than a realistic prospect of success, were probably instrumental in turning Heuss's thoughts to his home town of Heilbronn as a possible constituency for Naumann.

A bustling if rather inaccessible Swabian market town, Heilbronn was developing as an industrial centre but was a long way from Naumann's Berlin base and had a fearsome reputation for shunning 'outsiders'. The sitting member was a local man, a conservative agrarian elected on the votes of the wine-growers whose hillside vineyards surrounded the town. In the absence of anything more promising, however, Heuss began to explore the possibilities of establishing Naumann as a potential candidate, and soon drew encouragement from the editor of the local newspaper, Ernst Jäckh (1875–1959) of the *Neckar Zeitung*, who had been a Naumannite since the days of the NSV.

Heuss had met Jäckh for the first time in the autumn of 1902. The 27 year old Swabian had taken over the editorial reins in Heilbronn just as Heuss was about to leave for university in Munich. The precocious Heuss had asked to become the paper's unofficial 'Munich correspondent' and Jäckh, recognising a kindred spirit, had agreed. Heuss and Jäckh soon became close friends and their paths were to cross regularly for the next three decades, with both men playing key roles in the Werkbund, in the ups and downs of left liberal politics and in numerous publishing ventures: when Jäckh left Heilbronn in 1912 to become Executive Secretary of the DWB, it was Heuss who took over as editor of the *Neckar Zeitung*. Back in the autumn of 1906, however, it was clear to both men that if their political mentor was to stand a chance in Heilbronn he would require the backing of all the town's liberal notables, and not just the hard core of Naumannites who remained from the days of the NSV.

The principal liberal party in Heilbronn, as in much of south west Germany, was the German People's Party (known locally as the 'Democrats'), which worked closely with the Freisinnige Vereinigung in the Reichstag and contained a fair sprinkling of former National Socials in its own ranks. If Heuss's plan was to be successful, however, Naumann would also require the backing of any local supporters of the other left liberal faction, the Freisinnige Volkspartei, and, if possible, the local national liberals of the 'German Party' too. Heuss had been cheered by a joint meeting organised by all the liberal parties in Heilbronn in early 1905, and tentative moves towards liberal unity at a national level following the death of the Freisinnige Volkspartei's irascible leader Eugen Richter in March 1906. Heuss's negotiations were still in their infancy, however, when Chancellor Bülow unexpectedly dissolved the Reichstag on 13 December, paving the way for a General Election in the first month of 1907.

The speed of events forced Naumann's office to act quickly. Heuss was dispatched to Heilbronn with 300 Marks and a brief to sort something out as soon as possible, while colleagues assessed the chances of putting up Naumann in other constituencies around the *Reich*. Naumann's prospects in Heilbronn received a considerable boost when an extraordinary meeting of the Democrats unanimously backed his candidature. Particularly important was the support given to the man from Berlin by Peter Bruckmann, the silverware manufacturer described by Jäckh as the *geborene Herrgott* of Heilbronn.[1] Bruckmann & Sons was the town's biggest employer (730 workers in 1905) and had been producing high-quality silverware since 1805, during which time the Bruckmanns had advanced to being one of the town's leading families.

Since his election to the town council in 1895, Peter Bruckmann (1865–1937) had gained a reputation as a liberal and a democrat, and played a prominent part in the organisational life of the town, including the Chamber of Commerce, the Württemberg Arts and Crafts association and the Heilbronn Artists' Club. Bruckmann always received one of the highest polls in town council elections and was held in high esteem by his own work force, not least for his pioneering support of works' councils.[2]

Heuss was well aware of Bruckmann's qualities and importance to the town, having grown up in a house situated directly opposite the Bruckmann & Sons factory in the Lerchenstraße. Indeed, one of the childhood memories recalled by Heuss in his autobiography was of the strange, darkly-dressed 'artists' arriving to deliver their designs to Bruckmann, for the Heilbronn company was one of the first to ditch the historical pattern books and commission leading contemporary artists to design its cutlery and candlesticks. Bruckmann & Sons were duly to be found amongst the founder members of the Werkbund, an organisation which Peter Bruckmann chaired, off and on, from 1909 to 1932.

Bruckmann's endorsement of Naumann's candidature helped swing many of the town's *Honoratioren* behind the charismatic outsider and alternative plans for Naumann to stand in Colmar were quickly dropped. Heuss had been unable to reach a binding agreement with the German Party, which was split between backing Naumann and the candidate of the Agrarian League. Nevertheless, with the crucial backing of the Democrats, together with the Young Liberals and the Freisinnige Volkspartei, which had adopted a more hawkish foreign policy line and had therefore moved closer to Naumann's Freisinnige Vereinigung, Naumann entered the first round of voting with a reasonable chance of reaching the 'run off' election. On the eve of polling day the candidate of the Catholic Centre withdrew,

1. E. Jäckh, *Der goldene Pflug. Lebensernte eines Weltbürgers*, Stuttgart, 1954, p.90.
2. SA Heilbronn, Personal files: Bruckmann – P47–1, P47–2.

pledging his support to the Agrarian, who duly topped the poll with 11,529 votes to Naumann's 9,709 and the SPD's 9,476.[3]

It was then that the real election campaign began, with Naumann's hopes resting on the number of Social Democrats who could be persuaded to vote liberal in the 'run off'. The campaign attracted considerable attention, not least for the 'American' methods used by Ernst Jäckh to canvass support.[4] Cars supplied by local employers toured the constituency with loud hailers and prominent figures from public life were invited to express their support for Naumann in the pages of the *Neckar Zeitung*. In his memoirs Theodor Heuss recalled that the SPD gave only tacit support to Naumann on the second ballot, but James Clark Hunt believes the Social Democrat leadership in Stuttgart openly called on socialists to vote for Naumann.[5] Either way, enough SPD supporters voted for Naumann in the 'run off' to ensure that he beat his Agrarian League opponent by around 1,500 votes (15,695 to 14,178).

Naumann's victory was a cause of great rejoicing, not only for Heuss, Jäckh, Bruckmann and Dohrn, who had all been active in the campaign, but for many progressives elsewhere in Germany, who saw the events in Heilbronn as an example of what could be achieved by a reformist block stretching from the National Liberals to the Social Democrats, or, in the memorable phrase used by Naumann at the 1901 NSV congress, 'from Bassermann to Bebel'. In particular, Naumann's success gave new impetus to moves for liberal unity, and was a major stepping stone on the way to the formation of the Fortschrittliche Volkspartei (FVP) in 1910, which finally brought together the Freisinnige Vereinigung, Freisinnige Volkspartei and the south German Democrats in a single left liberal party.

In retrospect, of course, Naumann's victory in Heilbronn was another false dawn for Wilhelmine Germany's liberal reformers. The 1907 General Election – the infamous *Hottentot* elections – saw a nationwide swing against the SPD which briefly benefited the left liberals but which would be reversed five years later. In 1912 Heilbronn would fall to the SPD along

---

3. Details of election campaign in T. Heuss, *Erinnerungen 1905–33*, Tübingen, 1963, pp.54–64; T. Heuss, *Friedrich Naumann. Der Mann. Das Werk. Die Zeit*, pp.323–325, Berlin, 1937; also E. Jäckh, *Der goldene Pflug*. The left liberals were past masters at winning run-off elections. Indeed, in the 1903 and 1912 Reichstag elections every single left liberal deputy had to go through a second ballot to win a seat.

4. See the campaign leaflet of Naumann's agrarian opponent, Dr. Wolff, which describes, albeit in exaggerated terms, Naumann's 'truly American agitation', with 'hundreds of hirelings in automobiles' and 'numerous testimonies from liberal women, pastors and professors from all corners of the Reich'. ZStA Potsdam, Nachlaß Naumann 90 Na 3–221 p.11.

5. J.C. Hunt, *The People's Party in Württemberg and Southern Germany*, Stuttgart, 1975, p.129. The pro-SPD *Schwäbische Tagwacht* certainly carried a firm recommendation for Social Democrats to vote for Naumann. ZStA Potsdam Nachlaß Naumann 90 Na 3–221 p.9.

with 109 other Reichstag seats and Naumann, who was to turn down the offer of a 'safe' Munich seat in favour of his Werkbund colleague Kerschensteiner, would even fail to reach the second ballot.[6] At the end of 1907 however, Naumann and his supporters had no reason to be burdened by such gloomy prophecies: not only was Naumann safely ensconced in the Reichstag – which, for all its constitutional constraints was still the focus of national political life – but the Werkbund was at last up and running too, with Naumann's 'Heilbronn connection' playing key roles in both.

Existing accounts of the Werkbund and its members have struggled to come to terms with Naumann's political activities. Although most authors mention his membership of the Reichstag, many fail to place him in the right party. Stanford Anderson, in his thesis on Peter Behrens, refers to 'the nationalist and social democratic politician Friedrich Naumann'[7]; Kenneth Frampton's *Modern Architecture* mentions Naumann as a 'Christian-Social Democrat'[8]; the Werkbund Archive's own publication *Packeis und Preßglas* states that 'the Freisinnige Volkspartei was the party which was particularly close to the DWB',[9] whilst the same Werkbund Archive speaks in another pamphlet of 'Friedrich Naumann's national-liberal circle'.[10] If these errors highlight the tendency of art historians to underestimate the importance of historical accuracy, then the silent response of political historians, such as Naumann's most recent biographer Peter Theiner, to Naumann's 'artistic' activities is even more alarming.[11] Far from being an irrelevant self-indulgence, the Werkbund and its preoccupations were central to the new vision of Germany propagated by Naumann and his followers.

6. Naumann had 'a stimulating influence on the intellectual life of the whole town' (*Die Hilfe*, 18 Jan. 1912) and in 1912, as the official FVP candidate, he was able to increase his vote by 26%, but the SPD vote rose even more impressively (up 30%). In the first round of voting the SPD therefore topped the poll, but Naumann was unexpectedly beaten into third place, receiving a few dozen votes less than the agrarian candidate. The SPD comfortably took the run-off. However Naumann returned to the Reichstag a year later after a by-election victory in Waldeck-Pyrmont, when he beat an anti-semite in the second ballot (6,593 to 6,327 votes). Naumann owed his narrow victory to Gustav Stresemann, who had appealed to local National Liberals to vote for the FVP in the run-off. Incidentally, Heilbronn supporters helped Naumann's by-election campaign by contributing 1,019 Marks to his fighting fund (*Die Hilfe*, 14 Aug. 1913 p.526). See also letter from Naumann to Heuss (28 April 1913) in Nachlaß Naumann 90 Na 3–5 p.56.

7. S. Anderson, 'Peter Behrens and the New Architecture of Germany', in *Oppositions*, vol.11 (1977), p.63.

8. K. Frampton, *Modern Architecture. A Critical History*, London, 1985, p.110.

9. E. Siepmann & A. Thiekötter (eds), *Packeis und Preßglas*, Werkbund – Archiv 16, Lahn-Gießen, 1987, p.310.

10. 'Begleitheft zur Ausstellung Packeis und Preßglas', Berlin, 1987, p.44.

11. P. Theiner, *Sozialer Liberalismus und deutsche Weltopolitik*, Baden Baden, 1983, fails to mention the DWB once in three hundred pages.

The concept of *Qualitätsarbeit*, developed by Naumann and others in the years before the formation of the DWB, and propagated with such vigour by that organisation after 1907, was an integral part of Naumann's economic, social and foreign policy strategy. The new industrial architecture produced by DWB members in Wilhelmine Germany was a highly-visible demonstration of *Qualitätsarbeit* in action and helps to reveal those sectors of industry in which Naumann's reformist ideas made most impact. This chapter examines the origins and evolution of the *Qualitätsarbeit* idea, its place in Naumann's political programme and its role within the Werkbund. Firstly, however, we must sketch the broad outlines of Naumann's unusual political career.

It is surely significant that Wilhelmine Germany's most charismatic and influential liberal politician had no background or tradition in liberal politics. The son of a vicar, Friedrich Naumann's training and early social environment was that of the Protestant church. After studying theology and philosophy at university, Naumann became a social worker in Hamburg, employed by a German precursor to the Salvation Army, the 'Inner Mission'. In 1885 he returned from Hamburg to attend the Leipzig Clerical College, where he fell under the influence of the prominent Conservative politician and court chaplain Adolf Stoecker (1835–1909). Stoecker, who had founded the Verein für Sozialpolitik in 1872 and the Christian-Social Workers' Party six years later, was viewed by some as the 'New Luther', and was not afraid to campaign for social welfare legislation in the political arena. Naumann was undoubtedly attracted by many of Stoecker's ideas, but later he was anxious to distance himself from Stoecker's increasingly right-wing and anti-semitic activities.

From 1886 to 1890 Naumann served as a vicar in the small industrial community of Langenberg, Saxony. In an attempt to relate to his working-class parishioners he studied the works of Marx, Bebel, and Lassalle, and in return recommended the Bible as a 'Workers' Book'. Naumann's first brush with authority came with the publication of his pamphlet 'The Worker's Catechism, or the True Socialism'. The frosty response of the church elders probably convinced him that he was not well-suited to the life of a vicar and in 1890 he moved to Frankfurt to rejoin the 'Inner Mission'.

In Frankfurt Naumann became active in both the Evangelical Workers' Unions and the Evangelical Social Congress, where he first met the likes of Paul Göhre, Hans Delbrück and Max Weber (1864–1920). Weber's investigations into the living and working conditions of agricultural labourers shocked Naumann and convinced him of the need to confront the excesses and hypocrisies of the *Junker* class: any lingering attachment to the German Conservative Party as an instrument of reform disappeared in the early 1890s. Instead, Naumann was to find fresh inspiration in the work of Paul Göhre (1864–1928), the young theologian who aroused great public interest in social welfare issues after writing a book based on his experiences as an 'undercover' factory worker in Leipzig, and Charles Hallgarten (1838–1908), a liberal Frankfurt banker whom he first met in 1894.

Hallgarten was a German Jew who had emigrated to the United States in mid-century and made his fortune with the Hallgarten & Co. bank of New York City. In Germany Hallgarten had many influential contacts in banking and industry, and was a contributor to numerous progressive political and cultural causes. Naumann first received financial assistance from Hallgarten to launch his new weekly journal *Die Hilfe* in December 1894, and thereafter enjoyed a long association with the banker, who contributed large sums to all Naumann's subsequent enterprises.[12] However, Hallgarten gave Naumann more than an injection of cash: the earnest young cleric benefited from being introduced into a new social world, and the sophisticated élite of Frankfurt's banking circles were in turn intrigued by Naumann and his visionary schemes.

Although it is ludicrous to suggest, as Naumann's East German biographer Gertrude Theodor has done,[13] that in 1894 he became a 'tool' of a faction of monopoly capitalism, it is certainly true that from the mid-1890s Naumann changed the emphasis of his activities and concerns.[14] With his new Frankfurt friends came new ideas, many from America, on trade policy, industrial organisation and the prospects opened up by technological innovation. Naumann became more overtly political in his writing and began to criticise many areas of government policy. He was perturbed by the failure of the *Reich* administration to maintain the momentum of social welfare legislation that had characterised the immediate post-Bismarck era, but he also began to write on wider issues of economic and foreign policy too. The essay collection *Was heißt Christlich-Sozial?*, which appeared in 1896, was Naumann's most political publication yet, and revealed his intention to enter the party political arena.

Naumann was well aware of the dangers of launching yet another small party in the fragmented centre of German politics and knew only too well the deep-seated distaste for party politics in the educated middle-classes,

12. Naumann's correspondence with Hallgarten (Nachlaß Naumann 90 Na 3–147) gives some indication of the politician's debt to the banker, containing a number of requests for money and profuse thanks for services rendered in the past. Some years later Naumann wrote to Hallgarten's son (10 Nov. 1915), confirming that 'in my hardest time he supported and backed me tremendously' (Nachlaß Naumann 90 Na 3–147 p.32).
13. G. Theodor, *Friedrich Naumann oder des Prophet des Profits*, East Berlin, 1957.
14. As Naumann's old friend Martin Rade wrote: 'when he left Frankfurt he was no longer the same person who had come here'. (Nachlaß Naumann 90 Na 3–285 p.91. 'Die Verhandlungen des 36. Evangelisch-Sozialen Kongresses').

who formed a large part of his natural constituency. With this in mind, Naumann hit upon the rather dubious notion of founding a 'political association preparatory to a party'. The National-Social Union was established at a congress in Erfurt late in 1896, with the organisational affairs handled by Naumann's 'first lieutenant', Martin Wenck (1862–1931). The NSV's initial manifesto, sometimes known as the 'National Social catechism' was issued on 25 November 1896, and opened with a powerful statement of intent:

> We are nationalists, in the sense that we believe that the economic and political expansion of the German nation outwards is a prerequisite for all the great social reforms that are needed internally. At the same time, however, we are convinced that this power in foreign affairs cannot be sustained in the long term without the support of a politically-aware population. Therefore we aim for a policy of strength abroad and reform at home.[15]

Throughout the next twenty years the concept of 'strength abroad and reform at home' remained at the heart of Naumann's political credo. The NSV supported the colonial idea, national military service and the expansion of the German naval fleet, arguing that 'the struggle for the world market is a struggle for existence'. It took heart from the *Reich*'s growing population, which it compared to the fate of the 'sinking peoples' of Spain and Italy. Growth – both demographic and economic – was the key to Germany's future, and nothing should be tolerated which threatened to impede the expanding nation's destiny. At the same time, however, the Union stressed the importance of integrating the growing masses into the life of the nation, and demanded electoral reform at state and local level. Naumann called on the 'representatives of German education' to join in the political struggle of German labour 'for the common good' and against 'the supremacy of existing property rights'. The NSV was subsequently accused by the Right of being 'soft' on the socialist threat, as it campaigned against the notorious *Zuchthausvorlage* and expressed support for the major Hamburg dock workers' strike of 1896–7.

The NSV programme contained measures for land reform and women's rights, but the religious element, which had still been prominent in Naumann's thought at the launch of the NSV, gradually declined in importance. The pivotal role of the Christian faith in Naumann's programme of political and social reform was largely replaced by an equally strong belief in the benevolent power of the nation state. In the late 1890s many young men joined the Union as a refreshing alternative

15. F. Naumann, 'National-sozialer Katechismus', in *Werke*, Cologne, 1964–69, vol.5, p.199. For the NSV see Dieter Düding's book *Der Nationalsoziale Verein 1896–1903*, Munich, 1972.

to the established political parties. In 1897 Naumann transferred his base from Frankfurt to Berlin, to be closer to the heart of political life, and at the same time attempted to cash in on the success of *Die Hilfe* by publishing a daily newspaper called *Die Zeit*.

The paper failed, but Naumann was soon established as a high-profile political figure, surrounded by a small but dedicated clique of committed followers. Naumann always disliked the 'personality cult' aspects of his support, but it was to remain with him until his death in 1919. Naumann's best-known NSV disciples remained 'Naumannites' in the public eye, long after many of them had joined other political parties: Paul Göhre, who joined the SPD in 1901; Max Maurenbrecher (1874–1930); Hellmut von Gerlach (1866–1935); and Adolf Damaschke (1865–1935), all first generation Naumannites, later found great difficulty in emerging from the great man's shadow. Only Gustav Stresemann (1878–1929), representative of the Dresden branch at the 1901 NSV conference in Frankfurt, appeared at ease in forging a new career away from his political teacher.

Naumann paid a brief return visit to Frankfurt in 1898 to stand for the NSV in that year's General Election, but like all the National Social candidates he failed to win a Reichstag seat. Nevertheless his writing and publishing career continued to flourish and in 1900 the book *Demokratie und Kaisertum* – subtitled 'a handbook for domestic politics' – appeared, further enhancing Naumann's reputation as one of the most original thinkers in German politics. In it he expounded on his theory of a *demokratisches Volkskaisertum* and argued that democratic reform was perfectly possible under the monarchy. He also endeavoured to describe the crucial role the working class should play in securing Germany's future as a modern, industrial nation.

Naumann was convinced that the majority of workers, including active members of the labour movement, did not seriously believe in the SPD's Marxist rhetoric, and could be integrated into a reformed *Reich* without recourse to revolution. This could be of great benefit to the nation in future international power struggles: 'People who have something to lose', he argued, 'fight differently and better than those who have nothing to lose but their chains'.[16] With this in mind, he observed the struggles of the 'Revisionists' in the SPD closely, and frequently used his press accreditation to attend SPD conferences. In the summer of 1901 *Die Zeit* was re-launched as a weekly journal. Both *Die Zeit* and *Die Hilfe* were able to feature long articles on art, architecture and aesthetics – many written by Naumann himself – as well as politics and religion. Contributors to the journals included the colonialist Paul Rohrbach (1869–1956), the banker Hjalmar Schacht (1877–1970) and the art historian Paul Schubring,

16. F. Naumann, 'Demokratie und Kaisertum', in *Werke*, vol.2, p.121.

all future members of the Werkbund. The success of Naumann's publishing ventures was in marked contrast to the political fortunes of the NSV, which had failed to turn its good publicity to political advantage. On 1 October 1902 the NSV had just 2,704 paid up members.

Between 1900 and 1902 Naumann engaged in many long discussions with the other centre-left political parties, as he attempted to reach electoral agreements for the 1903 General Election. He was all too conscious of the fact that the NSV could not afford a repeat of 1898's polling-day whitewash. Eugen Richter's Freisinnige Volkspartei rejected Naumann's advances because of the NSV's aggressive foreign and colonial policy, but some headway was made in discussions with the other main left liberal party, the Freisinnige Vereinigung. The NSV co-operated effectively with the latter on the controversial trade tariff issue in 1902.

When polling-day arrived on 16 June 1903 Naumann stood in the north German constituency of Oldenburg, a stronghold of the Richter group. Despite a well-fought campaign and support from the Freisinnige Vereinigung, Naumann was beaten convincingly, as indeed were all other NSV candidates with the exception of Gerlach, who won in the university town of Marburg. Naumann was quick to grasp the voters' message. As he told his disappointed supporters:

> We are not in a position to be able to found the new party. That is bitter knowledge, but it is knowledge nevertheless. It is now not a case of 'giving it one more try' as a party, but rather of how to keep alive the representation of a distinctive strain of political thought, which should not die, just because it does not yet have the strength to build parties.[17]

At the annual NSV conference, held at Göttingen in August, the majority of members voted to begin moves to merge with the Freisinnige Vereinigung, although some prominent activists opted to move in different directions: Maurenbrecher followed Göhre into the SPD, whilst Damaschke left party politics altogether to concentrate on the Land Reform Movement, which he led with distinction for many years. Naumann admitted that by joining one of the left liberal parties, the National Socials were having to change course: 'If we venture into the structure of German liberalism then we will inevitably become something different from that which we had originally intended.'[18]

No one was more pleased to see Naumann join the Freisinnige Vereinigung than his old Frankfurt banking friend Charles Hallgarten, who was one of the party's principal paymasters. The party had been formed in 1892, as a splinter from the Deutsch-Freisinnige Partei, and was led by

17. F. Naumann, 'Die Niederlage', in *Werke*, vol.5, p.299.
18. F. Naumann, 'Die Zukunft unseres Vereins', in *Werke*, vol.5, p.314.

the lawyers Rickert and Barth. Hallgarten was not the only banker to have a close interest in the party: one of its founders was the Deutsche Bank director George von Siemens (1839–1901) and in 1898 no fewer than five of its thirteen Reichstag deputies were paid employees or consultants of the Deutsche Bank, including both Rickert and Barth. Following the death of George von Siemens in 1901, the parliamentary faction of the party was led by Karl Schrader (1834–1913), another Deutsche Bank director and a friend of Naumann. It was hardly surprising, then, that the Freisinnige Vereinigung was nicknamed the 'Bankers Party' by the electorate. It is interesting to note that the Deutsche Bank had particularly close links with the newer, emerging sectors of German industry; sectors which, as we shall see, were later to be particularly prominent in the Werkbund. Naumann's participation in the Freisinnige Vereinigung, and long-term identification with the economic interests of this 'new' industrial faction, no doubt helped to ease mutual suspicions when the DWB began to court large industrial firms after 1907.

Not everyone welcomed Naumann and the National Socials to the party with open arms. The Freisinnige Vereinigung was, after all, the closest of the German liberal factions to the traditions of classical, Manchester liberalism. Naumann on the other hand was an interventionist, schooled on the ideas of Christian charity and Socialism, with no great faith in free trade but a Weberian trust in 'rational' bureaucracy. Shortly before he joined the Freisinnige Vereinigung Naumann had written:

> All the old liberal polemic against socialism was based on the idea that 'it is out of the question and dangerous to hamper the free interplay of market forces'. That is now history. The free interplay of market forces in the old sense no longer exists. Today the struggles of the syndicates, co-operatives and federations have taken the place of the old personal battles, and nowadays one hears in the AGMs of the syndicates the sort of ideas that used to be branded as 'socialist' . . . The transition from capitalists to capitalism has theoretically brought capitalists and socialists closer together.[19]

Naumann was convinced that contemporary economic reconstruction was making Marxism irrelevant and the class-struggle unnecessary. The syndicates and cartels represented the beginnings of an efficient capitalist economy, in which an element of planning was in-built. Moreover the typical modern manager was no longer a cynical owner-exploiter but an anonymous employee, whose interest in the success of the company was identical with that of the shop-floor worker. At the back of Naumann's mind was a political scenario which envisaged the eventual creation of a two or three-party system, in which the two 'sides' of industry would unite

---

19. F. Naumann, 'Neudeutsche Wirtschaftspolitik', in *Werke*, vol.3, p.438.

for reasons of mutual benefit to oppose the reactionary and agrarian forces that remained so powerful in German political life. For, above all else, Friedrich Naumann's political activity was marked by two characteristics that had long been absent from the German liberal parties: a heightened awareness of the need to achieve power as a prerequisite for political action; and a fascination with the technicalities of political organisation. Naumann spent much of the next decade trying to impress on his new colleagues the importance of unity. As he wrote in a 1909 essay, 'power is organisation'.[20]

Although the leadership of the Freisinnige Vereinigung was closely associated with the world of high finance and modern big business, it naturally relied on a more heterogeneous constituency for its electoral support. Academics, civil servants, Protestant clergymen and professionals, hanseatic traders and some workers formed the bulk of the party's support. Small shopkeepers, artisans and craftsmen tended to vote for the rival Freisinnige Volkspartei, with its more pronounced anti-socialist line. Both left liberal parties relied heavily on support from the towns. In Germany's rural districts, the parties faced a constant battle for survival.[21] One section of the community that seemed to give considerable support to the Freisinnige Vereinigung, and the Naumannites in particular, was the architectural profession. Even before the idea of the Werkbund had been floated, Naumann was a popular and respected figure amongst young architects.

Fritz Schumacher, for instance, recalled that as a student he cared little for politics, although he did attend a few SPD rallies out of curiosity. He had then learnt of Naumann's efforts to 'build serious bridges to the Social Democrats':

> In large sections of the German working class, national feeling and religious need were far from suffocated; to create a party that represented these people's interests appeared to me to be one of the most vital tasks of the time. I therefore allied myself to the enthusiastic little band who supported this aim of Naumann's.[22]

Schumacher wrote that he had 'studied the classics of Socialism' – Lassalle, Marx, Engels, Bebel – but was 'bitterly disappointed' when he compared them to Fichte or Naumann. Shortly before his death in 1947 he added:

20. F. Naumann, 'Von wem werden wir regiert?', in *Werke*, vol.2, p.396.
21. For the social composition of the left liberal parties, see Chapter One of Alastair Thompson's 'Left Liberals in German State and Society', PhD thesis, London University Birkbeck College, 1989.
22. F. Schumacher, *Selbstgespräche. Erinnerungen und Betrachtungen*, Hamburg, 1949, p.85.

I have never understood why, and it still pains me that Naumann did not make the political breakthrough. Perhaps the reason was that he was not single-minded and hard enough to be a politician, because in personal contact the artistic side of his character would come through. We often met to discuss artistic matters, and had some arguments too, but that was by the by: politically, I remained true to his national and social ideas to the day he died.[23]

Other DWB architects to identify with Naumann's political aims included Richard Riemerschmid, who designed the masthead of Naumann's *Die Hilfe*, Theodor Fischer and Oswin Hempel. The young Walter Gropius and Eric Mendelsohn both read *Die Hilfe*,[24] whilst other DWB architects like Paul Bonatz, Peter Behrens and Bruno Paul regularly attended 'round table' discussions with leading Naumannites. The DWB landscape gardener Leberecht Migge, responsible for designing the grounds of Muthesius's Seidenweberei Michels in Potsdam, dedicated his best-known book to Naumann, claiming in a letter to the politician; 'one could say this book is *your product*. It is perhaps the first . . . attempt [to interpret] the spirit and the world view you have imparted to so many young Germans'.[25]

One reason why Naumann and his publications appealed to architects was undoubtedly the great interest and knowledge the politician showed in aesthetic and technological issues. From the mid-1890s Naumann wrote regular articles and reviews on art and architecture, revealing a deep understanding of the creative process and offering some perceptive insights into future trends. Many of his articles were reissued in a successful 1909 collection entitled *Form und Farbe*, and when the time came for his collected works to be republished in the 1960s a thick volume was devoted solely to essays on the arts. Like Schultze-Naumburg, Avenarius and Lichtwark, Naumann was one of the great turn-of-the-century art educators, but his work was refreshingly free of the school-masterly tone of his contemporaries. Just as his political writings exuded an air of great optimism about the future prospects for domestic reform and external strength, so Naumann's aesthetic essays were invariably positive in tone, proclaiming the dawn of the 'machine age' and highlighting the contribution new technologies could make to social progress.

Naumann was, for example, one of the first German commentators to see a promising future for high-rise buildings (1900), for great assembly halls in steel and glass, and for the use of concrete and glass-bricks as construction materials (1896). Naumann wrote on the glory of the Eiffel Tower, but he could also wax lyrical about 'iron architecture' closer to home, describing the beauty of 'an evening over Dortmund and

23. F. Schumacher, *ibid.*, p.85.
24. K. Junghanns, *Der Deutsche Werkbund*, East Berlin, 1982, p.12.
25. Letter Migge to Naumann (18 June 1913) in Nachlaß Naumann 90 Na 3–267 p.13.

Bochum'.[26] He also spoke fondly of the weighty iron framework of the Berlin elevated railway, which he described as 'more powerful than the judgements of Solomon.'[27] One of the most popular features in *Die Hilfe* and *Die Zeit* were his regular 'letters from the exhibitions'. Writing from the major Düsseldorf exhibition of 1902, he praised the comparatively plain pavilion of the GHH:

> As simple as the decision may appear, it is actually very rare and valuable to build in a way that does not attempt to portray something else. It takes a lot of trouble to be truthful in architecture. But when such a building succeeds it has the power to influence the whole of intellectual life. It stands like a warning to the conscience, calling for truth to one's principles in the midst of all these half-hearted, botched-up structures . . . Whoever takes this to their heart can no longer bear the false, decorative tendencies. It is as if this building has already been touched by the spirit of a purer future, beyond the period of Wilhelm II.[28]

Elsewhere he wrote about the aesthetic pleasures of fast trains and the motor car. At the same time, however, his fierce nationalism made him a defiant defender of the old German script, despite the growing fashion for Latin characters in intellectual and artistic circles.[29]

Naumann wrote intelligently about fine art, but his real passion was the interaction between the arts and society, and in particular the economic and social benefits applied art could bring to the German nation as a whole. In a *Kunstwart* essay entitled 'Art in the Machine Age' (1904), and a further lecture given two years later on 'Art and Industry', Naumann introduced many of the ideas which were soon to surface as Werkbund preoccupations. Yet these years also saw the publication of Naumann's major work on the national economy, which was developed from a series of lectures given in 1901 and finally published in 1906. The book was entitled *New German Economic Policy* and it dismissed many of the sacred cows of classical liberalism, proclaiming that 'there are no eternal truths in economic policy, no system and no legislation which suits every nation at every time'.[30] The book was intended as an introductory guide to contemporary economic matters for the layman, but this did not stop the specialists from debating the issues it raised. Naumann was not an economist and he was duly criticised for his highly-subjective, political approach to the subject, but the book proved popular, particularly in Japan, where it was published with

26. F. Naumann, 'Die Kunst im Zeitalter der Maschine', in *Werke*, vol.6, p.194.

27. F. Naumann, *ibid.*, p.196.

28. F. Naumann, 'Düsseldorfer Industrie-Ausstellung', in *Werke*, vol.6, p.410.

29. In a letter to Cäsar Flaischlen (15 Feb. 1911) Naumann writes: 'It is quite correct if Dr Heuss has informed you that I am personally a convinced supporter of the German script'. Nachlaß Naumann 90 Na 3–4 p.36.

30. F. Naumann, quoted by T. Heuss in *Friedrich Naumann*, p.257.

state support.

New German Economic Policy owed a considerable debt to the theories of Lujo Brentano and other young social scientists of the Verein für Sozialpolitik, such as Max Weber and Werner Sombart (1863–1941). It highlighted in particular the human aspects of the national economy, arguing that the 'working class must be given fresh air, if it is to remain healthy', and posing the question, 'how can industrial vassals become industrial citizens?' One chapter investigated the possibilities of encouraging work force loyalty within firms – *Betriebspatriotismus* – without coercion or false paternalism. The influence of this work on the Werkbund industrial architects was considerable, if the tone and content of Walter Gropius's famous pre-war essays are anything to go by. Naumann was intrigued by the efforts of some progressive factory owners, most notably the Venetian-blinds manufacturer Heinrich Freese (1853–1944), to introduce works' councils and profit-sharing schemes to their businesses, and wrote enthusiastically about such experiments in 'factory democracy'.

Freese – himself a left liberal politician – had made the first moves toward works' councils in 1879, conscious of the contradictions that had grown up between his political rhetoric and his own business practice. He began what he termed the 'constitutional system' in 1884, with a ten man works' council discussing working conditions, holiday times and other issues at his Berlin factory. The council members were elected by secret shop-floor ballots and all meetings were open to other workers too. Freese was allowed to address the meetings whenever he wished. In 1890 the council was increased in size to fifteen, with eleven members elected as before and four delegated by Freese – a right he gave up in 1909. Meetings were held quarterly, and the council's achievements included the abolition of night shifts at the factory, the gradual introduction of an eight-hour day and successful bi-annual wage negotiations. No agreement could be found on the controversial issue of the May Day holiday, but Freese conceded the right of workers to apply for the day off as part of their holidays. Freese always stressed that the existence of works' councils should not affect workers' wider trade union rights.

Freese's pioneering steps in industrial democracy received a certain legitimation in the national *Gewerbeordnung* of 1891, which formally established the legal status of works' councils. Although the legislation was modest, Freese believed it marked an important step on the road 'from absolutism to constitutionalism' in the factory hall. In 1890 Freese introduced an element of profit sharing for workers, based on an earlier scheme for the company's salaried employees, but profit sharing was slow to develop in Germany: just 29 companies offered similar schemes in Germany by 1899, compared to 100 in Britain and 119 in France. The number had risen to 42 in 1902.[31] Freese's well-developed sense of self-publicity – he wrote at least four books on his 'constitutional factory'[32] – ensured that he was the best known early exponent of German industrial democracy, but Naumann was also most impressed by the efforts of Ernst Abbé (1840–1905), the founder of the Carl Zeiß optical firm in Jena.

The Concept of *Qualitätsarbeit*

If the 'constitutional factory' was one method of improving the lives of industrial workers, then another was to make fundamental changes to the process and purpose of factory work itself. To this end, Naumann began to develop the concept of *Qualitätsarbeit*. Since the economic and social strategy associated with this idea subsequently formed the intellectual foundation for much of the Werkbund's mould-breaking industrial architecture, it is worth examining its evolution in more depth. There was nothing new, of course, in manufacturers describing their wares as 'quality' products, nor was Naumann the first to urge a greater emphasis on quality goods in German exports, but by building a whole economic and social reform strategy around the idea, Naumann gave the term a new meaning and significance. Writing in 1924, Günther Freiherr von Pechmann, assessed Naumann's importance thus:

> The term 'quality work' first appeared after the turn of the century, in the columns of specialist manufacturing journals, in economic literature, in the expressions of politicians and in parliamentary reports ... It would be meaningless to ascertain who used the word first, and in what context. More important is the question, who first filled it with a powerful and attractive content ... That was Friedrich Naumann. In nearly every one of his economic and political speeches and essays he expressed the importance which he attached to a qualitative improvement of German manufacturing work.[33]

Whereas the term 'quality' had long been used in manufacturing to signify a product that was made with high-class materials and to the best functional specifications, Naumann chose the term 'quality work' because it also implied a judgement of the manufacturing process itself. In other words, *Qualitätsarbeit* made the connection between the product and the

---

31. Figures quoted by H. Freese in *Die konstitutionelle Fabrik*, Jena, 1909, p.70.

32. *Fabrikantenglück!* (1889); *Das konstitutionelle System im Fabrikbetriebe* (1903); *Die Gewinnbeteiligung der Angestellten* (1905); *Die konstitutionelle Fabrik* (1909) etc. See also H.J. Teuteberg, *Die Geschichte der industriellen Mitbestimmung in Deutschland*, Tübingen, 1961.

33. G. Freiherr von Pechmann, *Die Qualitätsarbeit*, Frankfurt, 1924, p.19. For a recent study of the history of German 'quality work', and much else besides, see J. Campbell, *Joy in Work, German Work*, Princeton, 1989.

producer: quality work required quality workers. In this way, Naumann was able to combine his economic conviction that the *Reich* must improve the value of its exports, with his social concern for the lives of the working masses. Germany, with its lack of natural resources and temperate climate, its expensive but well-trained and expanding work force, and its tradition of scientific innovation, was for Naumann 'the ideal land for the manufacture of finished products'. In *New German Economic Policy* he examined the economic and social benefits to be gained by an improvement in the quality of German manufacturing. His conclusion was that 'all lesser goods swindle entrepreneurs, workers and salesmen alike, because they have all wasted their efforts on something that is simply not worth it. We can leave that sort of work to the half-educated peoples.'[34]

For Naumann the essence of a quality product naturally included first-class materials, good workmanship, and high functional performance, but he also stressed the particular importance of 'form' and appearance; the unquantifiable factor which later became known as 'design'. In his 1902 lecture on 'The Economic Consequences of Population Growth' he argued:

> ... if we do not want to become a people of sinking quality then we must become the nation of the quality goods trade. With basic, cheap and common mass products we will not be able to meet the challenge that lies in the growing population figures ... We will not win that world market we are always talking about simply by making things properly and with good materials. What rules the market is to a large extent *taste*.[35]

Thus he was able to combine his economic and social concerns with his third great interest, applied art. As Naumann himself wrote: 'The more we turn to quality production, the greater the average standard of living will be for the Germans. This is the point where art and trade and social policy all meet.'[36]

Naumann was aware that in a consumer society the form and appearance of products would be as important as their intrinsic value. This applied not only to biscuits, confectionery and the like, where the packaging and advertising were vital elements in the success or failure of the product, but also to more complex items, like cookers and automobiles, where the showroom appearance was a decisive factor in the world marketplace. If Germany was to become a nation known for the quality of its manufactured goods it would have to use the cream of its artistic talents to design everything from the product, the packaging and the posters, to the plant in which it was all assembled. The aim must be a

---

34. F. Naumann, 'Neudeutsche Wirtschaftspolitik', in *Werke*, vol.3, p.188.
35. F. Naumann, quoted by G.v. Pechmann in *Die Qualitätsarbeit*, p.20
36. F. Naumann, 'Die Kunst im Zeitalter der Maschine', in *Werke*, vol.3, p.190.

distinctive national style, which could compete with the established cultural identities of the French and English. As Naumann put it:

> A nation which wants to earn billions from its labour must learn to see artistic questions in economic terms. We are not saying that art follows economic objectives, but we maintain that a well-developed sense of aesthetics can be very useful economically: not so much the arts themselves, although they are very important, but in the sense of the perfect *form* for every sort of production.[37]

Naumann believed Germany had two basic options for its future path to prosperity: *Abnutzungstheorie* – buying and selling large quantities of low value commodities, which would imply a low-wage economy with minimal social provision – or *Dauerhaftigkeitstheorie* – building up loyal markets abroad in high quality products, then using the foreign earnings to pay higher wages and expand the domestic market. His 1904 *Kunstwart* essay, 'Art in the Machine Age', offered another punchy and polemical summary of the *Qualitätsarbeit* strategy, and left little doubt as to which economic course Naumann preferred:

> There is nothing to be earned from cheap mass production. Of course, this has to be done, but with the talents of the Germans one could achieve so much more. This lesser work will sooner or later be taken over by the half-educated peoples. What will we be doing then? We shall either be a people whose style and taste has broken through around the world, or we will be scrapping it out with the Orientals to see who can produce the cheapest mass products, squeezed out of flesh, blood and iron.[38]

The situation could not be improved simply by providing a better education for engineers and draughtsmen, but would require a major cultural shift, the creation of 'a German national style of the machine age'. Unfortunately for Naumann, however, 'powerful forces' were working in the opposite direction:

> So-called 'heavy' industry has the fundamental aim of making the production of semi-finished goods the core of German economic life, and the syndicates of these industries sell their products cheaper abroad than they do at home. This has the effect of driving the lighter manufacturing industries, in which art and good taste could make the greatest contribution, out and over our borders. This is the trend which currently holds the upper hand, and its victory over the finished-goods industries in the battle over the trade tariffs has cemented its position.[39]

37. F. Naumann, 'Neudeutsche Wirtschaftspolitik', in *Werke*, vol.3, p.190.
38. F. Naumann, 'Die Kunst im Zeitalter der Maschine', in *Werke*, vol.6, p.191.
39. F. Naumann, *ibid.*, pp.191–192.

The struggle between these two industrial power-blocks, together with their allies and agents, continued throughout the following decade, and was fought out not only in company board rooms and parliamentary chambers but in the field of architecture too. A later chapter will examine this fascinating confrontation in detail, but Naumann's argument illustrates how it also impinged on the *Qualitätsarbeit* debate. It was a long-standing grievance of the manufacturing and processing industries that they should have to pay customs duty on the vital raw materials they imported, as well as paying high prices for domestically produced crude steel and coal. To make matters worse, these German heavy industries then sold the same resources to overseas customers at a discounted 'dumping' price. In the eyes of manufacturing industry such a policy, from a quarter which so loudly championed 'the protection of the national work', was a most curious demonstration of patriotism and one which could only harm Germany's long-term economic prospects.

In view of the ideas and interests Naumann had pursued in the first years of the century the foundation of the Werkbund in 1907 was a logical step for the politician. Of course, not all who joined the new organisation did so out of a commitment to Naumann's political and economic aims, nor can Naumann be given sole credit for setting it up,[40] but there was no mistaking his influence on the organisation when its first 'manifesto' appeared early in 1908. Written by Naumann himself, and published by *Die Hilfe*, *Deutsche Gewerbekunst* was a fifty page pamphlet which summarised the DWB's initial aims and intentions. Much of the text was taken up with attempts to define the essence of the new organisation:

> The Werkbund is not an employers' association by natural inclination, because it wants to attract artistically creative people from all company levels – including employees and workers – but it is in the nature of things that the employers will play a greater role than the workers. One could do worse, then, than to define the Werkbund . . . as an alliance of like-minded quality manufacturing enterprises.[41]

40. A well-documented confrontation between Hermann Muthesius and the 'Trade Association for the Economic Interests of the Arts and Crafts' is usually cited as the immediate background to the formation of the DWB. The so-called 'Muthesius Affair' flared up as a consequence of the perceived bias against producers of historically styled products at the 1906 Dresden exhibition, and was exacerbated by the 'provocative' appointment of Muthesius to a professorial chair in applied art at the Berlin 'Handelshochschule'. At the Trade Association's annual conference in June 1907 a group of progressive manufacturers demonstrated their support for Muthesius by walking out of the hall announcing their intention to form a new organisation of quality producers and designers. These firms duly made up the hard core of the Werkbund, when it was founded four months later. For details of the 'Muthesius Affair' see: J. Heskett, *Design in Germany 1870–1918*, London, 1986; and J. Campbell, *The German Werkbund*.

41. F. Naumann, *Deutsche Gewerbekunst*, Berlin, 1908, pp.29–30.

Elsewhere in the pamphlet Naumann compared the DWB to 'on the one hand a trade union' and on the other 'an industrial syndicate': 'the Werkbund is the trade union of the art-creators against those who corrupt the market'. He also saw a parallel with 'the attempts to make the idea of the German fleet more popular'.[42]

One of the principal themes in *Deutsche Gewerbekunst* was how one could restore 'the joy of work', because 'in the industrial age the nation which is able to generate the most satisfaction at work has the best prospect of attaining the creative leadership.' For this to be achieved, firms would have to ensure that 'the rise of the company is to the benefit of all concerned'[43]:

> Workers must be able to call the company 'our company'. Then they are interested not only in their wages but in the success of the company as a whole: in the treatment of valuable materials, in the use of the machines, in the increased output of the separate departments, in the flawless execution of the temporary work as well, in the co-operation of the different groups. The better the working spirit of a firm, the more likely it is that it will create a perfect product.[44]

Naumann, who wrote that if one treated a worker like a proletarian one could hardly complain if he then acted like one, warned the DWB member firms to respect the workers and their organisations:

> For the Werkbund member companies it should be a matter of course, and should not require special pressure from the Bund, that they do not dismiss the workers' organisations out of hand. This is ruled out anyway by the nature of the sort of businesses that are represented here, but if such a refusal to acknowledge any dealings with the unions should occur, it is my opinion that the Bund must exert a moral pressure and intervene with a warning. There is nothing less artistic than a deliberately antagonistic approach to the other people working in a company.[45]

On the question of workers' rights, Naumann saw a great difference between the attitude of the 'quality' manufacturers and that of heavy industry. Whereas a coal mine could pull in labour 'from Galicia or anywhere else', the quality manufacturer had no such 'reserve army' to call on. Indeed, the finer the product, the greater the skills required from the worker and the less easy he was to replace. Thus the quality manufacturer was not able to risk the sort of confrontational approach to labour that was common in heavy industry. For this reason, he believed,

42. F. Naumann, *ibid.*, p.44.
43. F. Naumann, *ibid.*, pp.31–32.
44. F. Naumann, *ibid.*, p.32.
45. F. Naumann, *ibid.*, p.39.

the trade unions had a much more stable footing amongst the skilled workers of quality manufacturing industry than in the 'primary' industries of coal, iron and steel. Although the DWB was to have no statutes on employment and trade union questions, Naumann insisted that 'the spirit of the organisation on labour questions must be emphatically liberal'.[46]

Naumann's liberal attitude towards the working class was the result of a series of long-term economic and political calculations. For Germany's economy to develop in the way he wished, there would have to be greatly increased domestic demand for quality products, and such an expanded market could only be created in conjunction with an improvement in living standards for the bulk of the population. As the producers and ultimate consumers of these goods, the workers had to be better trained and educated to appreciate quality. A poorly-fed, poorly-educated, and poorly-motivated work force would not be able to support a quality domestic market, let alone produce the sort of wares that could conquer and sustain foreign markets.

If workers' living standards improved and this was accompanied by a greater shop-floor involvement in company fortunes then the chances of the SPD dropping its revolutionary rhetoric would surely increase. Then the labour movement could begin to make a constructive contribution to domestic reform, perhaps as part of a new progressive *Volkspartei*. If, however, the confrontational attitudes of the coal barons – allied to the high grain tariffs of the agrarians – held sway, then the dangers of revolution would increase, the economy would be destabilised and Germany's chances of ever becoming a great power would be jeopardised.

The perceived threat of revolution from the left – and the variety of responses to it – coloured much of Naumann's writing. *Deutsche Gewerbekunst*, ostensibly a work on the DWB, also attempted to understand and explain the phenomenal growth of the SPD:

> What does the mass which follows socialism want? . . . On the one hand it strives for abstract things like education, culture, political influence and social respect, and on the other hand material things, such as better accommodation, fresh air and light . . . For either to come true however, it is essential that we turn ever more closely to the quality manufactures. It is only through these that the individual worker can achieve the personal values which make him a 'free' citizen, whilst we also attain the purchasing power which allows us to treat the mass of our people well . . .[47]

Naumann's strategy was not inspired by altruism, though the Christian values he preached in his youth did not disappear. He viewed any

46. F. Naumann, *ibid*., p.31.
47. F. Naumann, *ibid*., p.45.

concessions to the workers, be they financial or psychological, as sound investments for the future, rather than sacrifices for the sake of social peace. Above all, he knew that he would need the backing of the workers if he and his friends were ever to relieve the reactionary agrarians of political power. At the same time, however, he had to struggle to keep his own support interested in the prospects of achieving reform through party political activity.

An element within the DWB respected and endorsed Naumann's general aims but remained sceptical about the benefits of electoral involvement. The publisher Eugen Diederichs, an early disciple of Naumann who wished to 'liberate our political life from the party cliché and make the issues so accessible that the educated man is no longer disgusted by politics,'[48] typified many *Werkbündler* and *Heimatschützer* in his reluctance to recognise the existence of class conflict and class-based politics. Like many members of the Wilhelmine *Bildungsbürgertum* he preferred to entertain vague notions of restoring harmony to the *Volk* than to become involved in parliamentary 'horse-trading'.[49] Naumann acknowledged some of the problems in his 1908 essay, 'The Aesthete and Politics': 'He pays his taxes and expects to be governed in return. But in so doing he inadvertently becomes a helper for yesterday's men and a hindrance for the men of tomorrow.' He added: 'Present events in particular should make it quite clear to all who have open minds that there is a connection between creative art and creative politics.'[50]

At the DWB's first annual conference in June 1908 Naumann gave the keynote address, on the subject of 'The Ennobling of Manufacturing Work'. His speech, which reiterated the main themes of the *Qualitätsarbeit* strategy, was met with 'tumultuous, sustained and repeated applause'. The chairman's response was to close the sitting, adding, 'after this experience any further words are superfluous'.[51] Thereafter, Naumann's contributions to Werkbund conferences were invariably considered as centrepiece events. He was careful not to become too involved in the day-to-day debates and disputes of the organisation, adopting – in the words of Walter Gropius – 'a sort of moral leadership role'.[52] Friedrich Naumann's tireless espousal of 'quality work' naturally began to attract new supporters, many keen to back up his fine words with facts and figures, but also some who

---

48. E. Diederichs, *Leben und Werk*, Jena, 1936, p.195 (from a letter written in 1911).
49. For an account of Diederichs' political views see G. Stark, *Entrepeneurs of Ideology*, Chapel Hill, 1981, chp.3.
50. F. Naumann, 'Der ästhetische Mensch und die Politik', in *Werke*, vol.6, p.543.
51. 'Die Veredelung der gewerblichen Arbeit. Verhandlungen des DWB zu München am 11. und 12. Juli 1908', p.71.
52. W. Gropius in letter to K. Junghanns (1963) quoted by Junghanns in *Der Deutsche Werkbund*, p.175.

sought to appropriate his ideas for their own purposes.

Heinrich Waentig's *Economy and Art*, published in 1909, fell into the former category. As a professor of economics, and a DWB member, Waentig was all too conscious of the fact that Naumann seldom did the empirical groundwork that would be required if his ideas were to convince economists and politicians as well as artists and architects. His book attempted to support Naumann by analysing Germany's trade figures. The Reich had recorded a balance of trade deficit every year since Wilhelm II's accession to the throne, rising from 73 million Marks in 1888 to 1,895 million in 1907, with raw materials for industry accounting for half Germany's imports in 1907 (50.7%). The proportion of manufactured goods in German exports had risen dramatically, from 40.1% in 1873 to 70.2% in 1907, whilst exports of raw materials and semi-finished goods had declined from 34.4% to 21.9% in the same period. Exports of agricultural produce, food and meat had fallen even more markedly, from 25.5% of total exports in 1873 to just 7.9% in 1907.[53]

Waentig believed these figures indicated that in the foreseeable future only exports of manufactured goods could be expected to increase, and 'as has often been noted, Germany must turn her attention to the better quality products, since the newly emerging competition from countries with cheap labour and plenty of raw materials, will find it hardest to compete in this area.'[54] However, Waentig warned that one should not expect too much from high-quality 'art' goods, as the market was too small to make much impact on the overall trade figures.

A more detailed attempt to assess the economic value of *Qualitätsarbeit* was undertaken in 1909 by the 'Institut für exakte Wirtschaftsforschung' at Rostock University. The research programme, designed by Johannes Buschmann with the encouragement of the DWB, was based around a questionnaire, which was sent out to around 600 companies in a wide variety of fields. The companies were asked questions such as: 'On what does the quality of your products depend ?'; 'Is this quality production profitable, and if so, how profitable?'; and 'To what extent are artists involved in the design of your products?'[55] The companies were also asked to supply a wide range of statistics on the nature of their operations, which were then processed by the Buschmann team.

Their interim findings were presented at the DWB's second annual conference in Frankfurt, but it was clear that the researchers had made little headway in defining the nature and importance of *Qualitätsarbeit*. Irate

53. H. Waentig, *Wirtschaft und Kunst*, Jena, 1909, pp.406–408.
54. H. Waentig, *ibid.*, p.407.
55. See: DWB Jahresbericht 1908–09, p.16 (K.E.O. Archiv DWB/330–1). Verhandlungsbericht DWB 2. Jahresversammlung zu Frankfurt am Main .. 1909, pp.20–23 (Werkbund-Archiv).

Werkbund members queued up to highlight the shortcomings of the research, which had not been able to find a way of quantifying either the aesthetic or social components of a quality product. The DWB's Executive Secretary, Wolf Dohrn, was forced to intervene, and attempted to cool down the members by pointing out the tremendous difficulties involved in devising such an ambitious programme of study.[56] It came as no surprise, however, when the DWB subsequently dropped its interest in the Rostock research.

The difficulties in defining 'quality' were obvious, but this did not stop a variety of suggestions for the analysis and codification of quality goods. The foundation of an official *Materialprüfungsamt* at Großlichterfelde in 1904, where scientists and technicians could test material samples for strength, solidity and other characteristics, was seen by some as the model for a future test centre in which all manufactured products would be assessed for 'quality'. As Naumann pointed out, people had no difficulty in accepting the regular quality controls on milk, meat and other foodstuffs. The German *Farbenbuch*, compiled by the DWB in conjunction with the leading chemical companies Bayer and BASF – both Werkbund members – provided a list of permanent coloured dyes and paints of guaranteed quality. The Werkbund was also responsible for a series of guides on the characteristics and qualities of various materials: woods, precious stones, metals and so on. The tests and guides for material quality could not be matched in the aesthetic or social fields, but the decision of the DWB to allow member companies to use the Werkbund signet for advertising purposes – first introduced in conjunction with the Brussels World Exhibition of 1910 – found favour amongst many industrialists eager to demonstrate their own 'quality work'.

At the Werkbund's third annual conference, held in Berlin in June 1910, the Viennese *Hofrat* Adolf Vetter spoke on 'The Civic Importance of Quality Work'. He began with a look at the evolution of work and production, drawing attention to Ruskin's differentiation between 'work' and 'labour', and pointing out that the former was essentially the same concept as 'quality work'.[57] He then referred to the workshops of the AEG, which the DWB members had visited that afternoon, as a prime example of *Qualitätsarbeit* in action. His main message, however, was directed at the relationship between *Qualitätsarbeit* and the working class:

> I myself have no doubt that the Social Democrats could gain new strength and even greater prominence for the raising of the masses, if they began to take up the issue of the quality of work, in addition to such questions as higher wages,

---

56. Verhandlungsbericht 2. Jahresversammlung, ibid., p.22.
57. A. Vetter, 'Die staatsbürgerliche Bedeutung der Qualitätsarbeit', *Dürerbund Flugschriften*, no.87 (1911), p.8.

shorter working hours, and the recognition of their organisations . . . I really believe that the promotion of quality work can and will be an instrument for reconciliation in our turbulent time.[58]

Vetter's words recalled a rhetorical question posed by Robert Breuer at the first Werkbund conference in 1908: 'what would it mean if it was part of the dignity of labour not only to be politically and economically organised, but to constantly strive to raise the quality of German work?'[59]

The next major publication on *Qualitätsarbeit,* Heinrich Pudor's *Deutsche Qualitätsarbeit* – subtitled 'guidelines for a new development in German industry' – appeared in 1910, and was cold-shouldered by Naumann and the rest of the DWB. Pudor, who was closely linked to *Mittelstand* and *völkisch* circles and had written a series of books on naturism, had established a 'commission' to examine the theory of *Qualitätsarbeit* in 1909. Initially the DWB members Kerschensteiner, Müller and Hellwag had accepted invitations to join the commission, but they quickly withdrew once they had been 'suitably informed as to Pudor's character'. Later, Karl Ernst Osthaus also declined Pudor's advances.[60] These rebuttals did not stop Pudor using his book to claim the credit for inspiring much of the *Qualitätsarbeit* theory, which was repeated here in the new familiar form:

Made in Germany – therefore good, reliable, solid, no rubbish – that must be our motto. Just as the Renaissance produced such a blossoming of German art and science, so we must dig deep into the German spirit and soul to extract similar treasures for our trade and industry. The image of Bach or Dürer must become the badge of honour for German industry, and then the international market will open to us.[61]

Pudor, like Naumann, cited Germany's demographic explosion – the population increased by 855,000 in 1908, an annual growth rate of nearly 1.5% – as a major reason for a change in economic strategy. In the long-term, quality manufacturing offered the best prospects for absorbing the expanding work force:

The question of how we best feed our growing population is solved by refining our industry more and more, and by making ordinary manufacturing industry an *art industry* . . . But this 'aestheticisation' of industry can only occur when

58. A. Vetter, ibid., p.7.
59. 'Die Veredelung der gewerblichen Arbeit. Verhandlung des DWBs zu München am 11. und 12. Juli 1908', p.170.
60. Letter DWB to Karl Ernst Osthaus, 10 September 1909 (K.E.O. Archiv DWB 1/7).
61. H. Pudor, *Deutsche Qualitätsarbeit*, Leipzig, 1910, p.48.

German industrial products are fully trusted for their solidity and quality, giving the consumer a feeling of security.[62]

The economist Robert Pantzer, whose study on *Qualitätsarbeit* appeared in 1912, saw the eventual move of German industry towards greater reliance on first class manufactured goods as an inevitable consequence of the international division of labour. In addition to the cultural, climactic, and geographical reasons cited by Naumann, Pantzer believed ethnographic factors would play an important part in the future shape of the world economy, with certain races less suited to quality industrial production:

> When analysed closely, the competition from low-paid Asian workers in the world market appears not to be as dangerous as it is sometimes portrayed ... Experience has shown that these less civilised workers can only compete successfully in those areas where cruder and less complex articles are produced. Their intellectual and moral disposition is generally not sufficient to support anything better.[63]

Pantzer dismissed any suggestion that the apparent international division between 'raw material economies' and 'industrial economies' was not a permanent state of affairs. It had been pointed out that the primary producers of today could develop their own manufacturing industries tomorrow, but Pantzer cited Australia, Canada and Argentina as examples of countries which had neither the work force nor the climate to make this transition. The crucial factor in the international division of labour would be 'national characteristics', and in this regard Germany had nothing to fear:

> A certain superiority of the German race will probably remain for the foreseeable future in the general areas of hard work, staying power, strength, skill, inventiveness and good taste – it may even increase, although the levelling out process caused by modern transport and communications in this area should not be ignored.[64]

In the immediate pre-war years the emphasis of the *Qualitätsarbeit* discourse, both within and without the Werkbund, remained firmly on issues of international trade, and all thoughts of making industrial work a more rewarding experience – the social dimension of the *Qualitätsarbeit* theory – tended to be subsumed under a welter of trade statistics and

62. H. Pudor, *ibid.*, p.3.
63. R. Pantzer, *Zur Frage der Qualitätsverfeinerung oder Entfeinerung unseres Exports*, Berlin, 1912, p.60.
64. R. Pantzer, *ibid.*, p.63.

nationalist rhetoric. Naumann's three main contributions to the debate in these years also concentrated on the financial benefits of the strategy: 'Art and the National Economy' (address to the DWB conference, Vienna 1912); 'What does the Werkbund have to do with Trade?' (essay in DWB Yearbook 1913); and 'The Werkbund and the World Economy' (address to the DWB conference, Cologne 1914). Instead it was left to Helmuth Wolff, the head of the Office of Statistics in Halle, to remind Werkbund members of their full range of responsibilities. He told the DWB's fourth annual conference in Dresden (1911) that the organisation must seek reform in five areas, if it wished to make *Qualitätsarbeit* a reality. Wolff's five point plan for *Qualitätsarbeit* involved the creation of 'quality workplaces', 'quality cartels', 'quality middlemen', 'quality consumption' and, finally, legislation for quality. It was perhaps not surprising that some Werkbund supporters grew tired of what August Endell (1871–1925) dismissed as 'that wretched word "quality"'.[65] Nevertheless Wolff continued:

> For the quality workplaces, the exterior of the establishment, the management, and the workers must all satisfy certain requirements. The factory building, the works' courtyard, the machines, the store rooms, the internal transport system must all measure up to quality production. The management must be conducted impeccably, meeting the principles of both business and art. The workers must perform with a heightened sense of the joy of work, not just as the servants of machines but through the full use of their abilities . . .[66]

The actual impact of the DWB's *Qualitätsarbeit* strategy on industrial architecture is examined from a variety of perspectives over the coming chapters, which will investigate the 'quality workplace' in the context of industrial power struggles and economic rationalisation, as a form of advertising and as a means of achieving social reform. It is also most important to ascertain which companies chose to embrace the 'quality workplace', and for what reason. Firstly, however it is interesting to note that the 'Heilbronn connection' did not cease to function with the successful conclusion of Naumann's 1907 election campaign.

New Developments in Heilbronn

The relationships established or cemented in the course of that winter between Bruckmann and Naumann, Heuss and Jäckh, were at the heart

65. Endell made his remark at the DWB's 7th annual conference in Cologne on 4 July 1914. Printed in 'Die Werkbund-Arbeit der Zukunft . . . und Aussprache darüber', p.58.
66. H. Wolff, 'Die volkswirtschaftlichen Aufgaben des DWB', in Werkbund Yearbook, 1912, p.88.

of all DWB activity in the years to come. Admittedly, much of this activity was to take place hundreds of miles away from Heilbronn, as each man attempted to make his mark on the national stage, but the Werkbund's presence in the town was nevertheless maintained in other ways. Bruckmann ensured that the town's Chambers of Commerce and Handicraft both joined the Werkbund as corporate members. Other local industrialists, like the soap manufacturer Alfred Amann and the paper maker Carl Landerer joined the DWB, as did Johanna Rümelin, a member of the town's leading banking family. Rümelin also commissioned Hermann Muthesius to build a new villa for her in the town (c.1910). Bruckmann then managed to attract the Werkbund's first President, Theodor Fischer (1862–1938), to design the town's theatre (1911–13), after citizens had successfully raised over 600,000 Marks to cover the building costs. The value of the 'Heilbronn Connection' to the Werkbund was recognised at a special *Schwabentag*, held at the DWB's big Cologne exhibition in June 1914, but surprisingly, all subsequent Werkbund literature has ignored the town's crucial contribution to the movement.[67]

In 1908 the leading Heilbronn architect Emil Beutinger, who lived within fifty yards of both Bruckmann and Heuss, joined the DWB and soon he too became an important figure in the organisation, serving on a number of committees and founding the journal *Der Industriebau* in 1910. Beutinger, whose father was an engraver at Bruckmann & Sons, was a particularly close acquaintance of Peter Bruckmann.[68] This no doubt helped Beutinger in his campaign to become Mayor of Heilbronn in 1921, a post he held with distinction until his dismissal by the National Socialists in 1933. Beutinger was not a member of a political party, but identified with Naumann's political aims, and was backed in his election campaign by supporters of both the DDP and the SPD. In his major election speech he declared himself 'a democrat from inner conviction', convinced that 'only an educated working class can bring forth the level of achievement in our economy which is required for the recovery of German industry.'[69] His victory over a lawyer by 8,500 votes was seen as significant, for it was still comparatively rare for engineers and technicians to reach the premier post in German municipal government. In its obituary for Beutinger in 1957 the *Heilbronner Stimme* wrote:

67. The contribution of the Werkbund circle to Heilbronn is at least recognised in the town's street-naming policy, with Naumann, Jäckh, Heuss, Bruckmann and Beutinger all being honoured in this way.

68. According to Beutinger's son Erik (born 1906), Emil Beutinger knew Bruckmann 'very well'. Letter to the author, 7 Aug. 1989.

69. SA Heilbronn, Personal files: Beutinger – P 28/1. Quote from *Neckar Zeitung*, 9 July 1921.

It was he who far-sightedly freed the town from its tight historic girdle and who planned the wide through-roads. During his period of office the gas works were expanded, the abattoir was modernised, the main dairy was built and the water tower on the Wartburg was constructed.[70]

For the Nazi *Heilbronner Tagblatt* in 1933, however, he was nothing less than a 'municipal autocrat' and a 'typical representative of the Marxist-Democratic system.'[71]

The concentration of leading *Werkbündler* in Heilbronn made it a logical meeting place for the organisation's management organs. In October 1912, for instance, the executive and management committees of the DWB met at Heilbronn's town hall and later enjoyed the local *Herbstfeier*. Heilbronn was also selected as a conference centre by the Evangelical Social Congress and the Evangelical Workers' Unions, whose local branch secretary was one of Naumann's most loyal foot soldiers, Johannes Fischer (1880–1942). In 1911 Fischer and Naumann collaborated on a book entitled *As a Worker at the World Exhibition,* which purported to describe the impressions and emotions of a 'simple German worker' at the 1910 Brussels world exhibition. Fischer wrote of his pride when confronted with the German exhibition halls – designed by the DWB architects Peter Behrens, Martin Dülfer and Bruno Paul – but also of his disappointment that so few Germans could identify personally with the achievements on show. In his introduction Naumann attempted to place Fischer's gut-feelings in a political context:

> The Socialists have made many criticisms of the capitalist system and not without justification. But where they are wrong is to believe that by nationalising firms the problem would disappear from the world. Even in the biggest publically owned companies the individual is betrayed and sold, unless the individual knows something and is allowed to express it . . . All cultures based on slavery have finally gone to the wall because of the slave mentality. We must recognise the vital task before us, to regulate international communications, machine technology, and big business in such a way that the individual can perform his work with understanding and enjoyment.[72]

It was Ernst Jäckh, however, who could claim most credit for giving the 'Heilbronn Connection' a new lease of life. In 1907 Jäckh's sister Martha had married Hugo Borst (1881–1967), the business director of a major electrical component enterprise in nearby Stuttgart. The company

70. SA Heilbronn, Personal files: Beutinger – P28/2. Quote from *Heilbronner Stimme*, 24 Oct. 1957.
71. SA Heilbronn, Personal files: Beutinger – P28/2. Quote from *Heilbronner Tagblatt*, 24 June 1933.
72. F. Naumann preface to J. Fischer, *Als Arbeiter auf der Weltausstellung*, Munich, 1911.

had developed rapidly since the turn of the century under the shrewd tutelage of Borst's uncle Robert Bosch (1861–1942). Borst had two great interests – collecting works of modern art and studying new forms of industrial management. His duties at Bosch included devising the company's advertising strategy and commissioning artists for its poster campaigns. Meanwhile his uncle was not only an extremely rich man[73] with a growing reputation for generosity but a socially-aware employer and a manufacturer committed to quality production. In other words, both men were ideal candidates for Werkbund membership and once Jäckh had become Executive Secretary of the DWB in April 1912 he quickly ensured that the organisation's already impressive Swabian faction was enlarged by two. Bosch's contribution to the DWB and its campaigns – above all financial – has already been mentioned, and will be considered more fully in the next chapter.

As editor of the *Neckar Zeitung* Jäckh had also begun to develop a somewhat unlikely interest in the political affairs of Turkey; an interest cemented on a visit to that country in 1908–9, when he became caught up in the fortunes of the 'Young Turk' movement. On his return to Heilbronn, Jäckh wrote a 'Diary of the Young Turk Revolution' and began strenuous efforts to improve Germany's image in the Balkans and the Near East. He was particularly concerned that 'to the outside world Germany appears like a Prussian spiked helmet'.[74] It was also on his Near East tour that Jäckh first met the diplomat Alfred von Kiderlen-Wächter (1852–1912), another Swabian who was soon to become State Secretary in the *Reich* Foreign Office. Kiderlen, who had close links to the Württemberg Democrats, was an important 'contact' for Jäckh and the Werkbund; it was he who enthusiastically took up the suggestion of the *Legationsrat* Edmund Schüler that Peter Behrens should be entrusted with the design of the new German embassy in St. Petersburg.[75]

In 1911 the town hall in Heilbronn was the venue for the proclamation of a friendship pact between Germany and Turkey, signed to mark the visit of a party of Turkish notables to the *Reich*. The visit was organised by Jäckh in conjunction with the Foreign Office and was financed by leading German banks. Jäckh also established a German-Turkish Union to further improve relations between the two states. This organisation was housed

73. In 1913 Bosch was the most highly paid individual in Württemberg, with annual income of around four million Marks. At this time his personal fortune amounted to some twenty million Marks, thanks largely to the commercial success of the patented Bosck sparkplug. Figures from C.-M. Allmendinger, *Struktur, Aufgabe und Bedeutung der Stiftungen von Robert Bosch und seiner Firma*, Stuttgart, 1977, p.45.

74. E. Jäckh, *Der goldene Pflug*, p.98.

75. See T. Buddensieg, 'Die Kaiserlich Deutsche Botschaft in St. Petersburg von Peter Behrens', in M. Warnke (ed.), *Politische Architektur in Europa*, Cologne, 1984.

in the same Berlin apartment block as the Werkbund headquarters, which had moved to Berlin when Jäckh became its Executive Secretary. Jäckh's 60-room block on the Schöneberger Ufer thus became the nerve centre of a multifarious political and publishing empire, which by the early war years included the *Deutsche Gesellschaft 1914* (a political dining club), the Working Committee for *Mitteleuropa*, the journal *Deutsche Politik* (edited by Jäckh, Rohrbach and Philip Stein) and a wartime pamphlet series entitled *Der Deutsche Krieg*. Other Jäckh enterprises later to share rooms with the DWB included the German Association for the League of Nations and the 'Orient Institute'; all funded by Robert Bosch, the most generous German benefactor of his day. In 1919 Jäckh's 'residence' also witnessed the birth of the DDP, the party in which all the Werkbund leaders were to find their new republican home.

Bureaucratic centralisation was not the only way in which Jäckh tried to bring together his many and varied activities. He attempted, for instance, to boost exports of German *Qualitätsarbeit* to Turkey by introducing the DWB's *Deutsches Warenbuch* to influential Turkish consumers. The culmination of such efforts came with ambitious plans to build a huge 'House of Friendship' in the Islamic quarter of Istanbul, which would incorporate a theatre, library, club and exhibition rooms 'to demonstrate to the Turkish people, German character in science and art'.[76] The leading DWB architects – including Behrens, Gropius, Poelzig, Bonatz and Taut – were invited to submit designs in a closed competition, eventually won by German Bestelmeyer. The building was largely financed by the Bosch millions and a stone-laying ceremony was to be accompanied by a week of lectures from prominent Germans, including Friedrich Naumann. The ceremony was eventually performed in April 1917 by the Kaiser himself, accompanied by the Werkbund members Jäckh, Bosch and Schacht, together with other Naumannites like Erich Schairer (1887–1956, Heuss's successor as the editor of the *Neckar Zeitung* and later an assistant to Walther Rathenau) and Gottfried Traub of *Die Hilfe*. The worsening military and economic situation in Europe, however, ensured that building work was first shelved and then abandoned. After the war the funds intended for the 'House of Friendship' were transferred to the German Association for the League of Nations.

It has been suggested that Jäckh's memoirs are unreliable, since they appear to have been written with the sole intention of claiming an unfeasibly large role for their author in twentieth century history.[77] Certainly Jäckh was a vain and verbose name-dropper, but his gift for

76. E. Jäckh, *Der goldene Pflug*, p.323.
77. K. Wegner, 'Linksliberalismus im wilhelminischen Deutschland und in der Weimarer Republik', *Geschichte und Gesellschaft*, vol.4 (1978), p.127.

organisational efficiency and knack of attracting wealthy sponsors can hardly be doubted. It was for these talents, of course, that he was approached by the DWB to run its affairs in the first place. From 1912 Jäckh not only oversaw a considerable improvement in the Werkbund's financial position, but presided over a marked shift in the emphasis of the *Qualitätsarbeit* strategy, from the reform of the workplace to the conquest of the world market. As we have seen, both were integral elements of the *Qualitätsarbeit* concept, but it was the latter strand which was dominant between 1912 and 1914.

Hermann Muthesius was amongst the first to reflect this change in interest. Addressing the Werkbund's 1914 conference in Cologne, Muthesius referred to the new architectural forms which would be demanded by trade and industry in the twentieth century and stressed that these firms would be international in character:

> Now, the nation which is able to find these new forms of expression first will set the tone for all future developments. It will take over the leadership in the shaping of style and be victorious across the world, because with the internationalisation of our lives a certain uniformity in architectural forms across the globe will become manifest . . . It can be assumed that those forms which have been developed in the German movement for . . . industrial, commercial and transport buildings will also become the world forms. Good new hotels, new ships, department stores, schools and hospitals across the world are already being fitted out in approximately the same way, and the industrial buildings of America share the same spirit as those of Germany.[78]

By 1915, and the publication of Muthesius's 'The Future of the German Form' in Jäckh's *Der Deutsche Krieg* pamphlet series, the argument had become more chauvinistic:

> This 'German Form' will be more than just the term used in patriotic elation, it will become the world form. Today the ascendancy of the German peoples on this Earth is confirmed . . . It is not just a matter of ruling the world, it means more than just financing the world, or educating it, or swamping it with goods and products. It is a question of determining its appearance. Only when a nation accomplishes this act can it be said truly to stand at the summit of the world: Germany must be that nation.[79]

Muthesius's personal contribution to the German war effort included chairing the '*Vaterlandsdank*' appeal committee, which called on the public for donations of silver and gold. By March 1916 200,000 Marks

---

78. H. Muthesius in 'Die Werkbund-Arbeit der Zukunft', p.46.
79. H. Muthesius, 'Die Zukunft der deutschen Form', *Der Deutsche Krieg: Politische Flugschriften*, no.50 (1915), p.35.

worth of silver and 600,000 Marks worth of gold had been collected, and donors were each rewarded with an iron ring designed by Behrens and manufactured by Krupp.[80]

Muthesius was by no means the only Werkbund member to write a pamphlet for the *Deutsche Krieg* series: Naumann, Jäckh, Paquet, Schacht, Rohrbach, and Gustav Stresemann can all be found in the list of authors who penned these fifty-Pfennig papers. Jäckh's other major wartime publication, the weekly *Deutsche Politik*, was equally dominated by Werkbund members and Naumannites. In 1916, for example, Muthesius wrote on *Der Werkbundgedanke. Seine Grundlagen*, in which he argued that the ideas behind the movement had quickly become 'part of the common knowledge of the German people'.[81]

Another Jäckh enterprise, the occasional series of essays entitled *Weltkultur und Weltpolitik* which he published in conjunction with the Institute for Cultural Research in Vienna, included a notable essay on the DWB by the museum director Walter Riezler. *Die Kulturarbeit des Deutschen Werkbundes* appeared in 1916 – the year in which this remarkable cultural offensive reached a peak – and gave a wide-ranging review of the organisation's origins and prospects. He declared that the future duty of the DWB would be to 'serve the German fatherland and the spirit of the age, by organising all the forces available to it.'[82] Riezler drew great encouragement from the decision of the British Ministry of Trade to establish a 'British Werkbund': the Design and Industries Association, which was founded in May 1915 and did not attempt to hide its debt to the German model.

The keynote speech at the DWB's eighth annual conference, held at Bamberg in June 1916, was for once not given by Friedrich Naumann but by one of his most ardent followers, Ernst Jäckh. The previous year had seen the publication of Naumann's best-selling contribution to the *Mitteleuropa* debate, now Jäckh took up the theme himself in a lecture on 'Werkbund und Mitteleuropa'. The DWB's desire to secure new markets for German *Qualitätsarbeit* ensured that it had always showed a keen interest in the *Mitteleuropa* discourse. Moreover, Jäckh combined his Werkbund duties with the chairmanship of the 'Working Committee for *Mitteleuropa*'. He was quick to dispel the suspicion, however, that the topic of his paper was merely the result of a coincidental *Personalunion*. In fact, he argued, the DWB and the *Mitteleuropa* concept were nothing less than different manifestations of the same principle, that of the German or

80. G. Pollack, 'Die gesellschafts- und kulturpolitische Funktion des DWB', p.123.

81. H. Muthesius, 'Der Werkbundgedanke. Seine Grundlagen', in *Deutsche Politik. Wochenschrift für Welt- und Kulturpolitik*, 3 March 1916, p.459.

82. W. Riezler, 'Die Kulturarbeit des Deutschen Werkbundes', *Weltkultur und Weltpolitik*, no.7 (1916), p.11.

'organic' way.[83]

In their wartime writings Jäckh and Naumann were anxious to differentiate their concept of *Mitteleuropa* from both the unsubtle power-lust of the Pan-German League and the heavy-handed imperialism of Germany's enemies. The task that lay ahead of Germany was rather to convince the peoples of *Mitteleuropa* that their own best interests lay in closer co-operation with the *Reich*. This could not be achieved if Germany's image abroad was that of the spiked helmet and the Prussian military machine, but would require a more subtle promotion of German cultural and technological achievements.[84] The Werkbund was the ideal organisation to spearhead such a propaganda offensive. Plans for the 'House of Friendship' in Istanbul, various exhibitions in neutral countries (Denmark, Switzerland), the encouragement of Werkbund branches in Austria, Hungary, Holland, Switzerland and Scandinavia, and the widespread distribution of DWB publications overseas, must all be viewed in this context. It is difficult to gauge the mood of the rank and file DWB membership towards their leadership's active involvement in geopolitics – the Werkbund possessed no forum for ordinary members to voice an opinion on policy matters – but few who had followed Naumann's career since the 1890s could have been surprised by the zeal with which he and his acolytes threw themselves into the machinations of power politics after 1914. This did not mean, however, that the architectural aspect of the *Qualitätsarbeit* strategy – the 'quality workplace' – was lost altogether, and even at the height of the 'war aims' debate Emil Beutinger was moved to write:

> The importance of 'quality work' in our bid to conquer world markets is being stressed ever more strongly nowadays. This will only be possible, however, when factory districts show a different physiognomy than is often the case today; when the workers themselves are able to perceive that the clarity, cleanliness and excellence of all industrial plants is being guided by a sense of beauty, which shuns everything that is ugly and unfunctional.[85]

The next chapter investigates which German industrial firms took this message to heart.

83. E. Jäckh, 'Werkbund und Mitteleuropa', p.6.
84. Efforts to present a positive and progressive view of Germany in the states of *Mitteleuropa* became known in the Naumann circle as 'ethical imperialism', and were seen as vital if the damaging myths of 'sabre-rattling' German barbarians were to be dispelled. The phrase 'ethical imperialism' was first coined by the DWB member Paul Rohrbach, the Naumannites' principal foreign policy expert and a regular contributor to *Die Hilfe*. See R. Opitz, *Ideologie und Praxis des deutschen Sozialliberalismus 1917–33*, Cologne, 1973, p.44.
85. E. Beutinger, 'Die künstlerische Gestaltung der Imdustriebauten', *Dürerbund Flugschriften*, no.154, p.30.

5

German Industry and the 'Quality Workplace': Company Responses to the New Industrial Architecture

The avant-garde composer Edgard Varèse (1883–1965) once argued that it would be misleading to portray progressive artists as people 'ahead of their time'; it was rather a case, he believed, of the public in general living permanently 'behind the times'. This neat observation cannot, however, fully explain the process of innovation in architecture, the most public and prosaic of the arts, where members of the general population are involved in every stage of the creative process. Buildings, far more than musical, visual or literary compositions, are team efforts, dependent upon the interaction of a whole series of individuals and agencies, often far from 'artistic' in temperament and outlook.

If an architect is to translate his paper visions into bricks and mortar he requires, above all else, the active backing of a client. An architect without a client – be it an individual, institution or corporation – has little chance of making an impact, unless critical recognition arrives posthumously, as it did for the Italian futurist Antonio Sant'Elia. Clients can, of course, be a mixed blessing for the architect. A contract is always accompanied by another person's financial, functional and aesthetic specifications, which can present the innovative or experimental architect with particular problems. If, however, the adventurous architect is able to find a sympathetic patron, willing to invest trust and money in his ideas, then much can be achieved. Indeed, without the support of such people, creative change in the field of architecture could never be possible.

Art history can sometimes give the impression that a client's involvement in the building process is limited to the imposition of short-sighted budget constraints or misguided interference in the sacred act of creation, but this is in fact only half the story. From the initial choice of a particular architect onwards, the patron is a vital element in the architectural equation. The architects organised under the Werkbund banner were unusually fortunate to be offered the chance to put some of their aesthetic and social theories to the test; unlike their Heimatschutz colleagues, leading DWB architects were seldom short of commissions from commerce and industry. Indeed, the swift adoption of Werkbund ideas by influential sections of the economic and political mainstream is surely one of the crucial differences between the DWB and a host of other artistic or cultural reform movements active in early twentieth century Europe. The creative achievements of Behrens, Gropius, Poelzig *et. al.* in the field of industrial architecture would simply not have been possible without the encouragement of their commercial clients and political supporters. As Thomas Nipperdey noted in *Wie das Bürgertum die Moderne fand*

> The rise of modern architecture in Germany, which was an event of universal significance and – in view of the long-established conventionality of German architecture an astonishing occurrence, required the awakening of a bourgeoisie which was specifically modern and industrial in character . . . Only when artistic awakening and bourgeois awakening are taken together can the astonishing fact be explained that in the first decade of this century Germany – which, with the exception of music, had hitherto been rather traditional in the arts – suddenly leapt into the vanguard of modernism.[1]

The search for modern and dignified industrial buildings undertaken by the Werkbund architects was only one means by which Wilhelmine architects endeavoured to find an appropriate physiognomy for the world of industry. As we have seen, other architects persevered with the text book retrospection of historicism, or attempted to revive vernacular traditions in the name of Heimatschutz. The simultaneous pursuit of such a wide variety of approaches cannot be explained in terms of the architectural profession's internal schisms alone. Of course, architectural practitioners in Wilhelmine Germany were divided by a host of stylistic, generational and personal conflicts, but just as significant were the contrasting demands made on architects by the companies and institutions which commissioned them. This chapter turns the spotlight from the architects and the activists to the clients. It examines the motivation of industrial companies in their choice of architects or architectural styles. In particular, it looks at those companies which endorsed the reform ideas of the Werkbund and the concepts of 'quality work' and the 'quality workplace', either by joining the organisation or commissioning its architects for industrial building projects.

The specific circumstances surrounding the commissioning of an architect is seldom documented in company archives, often leaving both the method of selection and terms of engagement as matters of conjecture. Whilst it is just about possible to ascertain who built what, where and when – though even after 1900 this has its difficulties – any discussion of why

1. T. Nipperdey, *Wie das Bürgertum die Moderne fand*, Berlin, 1988, p.85 and p.73.

companies chose to work with a particular architect inevitably involves an element of speculation. Similarly, the source material does not allow an in depth assessment of the client's personal or corporate contribution to the details of particular building projects. Nevertheless by examining the available evidence it should at least be possible to throw more light upon the client's most important contribution to the building process: the initial choice of architect, and in particular the choice of DWB architects rather than more conventional building practitioners. This chapter then seeks to explain these findings by placing them in the wider context of the fundamental divisions which existed within the German industrial sector in the early decades of the twentieth century.

Amongst the enterprises active in the Werkbund were several firms controlled by men who professed a strong personal affinity for the social, economic and political ideas of Friedrich Naumann. Although some of the first industrialists to be associated with Naumann's ideas, including Abbé and Rösicke, were dead by 1907, a new generation of left liberal manufacturers soon emerged to take their place. The most prominent of these were the head of the Deutsche Werkstätten, Karl Schmidt-Hellerau, and the Heilbronn silverware manufacturer Peter Bruckmann. Both men were founder members of the DWB in October 1907. Schmidt-Hellerau, who had a finger in every *Lebensreform* pie, from the garden city movement to Heimatschutz and the Werkbund, was a close personal friend of Naumann, and was even able to persuade the politician to endorse Hellerau furniture in print.[2]

Meanwhile, as we have seen, Peter Bruckmann had first fallen under Naumann's spell during the dramatic 1907 Reichstag election campaign. Bruckmann was himself later elected to the Württemberg Landtag as the FVP member for Heilbronn and eventually became leader of the DDP in the state. He became chairman of the Werkbund in 1909 and was for a while personally responsible for keeping the organisation afloat. In 1911–12, for instance, he had to make a 6,000 Mark interest-free loan to cover a growing shortfall between the DWB's income and expenditure.[3] Bruckmann was also an important figure in the intellectual life of the movement. His lecture at the AGM of the Association of Württemberg Industrialists in January 1914, entitled 'The German Werkbund and Industry', was hailed as a definitive statement of the organisation's origins and aims, and as such

---

2. Naumann wrote 'Der deutsche Stil', which Schmidt-Hellerau initially wanted to be called 'Das deutsche Möbel', for the Deutsche Werkstätten (ZStA Potsdam Nachlaß Naumann 90 Na 3–4 p.145). Naumann held 2,000 Marks worth of shares in the Garden City project launched by Karl Schmidt-Hellerau (ZStA Potsdam Nachlaß Naumann 90 Na 3–136 pp.1–3).
3. 'Haushaltsplan für das Geschäftsjahr 1912–13' DWB Accounts in K.E.O. Archiv DWB 1/324.

was widely distributed in a special offprint. His contribution to the DWB was recognised in 1920, when he was awarded an honorary doctorate by Aachen University for his 'services to German *Qualitätsarbeit*'.

Bruckmann's pioneering support for works' councils is said to have earned him the nicknames *Betriebsräte Bruckmann* and 'Red Peter' from other local employers, who fought the introduction of 'industrial democracy' in their own enterprises. Writing in the *Heilbronner Chronik* of 4 April 1922 the Christian trade unionist and Naumannite Johannes Fischer addressed the theme of 'Peter Bruckmann and the Werkbund':

> From the beginning Bruckmann has had a fine psychological awareness of the consequences of the evolution of work on those who carry it out. He has always praised the invigorating effect of a working mentality and purpose which goes beyond mere questions of income, and where the personal-creative drive can at the same time find a satisfying and humane expression.[4]

In Bruckmann's own words, the 'artistic and commercial employees must shake hands: all those involved in an enterprise, from the "temps" and the last apprentice upwards, must be filled with joy and a sense of participation, in order to achieve good work.'[5] These archetypal Werkbund ideas could not, however, find a contemporary form of expression in the architecture of the Bruckmann & Sons factory, as the plant had undergone an extensive expansion at the turn of the century and did not require further enlargement before 1918. Nevertheless DWB members were closely involved in product design for the company and it was said of the buildings – which no longer stand – that 'the generous and extensive planning of the workshops was a gamble for which substantial financial sacrifices had to be made. Those in the know had considered the project risky'.[6]

Another prominent DWB industrialist with a long-standing interest in Naumann's political career was the Hanoverian biscuit manufacturer Hermann Bahlsen. We know of Bahlsen's 'feeling for Friedrich Naumann and his National Socialism' from one of the company's *Festschriften*,[7] though the extent of his support is not recorded. Certainly Bahlsen was committed enough to send free copies of Naumann's journal *Die Hilfe* to all his employees serving at the Front in 1914. *Die Hilfe*'s religious correspondent, and FVP parliamentarian, Gottfried Traub, responded with

---

4. SA Heilbronn, Personal files; Bruckmann – P 47/1. J. Fischer, 'Peter Bruckmann und der Werkbund' in *Heilbronner Chronik*, 4 April 1922.

5. P. Bruckmann quoted by Otto Haupt in 'Geheimrat Dr.Dr. Peter Bruckmann – Heilbronn. Ein Pionier der Wirtschaft, Politik und Kunst. Die Ansprachen bei der Gedenkstunde anläßlich seines 100. Geburtstages am 13. Januar 1965 im Großen Ratsaal der Stadt Heilbronn', pp.14–15.

6. Oberbürgermeister Meyle, Heilbronn, ibid., pp.5–6.

7. *H. Bahlsens Keksfabrik 1889–1964*, Hanover, 1963, p.11.

a personal letter to the company's war journal *Leibniz Feldpost* in 1916, in which he exclaimed 'how often I've wanted to write a small contribution for your newspaper!'[8] More significantly, Bahlsen's weekly peacetime publication, the *Leibniz Blätter*, carried frequent articles strongly Naumannite in tone and content. The articles, generally written by the personnel manager Martha Hohmeyer (1889–1961), addressed a broad spectrum of ethical, cultural and social issues, usually with a tendency to lapse into the moralising mode much favoured by Naumann's supporters. In June 1912, for instance, Hohmeyer wrote:

> Humane thinking – which means to 'live and let live', or to be liberal towards those who are less blessed with material things or have less power than one's self – is something which is being increasingly lost to our time. Socially and politically, this is the greatest danger! Today everyone wants to rule over everyone else and in so doing people forget that 'to rule' does not mean to exercise power but to delegate power![9]

A year later she argued:

> We must not feel driven by our work, but must drive the work ourselves. We cannot let work master our lives, we must master the work ourselves. People should be motivated to work harder of their own volition, since for us the value of work lies in the free will with which one tackles a task.[10]

Hermann Bahlsen was himself the probable author of a lead article in the 1 June 1912 issue of the *Leibniz Blätter*, on the theme of 'Education for Beauty', in which he discussed the concept of 'art for life':

> Art for life should not only be practised in one's hours of leisure or enjoyment. The whole point is that its spirit should permeate through work and thus make work a joy for people. The environment in which a person works and the quality of the items he is involved with are truly not irrelevant. From a cultural point of view a great deal can be achieved here, if good will is present in those areas where it is practicable to spread beauty. And the person who understands how to enjoy beauty, and lets it take effect on his senses, is a happy person![11]

We have already seen how these ideas were reflected in the new production and administration buildings designed by the DWB architect Karl Siebrecht in 1910–11, and the generous social welfare facilities they housed. The opening of the Hanover factory complex was undoubtedly a

---

8. 'Ein Brief von Pfarrer Traub', in *Leibniz Feldpost*, 15 Oct. 1916, p.3. (Bahlsen-Archiv).

9. 'Menschlich denken', in *Leibniz Blätter*, 15 June 1912, p.2. (Bahlsen-Archiv).

10. 'Persönliches Leben', in *Leibniz Blätter*, 9 Aug. 1913, p.2. (Bahlsen-Archiv).

11. 'Erziehung zur Schönheit', in *Leibniz Blätter*, 1 June 1912, p.1. (Bahlsen-Archiv).

major landmark in the history of the Bahlsen company – a firm only founded in July 1889 but already a market leader in the biscuit and wafer trade by 1914. The company's rapid rise was largely the result of Hermann Bahlsen's far-sighted plan to introduce British-style biscuits to the German market; an idea born during a five year sojourn in England during the 1880s. It may also have been in Great Britain that Bahlsen formed his benevolently paternalistic managerial style, which was at times reminiscent of the great Victorian confectioners Rowntree and Cadbury. Bahlsen certainly benefited from good industrial relations throughout the Wilhelmine period, despite the company's general hostility to trade union membership amongst its workers. Hermann Bahlsen considered both labour and employers' associations unnecessary and divisive. He rarely mixed socially with other manufacturers and refused all titles, turning down the chance of becoming a *Kommerzienrat* on more than one occasion.

The industrialist who was to become the DWB's principal benefactor was also an admirer of Friedrich Naumann's political vision. Robert Bosch, like Bahlsen a philanthropic patriarch and a self-made man, held a dominant position in his own highly successful company. Having spent his *Wanderjahre* in the workshops of Great Britain and North America, Bosch established a small electrical repair business at Stuttgart in 1886. As a skilled mechanic with an interest in electrical technology Bosch was able to build up a steady trade, making and repairing gadgets to order, but it was only when he decided to specialise in the production of motor ignition systems that the business really took off. After several changes of address in the 1890s, Bosch and his 45 employees moved in 1901 to purpose-built premises, erected in the back garden of a house Bosch had purchased on the edge of Stuttgart's old town.

The new building, one of the first in Württemberg to make use of reinforced concrete, was built with Robert Bosch's critical eye supervising every stage of the planning and construction process: he even made a special visit to Strasbourg to study early examples of reinforced concrete technology in action. Bosch's suspicion of academic architects, whom he believed to be guilty of neglecting the functional and hygienic aspects of building for the sake of fancy historicist façades, became well known. His 'ambition to be involved in the creation of model buildings', in which light and airy rooms and a logical layout were to be more important than the 'aesthetic formalism' of the academies, dates from this time, according to his biographer Theodor Heuss.[12] In later life Bosch took wry satisfaction from an invitation to become an honorary member of the Akademie für das Bauwesen.

12. T. Heuss, *Robert Bosch. Leben und Leistung*, Stuttgart, 1946, pp.141–142 and pp.201–203.

The first major customers for Bosch's magneto ignition system were manufacturers of stationary engines, but the automobile industry, developing both in Württemberg and further afield, became increasingly important to the company, as the Bosch technicians steadily improved the quality and reliability of their products. By 1906 – the year in which the company's 100,000th magneto ignition was produced – the work force had grown to a total of 562 blue- and white-collar employees. Like Hermann Bahlsen, Bosch's principal talent lay in the ability to see a gap in the market and to exploit it with a quality product, although both businesses were undoubtedly blessed with bountiful good fortune too. The similarities did not stop there, for Bosch was also something of a maverick industrialist, who long ignored the employers' associations and supported both the land reform movement and the campaign for homeopathic medicine.

The decade before the Great War was a time of uninterrupted growth and huge profits for Bosch. The work force expanded dramatically, passing 4,700 in 1914, and the product range was diversified to include headlamps and other car components. In addition to the local automobile producers, such as Daimler and Benz (both DWB members), Bosch was also able to supply foreign manufacturers like Fiat of Italy. Indeed, by 1914 88% of Bosch products were sold abroad. The Bosch factory spread inexorably, first onto neighbouring plots and then over a number of new sites scattered throughout the Stuttgart area, but on each occasion Bosch was present to ensure that the quality of the working environment would meet his strict specifications. The man in charge of building for Bosch was Gottlob Honold, an engineer with an 'inherent feeling for form' who gave his structures 'concise but convincing contours'.[13] Together they pioneered the introduction of air-conditioning systems and other technological innovations to ensure the best possible environment for the company's workers.

For all their similarities, and their shared conviction that 'the quality of the product is largely dependent on the conditions in which its makers have to work',[14] Bosch and Bahlsen had fundamentally different conceptions of the 'quality workplace'. Bosch was sceptical about the practical benefits 'art' could bring to shop-floor workers and certainly had no intention of hanging oil paintings on the walls of his Stuttgart factory. As an engineer Bosch despised any attempt to disguise or 'prettify' the true nature of a product or a building. Nevertheless his commitment to good materials and quality products was sufficient to override his lingering suspicion of architects. In 1912 Bosch joined the DWB, following an

13. T. Heuss, *ibid.*, p.609.
14. C. Matschoß (ed.), *Robert Bosch und sein Werk*, 1931, p.52.

approach by his Swabian compatriot Ernst Jäckh. Thereafter he regularly preached the virtues of *Sachlichkeit*, be it in architecture, product design, business or personal relationships. Indeed, an *unbedingtes Echtheitsgefühl* was for one observer the cornerstone of Bosch's whole life-work.[15]

Bosch was at times critical of what he considered to be the artistic excesses of the Werkbund – on a visit to the DWB's Weißenhof estate in 1927 he is supposed to have asked 'what are my honest products doing in your madhouse?'[16] – but Bosch's faith in the social and political role of the organisation was unshakeable. After a contented childhood in a rural Swabian family with strong liberal-democratic traditions, Bosch's apprentice years in the sweaty and cramped conditions of British and American machine shops were enough to convince him of the labour movement's legitimate role in the struggle for higher wages and better working conditions. As Bosch himself once put it:

> I was brought up a democrat. I worked as a mechanic and grew up as a man of the people. The socialist movement, which developed so strongly and confidently in the 1870s, exerted a powerful influence on me. The bourgeoisie, in its fear of socialism, became increasingly unable to see what was justifiable about it . . . In my despair at the bourgeoisie I sympathised with the socialist party.[17]

Bosch continued to consider himself a 'socialist' during the boom years of his own highly profitable business. Despite arguments with his neighbour and acquaintance, the SPD theoretician Karl Kautsky, over the validity of the Marxist 'Law of Surplus Value', and despite growing despair at the dogmatism of the SPD Left, Bosch refused to abandon his youthful ideals. In 1918, for instance, he advocated the benefits of *Kultursozialismus* and in 1921 he went as far as to claim, 'up until now I have always voted socialist'.[18] Whether this is strictly accurate has since been questioned; Allmendinger suggests that at election time Bosch was in fact a 'floating voter' between the SPD and the south German Democrats.[19] In answer to a wartime questionnaire, however, he left no doubt as to the colour of his politics, writing down the single word '*naumännisch*'.[20] Bosch proceeded to demonstrate what Heuss calls his 'respectful friendship' for Naumann

15. C. Matschoß (ed.), *ibid.*, p.9.
16. T. Heuss, *Robert Bosch*, p.703.
17. C. Matschoß (ed.), *Robert Bosch*, p.18.
18. R. Bosch, 'Lebenserinnerungen', unpublished 1921 manuscript, quoted by J. Mulert, 'Erfolgsbeteiligung und Vermögensbildung der Arbeitnehmer bei der Firma Robert Bosch zwischen 1886 und 1945', in *Tradition*, vol.30 (1985), p.4.
19. C.-M. Allmendinger, *Struktur, Aufgabe und Bedeutung der Stiftungen von Robert Bosch*, Stuttgart, 1977, p.85.
20. T. Heuss, *Robert Bosch*, p.313.

by using his war profits to finance a whole series of Naumannite enterprises, of which the DWB was only one.

Bosch's opinions on a wide range of issues were clearly very different from those associated with the 'Coal Barons' or the great steel industrialists of the time. For the right wing newspapers, like the *Post*, he was a figure of ridicule, a 'paid-up comrade' and a 'social fanatic'. Not surprisingly, Bosch rarely mixed socially with other industrialists and also made a point of not fraternising with the 'officer class', declining the title *Kommerzienrat* because he had no wish to become a notional 'advisor to the Crown'. He despised the Kaiser and 'Prussian values', which he compared unfavourably with those of the Swabians; the Bosch works could never have flourished in Berlin, he used to say.

His feeling for the labour movement – he was one of the first employers to recognise May Day as a public holiday and gave financial support to left-leaning publications such as the *Schwäbische Tagwacht* and the *Sozialistische Monatshefte* – inevitably marked out 'Red Bosch' as a rather different breed of industrialist. The contrast was nowhere more apparent than in Bosch's conciliatory attitude to the company work force. Whereas the Ruhr industrialists sought to control their workers through measures such as tied accommodation, employment 'Black Lists' and the like, 'Father Bosch' attempted to secure industrial peace by appealing to his workers' hearts, minds and pockets.

This did not mean, of course, that the Bosch works were run as a charity or friendly society. The Bosch company was in the extremely fortunate position of holding a near monopoly in the supply of a product in great demand. If it wished to meet the growing orders it had little option but to attract and maintain a large, skilled and contented work force. In the words of Robert Bosch's most famous dictum, 'I don't pay high wages because I have lots of money. I have lots of money because I pay high wages'. Large wage bills could in any case be passed on to customers, without threatening Bosch's market position, but Bosch was also aware of the long-term economic and social benefits that could be gained from an increasing number of wealthy consumers. An essay by Jürgen Mulert, which analyses the wage and profit-sharing policies of the company, reaches the conclusion that Bosch's wages were indeed amongst the highest in the Stuttgart area, but they declined in relative terms after World War One, as the company's dominant market position was challenged.[21]

Bosch followed in the footsteps of Freese and Abbé by reducing the working-hours of his employees, introducing the nine-hour day in 1894 and the eight-hour day for all workers on 1 August 1906. Once again, the prime motivation was a pragmatic calculation of the company's best

21. J. Mulert, 'Erfolgsbeteiligung', p.20.

interests rather than vague idealism, but the move proved popular with all concerned. Moreover, the Bosch work force faced no restrictions on trade union membership, with around 95% of employees unionised. Indeed, by the mid-1900s the works had become something of a 'closed shop' for the German Metalworkers Union. Even so, the working life at Bosch was far from easy, with shop-floor employees having to meet strict piecework rates and disciplinary regulations. As the left liberal *Frankfurter Zeitung* put it in 1913, Bosch's industrial relations policy was 'Social, but not Social Democratic':

> Bosch has introduced social, but not socialist, reforms in his enterprise, such as shorter working hours etc., and he generously supports every culturally progressive endeavour. However if anyone draws from this the conclusion that Bosch is a Social Democrat, he must have no idea that it is perfectly possible to be a big industrialist and still have a social conscience.[22]

Bosch's social concern was certainly genuine, however, and quite different in character from many other employers who professed an interest in *Sozialpolitik*. Despite the rapid increase in the Bosch workforce, for instance, an early decision was made not to build any company-owned housing estates, since this 'could limit the freedom of the employee to decide his own circumstances'.[23] Instead Bosch generously supported housing schemes for the 'less well-off classes' in general, founding the 'Schwäbische Siedlungsverein' with an anonymous million Mark donation in 1915.

From October 1900 Bosch was assisted in the running of the business by his nineteen year-old nephew Hugo Borst, later to become Ernst Jäckh's brother-in-law. Borst was responsible for building up the company's sales department and played an increasingly important role in the organisation of production at the Stuttgart works. He was also a frequent visitor to the United States, where he met F.W. Taylor and became a convert to the principles of 'Scientific Management'. The consequences of Borst's involvement with 'Taylorism' are examined in the next chapter, but he also made a notable contribution to the success of the Bosch enterprise by masterminding the company's advertising campaigns over many years. As a patron of Stuttgart's avant-garde art circles Borst had many contacts with leading living artists and soon built up an impressive collection of contemporary Germanic art, including paintings by Munch, Pankok, Hodler, Itten, Baumeister and Schlemmer, and sculptures by Marcks and Kolbe. Borst brought his interest in modern art to bear on the company's acclaimed publicity posters, with successful designs coming from, amongst

---

22. *Frankfurter Zeitung*, 1 Feb. 1913, quoted in J. Mulert, ibid., p.7.
23. T. Heuss, *Robert Bosch*, p.297.

others, the Werkbund member Lucian Bernhard. Borst himself became an individual member of the DWB in 1912. In an essay entitled 'How I became a Collector' he later recalled:

> My increasing preoccupation with the world of art actually came to be an advantage in my day job as this involved the planning and running of the complete advertising strategy of the company for which I worked, including all correspondence with poster artists. I had a similar influence – in contact with architects – on the architectural design of the many sales offices and factories erected in the majority of European countries and in North America.[24]

Borst's memoirs also suggest another possible reason for the particular popularity of Werkbund ideas in south western Germany: 'Swabia, with its great appreciation of the genuine, the permanent and the beautiful, with its sense of form and feeling for the sensitive hand of the creative artist, has a special need to advance and fertilise its handicrafts and its powerfully expanding industries through the medium of art.'[25]

In 1917 the company became the 'Robert Bosch AG', and the contribution of both Hugo Borst and Gottlob Honold was recognised, with both men becoming major shareholders as well as directors of the firm. The reorganisation of the business coincided with the Bosch work force passing a total of 7,000 for the first time. Two years later Bosch offered a summary of his social and economic principles which would surely have met with Naumann's full agreement:

> The most heartfelt aspiration of a *Volksgemeinschaft* united in freedom must be the full and effective deployment of all the valuable talents of the individual, and to ensure that these talents can perform at maximum efficiency in every area of life, including the economy . . . The basis of a free and sensible economic order is the achievement of the highest possible productivity. For this to be possible it is not only important that as many goods as possible are produced, but that they are produced as well and as reasonably as possible.[26]

Carl Benscheidt and the Fagus-Werk: Architecture as Advertisement

The Fagus shoe-last factory is now inseparable from the name of its architect Walter Gropius, but the dominant figure in the company's history was actually its founder and long-standing managing director Carl

24. H. Borst, *Wie ich Sammler wurde. Erinnerungen und Bekenntnisse*, Stuttgart, 1941, p.9.

25. H. Borst, *ibid.*, p.24.

26. J. Mulert, 'Erfolgsbeteiligung', p.6.

Benscheidt, who was born on 17 January 1857 in the small Sauerland farming community of Halver. Although the first-born of eleven children, he was considered unsuitable to take over the running of the family small-holding because of a weak childhood constitution, which also barred him from military service. It was only as a college student that Benscheidt was finally able to put an end to his health problems, thanks largely to a course of treatment recommended by a natural health specialist.

Whilst on his fitness programme of bare-foot runs and frequent baths, Benscheidt became fascinated by the world of health, and though finance was not forthcoming to study medicine at university, he was able find a job in a natural health resort near Ljubljana . One of the most common complaints he encountered amongst the spa guests was that of bad feet, exacerbated by ill-fitting footwear. In a number of newspaper articles Benscheidt called for a reform of the shoe-making industry, and in particular for a shoe-last which more closely resembled the natural shape of the foot.

When the industry failed to respond to Benscheidt's suggestions, he began to carve individual wooden shoe-lasts for personal customers, and then established his own small workshop in Hanover to produce both lasts and shoes. The business expanded steadily, employing up to twelve cobblers and enjoying a growing reputation in and around the city. Benscheidt soon came to the attention of Carl Behrens, whose factory in Alfeld had been manufacturing shoe-lasts since 1858 and who was struck by Benscheidt's new approach to the design of the product. After long negotiations Benscheidt accepted an offer to become technical manager of the Alfeld company in 1887. When Carl Behrens died nine years later the ownership of the company passed in to the hands of the Behrens family, and Benscheidt become works' manager, with overall responsibility for the day-to-day running of the factory.

The C. Behrens factory underwent a major expansion in 1897, planned by Benscheidt and his business manager Wilhelm Bartram, and involving the erection of a new production building, designed by the Hanover-based architect Eduard Werner. The new building was a conventional red-brick industrial structure, with limited historicist ornamentation. The early years of the twentieth century were profitable ones for the shoe-last industry in general and for Benscheidt personally. He was by now a director and shareholder in the Behrens company, but towards the end of the 1900s he fell out with one of the owners, possibly Behrens's son Carl junior, and on 2 October 1910 he announced his resignation from the firm.

Benscheidt appears to have been considering the possibility of establishing his own shoe-last business for some time. Only a week after leaving the Behrens company, he had departed with his eldest son on a mission to secure American backing for just such an enterprise. In

November he began to contact wood suppliers, having already approached the architect Werner to draw up plans for a new factory, which was to be built on a site alongside the main Hanover-Göttingen railway line. Benscheidt's new company – known as the 'Fagus GmbH' after the latin name for the beech tree – was eventually registered on 28 March 1911, and the foundation stone was laid on 29 May 1911. As we have seen however, the architect was no longer to be Eduard Werner but Walter Gropius, whose eye-catching proposals for the design of the factory façades had so obviously appealed to Benscheidt.

'Fagus' began life as a modest enterprise: with a work force of sixty and a daily output of around 1,500 lasts it was one of the smallest of twenty similar factories in Germany, which at that time led the world in the production of shoe-lasts. Despite its small size and the close proximity of one of its biggest rivals, however, the company had every reason to be optimistic about its prospects. Benscheidt had a proven record of innovation in the industry, and was working on the first standardised measuring table for shoe-lasts. From the beginning, Fagus products would be designed to suit the needs of mechanised shoe production. Moreover, the good contacts Benscheidt had established with the American and British shoe-machinery industry whilst in his old job had been put to good use. Two Northampton-based companies were amongst the initial investors in Fagus, as was the United Shoe Machinery Company of Massachusetts, the American market leader in its field.[27] The latter firm invested 800,000 Marks in the new company, and made an undertaking to supply it with the latest production machinery.

The entry of the United States into the First World War raised questions about the American holding in Fagus. In 1917 the German government took over the shares on a temporary basis, before passing them on to Benscheidt and his son, but the company flourished nonetheless. The growing work force (it soon reached 500) were bound into a *Betriebsgemeinschaft* which Benscheidt liked to call the 'Fagus Family'. No white-collar workers at the factory ever received a contract; in the words of a 1947 pamphlet 'everything is built on devotion and trust'.[28] Benscheidt tried to maintain a personal relationship with every worker and always prided himself on being the first to arrive for work in the mornings. According to the trade union official Gustav Scharff, who began work at Fagus as a fourteen year old in April 1918, and remained until the end of the Second World War, Benscheidt was 'strict but consistent' in his expectations of the workers and a stickler for punctuality.[29] As at Bosch,

27. 'Fagus GmbH zu Alfeld', in *Alfelder Kreiszeitung*, 11 April 1911, p.2.
28. W. Barner, *Carl Benscheidt d.Ä. 1858–1947*, Hildesheim, 1947, p.3.
29. In a letter to the author, 15 Aug. 1988.

shopfloor employees received above average piecework rates and worked a basic eight-hour day, which was still considered rather unusual in German industry.

Indeed, although he was not a DWB member, Benscheidt had more in common with Bosch, Bahlsen and Bruckmann than just a surname beginning with the letter 'B'. For many years he had served as an independently minded *Bürgervorsteher* on Alfeld town council, and had been involved in a number of heated arguments with local notables and established interest groups. The titles of three pamphlets he published in the 1900s give some idea as to the controversial nature of these debates.[30] In November 1899, for instance, Benscheidt had founded the 'Gemeinnützige Bauverein Alfeld', a charitable housing association which aimed to build cheap and solid accommodation for the town's growing industrial population. It met with fierce opposition from many of the 6,000 townsfolk, who feared that the development of 'workers' barracks' would spoil the picturesque scenery. Leading local landowners even refused to sell their property to the association, which then had no option but to build its first settlement outside the town boundary. The association's two main pre-war developments of solid and attractive houses both reflected Benscheidt's support for the garden city movement.

It has been noted that Benscheidt possessed 'a deep social awareness' and was convinced that a successful business depended above all on a work force which was 'healthy, happy and housed'. The social and ethical concerns of his architect, Walter Gropius, are also well known. It is tempting therefore, to view Benscheidt's endorsement of Gropius's light and airy architecture as a further demonstration of the industrialist's social conscience in action. There are dangers, however, in attempting to explain the appearance of the factory in socio-political terms alone. Karin Wilhelm, for instance, suggests that the pioneering use of 'a democratic architectural form', the glass 'curtain wall', at Alfeld was the result of nothing less than a fundamental change in the ethos of manufacturers[31]; a change typified by Benscheidt's personal work ethic and progressive attitude to his workers.

She argues that in their rejection of the tradition of *architecture parlante* and the show-façade in favour of a transparent and neutral glass skin, Benscheidt and Gropius made the entire production process at the Fagus factory visible:

30. C. Benscheidt, 'Das "Privatinteresse" am Alfelder Bauverein und der Alfelder Bürgermeister Dr Hottenrott. Ein Wort zur Aufklärung und Rechtfertigung' (1905); 'Zur Abwehr und Aufklärung. Kritische Streiflichter auf das Alfelder Stadtregiment' (1908); 'Herr Senator Strobell. Eine Erwiderung auf dessen Broschüre – "Die Benscheidtsche Kampfesweise im Tageslicht"' (1908).

31. K. Wilhelm, *Walter Gropius, Industriearchitekt*, Brunswick, 1983, pp.62–65.

... by making the barrier between the inside and the outside a fluid one, the work of the factory is presented, even exhibited, not just opened up to the observer but submitted for his critical judgement.[32]

In other words, not only was the purpose of Benscheidt's business open for all to see but the factory would be subject to the democratic control of outside scrutiny. The removal of the masonry barrier which had hitherto marked the boundary between the internal realm of the private industrialist and the world outside meant that the Fagus building 'formulated a determinedly democratic principle'. At the same time it also removed the need for a symbolic architectural language to portray the world of industry, something which had characterised all industrial buildings up to, and including, Peter Behrens's AEG turbine factory.

Wilhelm points out that Benscheidt's own sparsely furnished office, which deliberately avoided the imposing leather chairs and daunting desk of industrial folklore, was only separated from the remaining second-floor office space by a thin transparent membrane. In view of this, and since the glass walls of the main building enclosed both production and administration areas alike, without any external sign of the division of labour, the Fagus factory can be said to demonstrate 'a new relationship between the factory owner and industrial work':

> Here we find the first architectural fruits of that *bürgerlichen Wirtschaftsethos* which Max Weber felt was characterised by the fact that entrepreneurs and workers found themselves united in the treatment of work as a vocation.[33]

On a symbolic level there is a good deal of truth in Wilhelm's thesis. Few would disagree in principle with her general assertion that 'out of the horrors of the nineteenth century and the "bloodsucking" capitalists (Marx) there had come a new type of entrepreneur',[34] of which Benscheidt was certainly one, but it is important not to lose sight of the realities of the Fagus case. Even before the erection of a porter's lodge and large iron gate in the 1920s the factory was definitely not accessible to members of the public, and production areas were not visible from the road which skirted the site. The large glazed areas may have been more transparent than brick or stone, but even those people with access to the complex would have struggled to 'observe' anything through the highly-reflective windows of the main building. Indeed, it was much easier for management to gaze out of their second-floor office windows to survey and 'control' their

32. K. Wilhelm, *ibid.*, p.64.
33. K. Wilhelm, *ibid.*, p.63.
34. K. Wilhelm in W. Herzogenrath, D. Teuber, A. Thiekötter (eds), *Der westdeutsche Impuls. Die DWB Ausstellung Cöln 1914*, Cologne, 1984, p.146.

employees than vice versa, as Wilhelm seems to suggest.

Fortunately, however, there is also a more sober explanation for the radical appearance of the factory. It is worth beginning with a closer look at its precise location. The *Alfelder Kreiszeitung* of 16 November 1910 carried the first report on Benscheidt's intention to 'go it alone', which at the time amounted to a major news story in the small country town:

> For the building site of the new factory complex the company has purchased an area of pasture on the New Meadow . . . from the present owner Mr L. Menge for the price of 140,000 Marks. As the plot measures 11 *Morgen* and 11 rods, it works out at a price of 12,720 Marks per *Morgen*; a price which at first sight appears very high, and one which has certainly never been agreed to in Alfeld before.[35]

The land was expensive because it had been exceedingly marshy and required extensive earth in-filling prior to the sale. Eventually some two metres of soil were added to provide a site suitable for building. Even with its easy access to the main railway line, however, the plot was hardly ideal for industrial development. Indeed, with plenty of land available in the wide Leine valley, it appears surprising that Benscheidt should choose to build his 'model' factory where he did. The decision can only be explained in terms of the close proximity of the C.Behrens factory, which stood about one hundred yards to the south on the opposite side of the tracks; Menge's plot on the New Meadow was the closest available land to Benscheidt's previous employer. Although the precise nature of Benscheidt's decision to leave the Behrens company is not known, it is clear from his choice of building site that Benscheidt had no intention of shirking a direct comparison with his former colleagues. With this in mind, his decision to give the young and radical Gropius a chance to design his factory façades appears more understandable.

As we have seen, Eduard Werner had built extensively for C. Behrens in 1897. Although his proposals for the Fagus factory thirteen years later showed that time had not passed him by – with its flat roof and ornament-free façade, the building would have been the most modern yet seen in Alfeld – Benscheidt doubted whether Werner's red-brick, utilitarian design would be sufficiently different to distinguish his new business from that of his old employers. On 12 January Benscheidt wrote in reply to Gropius's initial enquiry:

> As far as the internal layout and shape of the buildings is concerned this man [i.e. Werner] has such experience that I don't think I am likely to find anything

35. 'Neue Fabrikanlage im Industriestädtchen Alfeld a.L.' in *Alfelder Kreiszeitung*, 16 Nov. 1910, p.2.

Figure 35 C. Behrens shoe-last factory, Alfeld a.d. Leine 1897
Arch. E. Werner. Present condition

better. With regard to the external appearance of the buildings I feel rather differently, and the gentleman in question may not be able to meet my wishes fully.[36]

Werner's suggested layout was a perfectly acceptable demonstration of a functional and modern approach to manufacturing: Benscheidt refused Gropius permission to alter this aspect of Werner's plan. What Benscheidt wanted from Gropius was the one thing Werner could not supply – an eye-catching, high-tech façade, which would not only set the Fagus factory apart from its neighbours in Alfeld, but from anything yet seen in Germany. The importance of the local rivalry is highlighted by the fact that the building's most imposing façade did not face west to the main factory entrance, or north down the Leine valley to Hanover, but 'backwards' to the C.Behrens plant. In a letter dated 13 February 1911 Gropius wrote to his client:

> At the moment the main prospect is directed towards the Behrens factory. It would appear to me to be much better if the entire factory could be erected as a mirror image of the existing project. Then the attractive main façade would lie with a clear view towards Hanover. I cannot see any technical disadvantage coming from this.[37]

Significantly, Benscheidt refused to countenance any such suggestion. Although it may seem ironic that the arch-functionalist Gropius should be employed simply to provide an effective façade for the factory, this was in essence the nature of his task. Benscheidt knew that if his Fagus-Werk was going to compete with C. Behrens and the other established shoe-last manufacturers it would have to highlight its innovative ideas and fresh approach to the product. Gropius's ultra-modern façades would help to emphasise the new company's image, both to visiting reps and passing travellers, and also to the outside world via the medium of the company's publicity and advertising material.

Architecture had been used as a form of advertising before, of course, but seldom had a marketing strategy been conceived in such all-embracing terms. The obvious example of where this had already happened – Peter Behrens's new 'corporate identity' for the AEG – was almost certainly in Benscheidt's mind as the model for his Fagus project. Indeed, the reference made in Gropius's initial letter to his time with Behrens in Berlin may have struck a crucial chord with the entrepreneur, although the example of the United Shoe Machinery Company, with its modern 'daylight' factory in

---

36. C. Benscheidt quoted by H. Weber, *Walter Gropius und das Faguswerk*, Munich, 1961, p.30.
37. W. Gropius quoted by H. Weber, *ibid.*, p.43.

Beverly, Massachusetts, could also have influenced Benscheidt's thinking.[38] Either way, the entire Fagus complex was clearly employed to demonstrate to visitors and passers-by the modernity of the entrepreneur's state-of-the-art American machinery and the quality of his shoe-lasts. Moreover its advertising function went beyond a static existence as a three-dimensional billboard in the Hanoverian countryside. Views of the factory were reproduced, adapted and multiplied to help sell the product around the world, and continue to do so today, in the service of its current owners.

The importance of 'corporate identity' to Benscheidt is highlighted by his decision to commission another DWB member, the Berlin graphic artist M. Hertwig, to produce a distinctive 'logo' for the new company. As well as adorning all the company's publicity material the result was painted in large letters on the side of the factory chimney, leaving passing travellers in no doubt as to the plant's identity. Even the name 'Fagus' itself was chosen for its memorably 'catchy' quality. As the *Alfelder Kreiszeitung* noted on 11 April 1911:

> Latterly, short and pithy company names have become all the rage and one cannot deny that the name 'Fagus' has the virtue of brevity, whilst at the same time remaining in the mind. Any confusion with the *Alfelder Schuhleistenfabrik C. Behrens* is certainly out of the question. Furthermore it will be easy for the firm to stamp its name, rather than the usual trade mark (at Behrens, of course, the beech leaf), on every completed product. The advantage of this should not be underestimated.[39]

As we have seen, the DWB concentrated its rhetorical fire on the social and political benefits which could be gained from the 'quality workplace', but Werkbund architects and designers had no objection if commissions were also forthcoming for less morally uplifting motives. The *Werkbündler* were well aware that few businesses would consider the extra costs involved in commissioning a creative architect without some prospect of a return on their investment. Indeed, the leading DWB architects never wasted an opportunity to stress the commercial advantages which a striking contemporary building could bring to publicity-conscious companies. Gropius himself wrote in the 1913 DWB Yearbook:

38. See R. Banham, *A Concrete Atlantis. US Industrial Building and European Modern Architecture*, Cambridge Mass., 1986. Daniel Nelson writes that the United Shoe Machinery plant was built in 1903–4, and was the first major factory to be built with reinforced concrete in the United States. It consisted of 'three parallel four-storey concrete buildings, smaller buildings that connected the main structures and a foundry and a forge shop. Windows covered nearly the entire wall space of the three main buildings. The Beverly factory attracted widespread attention and started a trend that spread to other industries in the following years.' D. Nelson, *Managers and Workers. Origins of the New Factory System in the United States 1800–1920*, Wisconsin, 1975, p.16.

39. 'Fagus GmbH zu Alfeld', in *Alfelder Kreiszeitung*, 11 April 1911, p.2.

The greater the freedom and originality of the architectural forms, the more publicity-power a building will possess for its owners, and the better it will meet the advertising intentions of its managers. A worthy appearance allows one to draw appropriate conclusions for the character of the enterprise as a whole. The artistic beauty of a factory building, an imaginative, memorable silhouette, grabs the attention of the public far more intensively than a sea of advertising hoardings or firm name-signs, which force themselves upon the tired eye and only serve to deaden the senses.[40]

Carl Benscheidt was by no means the only Wilhelmine industrialist to recognise this argument. Even Hermann Bahlsen, whose company took the social message of the 'quality workplace' so clearly to heart, viewed the promotional and public relations potential of Siebrecht's buildings as an integral part of the company's calculations. This is indicated not only by numerous articles in the *Leibniz Blätter*, but also by the swiftness with which the company made use of the new buildings as an important element in its poster and publicity programme. Otto Obermeier's famous poster of 1911, for instance, featured a 'Bahlsen Boy', laden down with biscuits, striding over the recently completed administrative building. It was followed a year later by an advertisement designed by Robert Fricke, depicting a packet of Bahlsen's *Leibniz-Keks* superimposed upon an illustration of the new factory building. At the same time, paintings of both the factory and the administrative buildings were represented in the first series of 'artist stamps', which the public could obtain by collecting a dozen tokens from biscuit packet wrappers.

Furthermore, the Henkell headquarters by Paul Bonatz, Muthesius's Michels factory and Wagner's Kaffee Hag complex were all featured in the advertising of the respective companies before World War One. In each instance the factory building was employed in the manner of a trade mark, as a guarantee of identity, quality and modernity for the consumer. The 'Hag' advertisement, for example, depicted a huge packet of decaffeinated coffee looming above the sunlit silhouette of the Bremen factory, and was placed in a number of popular journals, such as *Die Woche*.

Illustrated magazines of this type, which owed their very existence to the desire of companies like the Kaffee Handels-AG to 'speak' directly to a growing number of consumers with disposable income, multiplied vigorously in the last years of the nineteenth century. With registered trade marks receiving official protection in Germany from 1874, manufacturers of 'luxury' provisions, household goods and durables increasingly turned to designers and graphic artists to provide their 'brand names' with instantly recognisable identities, which could leap at the consumer from

---

40. W. Gropius, 'Die Entwicklung moderner Industriebaukunst', in Werkbund Yearbook, 1913, p.20.

Figure 36 Henkell champagne advertisement, featuring Bonatz's building, c. 1910

the magazine pages and the shop shelves. Kaffee Hag backed up their product with a series of well-designed coffee cups, pots and milk jars, each with the distinctive Hag 'logo'. It is surely no coincidence that many of the companies which led the way in this sort of innovative advertising and packaging – Hag, Henkell, Bahlsen – took a similarly adventurous approach to the architecture of their factories and offices.

The clean, uncluttered lines favoured by the Werkbund architects and designers matched the desire of progressive manufacturers for well-defined and distinctive product identities. One major reason why DWB architects were more successful in capturing industrial and commercial commissions than their *Heimatstil* colleagues lay in the more appropriate aesthetic language they could offer for the places and products of modern mass manufacturing. The modest neo-vernacular revivalism proposed in the name of Heimatschutz was by its very nature intended to be inconspicuous, traditional, and to 'blend in' with the surroundings. Industry, on the other hand, was often looking for precisely the opposite; buildings which were eye-catching, original and imposing. Although, as we have seen, local building contractors and the planners together ensured that small industrial installations outside the major urban centres were frequently 'traditional' in character, there were remarkably few instances of more substantial industrial enterprises choosing to commission a Heimatschutz architect. Unless an industrialist had a strong personal commitment to Heimatschutz ideas, a company was unlikely to consider this option.

If the popularity of the Werkbund aesthetic amongst manufacturers was good news for DWB designers and architects, it was also a source of considerable disquiet for some who had initially expressed sympathy for the organisation's wider social aims. Most prominent of the critics was the economic theorist and writer Werner Sombart (1863–1941), an early supporter of the Werkbund who resigned his membership in 1910:

> It is a sad sign of the times that poor, hungry artists must place their talents at the disposal of some insecticide manufacturer, just so that he can extol the virtues of his product in beauty. Art in the service of advertising is one of the many basic aberrations of our culture.[41]

He was backed up by the art critic Wilhelm Schäfer. In an article on the Werkbund's major Cologne exhibition of 1914 he complained that 'our famous name artists have, with a few exceptions, become the trade marks of big business.'[42] In his review of the same event, which included a

---

41. W. Sombart, quoted by H. Väth-Hinz in *Odol. Reklame-Kunst um 1900*, Lahn-Gießen, 1985, p.10.
42. W. Schäfer, 'Die DWB Ausstellung in Köln,', in *Die Rheinlande*, vol.14 (1914), p.302.

retrospective display of the Werkbund's leading figures – known in some quarters as the 'Twelve Apostles' – Julius Meier-Graefe struck a similarly disapproving tone:

> Today the 'artists' are no longer 'apostles' but business people, and very shrewd ones too. They are raking in industry's thanks in the form of hard cash. There is no need to celebrate them as cultural heroes any more, because their activities have precious little to do with culture, or at least with the sort of culture that is worth talking about.[43]

Others took a more sanguine view. On 24 July 1910 Adolf Saager addressed the 'alliance between artists and businessman' in Naumann's *Die Hilfe*:

> This alliance has proved to be so productive, and is so much in step with the needs of the time, that one can already be as bold as to suggest that the artist has become indispensable for the businessman. The conservative industrialist, who in his proud self-confidence tries to do without the aid of the artist, will soon be overtaken by his more progressive competitor, for art has become the fashion.[44]

When companies commissioned progressive artists or architects, however, it was seldom just a case of 'following the fashion'. Although the talents of Werkbund designers were indeed enlisted on occasion to boost the prospects of a particular product in the marketplace, most firms which approached DWB members were motivated by a more general desire to promote their public image. For an enterprise to be associated with fresh and innovative ideas in the art world was attractive in itself of course, but the Werkbund's well publicised views on the need for social reform at the workplace and the promotion of quality in the economy, gave forward-thinking manufacturers an added incentive to become identified with the organisation.

At the end of 1907 the DWB membership included 143 commercial enterprises, mostly modest in size and often craft-based in character. Six years later this figure had moved well past the 300-mark, and read like a 'Who's Who' of German manufacturing, including AEG, BASF, Bayer, Benz, Bosch, Continental, Daimler, Degussa, Humboldt, Mannesmann, and MAN, in addition to a host of medium-sized companies throughout the *Reich*. Only small independent businesses were comparatively thin on the ground, unable to afford the extra costs involved in changing their product portfolio and introducing new machinery to meet Werkbund quality criteria, or indeed to commission high-profile architects for their

43. J. Meier-Graefe, 'Kunstbummel', in *Frankfurter Zeitung*, 21 July 1914.
44. A. Saager, 'Kunst und Kaufmann', in *Die Hilfe*, 24 July 1910, p.468.

building projects. The DWB's Helmuth Wolff had little sympathy: 'It is in the large firm that we see the future and the basis of manufacturing work for mass requirements . . . For us it is the manufacturing production of big businesses which we need to win over for *Qualitätsarbeit*'.[45]

The leading DWB firms specialised in a wide range of products, but nearly all belonged to that section of German industry variously described as the 'new', 'modern', 'flexible' or 'American' faction, which encompassed not only companies in the chemical and electrical engineering sectors, but the automobile industry, machine building and lighter manufacturing enterprises as well. These firms were united in the production of quality finished goods, often for export, and a heavy consumption of raw- or semi-finished materials, of the sort frequently supplied by syndicates and cartels. The contrasting interests of the major processing and manufacturing firms on the one hand, and the producers of coal, iron and steel on the other, were to be found at the root of most conflicts within pre-war German industry.

Individual entrepreneurs with a personal faith in Naumannite politics were certainly not the only industrialists to voice dissatisfaction with important aspects of the social, economic and political climate of the Wilhelmine era. Processing industries, and especially quality goods' manufacturers, had for some time been opposed to many of the policies favoured by primary producers in both industry and agriculture. Moreover they strongly resented the 'special relationship' which the suppliers of 'rye and iron' appeared to enjoy with the Prussian state, and were anxious to dismiss any notion that heavy industrialists and large landowners were alone responsible for securing the national wealth. They pointed to the growing contribution of manufacturing exports to German prosperity, and the rapid expansion of the electrical engineering and chemical industries, as indications of a fundamental shift in the industrial balance of power.

Manufacturers were well aware of heavy industry's fondness for ostentatious historicism, and the vainglorious desire of the great concerns to ape the mannerisms of state architecture, but they also knew that behind the show-façades heavy industrial buildings were often utilitarian and shabby, revealing scant regard for the sensibilities of the workers. Therefore once an alternative had been revealed, in the shape of the Werkbund and its 'quality workplace', many of the 'new' industrial firms were eager to embrace it. The artist-designed factory offered an opportunity for modern manufacturing companies to build a distinctive identity, both individually and collectively, at a time when successful industrialists no longer felt compelled to articulate their achievements in the language of

45. H. Wolff, 'Die volkswirtschaftlichen Aufgaben des DWB', in Werkbund Yearbook, 1912, p.88.

pre-industrial societies.

The 'new' industrial faction, whose enterprises were based largely on technological innovations, had for a while been seeking to establish a connection in people's minds between progressive product development and progressive social policies. An important contribution could be made by an architecture which was capable of expressing not only a different managerial ethos and a revised relationship with the Wilhelmine state, but also a vision of a peaceful and prosperous industrial future for managers and workers alike. The introduction of 'culture' into the industrial environment would, it was hoped, leave people in little doubt as to the changed character and quality of the nation's new industrial masters. At the same time, of course, these companies also hoped that the new aesthetic language would help to win consumers and build markets, by developing functional forms for mass-produced objects which were both attractive to users and cost-efficient for manufacturers.

Thus the DWB became very much part of the struggle for power and influence within German industry, lining up alongside the pressure-groups, professional lobbyists and politicians, who were increasingly engaged to fight the industrialists' battles 'by proxy'. In the first decade of the twentieth century the divisions within German industry, which were to have such fateful consequences for the evolution of stable bourgeois political parties and the modernisation of society, also came to be mirrored in the conflicting architectural styles of Germany's factory towns and cities. This was a short-lived phenomenon, to be sure; the distinctions soon became blurred, as the heavy industrial concerns gradually expanded into the area of quality manufacturing themselves and became more aware of the benefits modern design could bring. Not only did the Friedrich Krupp AG join the DWB in 1913, but Werkbund architects like Hans Erberich and Alfred Fischer even began to receive commissions for pit-head buildings from some of the smaller mining companies in the immediate pre-war years.[46]

By the 1920s and 1930s German pit-head installations were at the forefront of architectural innovation. Despite this, however, it is clear that the DWB retained particularly close links to the personalities and pressure-groups of the 'new' industrial faction. The following pages examine this relationship in more depth.

---

46. The Cologne architect Hans Erberich designed the pit-head buildings for the Gewerkschaft Barmen at Sprockhövel (1908–10). The pit had a short life, being closed down eight years later due to poor ventilation and flooding. He also worked on coal mine complexes in Rumania and Silesia, and designed benzol extraction plants for a couple of Krupp pits in the Ruhr. Alfred Fischer (1881–1968), who became a leading figure in coal-mine architecture in the 1920s, built the Schachtanlage Emil near Essen in 1912–13 (purchased by Mannesmann in December 1912), and the machine hall of the Zeche Sachsen near Hamm in 1914 (owned by the Mansfeldsche Gewerkschaft).

Figure 37 Zeche Sachsen, machine hall, Hamm-Heeßen 1914
Arch. A. Fischer. Present condition

The Struggle for Power and Influence: German Industry before World War One

> On the eve of the First World War 'the bourgeoisie' no longer existed as a class or social stratum. It had splintered into a number of separate groups for which no overall social category applies. This fragmentation of the old bourgeoisie resulted from the divergence of economic, social and political interests . . . since the 1870s.[47]

The fissures within the German bourgeoisie, referred to here by Karl Erich Born, were nowhere more apparent than in that part of the population which had so successfully masterminded the advance of industry in the second half of the nineteenth century. Even against a background of steady economic growth and high profits, Wilhelmine industrialists found themselves divided by more than the predictable personality clashes and competitive intrigues. Fundamental differences existed in such key areas as the desired direction of government fiscal and foreign policy, the future role of cartels and the appropriate response to the labour movement; issues which could not be resolved in abstract ideological terms, and which were viewed very differently from sector to sector, and even from company to company.

Of course, industrialists also held much in common too – not least, a shared conviction that their voice was not heard loudly enough in government – but the differences were sufficient to provoke the creation of a clutch of competing pressure-groups, each claiming to represent the best interests of German industry and, by implication, of the German nation as a whole. The pressure-groups employed a wide variety of techniques to get their message across, involving the lobbying of legislators and bureaucrats, the setting-up of electoral funds for sympathetic parliamentary candidates, and the dissemination of propaganda to win over new members and public opinion.

The first and biggest industrial pressure-group, the Centralverband deutscher Industrieller (CVDI), had been founded in 1876, at a time when depressed economic conditions had placed an unprecedented strain on the liberal doctrines of free trade and *laissez-faire*. The ironmasters of the Ruhr and South German textile industrialists, who were most prominent at the association's birth, were anxious to secure government protection for their industries, and were generously rewarded in the form of the 1879 tariffs.

---

47. K.E. Born, quoted by H.Nussbaum in *Unternehmer gegen Monopole*, East Berlin, 1966, p.8.

In return the CVDI played a leading role in establishing Bismarck's alliance of 'rye and iron', and thereafter continued to enjoy a close relationship with the *Reich* administration.[48]

Once it had achieved its initial aim of tariff protection, the CVDI broadened its horizons to become an administrative focal point for German industry as a whole, developing services such as a central fund for strike-bound employers. It claimed to be a mouthpiece for all sectors of industry, a *Verband der Verbände*, but it was the heavy industrialists of the Ruhr who usually had the last word, often through the person of H.A. Bueck (1830–1916), for many years Executive Secretary of both the CVDI and the metal-makers' association. As the organisation evolved from an association of notables to a central confederation of delegated interests, however, dissident voices began to be heard. The chemical industry's Chemieverein, which had joined the CVDI in 1882, walked out just seven years later, complaining that the organisation had a bitter 'iron after-taste'.

Meanwhile, other industrialists were beginning to express their dissatisfaction with the high tariff policy, which not only increased the cost of raw materials and the size of wage bills, but threatened to provoke international retaliation and hence damage German exports. It was these export-oriented manufacturers who played the leading role in the formation of a rival pressure-group, the Bund der Industriellen (BdI) in 1895. The BdI's early years, in which it attempted to remain politically-neutral and attract a mass individual membership from a wide range of industries, were largely unsuccessful. After the turn of the century, however, it gained more members and greater prominence as the focal point for a number of regional manufacturers' organisations, such as Stresemann's Association of Saxon Industrialists (VSI), and equivalent bodies in Baden, Württemberg and elsewhere.[49] As the *Qualitätsarbeit* debate showed, the arguments of these export-oriented industries were always to the fore in the Werkbund.

However, the divisions within German industry were not limited to conflicting approaches on the tariff question. Opinions were similarly divided on the merits of cartels and syndicates, which had proved increasingly attractive to producers of petrol, alcohol, sugar, paper and spun cotton as well as coal, coke, crude iron and steel, but were a cause of great concern to their consumers further along the chain of production,

---

48. See H. Kaelble, *Industrielle Interessenpolitik in der wilhelminischen Gesellschaft: CVDI 1895–1914*, Berlin, 1967. Also T. Nipperdey, 'Interessenverbände und Parteien in Deutschland vor dem ersten Weltkrieg' in *Politische Vierteljahresschrift*, vol. 1 (1960/61), p.262.

49. See H.-P. Ullmann, *Der Bund der Industriellen*, Göttingen, 1976. Also D. Stegmann, 'Linksliberale Bankiers, Kaufleute und Industrielle 1890–1900. Ein Beitrag zur Vorgeschichte des Handelsvertragsvereins', in *Tradition*, vol.21 (1976).

the finished goods' manufacturers. Their objections were practical rather than theoretical, for it was clear that industries fabricating a wide variety of complicated items for individual consumption had little prospect of being able to emulate the primary producers, much fewer in number but generally much larger, who were often concentrated in particular regions and whose products were invariably sold in bulk. Thus, whilst the heavy industrialists lobbied for legislation to encourage cartelisation, the processing industries used the BdI to fight a fierce rearguard action, highlighting the long-term economic costs of the strategy to Germany's future.

Steep rises in raw material prices, resulting in part from government fiscal policy but especially from the activities of the cartels, were a particular feature of the Werkbund's genesis years of 1906–9.[50] It appeared to the finished goods' manufacturers that whenever the primary industries hit a crisis their losses were automatically passed on to manufacturing consumers via artificially high cartel prices. Emil Kirdorf's Rhenish-Westphalian Coal Syndicate was frequently singled out for the harshest criticism. Even the highly concentrated electrical engineering and chemical sectors found it difficult to escape the full impact of the soaring raw material costs. For south western industrialists, such as those in Heilbronn, an added burden came in the form of the 'Kohlenkontor', a cartel of Rhine coal traders and transporters established by the coal syndicate in 1903. The sense of vulnerability engendered by a reliance on cartelised suppliers provoked the processing industries into a number of responses, which ranged from their own experiments in cartel-style arrangements or vertical integration to a renewed search for political influence. This included a public relations offensive in which architecture played an integral part. Friedrich Naumann, writing in *Die Hilfe*, summed up the mood of the typical entrepreneur in this sector: 'He is prepared, if it is unavoidable, to be a member of an association, but he does not like to be a vassal of the coal- and syndicate masters, for this damages both his self-respect and his own economic interests.'[51]

Another area in which industry was manifestly divided was on the vexed question of tactics for tackling the seemingly unstoppable rise of the SPD and the trade union movement. Many manufacturers saw little option but to seek an accommodation with the workers, fearing that the confrontational approach favoured by heavy industrial concerns would inevitably lead to the sort of protracted disputes they were least equipped to fight; for them, long strikes meant lost markets. Moreover manufacturers of finished goods could not pursue an aggressive 'hire and fire' policy

50. See H. Nussbaum, *Unternehmer gegen Monopole*, pp.58–59.
51. F. Naumann, 'Industrielle Strömungen', in *Die Hilfe*, vol.38 (1913), p.595.

because of their greater reliance upon skilled and semi-skilled workers, and they seldom enjoyed the benefits of economic self-sufficiency gained by heavy industry through vertical integration. So, whilst heavy industrial spokesmen were happy to back a succession of draconian proposals to curtail workers' rights, to slow the introduction of social-welfare policies, and even to establish an 'Imperial League against Social Democracy', other industrialists preferred to pursue more subtle or 'flexible' paths to secure industrial peace, ranging from 'yellow' company unions and paternalistic welfare schemes to genuine attempts at securing 'factory democracy' and the 'quality workplace'.

In the summer of 1897 representatives of the export-oriented manufacturers, including the BdI and the Chemieverein, joined the big banks and leading Hanseatic traders to form the 'Centralstelle zur Vorbereitung von Handelsverträgen', in which heavy industry was conspicuous only by its absence. Then, in March 1900, the shipping magnate Albert Ballin went one stage further by proposing a 'big, strong alliance of trade, industry and shipping' which would be as 'powerful, loud and uncomfortable' as the Agrarian League. Although unable to live up to its billing, the Handelsvertragsverein (HVV), founded in Berlin on 11 November 1900, did succeed in bringing together the chemical, machine-building, electrical engineering and steel-working industries to back a manifesto strongly critical of both the agrarians and the heavy industrialists. The document, written by Georg von Siemens, rejected any major change to the policy of trade agreements established under Caprivi's chancellorship, which had for once generally benefited the lighter industries. Prominent members of the HVV included representatives of BASF (Brunck), Bayer (Boettinger), AEG (Rathenau, Jordan) and Norddeutscher Lloyd.

By now it had become clear to most contemporary commentators that German industry was fundamentally split, shifting boundaries and changing allegiances notwithstanding. A spokesman for the Chambers of Commerce wrote:

> Recently it has become increasingly evident that German industry is divided into two camps, whose wishes and requirements differ to a greater or lesser extent in most areas of economic life. On the one side stand the cartelised, capital-intensive producers of raw materials and intermediate goods, on the other the labour-intensive, mostly export-oriented manufacturers of finished products.[52]

The case for the latter was put forward strongly in the Reichstag by the Freisinnige Vereinigung, whose deputies Schrader, von Siemens and

52. Quoted in H. Nussbaum, *Unternehmer gegen Monopole*, p.156.

Gothein all held executive roles in the HVV, which soon boasted over 16,000 members. They failed, however, to exert much influence on the 1902 tariff bill or the revised trade treaties of 1905–6, not least because the committee which advised the government on customs policy, the Wirtschaftliche Ausschuß, was dominated by CVDI appointees.

At the heart of many of these disputes was the pace of Germany's transition from an *Agrarstaat* to an *Industriestaat*, and the appropriate role of the old élites in that process. The policy of a *Sammlung* between agrarian and industrial interests, re-activated by the Prussian Finance Minister Miquel in 1897 to secure a conservative alliance in time for the following year's Reichstag elections, lacked the stability and longevity of the original bond of 'rye and iron', but heavy industry and the *Junker* continued to turn to each other for support when it was in their own best interests to do so. Indeed, with heavy industry rapidly losing its voice in the Reichstag – a consequence of the SPD's triumphant advance in the urban centres – the votes of the predominantly agrarian Conservative party became crucial if tariffs were to be maintained, expensive social policy initiatives blocked and 'latent parliamentary rule' nipped in the bud.

Heavy industry's reliance on agrarian support was in part the result of a growing frustration with the leadership of the National Liberal Party. Although heavy industrialists in some areas had been prominent in setting up the Free Conservatives, the leading figures from the world of coal and steel were still mostly to be found on the National Liberals' right wing, particularly in the party's Prussian Landtag faction and in the council chambers of the Ruhr. In the decade before the First World War, however, the heavy industrial clique, which had adopted the 'Old Liberal' tag, became increasingly detached from the party's centre and left, as Bassermann and Stresemann attempted to pursue a course of moderate reform. The leadership's cautious support for social policy initiatives and frequent attacks on the practices of the coal syndicate were condemned by heavy industrial spokesmen like Bueck and Tille as 'half socialist', but the rival industrial camp made no secret of their preference for this version of National Liberalism. Indeed, as we have seen, many even sympathised with the more far-reaching demands of Naumann's Freisinnige Vereinigung. Consequently, industry's internal struggles came to severely hamper party cohesion in bourgeois politics.

The nature of industry's internal power struggle changed somewhat in the years before the war: vertical integration, which gave many of the heavy industrial concerns an interest in manufacturing, muddied the distinctions between the export-oriented industries and the supporters of protectionism. At the same time the 'new' industrial faction began to expand into the domain of the heavy industrialists, as the struggle for the electricity supply industry between Stinnes and Thyssen's RWE and the

AEG indicates. The net effect of these changes, however, was certainly not a diminution of industrial rivalries. Indeed, the great industrial concerns were now of such a size that they could themselves operate in the manner of pressure-groups, thereby further adding to the general clamour of voices seeking to be heard in the corridors of power.

The cacophony in the lobby was an indication of the complexity of the issues which divided German industry. The two 'camps' were never monolithic blocks, but loose amalgamations, with their own conflicts and contradictions. By no means all the BdI's predominantly medium-sized manufacturers could be ascribed to the 'new' industrial faction – a large number were in stagnating sectors – and of those that could, many had little in common with the highly-concentrated giants of the Chemieverein, which itself attempted to steer an independent course between CVDI and BdI. Nevertheless, most differences were outweighed by the shared distrust of heavy industrial motives and the careful cultivation of a common enemy, the East Elbian *Junker.* In fact, the political ideology of the 'new' industrial faction cast the agrarians in a strikingly similar role to that played by the 'socialist threat' in the demonology of the heavy industrialists; as the main impediment to a bright and prosperous future for German industry. It comes as no surprise therefore, to find heavy industry's on-off affair with the agrarian lobby as a long-standing source of anger and frustration for the BdI, Chemieverein, HVV and left liberals alike.

It was a dispute with conservative landed interests, over the Bülow administration's attempted re-organisation of the *Reich*'s fund raising mechanisms, which led to the formation of the most interesting industrial pressure-group of the pre-war period, the 'Hansabund für Gewerbe, Handel und Industrie' in 1909.[53] The Hansabund (HB) was founded when 2,400 delegates, representing 109 trade organisations and 244 industrial *Verbände*, gathered in Berlin on 12 June 1909 for a rally called by the liberal banker Jacob Rießer to condemn the government's amended Finance Bill, which was about to receive a controversial second reading. The HB aimed 'to raise the civic importance and economic situation of the German bourgeoisie', by tackling the disparity which had become evident between the economic and political development of the nation. It was conceived as both an umbrella organisation of industrial pressure-groups and a mass movement of individual members, to include the 'new middle class' of white collar employees and technicians. Six weeks after the founding congress there were already 58 local groups in existence and at the end of its first year it claimed some 220,000 members, with strongholds in Berlin, Saxony, Württemberg and the Hanseatic ports.

53. See S. Mielke, *Der Hansa-Bund für Gewerbe, Handel und Industrie*, Göttingen, 1976. Also D. Stegmann, *Die Erben Bismarcks*, Cologne, 1970.

As well as embracing those sectors of industry, banking and shipping which had already become identified with the HVV, the HB was notable for involving the heavy industrial CVDI at its launch. This rare co-operation between two industrial 'camps' showed the depth of anger at the agrarians behaviour on the financial reform issue and ensured that the HB was for a while front-page news in the liberal press; the *Vossische Zeitung* even termed it an 'historical turning point for the German bourgeoisie'.[54] In fact, however, the differences between the factions were apparent from the beginning, with the majority favouring an aggressive anti-agrarian stance, whilst the CVDI leadership – which had joined the HB as a 'tactical manoeuvre' – argued for a stronger anti-socialist line. The CVDI member Emil Kirdorf even went as far as to call the Hansabund a 'stillborn child'. In 1911 many, but not all, of the CVDI representatives left the HB in protest at its leftward course, and though it remained a thorn in the side of both agrarian and industrial conservatism, the HB's impact on German political life was never quite able to match the high expectations of its founders.

Indeed, the efforts of quality manufacturers and the 'new' industrial faction to secure a political influence and public respect commensurate with their contribution to the nation's wealth were usually unsuccessful before World War One. Nevertheless the endeavours of the BdI, HVV and HB to establish an alternative voice for German industry, more in tune with the changing economic, social and political climate of the early twentieth century, were rightly viewed by contemporaries as matters of considerable significance. Certainly any study of industrial architecture in the Wilhelmine period cannot afford to ignore the pressure-groups, and not simply because their activities were a central feature of industrial life at this time. In the light of what is already known about the Werkbund's politics and personalities it comes as no surprise to find a close correlation between the industrial sectors which supported the DWB and those that backed the BdI, HVV, and HB. A more detailed look at these pressure-groups, however, reveals an impressive number of further direct and hitherto disregarded links between the movement for *Qualitätsarbeit* and the 'new' industrial faction's wider campaigns.

Only one of the DWB's major manufacturing members to join before 1913 was identified with the largest industrial pressure-group of the Wilhelmine era, the CVDI. This was the Bavarian engineering company Maschinenfabrik Augsburg-Nürnberg (MAN), whose director Anton von Rieppel (1852–1926) was both an early supporter of the DWB and a member of the CVDI management from 1901. Von Rieppel's personal interest in the Werkbund – he held individual membership in addition to

54. Quoted by S. Mielke, *Der Hansa-Bund*, p.32.

his involvement through the company – was not surprising, for he had made his reputation as a talented designer of bridges and industrial installations at the Gustavsburger Brückenbauanstalt. He had always shown a special interest in the aesthetic impact of engineering structures and his spectacular Müngsten railway bridge between Remscheid and Solingen was regarded as one of the wonders of the age. Under von Rieppel's management – he rose from being a minor assistant in an engineer's office to become General Director of the whole concern in 1913 – MAN maintained a high standard in its building projects. A number of its commissions, such as Homburg railway station, Vohwinkel engine shed, and Wülfel iron works, were illustrated in the Werkbund yearbooks.

Von Rieppel served as an elected member of the DWB Management Committee, but he also held a host of important industrial posts, including the chairmanship of the German Metalworkers Association and the Bavarian Association of Industrialists. Although to the right of the DWB leadership on most political issues – he had close links to Hugenberg and joined the Deutscher Vaterlandspartei in 1917 – von Rieppel was nevertheless a critic of the heavy industrial cartels and the antics of the Agrarian League. In his monograph on the CVDI Hartmut Kaelble describes von Rieppel as a leader of the 'medium-sized manufacturers', one of three main factions to emerge in the CVDI as its ideological unity began to decay after 1900. These industrialists, who sometimes came from large companies but represented sectors that were characterised by medium-sized enterprises (metal-working, machine building), were often to be found in opposition to the other two factions; the 'agrarian industrialists' (sugar refiners, grain mill owners, landowning industrialists from Upper Silesia etc.) and the 'cartel directors', amongst whom Kirdorf was the dominant personality.

Indeed, on a wide range of issues the 'medium-sized manufacturers' of the CVDI like MAN had more in common with the BdI than with other factions of their own pressure-group. Von Rieppel was prominent in the campaign against raw material cartels for instance, and was particularly critical of the Pig Iron Syndicate. Moreover, the CVDI's 'medium-sized manufacturers' had from the beginning opposed Miquel's *Sammlung*, and were more enthusiastic about the formation of the HB in 1909 than many other CVDI members. Whilst Feldman is correct to point out that von Rieppel did not object to CVDI policy enough to actually leave the organisation for the BdI,[55] the MAN company was certainly less of an anomaly within the DWB membership than it initially appears.

55. G. Feldman, 'The large firm in the German industrial system. The MAN, 1900–25', in D. Stegmann, B. Wendt, P.C. Witt (eds), *Industrielle Gesellschaft und politisches System*, Bonn, 1978.

The Werkbund's links with the BdI were much greater, both in quality and quantity, than those with the CVDI. Gustav Stresemann, leader of the BdI-affiliated VSI and executive chairman of the BdI from 1911, became a DWB member around 1910. Like his former mentor Friedrich Naumann, Stresemann was first elected to the Reichstag at the 1907 elections, as the National Liberal member for Annaberg in Saxony, and soon became a prominent figure in liberal politics. Although their personal relationship was cool, Stresemann and Naumann shared many of the same political precepts, not least the conviction that industry needed to acquire a mass electoral following, if it was to overcome the discrepancy between its economic and political standing. Stresemann believed this was possible if two long-term social processes could be accelerated, namely the 'bourgeoisification' of the working class and the creation of a specific group identity for white-collar employees. Stresemann pursued these aims in a number of ways through both his political and industrial activities: by supporting state social-welfare programmes; by repeatedly emphasising the 'common interest' of workers with their employers; and by highlighting the reformist potential of expansionist foreign policies.

Stresemann and other BdI industrialists were well aware of the 'beneficial consequences' of boosting 'the consumption of the masses', and therefore lobbied against any measures which would reduce the 'purchasing power of the bulk of the population'.[56] In return, they hoped for political support in the struggle against the heavy industrialists and the agrarians. Stresemann made it clear that manufacturing industry could not afford to be a 'flaming beacon which stands out clearly, visible in every corner of the country' without at the same time possessing the 'solid foundation which is necessary if the millions who are dependent on it are to feel at one with its interests'.[57] In order to build this 'solid foundation' of a partnership between capital and labour Stresemann backed a variety of approaches, of which the new industrial architecture of the DWB was clearly one.

Whether Stresemann attached particular importance to the Werkbund approach is another matter, for whilst he sat on the Honorary Committee for the 1914 DWB exhibition, he appears to have played no part in the organisation's policy-forming processes and never spoke at a DWB meeting. However, other BdI leaders were more demonstrative in their support. Fritz Gugenheim (b.1859), who sat alongside Stresemann on the BdI's governing board, was the founder of the Seidenweberei Michels and the man who commissioned Hermann Muthesius for a new factory near Potsdam in 1913. He was also a member of the Permanent Commission

---

56. BdI Yearbook 1908 quoted by H.-P. Ullmann, *Der Bund der Industriellen*, p.107.
57. G. Stresemann quoted by H.-P. Ullman,, *ibid.*, p.107.

on Exhibitions for German Industry and the Honorary Committee for the 1914 DWB exhibition. Although many textile businesses were involved in the birth of the CVDI, the industry's loyalties were actually divided, between those firms specialising in spinning and those in weaving. The former, including the cotton spinning and woollen industries, continued to support the CVDI and identify with the raw material producers, whilst the more complicated weaving and finishing firms such as Michels increasingly aligned themselves with the processing industries in the BdI. This split was exacerbated at the turn of the century when spinning industries began to form cartels and their prime consumers, the weaving firms, were unable to follow suit. In the difficult economic circumstances of 1907–09 Michels, and other companies manufacturing high-quality finished textile products, were vociferous in their opposition to the CVDI and the cartels.

Gugenheim was accompanied on the BdI governing board by two other industrialists whose companies were DWB members, David Heilner (b.1876) of the Germania Linoleum-Werke, Bietigheim near Stuttgart, and Nicolaus Eich (1866–1919) of the Mannesmann-Röhrenwerke, Düsseldorf. Heilner was a leading figure in the Association of Württemberg Industrialists and a supporter of the south German Democrats and later the FVP. He was a close friend of Peter Bruckmann and commissioned various DWB artists to supply linoleum designs for the firm, which he had co-founded in 1899. Eich, meanwhile, joined the BdI's governing board in 1911, having already served for over a decade as the chairman of the Mannesmann tubing company. As we have seen, Mannesmann was a DWB member and had chosen Peter Behrens to build its headquarters in Düsseldorf. Another Werkbund man, Willi Roerts of Hanover, designed advertisements for the firm, which appeared in numerous publications including the DWB Yearbooks. Eich's personal politics were liberal – he voted for the DDP in the Weimar National Assembly elections – and he was a fierce critic of the heavy industrial old guard. As he wrote in 1918:

Until now Rhenish-Westphalian industry has been embodied by Messrs. Kirdorf, Thyssen and Stinnes . . . These autocratic men, who have their business origins in a time which must be considered long out of date, have not brought any of their tremendous influence to bear . . . on the workers' valid desire to see that their interests are also represented.[58]

The Mannesmann company had in fact joined the CVDI in 1907, but long-standing differences with the established heavy industrial concerns and their expansionist tendencies made it rethink its position and in 1911

58. N.Eich letter to Steinthal 12 Dec. 1918, quoted by H. Pogge von Strandmann in *Unternehmenspolitik und Unternehmensführung*, Düsseldorf, 1978, p.146.

it switched to the BdI, where Eich was immediately offered a number of executive positions. Mannesmann's great product innovation, the seamless steel tube, had faced a protracted struggle for acceptance from the great 'mixed' enterprises such as Thyssen, which not only supplied the company with raw materials at cartel prices but produced their own welded tubes of an inferior quality. Once it became clear that Mannesmann's product could not be held back by restrictive cartel quotas, the Düsseldorf based enterprise inevitably faced a bruising battle to maintain its independence from the vertically-expanding 'mixed' concerns.[59]

Rather than remain a vulnerable 'pure' rolling mill operation, Mannesmann launched a 'defensive' vertical expansion of its own, to secure a reliable flow of raw materials, particularly of crude iron and coal. Eich received backing in this aggressive strategic response from the AEG's Walther Rathenau, a member of the Mannesmann supervisory board and another man seriously perturbed by the heavy industrial 'threat' to manufacturing industry. Viewed in this light, Mannesmann's endorsement of the Werkbund and the modern architecture of Peter Behrens in 1911–12 appears to have been an integral element in the company's pugnacious response to the acquisitive gaze of the mixed concerns like Thyssen, Kirdorf's GBAG or Stinnes' DLBAG, whose architectural identity had long been established on very different lines.

The majority of firms affiliated to the BdI were much smaller operations than Mannesmann, but many came from sectors generally favourable to the Werkbund. Trade organisations with BdI membership in 1913 included: the German Book Printers' Association, Leipzig; the Association of German Sekt Producers, Mainz; the Association of German Silk Weavers, Düsseldorf; the Association of Poster Makers, Berlin; the Association of Advertising Interests, Mannheim; the Association of German Cake and Biscuit Manufacturers; and the Association of German Shoe Last Factories, Alfeld. At the same time, however, a number of industrialists from large-scale enterprises identified with the BdI, including both Rathenau and Bosch. It was fitting then that a BdI leader, the future Executive Secretary Rudolf Schneider, should have been chosen to give industry's view on the theme of 'Art and Industry' at the DWB's second annual conference in Frankfurt. In his speech at the Akademie für Sozialwissenschaften Schneider welcomed the decision of AEG to take on Behrens as 'artistic advisor', but warned that it would not be easy for all companies to follow suit:

> The small and medium-sized businesses of the finished goods industries will only be able to put the AEG course into action gradually, and they must first

59. See H. Pogge von Strandmann *ibid.*

find themselves a suitable field of *Qualitätsarbeit*. In the preparation and cultivation of this field, however, the DWB can give valuable support. It is in a position to work directly on the consumer, to create a need, a demand, which the finished goods industry must then meet – something it will certainly enjoy doing.[60]

At the same conference three leading industrialists were elected to the DWB's Management Committee – Immerheiser (BASF), Jordan (AEG) and Rieppel (MAN) – thus marking formally the increased importance of big business in the organisation. A year later, in June 1910, the two leading BdI regional associations, from Saxony and Württemberg, made a joint visit to the Brussels World Exhibition, where the DWB had been responsible for co-ordinating the German contribution. The industrialists were welcomed by Stresemann, who gave papers on 'Administration and Industry' and 'World Exhibitions and Industry'. In the run up to the exhibition the VSI had advised all its members to consider working with 'artists',[61] and both the VSI and BdI were listed in the DWB's annual reports as 'standing in regular correspondence with the Werkbund'. Other associations and pressure-groups listed in this way included the Deutsche Handelstag, the Association of Württemberg Industrialists and the Permanent Commission on Exhibitions for German Industry, but not the CVDI.

The BdI industrialists who supported the DWB also turned up in leading positions in the Hansabund. David Heilner sat on the HB 'Executive' from 1909, Nicolaus Eich from 1912 and Gustav Stresemann from the same year, when they were also joined by Ludw. Loewe's Walter Waldschmidt, head of the HB in Berlin. Anton von Rieppel served from 1909–11, Carl Duisberg of Bayer and Georg Plate from Norddeutscher Lloyd both from 1909. Emil Rathenau of the AEG made a major speech at the founding congress of the HB and subsequent members of the organisation's 'General Committee' included Gugenheim (Michels), Boettinger (Bayer), von Brunck (BASF) and Vischer (Daimler). Other *Werkbündler* to play key roles in the HB included Peter Bruckmann (head of HB in Heilbronn), Josef Neven du Mont (head of HB in Cologne), and Friedrich Naumann, who championed the HB in the Reichstag. Indeed, after its foundation in 1910 Naumann's new united left liberal party, the FVP, came to rely greatly on financial assistance from the HB, a fact which partly explains the very close ties between the FVP and HB; fifteen members of the eighteen-man FVP management committee were HB members, as were 90% of the FVP Reichstag faction.

Meanwhile, the links between the DWB and the HB took more concrete

60. Verhandlungsbericht 2. Jahresversammlung, p.12 (Werkbund Archiv).
61. *Kunstgewerbeblatt*, vol.20 (1909), p.230.

form in October 1911 when the two organisations co-operated in the establishment of the 'Hansabund Submissionszentrale'. This central exchange, set up to offer reliable advice and useful contacts to public and private clients with an interest in putting work out to tender for architects, builders, engineers, interior designers and the like, evolved from the DWB's 'Kommission für das Submissionswesen', which was chaired by the architect Emil Beutinger. Thirty leading trade, commercial and professional associations agreed to take part in the service, which was seen by the DWB as a potential source of new opportunities for its members, and one which could help to make quality count in competitive tendering. At the same time the *Submissionszentrale* also lobbied the Reichstag for legislation to regulate and standardise tendering practices, which it believed to be in the best interest of all concerned.

The partnership of HB and DWB was again in evidence in the summer of 1914, when the annual conference of the Hansabund was arranged to coincide with the major DWB exhibition in Cologne. Formal conference sessions were held in Behrens's *Festhalle* and HB delegates had plenty of opportunity to tour the extensive showground. As for the heavy industrial concerns, many of whose representatives had stormed out of the HB three years earlier, their impact on the exhibition was minimal. With the exception of the Krupp AG – which at the DWB's behest donated 25,000 Marks towards the cost of the mammoth undertaking[62] – the famous names of German coal, iron and steel production were largely absent from the Cologne riverside site. It is true that industrialists from both 'camps' were invited onto the 'Honorary Committee', but this had little practical function. More significant were the smaller committees set up to co-ordinate detailed aspects of the exhibition. The 'Industry Committee', for instance, was responsible for the 'model factory' – designed by Gropius – and its quality industrial exhibits. The committee brought together the industrialists Carl Duisberg, Nicolaus Eich and Paul Jordan, plus Rhazen (Gasmotorenfabrik Deutz, Cologne), Zörner (Maschinenbauanstalt Humboldt, Cologne) and von Bodenhausen-Degener (Fr. Krupp AG, Essen) with the architects Gropius, Behrens, Fischer and van de Velde.

Another pavilion, this time designed by Hermann Muthesius, was erected to house the 'Colour Show', and was produced and financed by two Werkbund firms from the chemical industry, Bayer and BASF,[63] whilst the German glass industry sponsored the remarkable 'Glasshouse',

---

62. HA Krupp WA IV 1541 V.3361 (DWB-Ausstellung Köln) pp.153–4, p.156.

63. The links between the chemical industry and Werkbund architects were maintained in the Weimar republic. In 1919 the Düsseldorf DWB member Emil Fahrenkamp (1885–1966) designed a pill factory for Bayer in Leverkusen. A year later Peter Behrens began work on the headquarters of the Hoechst chemical company near Frankfurt. Then, in 1929–30 Hans Poelzig built the huge Frankfurt home of the IG Farben.

designed by Bruno Taut. The great heavy industrial concerns made no such contribution, in marked contrast to the last major industrial exhibition held on the banks of the Rhine – at Düsseldorf in 1902 – when the pavilions of the GHH, Krupp, Hörder Verein, Bergbaulicher Verein and others had dominated the site. Indeed, there could be no better illustration of the structural shift which had occurred in German industry at the start of the century than in the comparison of these two events. Perhaps the author of the initial 'Proclamation' for the Cologne exhibition had this very fact in mind when he wrote:

> If our great industries, and above all the electrical and chemical industry, have founded anew the international reputation of German work and prepared the ground for our economic and political status in the world, so any further significant advance will depend on whether we are capable of going beyond the technical-scientific quality of those achievements to reach the heights of a truly artistic quality and form.[64]

Nevertheless, one of the DWB's prime motivations in holding its first proper exhibition at Cologne was, in Ernst Jäckh's phrase, to 'gain entry into an area which has become the richest and economically most powerful in Germany'.[65] In this aim at least, Jäckh was to be frustrated, for the heavy industrial concerns of the Rhine and Ruhr continued to play a disproportionately small role in Werkbund affairs. As late as 1926 the secretary of the Düsseldorf Chamber of Commerce wrote in the *Kölnische Zeitung*:

> No sooner was the war at an end than the Werkbund began afresh in its efforts to translate aspirations into reality. Recently it has put out its feelers towards the Rhenish-Westphalian industrial region, the workshop of the west. It held its main conference in Essen, in heavy industry's realm. At the same time it visited Duisburg and its docks, Krefeld . . . and Düsseldorf, seat of the iron and steel working industries. This visit to the west certainly had a serious reason, for the Werkbund is once again looking for contact with industry . . . For the time being, however, it appears that the Werkbund has not succeeded in making this contact.[66]

The reticence shown by the great heavy industrial concerns towards the DWB as an organisation could no longer be put down to ignorance or a lack of interest in the merits of *Qualitätsarbeit*. By the early years of the Weimar Republic all the 'mixed' concerns of the Ruhr had some

---

64. Aufruf des 'Vereins zur Veranstaltung der DWB-Ausstellung Köln 1914, e.V.' in *Deutsche Bauzeitung*, vol.43 (1913), p.398.
65. E. Jäckh, '5. Jahresbericht des DWBs' in Werkbund Yearbook, 1913, p.105.
66. J. Wilden, 'Der Werkbund-Gedanke in der rheinisch-westfälischen Industrie', in *Kölnische Zeitung*, 14 July 1926.

involvement with the manufacture of finished goods and all possessed a reasonable understanding of the benefits which could be gained by good design and marketing. Similarly, most heavy industrialists were well aware of the widely-reported achievements of the leading DWB architects and were no longer ill-disposed towards offering them commissions for pit-head complexes, administrative buildings or factory halls. Indeed, historicist industrial architecture had been another fatal casualty of the Great War. Moreover the crude anti-socialism of Kirdorf and Stumm had, in part at least, given way to a more flexible approach to industrial relations and the 'quality workplace' was no longer considered an expensive extravagance by heavy industry. Yet the Werkbund itself remained an object of suspicion in heavy industrial circles. This was surely a legacy of the DWB's early years, in which it was clearly, and correctly, perceived to be a part of the pressure-group activity of the rival industrial 'camp'. Such were the personal and organisational links between the DWB, HB, BdI and left liberal politics that the Werkbund had little real prospect of ever attracting heavy industrial finance to subsidise its activities.

Industrial clients approached the Werkbund and commissioned its architects for a number of reasons – out of political conviction or social conscience, as a form of advertising or a means of image building – with the precise combination of factors different on each occasion. The DWB companies did, however, have much in common: they were innovative, rapidly expanding and publicity conscious; they were to be found in the principal growth areas of the economy, or else were market leaders in more stable sectors; above all, they were companies which sought to distinguish themselves from the industrial status quo.

Angered by tariff policy and cartelisation, worried by the rise of the labour movement, and frustrated by their own impotence, yet all too conscious of their contribution to the national wealth, they had become engaged at the turn of the century in a struggle for power and influence in the Wilhelmine state. Their pressure-groups, lobbyists and political spokesmen fought a fierce war of words and statistics, but in 1907 they found a new weapon, architecture. In the immediate pre-war years it was often deployed in the front line, directed at both the agrarians on the eastern front and the heavy industrialists in the west. The 'quality workplace' gave capitalism a human face; the Werkbund companies hoped it would also give it a prosperous future.

6

Inside the 'Quality Workplace': The Werkbund and the Workers

As the First World War entered its final year, the Werkbund came under fire from within its own ranks. In a series of articles for the intellectual journal *Die Tat*, leading *Werkbündler* began to express fundamental doubts about the organisation's chosen course. Adolf Behne, a writer who had made his name as a champion of the new industrial architecture, did not attempt to hide his own personal disappointment. Despite a decade 'of artistic town planning, artistic factory buildings, artistic school rooms and artistic advertisements, of artistic fashion magazines, artistic vases and artistic village streets', he lamented, 'the world has not become one jot more beautiful'. The reform movement's zeal to provide biscuits and chocolate with 'artistic' wrappers was, moreover, nothing short of 'absurd', leading him to conclude that 'any fusion between art and civil, political or commercial life will inevitably be pulled down to the level of sentimentality'.[1]

The respected Berlin publicist Bruno Rauecker was equally critical in his article, which attacked the DWB's failure to match its fine words with deeds, most notably in the field of social policy. He wrote:

> The maxim that 'the improvement of the working man depends on an improvement in the quality of work' has been used ad nauseam by the leaders of the Bund, but has anything been done in practice? The free trade unions and the Social Democratic Party regard the Werkbund – the 'employers' organisation' – with suspicion . . . wages, methods of payment, working hours, the joy of work, homeliness, old age and pensions – these are the focus of social and ethical aspirations, but does the Werkbund really understand the connections between them?[2]

It was a valid question, because the DWB appeared to have made little headway in developing the social component of its 'quality work'

---

1. A. Behne, 'Kritik des Werkbundes', in *Die Tat*, vol.9 (1917/18), p.430.
2. B. Rauecker, 'Nochmals zur Kritik des Werkbundes', in *Die Tat*, vol.9 (1917/18), p.887.

programme. While many of its ideas on architecture and design had been pursued enthusiastically by German manufacturing industry, the concept of *Qualitätsarbeit* remained vague and ill-defined. Having opened a lively debate on the purpose and practices of industrial production, the Werkbund had then seemed quite content to drop the subject once more, as if in fear of offending its important friends in industry and big business.

If this was hardly likely to endear the organisation to labour leaders, then *Werkbündler* could in return point with some justification to the dismissive reaction their reformist ideas had met with on the orthodox left, where any attempt to prolong the life of the old economic and political order was condemned out of hand. SPD hardliners had consistently expressed their opposition to any 'marriage' of art and industry on capitalism's terms. In a speech to the Prussian parliament in 1910, for instance, Karl Liebknecht proclaimed:

> our art [has become] Americanised . . . industrialised. Art has been caught in the maelstrom of capitalism to such an extent that all those who have a real need for a pure, untouched art are deeply shocked, and view future developments in this regard with very great misgivings.[3]

Liebknecht did not mention the Werkbund by name, but his disapproval of the ideas it represented was obvious. A year later he launched another attack on what he termed the 'Americanisation' of art:

> it describes a phenomenon that we come up against daily: that art stands in the service of capital, in the service of the ruling powers, that art is being exploited in order to preserve those attitudes and beliefs which are convenient for the ruling classes, that capital and the political powers are seeking to use their material influence to subjugate art to their will.[4]

In view of such implacable opposition, the fervent hope expressed by the revisionist SPD art critic and Werkbund member Robert Breuer at the DWB's first annual conference, that the average German worker should add 'quality work' to his list of economic and political demands, appeared destined to remain unfulfilled.

This chapter shifts the focus of attention from the external to the internal politics of the so-called 'quality workplace', the architectural embodiment of the 'quality work' programme. It considers the uneasy relationship between the Werkbund and the people who ostensibly had most to gain from the reform of factory architecture, the shopfloor workers of German

3. K. Liebknecht speech 28 April 1910, quoted by G. Pollak, 'Die gesellschafts- und kulturpolitische Funktion des Deutschen Werkbundes', PhD thesis, Weimar, 1971, note 324.
4. K. Liebknecht speech 15 March 1911, quoted by G. Pollak, ibid., p.134.

industry. Above all, however, it attempts to look beyond the idealist rhetoric of *Qualitätsarbeit* to the realities of modern manufacturing, at a time when the increasing use of 'American' methods had left little room for sentiment.

It would be all too easy, amidst the hit-parade of heroic technological, entrepreneurial and artistic achievements, which so characterised this stage of German industrialisation, to neglect the vital but unrecorded contribution to national prosperity made by countless individuals on shopfloors and at office desks throughout the country. Yet, if the pronouncements of the DWB's leadership were to be believed, it was a concern for precisely these people which had inspired the reform movement in the first place. The chapter begins, therefore, by taking a closer look at the DWB's attitude to organised labour, and the tenor of the working class response.

The established links between Friedrich Naumann and the Evangelical Workers' Unions ensured that the DWB's efforts always received a fair hearing in the Christian trade union movement. Indeed, the Evangelical Workers' Unions held their 1914 conference at Cologne to coincide with the Werkbund exhibition, and took the socio-political importance of 'quality work' as the main theme of their debates. Yet the DWB did not appear to build on these cordial relations. There is no record of formal discussions between the DWB and the Christian labour movement, nor indeed with the liberal Hirsch-Duncker trade unions. The only formal ties between the Werkbund and employees' organisations were with white-collar clerical associations, such as the Association of German Commercial employees (Verband deutscher Handlungsgehilfen), and the German National Association of Commercial Employees (Deutschnationaler Handlungsgehilfen-Verband),[5] which were both listed as 'standing in regular correspondence'.

There were no such contacts with the largest section of organised labour, the 'free' or socialist trade unions. Moreover, when individual DWB employers, such as the Leipzig printing firm Poeschel and Trepte, did attempt to co-operate with the trade unions in the establishment of technical and aesthetic training courses for their workers, the Werkbund's leadership failed to take up the initiative. An offer by the DWB executive to act as a 'conciliation service' between employers and workers in the development of such schemes appears to have gone no further than an internal memorandum.[6]

---

5. For the Deutschnationale Handlungsgehilfen-Verband see Iris Hamel's book *Völkischer Verband und nationale Gesellschaft. Der DHV 1893–1933*, Frankfurt, 1967. The organisation was founded in 1893 and by 1913 had 148,000 members. It evolved from being a small anti-semitic grouping to become Germany's largest white-collar union.

6. 'Denkschrift über die Organisation und die Arbeit des DWB..' (1907) in K. Junghanns, *Der Deutsche Werkbund. Das erste Jahrzehnt*, East Berlin, 1982, p.148.

One should not be surprised, however, that the Werkbund found it easier to deal with company executives and marketing managers than representatives of the wider workforce. Throughout the Wilhelmine era, relations between bourgeois and working class organisations were marked by mutual mistrust and genuine fear. Those who did attempt to build bridges between the classes risked criticism or condemnation from colleagues on their own 'side'. Indeed, within the Werkbund itself there were many who did not share the progressive political and social views of the Naumannites, and others who considered Naumann well-meaning but naive. Karl Ernst Osthaus, who once described 'the masses' as 'eternally unproductive and unteachable', was certainly one.[7]

Nevertheless, a degree of interaction between the Werkbund and the labour movement did occur. The most notable example concerned the design of furniture for working-class households. The large furniture 'workshops', such as the Deutsche Werkstätten, had been producing simple machine-made furniture for less well-off consumers since the turn of the century, and a number of DWB designers had become involved. In 1911 Robert Breuer, who wrote for both *Vorwärts* and Naumann's *Die Hilfe*, and who joined the Werkbund in its first year, had the idea of staging an exhibition of such furniture at the headquarters of the free trade unions in Berlin. The plan was warmly received and a committee was quickly established to co-ordinate the project. Its members included the union leader Sassenbach and the SPD politician Paul Göhre.

As Theodor Heuss noted in his review for *Die Hilfe*, the exhibition's setting, in the very heart of the trade union realm, gave the whole enterprise something amounting to 'the party's blessing'.[8] The exhibition proved popular – 20,000 Marks worth of furniture was sold and many more people came to look – and the idea was repeated in subsequent years. In 1913, for instance, it was possible to purchase from the *Gewerkschaftshaus* a complete set of furniture designed by Peter Behrens (for a living room, bedroom and kitchen) at a total cost of 884 Marks. Of course, not all workers were impressed: at a similar show held in Hamburg two years earlier many considered the furniture too plain and expensive, dubbing it *Armeleutekunst*.[9] Even so, *Werkbündler* like Heuss drew great encouragement from such events, which appeared to open up a new market for products that were 'simple in form, excellent in construction and made in a workshop with high wages'.[10]

Robert Breuer, who was at the heart of most efforts to bring the

---

7. K.E. Osthaus, in a letter to E. Joel 9 Feb. 1916, quoted in H. Hesse-Frielinghaus (ed.), *Karl Ernst Osthaus – Leben und Werk*, Recklinghausen, 1971, p.335.
8. T. Heuss, 'Der Hausrat des Proletariers', in *Die Hilfe*, vol.20 (1911), p.318.
9. K. Junghanns, *Der Deutsche Werkbund*, p.38.
10. T. Heuss, 'Der Hausrat des Proletariers', p.318.

Werkbund and the labour movement together, was also a frequent speaker at DWB meetings. In a debate held at the Munich conference of 1908, for instance, he pointed out that proposals to improve the provision of skill-training for workers, seen by the DWB as a long-term method of enhancing the quality of manufactured goods, would fare better if the support of trade union leaders could be secured: 'who knows the instincts of workers better than those people who head their organisations?', he asked. Breuer warned, however, that the DWB would first have to convince the workers of the pecuniary benefits of *Qualitätsarbeit*:

> Only then, when the industrial workers have to say to themselves, 'the men from the Werkbund don't just want to give us a better education, they also want to see that our best work is rewarded with higher wages', only then will the trust be won which is necessary for successful training. Then, but only then, is it possible to win over the trust of their organisations.[11]

This trust was never really won, but considerable interest was nevertheless shown in the DWB by some of the Left's leading journals. The *Sozialistische Monatshefte*, the journal of the SPD's revisionist wing, carried regular features on the reform movement in the applied arts, including at least six articles on various aspects of the DWB between 1908 and 1914.[12] Indeed, the journal's sympathetic coverage of such issues may have been decisive in persuading Robert Bosch to provide it with financial aid in the early years of the Weimar Republic. Another SPD weekly, *Die neue Zeit*, included an article entitled 'Die Kunstindustrie und das Qualitätsproblem', written by a prominent *Werkbündler*, J.A. Lux, in 1909.[13]

Three years later, Heinz Sperber wrote on the new industrial architecture in the mass-circulation SPD newspaper *Vorwärts*, admitting that 'some new factories' were 'logical and spacious . . . designed with regard to the most recent advances (baths, water closets, ventilators, electric lights etc.)', amenities which were 'still lacking in the homes of millions of workers.' Sperber believed that such factories pointed 'the way to the future' and suggested that capitalism was 'treading the path of modern proletarian

11. R. Breuer in 'Die Veredelung der gewerblichen Arbeit', 1908, p.170.

12. 1908, issue 1, on the Muthesius controversy; 1911, issue 15, on Bruno Paul, also an article on Hamburg workers and furniture made in Hellerau; 1912, issue 16, on workers' furniture exhibition; 1913, issue 19 on Richard Riemerschmid; 1914, issue 14 on the transport display at the DWB exhibition, and issue 20, on conference debates at the same event; 1916, issue 22, Adolf Behne on architecture. For the *Sozialistische Monatshefte* in general, see Roger Fletcher's *Revisionism and Empire. Socialist Imperialism in Germany, 1897–1914*, London, 1984.

13. J.A. Lux, 'Die Kunstindustrie und das Qualitätsproblem', in *Die neue Zeit*, vol.27 (1909), p.769.

architecture'.[14] This view was shared by Robert Breuer, who even went as far as to claim:

> reinforced concrete and democracy belong together. The reinforced concrete style is already being developed in the structures and instruments of the new masses, in factories, bridges, railway stations, department stores and assembly halls.[15]

The 'Quality Workplace': Theory and Practice

The pages of the Werkbund yearbooks and pro-DWB journals like *Der Industriebau* offer little insight into the real conditions and practices of working life within the great halls of the new model factories. The buildings and their products are presented reverentially, like paintings in a gallery, with any smoke, sweat and steam carefully filtered from view. Views of façades far outnumber internal shots, whilst shopfloor areas are noticeably and unnaturally clear of workers. People only invade the frame as indistinct and peripheral objects, as human yardsticks to illustrate the massive scale of the modern factory. Toiling armies of workmen and fuming chimneys, hitherto indispensable elements in pictorial images of industrial wealth creation, have been replaced by orderly rows of silent machinery and the play of light over simple, yet imposing, architectonic forms. The photographs naturally express the desire of the DWB companies to appear clean and modern, but they also communicate a powerful sense of self-reliance, as if industry was celebrating its emancipation from the burden of human fallibility.

Anyone who studies the photographs could be forgiven for reaching a second conclusion too; the *Werkbündler* created architecture first and 'workplaces' second. That is to say, a striking façade appears to have been a more important factor in the design brief than the quality of the internal working environment. This may well have been true, but it does not necessarily expose the 'quality workplace' as a fiction. Firstly, because the external physiognomy of an industrial plant was always considered an integral part of the 'quality workplace', and secondly, because the Werkbund's definition of the concept was, of course, broader than bricks and mortar. It was often taken, for example, to include such things as shorter working hours, reasonable wages and generous social welfare provision, and it was always viewed in tandem with reforms in the area of production; in other words, the introduction of 'quality work'.

Since it was clearly not within the powers of even the most talented

---

14. H. Sperber, in *Vorwärts*, 15 June 1912, quoted by T. Buddensieg in *Industriekultur. Peter Behrens and the AEG*, Cambridge Mass., 1984, p.41.
15. R. Breuer, 'Die Breslauer Ausstellung', in *Die Hilfe*, vol.22 (1913), p.347.

architect to ensure that a new industrial building met all these criteria, responsibility for the realisation of the 'quality workplace' was in effect passed on to industry itself. This inevitably meant that the transition of the 'quality workplace' from theory to practice was a patchy and uneven process, with some firms more willing than others to initiate improvements. Naumann had once suggested that companies which were not 'emphatically liberal' in their approach to the workforce would have no place in the Werkbund, but in practice the DWB did not attempt to interfere in the affairs of its member companies. There was in any case little it could do, since its only sanction – the threat of expulsion – would cause little loss of sleep in company boardrooms.

The consequence of this was clear; companies took from the Werkbund's broad palate of ideas the things they wanted, and left – without fear of censure – anything they did not. It was therefore possible for a 'model' Werkbund employer, such as Bahlsen, to display illiberal attitudes on issues such as trade union membership, and for other DWB companies (MAN, Bayer) to pursue precisely the sort of aggressive employment and industrial relations policies which the DWB had initially condemned. In view of this gap between the rhetoric of the Werkbund leaders and the actions of its member companies, it was hardly surprising that more socially-aware *Werkbündler* began to express serious concern about the organisation's direction. There was, however, precious little they could do.

The keenest disappointment was predictably felt by those who had joined the DWB with the greatest expectations. J.A. Lux, who had written in 1906 that 'the predominantly antagonistic relationship between employer and employee will be improved immediately, if the pursuit of quality becomes fundamental', was one of the first to leave the organisation.[16] Clearly, if the concepts of 'quality work' and the 'quality workplace' were really going to make any impact on German industrial relations, it would be as part of a much more gradual and subtle process. A process, moreover, in which the psychological response of the average worker to his changing role and environment would be crucial.

In fact, the most immediate concerns of manufacturing employees in the late 1900s appear not to have centred on the working environment at all, but on wages, working practices, and the introduction of new machinery. We know this from a number of investigations into working-class attitudes and aspirations carried out in later Wilhelmine Germany by academics and psychologists, with an interest in the 'social question'. One such survey, co-ordinated by the Berlin doctor Adolf Levenstein,

---

16. J.A. Lux, quoted by E. Haase in 'Zur Ideologiefunktion der ästhetischen Produkt- und Unweltgestaltung, dargestellt an der Arbeit und Wirkung des Deutschen Werkbundes', PhD thesis, East Berlin Humboldt University, p.71.

investigated the 'socio-psychological side of the modern large firm, and its psycho-physical effects on the workers'. Similar work was also carried out by members of the Verein für Sozialpolitik and the Institut für Arbeitsphysiologie, as the psychology and sociology of the factory community came under detailed scrutiny for the first time. Indeed, new academic disciplines, which would later offer useful insights into the design of factory and office environments, such as industrial psychology and *Betriebssoziologie*, had their origins in this period.

Levenstein, who was well respected in Naumann's circle, had sent out 8,000 questionnaires to workers in three categories (miners, textile workers, metal workers) between 1907 and 1911, and had achieved a response rate of over 63%, with many of the questions answered in great detail. His findings were published in 1912 and revealed that only in the sample of coalminers was there a frequent recurrence of 'environmental' complaints about working life. Some factory workers objected to the heat, dust or damp of their surroundings, but few linked these problems directly to the buildings in which they worked. One worker did, however, manage to find a memorable phrase, which perhaps helps to explain the attitude of studious disinterest demonstrated by some workers toward their factory environment: 'a cage is still a cage, even if it is a golden cage. The dog on a lead remains a dog, even if it receives the best possible food.'[17]

The sort of fears detected by the likes of Levenstein in the 1900s may well have been exacerbated by the widely-reported transfer to Germany of the latest American innovations in both the organisation and technology of industrial production. The American factory, with its conveyor belts, piece-work rates and output targets, was viewed with great suspicion on the shopfloor, but soon became an object of fascination for many *Werkbündler*. Indeed, in many people's minds the new industrial architecture was itself a manifestation of the 'Americanisation' of German industry. Clearly, all industrial architects had to take account of changes in production methods when planning the layout and spatial design of a factory building, but the DWB's interest and involvement in the 'Americanisation' debate ran much deeper.

It is important to remember that whilst the Werkbund was very much a product of German cultural and political life, it was not born into a vacuum. Neither the DWB's founders nor its member companies were insular in their outlook. With German industry's pre-eminence in Europe apparently assured, the attention of many Germans became fixed on the emerging superpower across the Atlantic. If Germany was to establish a stable footing in world markets, her industry would have to compete with

17. An anonymous textile worker from Forst, quoted in A. Levenstein, *Die Arbeiterfrage*, Munich, 1912, p.142.

the best the New World could offer. For this reason, all changes in American manufacturing were closely monitored, and any implications for German industry carefully digested. Amongst the keenest observers of transatlantic trends were many of the enterprises which chose to work with Werkbund architects.

We have already seen how the Ludw. Loewe company played a pioneering role in introducing aspects of American manufacturing to Germany. Emil Rathenau, founding father of their near neighbours AEG, was another to benefit from paying close attention to developments in the USA. He later recalled, 'the study of American methods increased my knowledge of modern work practices and served as a signpost for the direction in which I was to travel'.[18] Meanwhile, when Hermann Bahlsen introduced a conveyor belt at his Hanover factory in 1905, the giant abattoirs of Chicago were readily acknowledged as his inspiration. As for Carl Benscheidt's Fagus factory, the importance of the American connection can hardly be stressed too highly. It was certainly no coincidence that Walter Gropius referred to the Alfeld plant as 'an American shoe-last factory'. Most significant of all, however, is the fact that, in some respects at least, the Werkbund itself was pre-empted by developments on the other side of the Atlantic.

The American Model: The 'New Factory System'

In 1902 *Die Hilfe* ran a four-part feature on the National Cash Register Company (NCR) of Dayton, Ohio, under the title 'Wenn man den Geist der Arbeit erfaßt'.[19] The bulk of the article had already appeared in the English language journal *Review of Reviews*, but Naumann and his team clearly felt its content was of sufficient importance to merit a rapid translation. Introducing the series, A. Pohlmann wrote:

> The working conditions described here offer a key to the question how American industry can in some areas be so superior to ours. We in Germany still have a long way to go before we fully appreciate, as the Americans do, that the provision of welfare for workers, the raising of their status and the recognition of their valid wishes, are not costly indulgences, but measures which pay, at least in businesses where the quality of the work is important. The American does nothing out of love for his fellow man and everything for his own best interest, but he knows better than we do where his interests lie.[20]

18. Quoted by T. Buddensieg in preface to H. Rogge's *Fabrikwelt um die Jahrhundertwende am Beispiel der AEG Maschinenfabrik in Berlin-Wedding*, Cologne, 1983, p.28.
19. A. Pohlmann, 'Wenn man den Geist der Arbeit erfaßt', *Die Hilfe*, vol.8 (1902).
20. A. Pohlmann, ibid., p.6.

The NCR company, which employed 3,000 workers by the turn of the century, was not only a highly successful enterprise, expanding on the back of a rapid rise in demand for modern cash registers, but, along with H.J. Heinz of Pittsburgh, was also the most prominent name in the American movement for 'industrial betterment'. The movement, described by Samuel Haber as 'an uneven and varying mixture of philanthropy, humanitarianism, and commercial shrewdness',[21] was dominated by religious entrepreneurs such as John H. Patterson, NCR's founder and president, who coined the catchprase 'It pays!' to sum up his attitude to company welfare work. Patterson, who was a leading member of the League For Social Service, believed human happiness could be turned into a business asset. Haber writes:

> One of the important aims of these schemes was to prevent 'labour troubles' and get better work from the workman. This was to be accomplished by providing lunchrooms, bathhouses, hospital clinics, safety training, recreational facilities, thrift clubs, benefit funds, profit-sharing plans, and Ruskinesque garden cities.[22]

Support for the 'industrial betterment' movement in the United States came from companies in a variety of sectors, but as in Germany and Great Britain, the pioneers of factory reform were seldom to be found in heavy industry. As Charles Maier has noted:

> those entrepreneurs identified with benevolent labour relations often headed firms that depended upon light manufacture, where the plant still remained a conglomeration of ateliers . . . and workers might assemble small motors, or packaged sweets . . . Conversely, this style of labour relations was also compatible with the less labour-intensive, continuous flow production of the chemical industry, or with far-flung electrical concerns that owned factories to assemble motors and insulators as well as generating plants that needed minimal supervision. Rarely, however, did the heavy iron and steel manufacturing industries that employed masses of men on large scale semi-skilled production provide the incentive for the paternalism of a Rowntree or others.[23]

The particular characteristics of the NCR operation were described in admiring tones by *Die Hilfe*. From the article one learns, for instance, that the company kept its workforce informed by publishing four different

21. S. Haber, *Efficiency and Uplift. Scientific Management in the Progressive Era, 1890–1920*, Chicago, 1964, p.18.
22. S. Haber, *ibid.*, p.19.
23. C. Maier, 'The Factory as Society. Ideologies of Industrial Management', in R. Bullen, H. Pogge von Strandmann, A. Polonsky (eds), *Ideas into Politics. Aspects of European History*, London, 1984, p.149.

newspapers and magazines, and provided employees with 'suggestion boxes', so that good ideas could be rewarded with substantial cash sums. There was also generous encouragement for worker education programmes, which centred around a collection of six thousand photographic slides of beautiful objects, assembled by the company president and shown at regular evening classes.

The overall relationship between management and trade unions at NCR was adjudged to be 'entirely friendly'. Indeed, workers invariably referred to the company as 'our company', and were positively encouraged to join a union. The workplace itself, built in 1896, was described as 'a model establishment of order and cleanliness', where 'great importance' was placed on 'rooms flooded by sunlight'. The windows were 'huge' and all rooms were painted yellow, enlivened by flowers both inside and out. The final instalment of the article concluded with the words:

> May everyone who walks through our black, sooty and ugly factory districts, past the bare walls of the factories and their surrounding slag heaps, say to themselves: the workplaces of the people do not have to look like this. An American model plant has shown that the raising of workers' status, the advancement of their organisations, cleanliness, the cultivation of welfare and beauty, are not just good things in themselves, but things which pay.[24]

One cannot know for sure what influence *Die Hilfe*'s four-part feature on NCR, or indeed knowledge of other American examples, had on the emergence of the Werkbund from the Naumann circle, but the similarities between the movement for 'industrial betterment' and the efforts of German reformers are obvious. There was, of course, a significant difference as well, for the American movement did not involve the artistic impulse which was such an integral part of the DWB, but the *Hilfe* article is nevertheless instructive. The awestruck tone adopted by the writer Pohlmann reflects perfectly the admiration felt by many Naumannites for the recent achievements of American capitalism. When Naumann's party colleague Theodor Barth wrote down his impressions of the New World in 1907, for instance, he was moved to quote Goethe's famous line: 'Amerika, du hast es besser als unser Kontinent, der alte, hast keine verfallenen Schlösser und keine Basalte'.

This sense of wonderment was very much in evidence in 1913, when the second Werkbund Yearbook included many photographs of American industrial installations. The illustrations, selected by Walter Gropius and depicting a range of US car factories and South American grain silos, then reappeared after the war in Le Corbusier's seminal work *Vers une architecture*, as if to confirm the important influence of American industrial

24. A. Pohlmann, 'Geist der Arbeit', p.7.

architecture on European modernism. Although these large industrial plants were perceived by Gropius and his contemporaries to be one of the distinctive and definitive features of America ('the motherland of industry' according to Gropius), they were still in fact a very recent phenomenon. The nineteenth century American factory had differed little in size and appearance from its European counterparts. It was only around the turn of the century that American factories began to assume hitherto unprecedented dimensions and characteristics.

Indeed, as Daniel Nelson has described, the internal and external landscape of the American industrial plant was 'transformed' between 1880 and 1915.[25] Electric lighting, or an increased level of natural light, together with the removal of power shafts and drive belts, led to greatly improved visibility, and similar progress was made on ventilation systems. Of particular interest to Gropius and other European modernists, however, was the low-key development of the so-called 'daylight factory' – 'multistoried reinforced concrete grids [which] served as the framework for window walls of glass'[26] – by architects such as Ernest Ransome, who designed the United Shoe Machinery plant at Beverly in 1903–06. 'Daylight factories' had become so widespread by 1911 that the *American Architect and Building News* could write: 'pure, clear, uncolored daylight – the sunshine of roofless fields . . . is becoming the possession of the American factory labourer'.[27]

These technological and architectural innovations were matched by less obvious but equally crucial changes in managerial practices. Since the turn of the century an increasing number of American accountants, engineers and factory managers had been emphasising the importance of order, planning and discipline in industrial production and administration. They called their new approach 'systematic' management, and recommended a greater use of job cards, time clocks, standardised parts and systemised purchasing, as well as measures to improve accounting and record keeping. Some large American companies also began to employ personnel directors and welfare secretaries to co-ordinate the relationship between management and workforce.

The technological, managerial and personnel elements of what Nelson terms the 'New Factory System' were all evident in the factories of the Detroit automobile industry. The plants designed by the German-born architect Albert Kahn (1869–1942) for Packard in 1905, for Pierce at Buffalo shortly after, and the 865-foot long factory for Ford at the Highland

25. D. Nelson, *Managers and Workers. Origins of the New Factory System in the United States, 1880–1920*, Wisconsin, 1975, p.33.

26. R. Banham, *A Concrete Atalantis. US Industrial Building and European Modern Architecture*, Cambridge Mass., 1986, introduction.

27. Quoted by R. Banham, *ibid.*, p.22.

Park site in 1908–10, were unlike any factories yet seen. The most potent symbol of the new system was undoubtedly the famous 'assembly line', opened at Highland Park on 1 April 1913, which came to embody the dawning of the age of 'mass production'. The combination of assembly line production, high wages, and an affordable machine product, which made up Henry Ford's philosophy of industry, gained both fame and notoriety in Europe after World War One.

'Fordism' was, however, only one aspect of the complex series of approaches to industrial production and labour relationships which became associated with 'Americanism' or 'Americanisation'. In fact, the American industrial innovation which received the greatest attention in pre-war Germany was a programme for the reform of factory organisation and labour discipline devised by the engineer Frederick W. Taylor (1856–1915). Taylor's first publication had appeared as early as 1895, but his most important works were *Shop Management* (1903) and *The Principles of Scientific Management* (1911). Taylor differed from proponents of 'industrial betterment' by concentrating on shopfloor working practices rather than social welfare provision, and at the same time went beyond supporters of 'systematic' management in the depth and complexity of his investigations. He believed that by analysing each stage of the production process 'scientifically' it would be possible to find an optimum level of human and mechanical performance, which would maximise output and eliminate inefficiency. For this reason he termed his programme 'scientific management':

> Like many of the systemizers, Taylor favoured the analogy between the organization and the machine. Taylor was not satisfied, however, simply with an orderly arrangement of parts. He wanted to know how well each component performed its task, and he intended to bring each component 'to its highest state of excellence'.[28]

In order to establish optimum performance levels, Taylor envisaged the setting up of planning departments within factories. The planners, who would have to be well versed in the methods of scientific management, would use time and motion studies and task instruction cards to restructure the pace and pattern of production. This process should take between three to five years to complete properly. The growth in productivity which would result from a more efficient use of resources would then benefit shareholders and employees alike, since wages and dividends would rise with output. Money would also become available for the sort of welfare schemes envisaged by the supporters of 'industrial betterment'. In this way

28. S. Haber, *Efficiency and Uplift*, p.21.

the interests of the shopfloor worker would become synonymous with those of the manager.

At the same time, however, wage scales would have to be revised to take account of productivity. Taylor believed that the introduction of piece-work rates would encourage the good worker and punish the inefficient. It would also mean that wages were worked out between the individual worker and his superior, rather than through a process of collective bargaining. Furthermore, employees would have to undergo an element of psychological and physical testing, in order to achieve a better allocation of tasks amongst the workforce. The guru of scientific management admitted that his programme required 'a complete mental revolution on both sides', but was certain of the long term benefits it would produce:

> The great revolution that takes place in the mental attitude of the two parties under scientific management is that both sides take their eyes of the division of the surplus as the all-important matter, and together turn their attention toward increasing the size of the surplus.[29]

As an engineer Taylor liked to portray himself as an honest broker, detached from the disputes of capital and labour. He believed that managerial decisions based on the 'objective' findings of his scientific research would be more acceptable to workers than the arbitrary dictates of old-style management. Indeed, the personal exercise of power would be eliminated altogether, for 'the man at the head of the business under scientific management is governed by rules and laws which have been developed through hundreds of experiments just as much as the workman is'.[30] In this way, he argued, the appliance of science could provide an escape route from the impasse of class confrontation.

It was no coincidence that the concept of scientific management had its origins in the highly-mechanised world of American manufacturing, where a method was required to force up human workrates in line with increasing mechanical productivity. Yet Taylor's message did not take long to spread across the Atlantic: the first German translation of a work by Taylor appeared in 1908, and the following year a German edition of *Shop Management* was published. The *Principles of Scientific Management* came out in Germany in 1913, just two years after it had first appeared in the USA. The books set out a programme which, as Maier has written,

29. F.W. Taylor quoted by C. Maier in 'Between Taylorism and Technocracy: European ideologies and the vision of industrial productivity in the 1920s', in *Journal of Contemporary History*, vol.5 (1970), p.32.

30. F.W. Taylor quoted by R. Bendix in *Work and Authority in Industry. Ideologies of Management in the Course of Industrialization*, New York, 1960, p.278.

'both demanded and promised much',[31] yet the main themes – efficiency, productivity, incentives – were simple enough to win converts quickly.

The disciples of scientific management soon included engineers, architects and forward-thinking entrepreneurs, but also some social reformers, who believed that Taylor's ideas could be transferred from the factory to society at large, that industrial efficiency could bring 'social efficiency' too. 'Taylorism', as scientific management inevitably became known, appealed to political thinkers on both the left and the right, but gained particular support from those groups which looked for solutions beyond *laissez-faire* liberalism and doctrinaire socialism. Indeed, the cultural and political impact of Taylorism in the first three decades of the twentieth century was rather more important than its influence on the shopfloor, where the number of companies to endorse all aspects of Taylor's programme remained small. The effects of 'scientific management' on industry should not, however, be underestimated, for as Maier writes:

> Theories of management are to the practice of business as theories of architecture are to building. Few buildings follow the canons of design announced by leading architects, even if they may incorporate individual elements. Still, architectural manifestos are crucial for orienting the profession to what might be their solutions if clients, money, and site constraints allowed. So, too, few industrial plants incorporate the doctrines of management experts as coherent ensembles. Very few factories, for example, were actually organised as Taylorite institutions before and after World War One, even in the United States. Nonetheless, Taylorism or scientific management dominated the discourse of industrial relations.[32]

Elements of Taylorism began to appear in German industry during the years 1902–08, most notably in those sectors engaged in direct competition with American companies: precision engineering, machine building and the like. Experiments in wage incentive schemes were particularly common here, but detailed knowledge of Taylor's work remained vague. Heidrun Homburg, who has written on the origins of Taylorism in Germany, believes it was only as a result of the 1907–8 depression that German companies became more interested in the principles of scientific management.[33] Amongst the first German industrialists to express admiration for Taylor's ideas were Neuhaus of Borsig and Perls of the

---

31. C. Maier, 'Between Taylorism and Technocracy', p.31.
32. C. Maier, 'Ideologies of Industrial Management', p.147.
33. H. Homburg, 'Anfänge des Taylorsystems in Deutschland vor dem Ersten Weltkrieg. Eine Problemskizze unter besonderer Berücksichtigung der Arbeitskämpfe bei Bosch 1913', in *Geschichte und Gesellschaft*, vol.4 (1978), p.170. See also J. Campbell, *Joy in Work, German Work: the National Debate 1800–1945*, Princeton, 1989.

Siemens-Schukert AG, but both doubted whether his programme could be introduced directly into the different social, economic and cultural climate of central Europe. One company that did manage to implement the Taylor programme in Germany, however, was Bosch of Stuttgart, where the business director and Werkbund member Hugo Borst was its great champion.

The Bosch company had in fact been attempting to organise its production along American lines for some time. In 1908, for instance, it had established a central office to set and monitor piece-work rates, and had rationalised a number of repetitive tasks, such as the preparation of technical drawings, by transferring responsibility from the shopfloor to specialist departments. In addition, all Bosch factories had been refitted with the latest in American autocratic production machinery. Early in 1913, however, Bosch's Hugo Borst went one stage further than other German industrialists, by setting out on a special mission to the United States with the aim of meeting F.W. Taylor personally.

Borst spent several days with Taylor in Philadelphia, and was shown around a number of small manufacturing companies which had introduced scientific management policies. On his return to Germany, Borst became a vociferous, though not uncritical, promulgator of Taylor's ideas, addressing everybody from the German Engineers' Association to the Evangelical Social Congress, and promoting Taylorism within the DWB as well. In one lecture he claimed he had been told 'twenty times' by Taylor to remember the following 'simple rule':

> Make the worker your friend and mean this friendship honestly and sincerely. Only when this spirit has entered your business, only when you have proved to the worker that your gain is his gain too, will he help you voluntarily to introduce the principles of scientific management.[34]

Borst believed that this rule was an essential pre-requisite of Taylor's stated goal of 'high wages and the lowest production costs', and was fundamental to his 'undoubted success' in America. 'Taylor considers himself a social reformer', Borst said, 'and all his friends in America see him in the same light'.[35] Whether all Borst's colleagues in the Werkbund agreed, however, remained to be seen.

The appeal of scientific management to *Werkbündler* was at first sight considerable. Taylor's programme offered to improve industrial relations without damaging profits, to increase output without raising costs, and, above all, to grant engineers and other 'specialists' a pivotal role in

34. H. Borst, 'Das sogenannte Taylor-System..' lecture given to the Württemberg branch of the VDI on 15 January 1914, pp.23–24.
35. H. Borst, ibid., p.24.

achieving industrial and social harmony. The psychological power of a plan which nailed its colours so clearly to the mast of modernity and the 'machine age' was, moreover, not to be underestimated. On the other hand, how could this method, which even supporters admitted was designed to remove any element of thought or individuality from the manufacturing process, be equated with the DWB's declared aim of 'spiritualising' or 'ennobling' industrial work? Turning workers into automatons seemed to some *Werkbündler* a most peculiar way of achieving 'quality work'.

In 1913 the pages of *Die Hilfe* reflected the strong feelings aroused by 'Taylorism' in a series of thoughtful and closely argued essays. Friedrich Naumann himself contributed a piece entitled 'The Human Machine', in which he praised the efficacy of Taylor's arguments, but voiced fears for the consequences:

> One cannot say that Taylor brings something completely new and unexpected, but he presents his ideas in such an understandable and common sense way, and shows their direct usefulness so incontrovertably, that much we already knew takes on a practical form for the first time . . . One cannot deny that great tasks still lie ahead. It is indeed true that much energy is wasted unnecessarily. The loss of human energy is even greater than that of electricity from powerlines: so much more could be done with these people! But, if it was, would they still be people?[36]

Naumann's rhetorical question hung in the air for much of the next decade, as the DWB waited to assess the effects of 'Taylorism' in action. Little had been resolved, however, by the time the Werkbund conference delegates gathered at Karlsruhe in 1924. Two years earlier, the DWB had taken 'Joy in Work' as the theme for its annual conference; now two days were to be set aside for a debate on scientific management and other aspects of 'Americanisation', in which the opposing sides were each given the opportunity to present a major set-piece paper. The 1924 DWB conference falls outside the scope of this study, of course, and has been looked at in more detail elsewhere,[37] but this particular debate is nevertheless worthy of comment here, since it highlights very clearly the different conceptions of 'quality work' which had always existed within the DWB.

Speaking on behalf of 'Taylorism' was the familiar figure of Hugo Borst, whilst his opponent was to be the educationalist, social scientist and left liberal politician Willy Hellpach, who had written extensively on the problems of making industrial labour a more satisfying experience. In his paper Borst conceded that shopfloor work in a mass production factory

---

36. F. Naumann, 'Die menschliche Maschine', in *Die Hilfe*, vol.22 (1913), pp.438–439.
37. See J. Campbell, *Joy in Work.*

was monotonous and repetitive, with precious little time for breaks or relaxation. Nevertheless, he argued, American-style mass production was both indispensable and desirable. For a start, not everyone had the sensibilities of a *Werkbündler*: many people were in fact looking for work that was neither creative nor challenging. To support this claim, he cited the experiences of both Henry Ford – 'for most people, having to think is a punishment' – and Hugo Münsterberg, whose aptitude tests and psycho-selection methods were much in vogue at the time.

Borst, who drew heavily on the Ford phenomenon, but also on his own experience at Bosch, suggested that increased efficiency would lead to shorter working hours and hence greater leisure time, which could then be put to constructive use by each individual worker. At the same time, improvements in efficiency and output would boost wages as well, thus allowing the industrial worker to become a valued consumer and an integrated citizen too. In short, there was nothing undesirable about a worker sacrificing eight hours a day to a relative mundane task, if he was able to enjoy the remaining sixteen with money in his pocket:

> If it is really so soulless for a worker to spend his entire working life making screws for bicycles, then at least he can expect some respect for his wish to own a bicycle himself, and have the time to put it to practical use.[38]

As a good *Werkbündler*, Borst tempered his 'American' vision with some sound words on the quality of the product and the working environment. The worker's well-being and freshness should be guaranteed by 'healthy, clean, light, dust-free, well heated and ventilated workrooms', enlivened where possible with 'happy colours, pictures or flowers', together with the usual array of welfare facilities. Nevertheless, it was clear that for Borst, 'quality work' did not really require 'quality workers' at all, if quality was to be measured by mental agility or practical skills. For Willy Hellpach, however, Borst's vision of 'mindless' machine work spelt great danger, not only for the industrial workplace, but for society as a whole.

Hellpach insisted that he was in no way a hopeless romantic, longing for a return to the 'good old days' of handicraft production, with its 'mythical' joy of work. What he wanted was a more reasonable, a more human way of structuring modern industrial production, so that 'mechanical work' could regain its meaning and its morality, and once

---

38. H. Borst, 'Mechanisierte Industriearbeit, muß sie im Gegensatz zu freier Arbeit Mensch und Kultur gefährden?', in H. Borst & W. Hellpach, *Das Problem der Industriearbeit*, Berlin, 1925, p.28.

again involve the 'whole person'.[39] The movement to 'spiritualise' industrial work, which Hellpach believed included the Christian trade unions and the *Werkbund* itself, should concern itself with the increasing division of labour, and attempt to find some way of restoring the meaning of work to the individual worker. In the long term, however, Hellpach hoped that fully-automised production would replace the need for assembly-line operatives altogether.

In retrospect we know, of course, that the reality of 'Taylorism' failed to live up to both the exaggerated expectations of its supporters and the dire warnings of its detractors. The Ford model soon lost its aura of infallibility too. More significant for us, however, is the fact that Borst and Hellpach could interpret 'quality work' in such different ways: Borst, the industrialist, was concerned with creating a good but affordable product, as efficiently as possible; Hellpach, the social reformer, sought changes to the nature of industrial work itself. If Hellpach's views more closely resembled the Werkbund's public rhetoric, it was Borst who more accurately reflected the actions of the DWB companies. In the final analysis, however, neither would have won many friends on the factory floor.

The fatal flaw in the reformist conception of 'quality work', as proposed by the Naumannites before World War One, was the assumption that the manufacture of a quality product necessarily required 'quality workers'. Of course, a high standard of workmanship would always be important, but new production technology made it possible to turn out ever greater quantities of well-designed and well-built products with an increasingly de-skilled workforce. Thus whilst companies like AEG and Bosch were able to make steady progress in improving the design and technical quality of their products, similar advances were not made in improving the quality of their workers.

The process of de-skilling which could result from the adoption of American production methods and technology was the direct cause of much labour unrest, including a particularly long and bitter strike at Bosch in 1913, led by the most highly skilled and experienced section of the

---

39. Hellpach's paper was short on practical suggestions, but it did make reference to Daimler's experiments in so-called 'group manufacturing', a subject on which Hellpach had already written a critically acclaimed book. Under their chief engineer Lang and an academic, Eugen Rosenstock, the Untertürkheim company had in 1919 attempted to alter the structure of manufacturing by devolving production into separate, self-contained workshops, with teams of workers co-operating to construct recognisable end-products, such as engines. The experiment failed in the difficult economic climate of the early 1920s. See J.Campbell, *Joy in Work*.

workforce, the toolmakers.[40] They objected not only to the increasingly 'murderous' tempo of work itself, but to the company policy of making redundant anyone who was unable to keep it up. After 1908, and particularly after the 1913 dispute, the profile of the Bosch workforce changed dramatically, with a significant number of older, skilled workers, including many trade union replaced by younger, semi-skilled men, and for the first time, low paid women as well. The proportion of skilled workers in the workforce fell from 64% in 1908 to 42% in 1910 and 33% in 1914, whilst in the course of 1913 the proportion of female labour nearly doubled, from 3.3% to 6.3%.[41]

Although it is not clear whether the 1913 strike was deliberately provoked by the company to speed up this restructuring process, it certainly brought an end to the age of innocence of 'Father Bosch' and his business, and one suspects, of many *Werkbündler* too. The claim made by Bruno Rauecker in 1912, that 'the goal of "quality work" is the same as that of the unions: the abolition, or at least diminution, of piece-work . . . because the quality product par excellence cannot be manufactured in a mad rush',[42] would have convinced few workers in 1912, and fewer still in 1913.

In view of their personal experiences, workers at Bosch could have been forgiven for thinking that the Werkbund programme of 'quality work' had more to do with economic rationalisation than with social reform; that the 'quality workplace' offered only a more subtle and efficient exploitation of the working class. However, such a conclusion would be justifiable only in part, for the development of improved working conditions usually stemmed from a complex mixture of motives, which certainly included the desire to increase output and profits, but also reflected some genuine concern for employee welfare too.

Interest in the well-being of workers had increased since the discovery of the 'human factor in business', and the belated realisation that the motivation of the workforce could be as crucial as the condition of the machinery. For the first time, employers were beginning to regard their workforce as a valuable resource; a commodity which could be improved with investment and would cost money to replace. It is possible, therefore, to find benefits for both sides of industry in the improved conditions of

40. For details of strike at Bosch see H. Homburg, 'Anfänge des Taylorsystems'; also U. Stolle, *Arbeiterpolitik im Betrieb. Frauen und Männer, Reformisten und Radikale, Fach- und Massenarbeiter bei Bayer, BASF, Bosch und in Solingen, 1900–1933*, Frankfurt, 1980; and T. Heuss, *Robert Bosch. Leben und Leistung*, Stuttgart, 1946.
41. H. Homburg, ibid., p.184. In the following decades the process of de-skilling was to some extent reversed, as a section of the workforce became 're-skilled' as technicians and machine supervisors.
42. B. Rauecker, 'Über einige Zusammenhänge zwischen Qualitätsarbeit und Sozialpolitik', in *Kunstgewerbeblatt*, vol.24 (1912), p.5.

the new model factories, albeit in unequal measure.

One should be wary, however, of the impression frequently conveyed by company sponsored publications, that improvements in working conditions were introduced in a spirit of managerial benevolence. As Roland Günter has pointed out, the industrialists of the day were particularly adept at dressing up straightforward business decisions in the guise of generous 'good deeds'.[43] It was not unusual, for instance, for the layout of a new factory, or the development of a company housing estate, to be presented to the outside world as a significant social concession, when commercial considerations had in fact been paramount. When companies commissioned DWB architects they were predictably quick to publicise the 'light, air and sun' which would henceforth enrich the lives of ordinary workers, but in so doing they told only half the story.

The use of reinforced concrete and steel as building materials, and the introduction of small electric motors for machinery, transformed the German factory as it had the American. The shape and form of industrial buildings could now be dictated by the pattern of production rather than the plan of the power shafts. The factory floor itself seemed to open up new possibilities as soon as it was realised that rows of load-bearing pillars and a tangled web of transmission equipment would not always be around to hamper visibility and movement. It was not only in factories designed by DWB architects that these changes occurred, of course, but such was the high publicity profile of the Werkbund buildings – and especially Behrens's AEG factories – that they came to symbolise perfectly the changing industrial environment.

The increased level of daylight was invariably the first aspect of the new factory architecture to be singled out by management for public consumption. It was understandable, but somewhat disingenuous, of company spokesmen to present this as a 'gift' to the ordinary worker. For, whilst the workforce undoubtedly enjoyed a factory environment less gloomy and sepulchral than before, management also benefited from being able to observe more closely the actions and movements of its employees. On the principle that 'it's the boss's eye which doubles the work, and not his hand'[44] it was now possible for supervisory personnel to move from the shopfloor to elevated glass control cabins (*Meisterstuben*), from where they could observe virtually the whole work area without obstruction. As Karl Ernst Osthaus – no great friend of the working man – put it in his *Frankfurter Zeitung* article on the AEG turbine factory:

43. R. Günter, 'Krupp in Essen', in M. Warnke (ed.), *Das Kunstwerk zwischen Wissenschaft und Weltanschauung*, Gütersloh, 1970, p.138.

44. See T. Engelhardt, 'Menschen nach Maß', in 'Leben und arbeiten im Industrie-zeitalter', catalogue, Germanisches Nationalmuseum, 1985, p.291.

From one point it is possible to have an uninterrupted view over the giant factory hall. Here the view is not hampered by any little shed where the foremen can have their midday snooze and hide their botched work. Everything is open for the eyes of the control.[45]

The flood of light through the windows of the Werkbund factories proved a mixed blessing for shopfloor workers in another way too. The desire of the DWB architects to take advantage of the possibilities opened up by new building technology at times overcame their practical good sense. At the AEG *Montagehalle*, part of the Brunnenstraße complex, for instance, Behrens's glass roof turned the building into a greenhouse in summer and a refrigerator in winter. It was later replaced by a more conventional concrete tiled roof with separate skylights. Similar problems were reported at Gropius's Fagus-Werk, where blinds were fitted during the 1920s to reduce the glare of sunlight through the glass 'curtain-wall'. Julius Posener has written of the Werkbund's 'craze' for light (*Lichtfimmel*):

> The completely glazed roof of the *Montagehalle* shows just how far this craze for light went . . . In reality it was an unwarranted imposition on the workers, although it was admittedly not intended as such. The intention of this new form of representation, representation through light, was this: look, *we* the management are giving the worker bright places of work, *we* are giving him the humane places of work demanded by socialism . . . the monumentality of the factory buildings was intended to give notice of the power of the company, the profusion of light the humanity . . .[46]

In this way the 'new' industries developed a different style of labour relations, dependent upon more subtle forms of control and motivation than had hitherto been the case. The essence of the employer-employee relationship remained intact, of course, but the authoritarian approach to labour questions which had characterised the first wave of German industrialisation, and which lived on in many heavy industrial concerns, appeared increasingly irrelevant to the needs of a changing society. Just as the overt domination of the workforce in nineteenth century industry had found architectural expression through the historical architecture of privilege and subjugation, so the new managerial style, with its reliance on 'American' methods and technological innovation, briefly became embodied in the industrial buildings of the German Werkbund.

The DWB was, however, very much an organisation of transition and contradiction, born with one foot in the nineteenth and one in the twentieth

45. K.E. Osthaus, 'Ein Fabrikbau von Peter Behrens', in *Frankfurter Zeitung*, 10 Feb. 1910.
46. J. Posener, *Berlin auf dem Wege zu einer neuen Architektur*, Munich, 1979, p.389.

century, and still unsure which way to fall. Its members became involved with industry at the cutting edge of capitalism and technological change, yet retained a naive faith in the power of art to provide solutions to social and economic dilemmas. They recognised the growing importance of world trade and an international style, yet sought solutions which were definitively German, compatible with all the best traditions of *Kultur*. It is this which distinguishes the industrial buildings of Behrens, Muthesius, Poelzig and even Gropius, from the work of their anonymous American contemporaries.

If American industrial architects were largely content to construct simple functional shells to house machinery in the most efficient manner, the *Werkbündler* attempted an altogether more ambitious synthesis. Striving self-consciously to 'ennoble' industrial production, whilst at the same time satisfying the practical requirements of manufacturers, and the supposed needs of the workforce, the DWB architects aimed high, and went as far as they could go. Ultimately, however, they appeared to be as much restricted by the economic and social realities of their time and place as anyone else. To launch a new aesthetic was one thing, to change the direction and emphasis of economic life was quite another. If *Qualitätsarbeit* was to become a reality, it could only be on industry's terms: the crucial decisions would be taken not on the shopfloor, nor in the architect's studio, but in company boardrooms across the *Reich*.

This no doubt came as a shock to some of the more unworldly *Werkbündler*, but Naumann and his closest followers were not easily deterred. Whilst the path of political reconciliation and peaceful reform had left the Naumannites some way from the summit, there were enough positive signs in the foothills of works' councils and local politics to keep spirits from flagging. Indeed, it is from this more modest perspective that the Werkbund ethos appears in its most flattering light. The next chapter looks in some depth at the impact of Werkbund ideas on an individual town in northern Germany.

7

Industrial Architecture and Municipal Politics: The Experience of a Single Town

The small industrial town of Delmenhorst, situated on the eastern fringe of the predominantly rural Oldenburg region, is at first sight an unlikely location in which to search for landmarks in the history of German design. The architectural tourist trail, which each year brings growing numbers of visitors to Behrens's AEG complex in Berlin, and even to little Alfeld in search of the Fagus-Werk, by-passes Delmenhorst altogether, preferring instead the rival attractions of Bremen, its historic Hanseatic neighbour. After many centuries as a minor staging post on the coach road to Oldenburg, and several decades as a dormitory town for Bremen-bound commuters, Delmenhorst has learnt to live with obscurity. Its absence from the guide books today arouses less concern in the local community than the levels of unemployment and crime, both rising as the town's economy enters a period of transition.

In the first decade of this century, however, Delmenhorst enjoyed an all too brief spell in the limelight, as a centre of artistic and political innovation. The rare but auspicious conjunction of a young left liberal mayor, a progressive local manufacturer, and an ambitious modern architect was responsible for this intriguing episode in the town's history, which has since been forgotten elsewhere in Germany, but at the time represented perhaps the most complete demonstration of the Werkbund idea in action. The particular combination of individuals and circumstances which makes the case of Delmenhorst so interesting, was of course unique, but the town's development was in other ways quite typical, illustrating many of the trends discussed in previous chapters. For this reason, the following pages examine Delmenhorst's industry, architecture and politics in the Wilhelmine period, focusing in particular on the relationship between the mayor Erich Koch, the industrialist Gustav Gericke, and the architect Heinz Stoffregen.

Delmenhorst's 'Unforeseen Advance'

Delmenhorst had been granted its first civic charter as early as 1371, but by the middle of the nineteenth century it was still little more than a village. With the exception of a few dozen men engaged in cork-cutting and cigar-making workshops, the two thousand inhabitants made their living servicing the needs of the surrounding countryside. The town's once imposing castle, the former seat of the Counts of Oldenburg-Delmenhorst and for centuries the focal point of the community, had long since fallen into decay. In 1855 Delmenhorst suffered the ultimate indignity of being downgraded to the status of the Grand Duchy of Oldenburg's 'second class' towns, which meant giving up many of its administrative powers to a central government official. Thereafter a sheriff or *Amtshauptmann* – the Oldenburg equivalent of the Prussian *Landrat* – ran the town's judicial and administrative affairs in the manner of the Duchy's rural districts.

It was not until the arrival of the railway in 1867 that Delmenhorst's fortunes began to improve.[1] The line, linking Bremen and Oldenburg, was an essential pre-requisite of the town's later development. The close proximity of Bremen, which had hitherto acted as a barrier to Delmenhorst's growth, was now to aid its industrial expansion. For, with a rail link in place, Delmenhorst was perfectly situated to take full advantage of the Hanseatic port's delayed integration into the German *Reich*. Bremen, like Hamburg, had always declined to become a member of the German Customs Union, and continued to uphold her independence even after unification. Freeport status, which had guaranteed the prosperity of Bremen's harbour for many centuries, was fiercely defended by the city's merchants, but only at the cost of stifling the development of local industry, since all goods manufactured in the *Hansestadt* were subject to import duty on entering Customs Union territory. In view of the particularly high tariffs levied upon finished goods, it was not surprising that Bremen industrialists soon began to look outside the city's boundaries for factory sites. Delmenhorst, just ten miles to the west, was the principal beneficiary. When Bremen did finally join the German customs zone in 1888, Delmenhorst was firmly established as an industrial centre.

The first major industrial enterprise to set up in Delmenhorst, on a plot of land next to the town's railway station, was a jute factory, founded by the Bremen businessmen Vogt and Wex, under the title 'Hanseatische Jute-Spinnerei und Weberei'. The factory, which employed 130 people to manufacture sacks and matting from Indian jute, opened in February 1871. At the same time, Delmenhorst's small cork-cutting industry, which also relied upon the import of raw materials through Bremen, was undergoing

---

1. For details of Delmenhorst's industrial development see H. Lübbing, 'Delmenhorsts Aufstieg zur Industriestadt', *Delmenhorster Schriften* – no. 1, Delmenhorst, 1971; also E. Grundig, 'Geschichte der Stadt Delmenhorst 1848–1945', vols 3–4, typewritten manuscript in SA Delmenhorst; G. von Lindern, *Kleine Chronik der Stadt Delmenhorst*, Oldenburg, 1971; and H. Saebens, *Delmenhorst. Werden einer Wirtschaftsstadt*, Delmenhorst, 1953.

a process of mechanisation, which boosted productivity tenfold, but also increased wastage rates to nearly 60%. As we shall see, the presence in Delmenhorst of both the jute and cork-cutting industries later made the town an ideal centre for linoleum manufacture.

The factory which was to become Delmenhorst's largest employer, the sprawling textile mill known as the 'Norddeutsche Wollkämmerei und Kammgarnspinnerei' (NW&K), was built on a thirteen hectare site to the north of the Bremen-Oldenburg railway line in 1884. The NW&K was the idea of the Bremen wool merchant Christian Lahusen, who owned vast sheep farms in South America and had purchased one of Europe's leading woollen mills at Neudeck, Bohemia, in 1873. Production began with 100 employees, but by 1891 this figure had already risen to 1,647, and by 1914 it had reached 3,300. Under Christian's son Carl (1858–1921) the NW&K developed into multinational concern, which at its height controlled one quarter of the world's woollen yarn production, before crashing ignominiously in the 1931 depression.[2] Around 20% of Delmenhorst's total population was employed at NW&K in the 1890s, but the headquarters of the Lahusen concern remained in Bremen, and with NW&K factories being established throughout central Europe, Delmenhorst never became as closely identified with the woollen industry as that statistic may suggest.

In fact, it was as a centre for linoleum production that the name of Delmenhorst was carried around the world.[3] Linoleum, invented by an Englishman, Frederick Walton in 1860, was the end product of a long and complicated process which combined oxidised linseed oil, ground cork and woven jute to create a hard wearing and hygienic floor covering, that could be coloured or decorated with inlaid designs. Large imports of English linoleum to Germany in the 1870s convinced the Bremen merchant Heinrich Bremer, the banker Georg Wolde and the Delmenhorst cork manufacturer J.C.Wieting, to set up a German linoleum factory in Delmenhorst. After negotiations with the leading English company in Staines, which was itself looking to establish a factory on the continent, Bremer and Wieting agreed on a joint enterprise: the German Linoleum Manufacturing Company Ltd. was founded in 1882 and a factory, fitted with the latest English machinery, was built on the northern outskirts of the town. The initial workforce of 62 soon doubled in size and by 1891

2. For the history of the NW&K see S. Auffarth & F. Stracke, 'Die Nordwolle. Neues Leben für ein Industriedenkmal', *Delmenhorster Schriften* – no. 10, Delmenhorst, 1982, pp.17–21.

3. The growth of the linoleum industry in Delmenhorst is recounted by G. von Lindern, 'Die Delmenhorster Linoleum-Industrie', in *Delmenhorster Heimatjahrbuch* 1932; E. Dürks, 'Die deutsche Linoleum-Industrie, unter besonderer Berücksichtigung der Fabriken in Delmenhorst', PhD thesis, Heidelberg University, 1919; H.G. Bodenbender, *Linoleum-Hanbuch. Ein praktischer Führer für Industrie und Handel*, Berlin, 1931.

the factory was producing 400,000 square metres of linoleum annually, with a value of around one million marks.[4]

In 1896 the factory's name was changed to the Deutsche Linoleumwerke Hansa AG, but the majority shareholding remained in British hands until the First World War. By this time two other large linoleum companies had become established in the town. The Delmenhorster Linoleumfabrik AG was formed in 1892, with 24 shareholders and a traditional merchants' symbol, the anchor, as its trade mark: the company quickly became known as the Anker-Marke. In addition to its successful lino designs, Anker also pioneered the development of lincrusta, a washable wall covering that enjoyed great popularity in hospitals and schools. A third linoleum factory, founded by the Bremen bank of E.C. Weyhausen, settled in Delmenhorst in 1898, and began production the following year. The Bremer Linoleumwerke AG Delmenhorst adopted the city of Bremen's traditional emblem, the key, as its trade mark, and was thus known as the Schlüssel-Marke.

Whilst the Hansa and Anker companies were soon attaining respectable profits, the Schlüssel-Marke at first struggled to make an impact, its foundation coinciding with the formation of two further German linoleum producers, the Germania Linoleumwerke in Bietigheim, and a similar company in Eberswalde. After failing to break even in 1901 and 1902, the Schlüssel operation underwent a major reorganisation, including a merger with a linoleum factory in Köpenick, and was eventually able to compete on equal terms with the other Delmenhorst manufacturers. Over-capacity in the German linoleum sector led to many attempts to regulate prices and production in the industry, including the creation in 1910 of a cartel of German linoleum factories, but such arrangements invariably proved short-lived.

The development of Delmenhorst as an industrial centre attracted a number of other businesses to the town. Small engineering companies, such as Gebrüder Wehrhahn (1894) and Friedrich Christoffers, each employed several dozen men to supply the linoleum and textile factories with machine tools and spare parts. An automobile factory, the Delmenhorster Wagenfabrik Carl Tönjes AG was founded in 1909, and saw its initial workforce of 120 soon rise to over 750. In the following year the Petersen margarine factory was opened, producing large quantities of the popular Sanella brand. Meanwhile, the cork and jute processing industries both expanded on the back of the linoleum industry, with no fewer than nine enterprises supplying ground cork waste to the Hansa, Anker and Schlüssel works before World War One.

The rapid growth of industry in Delmenhorst had far-reaching

---

4. H. Lübbing, 'Delmenhorsts Aufstieg', pp.11–12.

consequences for the town. Three new brick works had to be set up to meet the huge demand created by the local building boom. The population rose from 4,018 in 1871 to 16,569 in 1900 and 22,516 in 1910,[5] the sort of increase more usually associated with the heavy industrial Ruhr towns. Many of the workers who came to man the new industries were foreign, including Ukrainians, Poles, Czechs, and Croats. As a result the proportion of Catholics in the population rose from one twelfth in 1885 to one fifth in 1890, one quarter in 1900 and nearly one third in 1910.[6] Housing conditions worsened as the town struggled to keep up with the influx of workers, and both roads and public utilities were stretched to breaking point by the growing demands placed upon them. The changing character of the community was reflected in its architecture. The director of the Bremen Museum of Applied Art, Emil Högg (1867–1954), wrote in 1909:

> Delmenhorst was once a pretty, village-like country town, with a picturesque, homogenous character – one can still see this in the occasional humble building, now squashed anxiously between the ostentatious intruders of a more recent time. Then it became an industrial town and made its 'unforeseen advance'; vigorous building activity produced factories, housing estates, villas and department stores. Unfortunately this all occurred at a time which is now acknowledged to have been the absolute nadir of our architecture and our good taste, from which we are only just recovering. The results were predictably depressing.[7]

Erich Koch's 'Municipal Socialism'

In 1901 the burgeoning town gained a new mayor. The previous incumbent, Odo Willms, had been gravely ill for some time, and a junior barrister from Bremerhaven had been acting as his deputy. On the mayor's death, the *Amtshauptmann* of Delmenhorst, Rabben, had little hesitation in proposing the young deputy, Erich Koch (1875–1944), as Willms's permanent replacement. On 26 April 1901, a joint sitting of the town's *Magistrat* (a five man executive council) and the *Gesamtstadtrat* (the combined urban and rural district council), voted to accept the appointment, even though Koch had yet to complete his final examinations. Koch's age and inexperience were not considered a serious handicap, since the mayor of a 'second class' town possessed comparatively few responsibilities: it was the *Amtshauptmann* who pulled the strings. It did not take long for the ambitious and idealistic Koch to realise, however, that if the town was to tackle its mounting problems successfully, it would

5. Statistics from H. Saebens, *Delmenhorst*, p.13.
6. From H. Lübbing, 'Delmenhorsts Aufstieg', p.19.
7. Quoted by E. Grundig, 'Geschichte der Stadt Delmenhorst', p.833.

have to gain more control over its own affairs.[8]

From the beginning Koch impressed people with his competence and enthusiasm, and after much debate he was able to convince the Oldenburg state authorities that Delmenhorst should regain its 'first class' status. With the backing of *Amtshauptmann* Robben, the town became a self-governing borough on 1 May 1903, assuming widespread powers over most aspects of local administration, including planning, public utilities, policing and the magistrates courts. It was clear to Koch, however, that the new powers brought with them fresh responsibilities, which the town was as yet ill-equipped to meet.

One of Koch's first priorities was to ensure that a set of building regulations was drawn up for the town, to prevent the sort of shoddy speculative developments which had already disfigured some of its newer districts. A commission to investigate the issue had been established by the town council back in 1900, but the commission's deliberations were still far from complete when Koch took office. The new mayor recognised the urgency of the situation, but it was not until August 1904 that the town council was in a position to approve the new building code, and a further ten months before the regulations were finally in place. The wait was worthwhile, however, because Delmenhorst eventually gained an exemplary modern statute, covering all aspects of building, including a paragraph outlining conditions for industrial structures.[9]

In the meantime, Koch established a planning department at the town hall (1902), and advertised in the leading professional journals for a municipal architect, receiving no fewer than 102 applications. The town's first *Stadtbaumeister*, a civil engineer from Hagen, proved unsuited to the job, but his successor, a Thuringian called Karl Kühn, spent three decades in the post, between 1903 and 1933. Kühn (1884–1952) also served as the town's mayor for a brief period after World War Two. In the 1900s he worked closely with Erich Koch on many projects that were to change the face of the town. One of their most important acts was to ensure the civic purchase of some large areas of unbuilt land in the town centre, including the 1.5 hectare Neuer Markt, on which the heart of the new Delmenhorst was soon to rise.

In his first years as mayor, Koch supervised long overdue improvements to the sewerage system, roads, street lighting and drainage, and planned the provision of much needed public services. In 1906 he masterminded the foundation of the municipal savings bank, to help encourage thrift and

---

8. For Koch's time as Mayor of Delmenhorst see in particular H. Ivers, 'Erich Koch Wesers politische Tätigkeit als Bürgermeister von Delmenhorst', typewritten manuscript in SA Delmenhorst.

9. See E. Grundig, 'Geschichte der Stadt Delmenhorst', pp.790–796.

to provide a further source of income for the town. A year later the hitherto privately-owned gas works was acquired to supply the local population with light and energy. In 1908 the town council passed a plan to build a municipal water works and in 1910 the construction of a local electricity power station was also approved. This sort of rapid infrastructural modernisation, which was by no means uncommon in the urban centres of later Wilhelmine Germany, has been termed 'municipal socialism' by some historians.[10]

In fact, as Delmenhorst's mayor, Erich Koch always attempted to maintain a politically neutral stance, but at the same time never tried to hide his own strongly held political convictions. He would later rise to prominence as chairman of the DDP and serve under the name Koch-Weser as a minister in a number of Weimar cabinets, before being forced into exile by the National Socialists in 1933, but his early years in Delmenhorst were more than just a preamble to his later political career. As a member of the Freisinnige Vereinigung and an admirer of Friedrich Naumann's National Social movement, the young Koch proved himself to be an indefatigable worker for political reform and social reconciliation.

Koch first came to national attention in November 1902, when he was elected to the Oldenburg Landtag under most unusual circumstances. The elections in the Delmenhorst constituency, as elsewhere in the Duchy, had a one-class franchise, but were indirect. On this occasion SPD supporters managed to secure a majority in the electoral college which would determine the destiny of the five available seats. Instead of voting only for SPD candidates, however, the Social Democratic *Wahlmänner* kept to a pre-election agreement, and elected two left liberals, including Koch, as well as three men of their own. As *Die Hilfe* noted, under the headline 'A Remarkable Election', the decision of the civil servant Koch to actually accept a seat in this manner (*von Sozialdemokraten-Gnaden gewählt*) was almost as noteworthy as the voting behaviour of the SPD delegates who put him there. Kurt Klaus of *Die Hilfe* remarked:

> It is a good job that Herr Koch is not mayor of a Prussian town (although as such it is hardly likely that he would have been in the position of being elected to the Landtag by the Social Democrats!) because the *Landrat* and the *Regierungspräsident* would have subjected him to a most terrible interrogation. In Oldenburg they seem to have accepted his explanation without any fuss and consigned the matter to the vaults.[11]

10. Most notably Wolfgang Krabbe, Wolfgang Hofmann and Jürgen Reulecke. See, for instance, H. Croon, W. Hofmann, G. von Unruh (eds), *Kommunale Selbstverwaltung im Zeitalter der Industrialisierung*, Stuttgart, 1971.
11. K. Klaus, 'Eine bemerkenswerte Wahl' in *Die Hilfe*, vol.8 (1902), pp.2–3.

Koch viewed his election as 'an encouraging sign', indicating that when one co-operated with workers and put them in positions of responsibility, the faction within the SPD which 'sought a genuine raising of the working class' would be strengthened, at the cost of those who merely played with 'slogans and fantasies'. Kurt Klaus finished by praising Koch's 'lack of prejudice' and his 'intellectual freedom':

> He embodies the new political tendency, thankfully rising within the educated middle class, which regards the Social Democrats without the nervousness and insufferable impatience which used to be the norm, and which is inclined to assess them in more measured tones. He belongs to the optimists in his view of the Social Democrats.[12]

Koch saw his Oldenburg Landtag seat primarily as a platform from which to fight for the wider interests of Delmenhorst, rather than to engage in party politics, and this attitude appears to have won the respect of political opponents as well as friends. He was re-elected in the Landtag elections of 1904, 1905 and 1908, and on each occasion benefited from SPD votes. When Koch later left Delmenhorst to become Mayor of Bremerhaven, however, the co-operation between the town's liberal and socialist voters in Landtag elections broke down, and all five Delmenhorst seats fell to conservative agrarians from outlying country districts.

One of Koch's priorities as a member of the Landtag was to promote the cause of electoral reform. Nearly five years after he had first raised the issue, Koch succeeded in winning acceptance from the authorities in Oldenburg for town council elections in Delmenhorst to be fought on the basis of proportional representation. The new electoral law, devised by the town clerk Rudolf Königer, was passed by the *Gesamtstadtrat* in December 1907, making Delmenhorst the first town to introduce such a system anywhere in northern Germany. Town council elections had hitherto been straight contests between the notables' Bürgerverein and the SPD. The electoral support of the two blocks was roughly equal after 1900, and with half the council standing for re-election every two years, a handful of votes could bring a landslide victory to either side, as happened in 1906, when the SPD lost all its council seats.

The first election fought on the basis of proportional representation, in February 1908, produced a turnout of 87%. A separate catholic list stood for the first time and won one seat, whilst the SPD took six seats, and two *bürgerlich* lists gained five seats between them. Late in 1909 the town voted once more, with the SPD winning five seats, the Bürgerverein three, a separate left liberal list also three, and the catholics a single seat again.

12. K. Klaus, *ibid.*, p.3.

Thus at the end of 1909 the town council had eleven SPD members and thirteen non-socialists, with a similarly close state of affairs in the larger *Gesamtstadtrat*. The balance of power did not shift significantly again before 1918.[13] It was a testament to Koch's character and ability as mayor that he was able to maintain generally cordial relations with both sides of the council chamber throughout his time in Delmenhorst.

With the support of both bourgeois notables and Social Democrats, Koch was able to implement a number of initiatives in the field of social policy and health care, including the construction of a municipal sanatorium to deal with an abnormally high rate of tuberculosis in the area. Lung disease was an unfortunate side effect of the linoleum industry, which to this day discharges a particularly distinctive and powerful odour over the town. Koch was also active in the field of education policy, where he made his name as a supporter of co-educational schools. The record of his administration on housing issues was less impressive, however, failing to tackle the town's chronic housing crisis. Even so, a left liberal newspaper from Berlin, the *Welt am Montag*, wrote in 1909: 'small but fine, the town of Delmenhorst in Oldenburg, known only to the general public through its linoleum, deserves to be studied by every modern social policy specialist for its social institutions'.[14]

Koch's desire to create social harmony and encourage self-improvement in the new industrial community was reflected in his chairmanship of the town's Goethebund, a cultural and educational association whose vice chairman was the Social Democrat councillor Jan Schmidt. In fact, as we shall see, Koch's contribution to the cultural character of the town was every bit as significant as his impact on its political life. In view of his social and political convictions, it comes as no surprise to discover that Koch was particularly attracted by the reformist ethos of the Werkbund. His name duly appears in the DWB membership lists from 1910 onwards. Although the circumstances of Koch's introduction to the organisation are not known, it would seem reasonable to assume that he was initiated into the world of architecture and design by the local industrialist Gustav Gericke, a member of Delmenhorst's *Magistrat* since 1907 and on the DWB's board of directors from 1908.

Linoleum: A True *Kulturprodukt*?

Gustav Gericke (1864–1935) had been a director of Delmenhorst's Anker linoleum company since 1903, and had successfully steered the business

---

13. Delmenhorst's town council elections in this period are examined by E. Grundig, 'Geschichte der Stadt Delmenhorst', pp.18–21.
14. Quoted by E. Grundig, ibid., p.226.

into the vanguard of the artistic reform movement. The Anker company was an early member of the DWB, as were the Hansa works in Delmenhorst and the Germania in Bietigheim. Linoleum patterns by leading designers were a familiar sight in all DWB publications and exhibitions. Indeed, linoleum was in many ways the ideal object for Werkbund attention; as a by-product of the nineteenth century chemical industry it was not burdened by historical convention, yet it was still to find a convincing modern form. Ever since its introduction to Germany in the *Gründerzeit*, linoleum had borne the stigma of the surrogate, but it was believed that if its 'true character' could be tapped, a money-spinning quality product would emerge from the unassuming mixture of cork waste, jute and oxidised linseed oil.

For many years linoleum producers had themselves been responsible for perpetuating the 'surrogate' tag, by attempting to transfer popular carpet patterns directly onto the new material, or by imitating tiles or parquet-style wooden floors. However with the development of 'inlaid' linoleum, a process by which designs were imprinted into the linoleum rather than left on the surface as an oily film, new possibilities were opened up for more imaginative and durable patterns. The Anker company in Delmenhorst led the way by commissioning many modern artists and architects to submit suitable designs: the DWB members van de Velde, Behrens, Hoffmann, Müller, Vogeler, Paul and Riemerschmid all obliged.[15] Linoleum became the subject of aggressive marketing campaigns, which portrayed it as a true *Kulturprodukt*, more hygienic and practical than traditional floor coverings, and more in touch with the spirit of the age.

Peter Behrens had a particularly long and fruitful association with the Anker. In 1905 he designed a pavilion for the company as part of a highly acclaimed complex of buildings at the North West German Art Exhibition in Oldenburg. The Bremen art critic Karl Schäfer (1870–1942), writing in *Die Rheinlande*, praised both the white-washed, red tiled and symmetrical exterior, and the 'tastefully stage-managed' interior, which made an impressive architectural feature of the upright rolls of linoleum.[16] In its 15 August edition the *Delmenhorster Kreisblatt* also eulogised about the display:

The rolls of linoleum are subtly illuminated and arranged along both sides of the pavilion, with a most sensitive appreciation of the play of colours. They reflect the different tastes of the public, with different patterns and styles, but one must give special praise to the firm for its efforts to bring patterns to the

15. A Bonn art historian, Torsten Ziegler, is writing a PhD thesis on the linoleum patterns designed by leading German artists in the first decades of the twentieth century.
16. K. Schäfer, 'Die Nordwestdeutsche Kunstausstellung in Oldenburg', in *Die Rheinlande*, vol.5 (1905), pp.428–430.

Figure 38 Anker linoleum patterns by leading Werkbund designers, from Werkbund Yearbook, 1912

trade which are designed by leading artists, specifically for linoleum . . . The company's endeavours to ennoble and improve the taste of the public in this way have so far been a great success.[17]

The pavilion's positive reception convinced Gericke that Behrens should also be entrusted with the company's contribution to the third National Exhibition of the Applied Arts, held in Dresden the following year. The domed Anker pavilion proved to be one of the most talked about structures on the site. Behrens's 1972 biographer Hans-Joachim Kadatz described it as one of the 'acknowledged harbingers of the new conception of architecture'.[18] Behrens's third, and last, exhibition display for Anker was a room in the German pavilion at the 1910 Brussels world exhibition, which featured Behrens-designed furniture as well as linoleum patterns.

It was Behrens too who devised the Anker logo, which became such a fixture in arts journals and Werkbund publications before World War One, and which also adorned the main chimney of the company's Delmenhorst factory. Anker catalogues and brochures, such as the ones which appeared in 1906, 1907, 1909, 1912 and 1913, were regarded as works of art in their own right, and usually included a text from the aforementioned journalist Karl Schäfer, himself a DWB member. The company also owned a sales outlet in Hamburg, where the local DWB architect and teacher Hans Haller was responsible for designing the award-winning layout and window displays. All three Delmenhorst linoleum companies staged presentations at the 1914 Werkbund exhibition in Cologne.

Gericke played an active role in DWB affairs. At the organisation's first annual conference, at Munich in 1908, he was elected to the Werkbund's highest body, the board of directors, and served until 1914, when he stepped down to make way for Walter Gropius. In his address to the Munich conference Gericke acted as a spokesman for the DWB's industrial faction, stressing the difficulties inherent in the switch to 'quality work' and the need for members to remain patient. He told the audience:

> If the industrialists present today were to be put to the test, it is my conviction that hardly any of us would be able to say in all honesty 'I am already working fully in line with the constitution of the Werkbund'. Our entire manufacturing system simply cannot be changed overnight. The plants and quantities produced are too big, the comprehension of the consumer . . . too small.[19]

17. H. Fuchs, 'Landes-Ausstellung: Ausstellung der Delmenhorster Linoleumfabrik Anker-Marke' in *Delmenhorster Kreisblatt*, 15 Aug. 1905.

18. H.-J. Kadatz, *Peter Behrens. Architekt – Maler – Grafiker*, Leipzig, 1977, p.40.

19. G. Gericke, in 'Die Veredelung der Gewerblichen Arbeit im Zusammenwirken von Kunst, Industrie und Handwerk. Verhandlungen des Deutschem Werkbundes zu München am 11. und 12. Juli 1908', p.23.

Gericke was similarly blunt in his essay for the 1912 DWB Yearbook, entitled 'German Linoleum in the World Market', in which he admitted that the new German style was struggling to make an impact on foreign markets. Only in Austria and Switzerland, where the German reform movement had won many admirers, and in Belgium, where the 1910 World Exhibition had made a mark, had 'designer lino' achieved any great success. Consumers elsewhere appeared to prefer the cheaper British product, which was of poorer quality and continued to imitate other materials. Gericke acknowledged that for as long as this was the case, German manufacturers would find it difficult to concentrate solely on quality production. The future would depend to a great extent on the development of the American market, where a sales offensive for modern German products was now required.

For this reason Gericke was eager to support the travelling exhibition of the German Museum for Art in Trade and Commerce, which visited six American cities in 1912–13, and took with it many examples of Anker linoleum and lincrusta.[20] A year earlier Gericke had in fact joined the management committee of the museum, where he sat alongside Bruckmann, Osthaus and Muthesius.[21] Anker posters, letter-headings, advertisements and pattern books were dispatched to Hagen in great quantities, and formed the basis of many of the museum's other travelling exhibitions, including one devoted entirely to 'Wallpaper, Linoleum and Lincrusta'. In addition to the annual subscription of 200 Marks paid by his company, Gustav Gericke made unspecified private contributions towards the museum's upkeep.[22] It is interesting to note that the Hansa linoleum company was quick to follow Anker's lead in joining the museum, but the third Delmenhorst factory, Schlüssel, was typically slow to respond, only becoming a member in November 1913, and then contributing just twenty Marks annually.[23]

The Anker company was naturally quick to highlight examples of its products in use. The 1912 publicity brochure, for instance, featured photographs of two large houses recently built by Behrens in Hagen, where

20. 'Wanderausstellung des Deutschen Museums für Kunst in Handel und Gewerbe. Newark-Chicago-Indianapolis-Pittsburgh-Cincinnati-St. Louis', catalogue, Hagen 1912–13.

21. The Karl Ernst Osthaus Archiv in Hagen retains the entire correspondence between the Anker company and the German Museum for Art in Trade and Commerce (K.E.O. Archiv A/351). It amounts to some 72 pages for the years 1909 to 1914; a total which gives some indication of the Delmenhorst company's involvement in the enterprise. See K.E.O. Archiv A/351 p.26 for letter from Osthaus to Gericke, in which he invited the industrialist to join the Management Committee (1 Aug. 1911).

22. K.E.O. Archiv A/351 p.22 (18 July 1911).

23. K.E.O. Archiv DM/10-1 (29 June 1911) Anker; DM/11-1 (13 Sept. 1911) Hansa; DM/8-1 (14 Nov. 1913) Schlüssel.

linoleum floors had been installed. Anker linoleum could also be found in a Stockholm theatre, the royal library in Berlin and the crown court in Dresden.[24] Less conventionally, it was often used by Behrens as a covering for the living room tables and other furniture he designed for 'model' working class families, even though it proved unpopular amongst the targeted consumers, who resented the intrusion of a smelly and institutional surrogate into their *guten Stube*. As Uwe Henning has pointed out, this rather excessive use of linoleum must surely call into question the true intentions of Werkbund designers involved in such exercises.[25]

For all his links with the Anker company, Peter Behrens never built in the Delmenhorst area. The closest he came was in 1907, when he was approached by Gustav Gericke to design a Bismarck memorial on the Bookholzberg, a few miles from the town. Gericke and Koch were both members of the local 'Bismarck Memorial Committee', which held several public meetings in 1908 and 1909 to drum up support. Behrens's design was described by the *Delmenhorster Kreisblatt* as 'a sort of gigantic altar to the genius of Bismarck',[26] and it was also praised in the *Bremer Nachrichten* by Karl Schäfer, but although nearly 500 Bismarck memorials were erected in Germany before the First World War,[27] this one failed to make it off the drawing board. Gericke and Koch did not have to wait long, however, for another opportunity to leave their mark on the local landscape.

Heinz Stoffregen and the New Delmenhorst

A frequent target for both *Heimatschützer* and *Werkbündler* was the poor quality of architecture in the vicinity of railway stations, particularly in small country towns. Almost every community had gained a Station Road, a Bahnhofstraße, in the second half of the nineteenth century, and Delmenhorst was no exception. For the likes of Schultze-Naumburg and Muthesius, these streets invariably symbolised the degeneracy and pomposity of the *Gründerzeit*, with half-digested historical styles applied to the humblest of buildings, and the honest virtues of craftsmanship

24. N. Aschenbeck, 'Romantische Sachlichkeit. Dokumentation und Bewertung des Werks und der architektur-historischen Bedeutung des Bremer Architekten Heinz Stoffregen, unter besonderer Berücksichtigung seiner Zusammenarbeit mit Delmenhorster Industrie', typewritten manuscript in SA Delmenhorst, p.23.

25. U. Henning, in A. Thiekötter & E. Siepmann (eds), *Packeis und Preßglas. Von der Kunstgewerbebewegung zum Deutschen Werkbund*, Berlin, 1987, pp.311–312.

26. *Delmenhorster Kreisblatt*, 14 Jan. 1909. See also 'Bismarckdenkmal auf dem Bookholzberg', in *Delmenhorster Kreisblatt*, 10 Jan. 1909, and 'Aufruf', 13 Jan. 1909.

27. See L. Tittel, 'Monumentaldenkmäler 1870–1918', and H.-W. Hedinger 'Bismarck-Denkmäler und Bismarck-Verehrung', in E. Mai & S. Waetzold (eds), *Kunstverwaltung, Bau- und Denkmalpolitik im Kaiserreich*, Berlin, 1980.

subverted by the rigid formalism of the academies.[28] Delmenhorst's station, which stood some way to the north of the old town, was surrounded by fields when it opened in 1867. A straight cobbled road was laid to link the station to the town, and as the community expanded outwards so the familiar array of hotels, shops and workshops in historicist styles sprang up along its length.

At the town end of Delmenhorst's Bahnhofstraße however, something of a surprise awaited the visitor, for instead of leading directly to the main street, the road petered out into a maze of back lanes and courtyards. In the early 1900s the town council decided that access from the Bahnhofstraße to the main Langesstraße would have to be improved; a number of buildings were demolished and the Bahnhofsstraße was extended. In 1908 Mayor Erich Koch, no doubt aware of the criticisms levelled against such developments in the pages of widely-read journals like *Kunstwart* and *Die Hilfe*, set up a competition to attract suitable designs for the street's new buildings. He had already demonstrated an interest in planning and conservation issues by attempting to steer a 'Preservation Law' through the Oldenburg Landtag.

The panel of judges for the Bahnhofstraße competition was chaired by Koch himself, and also included the town clerk Königer, Anker's Gustav Gericke, the Oldenburg state architect Adolf Rauchheld, and the aforementioned Emil Högg. The members of the jury were all known as opponents of historicist architecture. Indeed, Rauchheld and Högg would soon join Gericke and Koch in the Werkbund. It is not surprising, then, that the favoured entries proved to be simple, functional and rather austere in character. Amongst the winners was a young architect from Bremen called Heinz Stoffregen, whose previous practical experience was limited to one house in Bremerhaven and one in Delmenhorst. As a result of the competition, Stoffregen (1879–1929) was invited to design two retail buildings for the street (no.4 and no.39), which were built in 1910 and 1913.

The Bahnhofstraße competition proved, however, to be only a dress rehearsal for a much bigger undertaking later that same year. The expansion of Delmenhorst's administrative responsibilities in the 1900s had put an intolerable strain on the two converted houses which had been accommodating the town's council staff since the turn of the century. The need for a purpose-built town hall, to house an increasing number of administrative departments, an archive, registry office and council chamber, was plain for all to see. In 1908 it was decided to combine the construction of a new town hall with a fire station, watertower and market

---

28. See, for example, H. Muthesius, *Stilarchitektur und Baukunst*, Mülheim, 1902, or P. Schultze-Naumburg, *Die Enststellung unseres Landes*, Munich, 1908.

hall. Once again a competition would be held to find the most appropriate plans.

The details were announced in the *Deutsche Bauzeitung* of 8 August, and the closing date was set for 15 December.[29] The competition was open to all architects living or born in the Grand Duchy of Oldenburg, the Prussian province of Hanover, or the Free City of Bremen. A total of 3,500 Marks worth of prizes were available to the best three entries. No particular style or material was specified, but the buildings should be 'simple, durable and dignified'. The Bahnhofstraße jury was to joined by the technical *Beigeordnete* of the city of Cologne, Carl Rehorst, a prominent figure in both the Werkbund and the Heimatschutz movement.[30] In his initial approach to Rehorst, Koch wrote: 'your aims and achievements in the field of architecture and town planning have my full support.'[31]

By the time the judges met on 28 December 1908, 51 entries had been received, of which fifteen were subjected to particularly close scrutiny. Two first prizes were eventually awarded, to the Berlin-based architect Emmingmann and to Heinz Stoffregen, one of the winners of the earlier Bahnhofstraße competition. Both men were informed of the judges' decision by telegrams despatched on 30 December.[32] It was clear from the panel's report, which was signed by all the judges, that Stoffregen's entry had won the plaudits for its architectural conception, whilst Emmingmann's contribution had impressed because of its layout. Stoffregen's design, entered under the title *Festgemauert*, received special praise for the architect's endeavour 'to solve the task in a thoroughly modern spirit'.[33] Delmenhorst's five-man *Magistrat*, including Koch and Gericke, recommended that Stoffregen should be entrusted with the commission, on the basis of Emmingmann's layout.

On 9 January Koch wrote a memorandum to the members of the *Gesamtstadtrat*, the combined town and district council, who would have to vote on the *Magistrat*'s recommendation during the following week. In it he praised the 'simplicity' of Stoffregen's architecture, and singled out the watertower as 'particularly successful'.[34] He reminded councillors that the construction of the watertower was a pressing concern, since the

29. *Deutsche Bauzeitung*, 8 Aug. 1908, p.440.

30. Bundesarchiv Nachlaß 12 Koch-Weser/175. 'Bedingungen und Programm für den Wettbewerb zur Erlangung von Skizzen für die Gestaltung und Bebauung des Marktplatzes und für den Neubau eines Rathauses und Spritzenhauses zu Delmenhorst'. See also SA Delmenhorst, File XIX. 13.652 100/2 (Rauthaus) p.9, list of judges.

31. SA Delmenhorst, File XIX. 13.652 100/2 (Rathaus) p.12, letter from Koch to Rehorst.

32. SA Delmenhorst, File XIX. 13.652 100/2 (Rathaus) p.27.

33. SA Delmenhorst, File XIX. 13.652 100/2 (Rathaus) p.38.

34. SA Delmenhorst, File XIX. 13.652 100/2 (Rathuas) p.33, memorandum from Koch to the members of the *Gesamtstadtrat*.

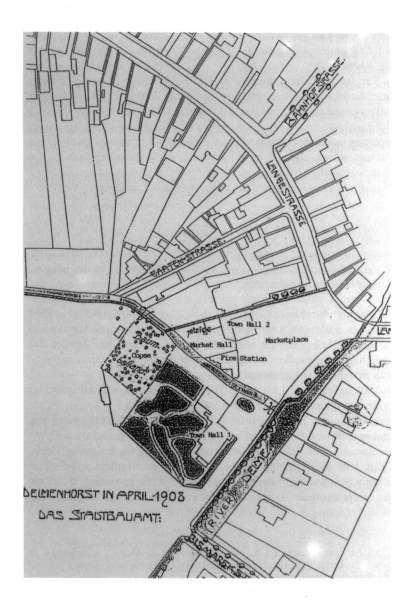

Figure 39 Plan of Delmenhorst in 1908. Note the newly-completed Bahnhofstraße extension and the two converted houses – separated by a stream – which accommodated the town's officials

new municipal waterworks would be ready in six months, and ideally the tower should be in place at the same time. When the council met on 14 January, to pass judgement on what was by far the largest municipal building project ever envisaged for the town, the debate was suitably highly-charged.

The strong feelings aroused by Stoffregen's plans were predictable, since the young architect, who was to join the DWB in the course of 1909, had proposed the most modern municipal buildings yet seen anywhere in Germany. At a time when journals such as the *Deutsche Bauzeitung* were reporting on new town halls in almost every edition – around one hundred German towns planned new town halls between 1900 and 1914 – historicism still held sway in this sector of architectural activity.[35] As Wilhelm Schäfer bemoaned in the pages of *Der Kunstwart* in 1908:

> If we were to line up all the German town hall buildings of the last twenty years, and consider them as symbols of our bourgeoisie at the turn of the century, I believe that even the simplest souls would find them rather comic. Nothing but stone buildings in German, French, Italian and recently even Assyrian Renaissance style (who knows any exceptions?), which look like anything but places of civic administration.[36]

Moderately progressive designs, such as Paul Bonatz's 1908 plan for a town hall in Barmen, were championed in the reform-minded sections of the architectural press, but stood little chance of selection.[37] Against this background, Delmenhorst's decision to choose Stoffregen's entry appeared both daring and controversial.

The crucial council meeting was opened by Koch, who bolstered his written report with some further words of support for Stoffregen, but the plans soon came under fire from councillor Vosteen of the Bürgerverein, who argued that the new town hall should not be 'mixed up with the waterworks'.[38] Would the planned watertower, with its stark modern form, 'fit in' with the neighbouring courthouse or school buildings, he asked. In reply, Koch stressed that the watertower had no particular 'style' and was scrupulously designed to be part of a complete ensemble of municipal buildings, adding that 'the whole business' had been 'more carefully tested

---

35. For further details see E. Mai, J. Paul, S. Waetzold (eds), *Das Rathaus im Kaiserreich*, Berlin, 1982. The only other town halls built in Wilhelmine Germany to reflect reformist architectural ideas were Hermann Billing's complex at Kiel (1904–11) and Pfeiffer & Großmann's town hall at Mülheim (1911–16).
36. W. Schäfer, 'Rathäuser', in *Der Kunstwart*, vol.22 (1908), pp.305–6.
37. W. Schäfer, 'Ein bürgerlicher Rathausbau', in *Die Rheinlande*, vol.8 (1908), pp.149–50.
38. The quotes from the town council meeting are all from the *Delmenhorster Kreisblatt*, 16 Jan. 1909.

Figure 40 H. Stoffregen's competition-winning design for Delmenhorst's municipal buildings, from *Architektonische Rundschau*, 1909. They were built between 1909 and 1914, based on an amended layout

and worked out than seldom anything'. Vosteen's colleague, Pape, conceded that this was the case, but nevertheless called for fresh designs to be submitted, since it was 'difficult to become accustomed to the New', as the 'shocking example' of the building for the municipal savings bank showed.

It was then the turn of the municipal architect, Kühn, to defend the scheme in a long speech, which questioned the competence of the councillors to pass judgement on the plans. Nevertheless, Pape repeated his criticisms, and was supported by the catholic member Leffers, an admirer of Gothic architecture, who stated that he would not be able to vote for the plan in its present form. He believed the town's building department should prepare its own design 'along the lines of the courthouse'. It was wrong that the taste of outside judges should be imposed on Delmenhorst, he argued.

Leffers received unexpected backing from the other side of the chamber when the leading SPD councillor Jan Schmidt attacked the town's savings bank and other modern buildings. Significantly, Schmidt recognised the important role played by Anker linoleum's Gustav Gericke in Delmenhorst's endorsement of the architectural reform movement: 'This aberration of taste, which has been imported by the Anker-Marke, will not last long', he told the council. He was especially critical of the planned use of rough-cast plaster on the town hall façade, which was a 'nonsense'. People would graze their hands as soon as they came up against the walls, and it would be necessary to provide a first-aid box for the injured!

This was too much for Gustav Gericke, who rose to offer fulsome praise for Stoffregen's plans. 'It is quite obvious', he told the chamber, that the town hall could not be built 'in the Gothic style'. Delmenhorst's recently completed Catholic church, which had been designed in the Gothic tradition, was certainly not a *Kulturwerk* by contemporary standards, and the courthouse was nothing more than an imitation of Renaissance architecture, riddled with errors. The divisions within the SPD faction over the issue then became apparent, with another prominent Social Democrat, August Jordan, siding with Gericke in favour of Stoffregen's design. The debate continued long into the night, but when the matter was finally put to the vote the *Magistrat*'s recommendation was passed by a majority of nine.

Stoffregen was quickly notified of the decision and began to tackle the details of the design. It was the watertower which took precedence and construction work here was soon underway, with the local building contractor Karl Twisterling securing the 71,000 Mark contract. Even so, the controversy surrounding the new buildings simmered on in the pages of the *Delmenhorster Kreisblatt*, where Stoffregen's initial plans had been published on 17 January. One correspondent wrote:

Should we allow the most attractive area which we possess in Delmenhorst to be disfigured by a watertower, together with a fire station, whose form and design is in many people's opinion anything but attractive. The men most responsible for this plan, the mayor and the municipal architect, can pack their bags and leave whenever it suits them, but for us the disfigurement of the beautiful marketplace and the payment of the bills will remain! Citizens it is not too late, pull yourselves together and protest against the building of the watertower and its incalculable consequences![39]

The construction of the forty-two metre tower, 'the first skyscraper in Delmenhorst' according to local wags, was delayed by a two month building workers' strike, but by the end of 1909 the colossus was taking shape. It was then that rumours began to circulate in the town that the tower's foundations were insufficient for its marshy site close to the banks of the River Delme. Bets were supposedly placed on the chances of the tower toppling over as soon as it was filled with water.[40] Although such claims were dismissed as nonsense, the authorities were worried enough to have a secret 'dress rehearsal' shortly before the tower's official opening; even town councillors were not informed as the giant tanks were filled for the first time. The tower stood firm, however, and on 29 April 1910 a ceremony was held to declare it open. Illuminated by a giant bonfire and a firework display, Delmenhorst's new 'trade mark' was visible for miles around.[41]

The watertower's stability stopped one aspect of the campaign against it, but opponents continued to criticise both the aesthetic quality of the building, and the need for a municipal waterworks at all. Some citizens refused to be connected to the new water system, and called for the dozen or so public water pumps to be retained, whilst others attacked the cost of 420,000 Marks, of which 82,000 had been spent on the tower alone. The building had its defenders too, however, and after one attack on its design in the *Kreisblatt*, a citizen wrote to the newspaper with tongue firmly in cheek:

Bravo! At last, another loud voice against the square watertower. It should be round of course and have a hat like a giant mushroom – all proper watertowers have that. And the price of 85,000 Marks is much too high, even 20,000 or 10,000 would be too high. All one has to do is build a simple timber framework and place a few empty petrol barrels on the top, that would cost 5,000 at the most . . . Poor people, if only you knew what was going to happen. The top of the tower is to be made 'out of bounds' for the public; it will be glazed all round and turned into a palm garden for the exclusive use of the ruling mayor![42]

39. Quoted by E. Grundig, 'Geschichte de Stadt Delmenhorst', p.834.
40. Story told by J. Mehrtens (ed.), *Alt Delmenhorst* , Delmenhorst, 1981.
41. Report of opening festivities in *Delmenhorster Kreisblatt*, 1 May 1910.
42. Quoted by E. Grundig, 'Geschichte der Stadt Delmenhorst', pp.834–5.

Figure 41 Watertower (shortly after completion), Delmenhorst 1909
Arch. H. Stoffregen. From a contemporary postcard, illustrated in *Delmenhorst in alten Ansichten*, European Library, Zaltbommel, Netherlands, 1976

Figure 42 Watertower (south-west elevation, with fire brigade tower), Delmenhorst
Arch. H. Stoffregen. Present condition

Stoffregen's 'square' watertower, with its powerful and compact character aroused interest in architectural circles too. The architect himself wrote an article on the building which was published, along with photographs, on the front page of *Der Industriebau* in 1913.[43] As we have seen, watertowers had been built in many shapes and sizes in the Wilhelmine era, but nothing could match the simplicity or purity of Stoffregen's composition, a logical progression from Olbrich's 1907 'Wedding Tower' at the artists' colony in Darmstadt. The tower was neither painted nor plastered, but the sensitivity of the architect ensured that it rose above 'naked' functionalism too. Its south-western aspect incorporated an unusual red brick structure, which was designed for fire brigade training purposes.

In October 1911 Gustav Gericke sent two plates of the watertower to the German Museum of Art in Trade and Commerce,[44] and it subsequently appeared in many of the exhibitions of 'model' industrial buildings. The watertower was not intended to stand in splendid isolation, however, and it was still far from certain whether the other municipal buildings, which were an integral part of Stoffregen's conception, would ever make it off the drawing board. In 1910 councillors had to decide whether stage two of the project should proceed as planned, with the construction of the fire station and municipal offices. It was clear from the debate that opposition to the scheme had not in fact diminished. The initial vote resulted in a tie, and a narrow majority in favour was only secured at the second attempt. The final go-ahead for the third, and most expensive, stage of the scheme was eventually given in April 1912, when the *Gesamtstadtrat* voted unanimously to approve the expenditure of 250,000 Marks on the new town hall itself.

Thereafter events moved quickly; foundations were laid in June and on 3 December the topping out ceremony was held. In late Spring 1914 one of the old town hall buildings was demolished and the authorities began to move into the new structure in June. The first sitting of the town council in its first purpose built chamber took place on 10 September 1914. Excluding the market hall, which was not finished until 1920, Delmenhorst's municipal centre had cost over 440,000 Marks to build.[45]

The town hall itself was a three-storey building with rough-cast plaster walls and steeply-pitched, tiled roofs.[46] It managed to combine functionality and dignity, without resorting to either historical quotation

43. 'Der Wassertum zu Delmenhorst', in *Der Industriebau*, vol.4 (1913), p.29.
44. K.E.O. Archiv A/351 p.37. (27 Oct. 1911).
45. E. Grundig, 'Geschichte der Stadt Delmenhorst', p.835.
46. The town hall is described in more detail by K. Dillschneider in 'Das Delmenhorster Rathaus', *Delmenhorster Schriften* – no.5, Delmenhorst, 1972. Also see N. Aschenbeck, 'Romantische Sachlichkeit'.

or daring experimentation. The projecting central axis of the north-east façade, the town hall's main entrance, was a particular tour de force, incorporating many decorative touches – including the town's coat of arms, sculptural representations of trade and industry and a gargoyle of the architect beneath its steep gable, without losing an air of sober rationality. Delmenhorst town hall was, moreover, a true *Gesamtkunstwerk*, with Stoffregen designing not only the buildings themselves, but the curtains, chairs, radiators, wardrobes, letter boxes, door handles and wastepaper baskets.

As Nils Aschenbeck notes, the spatial organisation of the municipal buildings was also remarkable:

> The layout shows a quite amazingly modern distribution of space . . . The division of the open areas and the grouping of the buildings is dynamic and asymmetric. In this it anticipates the spatial arrangement of the Bauhaus in Dessau.[47]

The sprawling area of under-used land which had hitherto lain in the heart of the town was neatly divided by the new municipal buildings into three separate and well-defined market spaces. Access to each was made possible by a series of arcades which linked the town hall to the fire station and to the circular market hall, as well as running underneath the watertower itself.

Emil Högg, one of the judges responsible for selecting Stoffregen's design, praised the town of Delmenhorst for its efforts 'to put right the architectural sins of the previous generation'. Writing in the *Kreisblatt* he acclaimed the new municipal complex:

> With this the town will receive a central and focal point, which can become influential in determining the character of future architectural changes and improvements, because it expresses perfectly the essence of a modern, aspiring industrial town. May other German towns take Delmenhorst as a model – most of them are badly in need of it.[48]

Mayor Koch, who had done so much to promote the project, was no longer in office when the town hall finally opened, having moved several years earlier to take up a similar post in his home town of Bremerhaven. His friend Gericke had also vacated his seat in the *Magistrat*, to concentrate on his business activities. Nevertheless the finished complex stood as a lasting reminder of Koch's period in office, which had permanently

---

47. N. Aschenbeck, ibid., pp.37–38.
48. E. Högg in the *Delmenhorster Kreisblatt*, 26 Jan. 1909.

Figure 43 Town hall (south-west elevation), Delmenhorst, designed 1908–9, built 1912–14. Arch. H. Stoffregen. Present condition

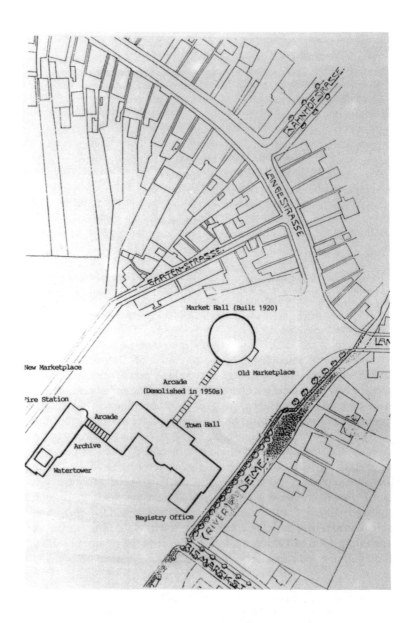

Figure 44 The location and layout of Delmenhorst's new municipal buildings

changed the character and appearance of the town. As Wolfgang Hofmann has written in his study of mayors in German politics:

> These opportunities for an active role in shaping the environment, which were grasped with great eagerness by many mayors, together with the peculiar conditions of a municipal official's career path – working up from town to town, securing re-election by achievement – were particularly important in furthering the infrastructural development of towns. Mayors would often leave a memorial to themselves in the form of a town hall or other municipal buildings.[49]

After a short period in Bremerhaven, Erich Koch went on to serve as Mayor of Kassel before entering political life on the national stage as Home Secretary in October 1919, but he continued to regard his time in Delmenhorst with particular affection. In 1928 he returned to the town to receive the freedom of the borough; an honour which would later be taken from him by the National Socialists. He told the audience at his award ceremony:

> Nowhere did I put in more work than in Delmenhorst. Here, where as a result of rapid growth everything was still like soft wax – politics, administration, town planning, education – I was able to knead with all my youthful energy. I am delighted that so many ideas, which I could only plan or begin back then, have today been realised.[50]

Koch-Weser's relationship with the town of Delmenhorst was undoubtedly special but by no means unique. A parallel example of co-operation between a local left liberal politician and the architectural avant-garde took place in Hagen, an industrial community not unlike Delmenhorst, at much the same time. Willi Cuno, the town's mayor from 1901 to 1925, had a Naumannite background and from 1906 a seat in the Reichstag too, having been elected as member for Hagen-Schwelm in succession to the late Eugen Richter. In many respects Cuno's period in office was marked by the same infrastructural and social reforms which characterised Koch's years in Delmenhorst. It was Cuno, for instance, who employed Hagen's first municipal architect, Ewald Figge, and implemented a new building code for the town. Figge, who served in Hagen from 1906 to 1929 was a leading figure in the reform of school building design and a member of the Werkbund.[51] He designed both the

49. W. Hofmann, *Zwischen Rathaus und Reichskanzlei*, Stuttgart, 1974, p.52. Other mayors who left a town hall as a 'memorial to themselves' included the National Liberal Tramm (Hanover), Adickes (Frankfurt) and the conservative Beutler (Dresden).

50. Quoted by N. Aschenbeck, 'Romantische Sachlichkeit', p.36.

51. See J.H. Müller (ed.), *Der westdeutsche Impuls 1900–1914. Die Folkwang-Idee des Karl Ernst Osthaus*, Hagen, 1984, pp.184–185, 204–205.

town's new library (1915) and an imposing city hall (1913–22), whose monumental dome dominated the town's sky-line until its destruction in World War Two.

Mayor Cuno was an enthusiastic supporter of Karl Ernst Osthaus's tireless efforts to put Hagen on the cultural map for the first time. He sat on the Management Committee of the German Museum for Art in Trade and Commerce, backed competitions to improve the aesthetic standard of shop-window displays in the town centre and on one occasion welcomed 400 members of the Werkbund on a Sunday excursion to Hagen. The most tangible result of the relationship between Osthaus and Cuno was, however, the large house built for the mayor by Peter Behrens at Osthaus's Hohenhagen development in 1909–10. The house, for which Osthaus met the 40,000 Mark construction costs, was rented to Cuno and was a curious mixture of the classical and the futuristic.

It is also worth mentioning that a decade or so later, another left liberal mayor, Fritz Hesse of the DDP and Mayor of Dessau from 1918, would be the saviour of Walter Gropius's Bauhaus, after the design school had been driven out of Weimar by hostile right wing politicians. Dessau, which like Delmenhorst and Hagen was a medium-sized industrial town with no tradition of cultural excellence, made a substantial investment to ensure the school became established on a site in the town. Mayor Hesse, to his credit, continued to champion the institution and practices of the Bauhaus long after it had become politically damaging to do so.

Heinz Stoffregen and the Anker-Marke

Meanwhile, back in Delmenhorst, Heinz Stoffregen was working on the details of the new town hall when he was approached by Gustav Gericke to tackle a very different kind of project; the design of a number of linoleum production buildings at the Anker factory, to the north of Delmenhorst railway station. The Anker-Marke had consistently out-performed the town's other linoleum producers during the 1900s, regularly paying annual dividends of over 20% to its shareholders[52], and embarking on an ambitious expansion plan at a time when other operations were facing an uncertain future. The company had also managed to secure a high profile in the everyday life of the town, with its achievements frequently praised in the pages of the *Kreisblatt*.

There were a number of reasons, therefore, why Anker should seek the skills of a progressive architect, with a growing local reputation, to design

52. See Jahresberichte der Handelskammer für das Herzogtum Oldenburg, 1904–14. The other Delmenhorst linoleum companies also paid reasonable dividends, but usually lower than those given by the Anker.

its factory buildings. Firstly, as a leading *Werkbündler*, Gericke had an obvious interest in furthering the reform of industrial architecture at a practical level. Secondly, as a prominent figure in the community and a member of the *Magistrat*, Gericke felt a personal responsibility to the town that his company's factory should in no way disfigure the local landscape. And thirdly, having become established as a major employer and ratepayer in the town, the Anker enterprise wished to express its new-found status and significance in architectural form.

As we have seen, Delmenhorst's biggest employer throughout this period was actually the NW&K textile concern, whose factory had spread over thirty hectares of land alongside the Bremen-Oldenburg railway line. By the 1900s, however, the linoleum industry could legitimately claim to have become more important to the town's fortunes. Whereas the family seat of the Lahusens and the NW&K administration had both remained in Bremen – which meant that neither contributed much to Delmenhorst's finances – the leading figures in the linoleum industry tended to live *and* work in the town.

Furthermore, whilst the NW&K relied to a large extent on 'imported' foreign labour or unskilled women workers, the linoleum factories employed skilled local men, and had a reputation for attracting the cream of the town's workforce. By 1911 the NW&K's 3,000 workers included around 2,000 men and women of foreign origin, mostly from eastern Europe. A similar proportion of immigrant workers (700 of 1,050) was employed at the jute factory, but at the linoleum works 'outsiders' stood little chance of finding employment.[53] If one wished to become a member of Delmenhorst's working class élite, family connections at the Anker, Hansa or Schlüssel were essential. Once a job at the linoleum works had been secured, however, credit in the town's shops seldom proved a problem.

The linoleum companies generally enjoyed better industrial relations than the jute factory or the NW&K, although the latter attempted to solve its labour problems by establishing a wide range of welfare services, including several tied-housing estates – more than one quarter of the workforce lived on site. The strictly authoritarian managerial style of the Lahusen concern was manifest in the foreboding façades of the 1884 factory, which was built by the Bremen architect Wilhelm Weyhe and later extended by Henrich Deetjen (1844–1916). Both men favoured a util-itarian red-brick architecture with Romanesque details, although Deetjen had originally made his name as the designer of Gothic churches. Deetjen, who was related to the Lahusen family through his mother, was appointed head of the building department at NW&K in 1897, and remained there

53. J. Mehrtens (ed.), *Alt Delmenhorst*, p.184.

Figure 45 NW&K machine hall, Delmenhorst 1902
Arch. H. Deetjen. Present condition

until his death nineteen years later. One of his most important projects was the design of the new machine hall, with its representative southern elevation, in 1902.[54]

In the 1900s Deetjen supervised a major extension to the works, which involved the addition of two further floors to the three-storey warehouse building of 1896, and the construction of a monumental watertower at its eastern end. The alterations, to buildings which overshadowed the railway line and were hence very much part of the public face of the company, kept rigidly to the original architectural conception of the 1884 NW&K factory. But, whilst the round-arched windows and rhythmic saw-tooth cornices were quite progressive in the architectural climate of the 1880s, by the time the additions were complete in 1910, the NW&K factory had already begun to appear as an aesthetic anachronism. The watertower, in particular, seemed to be a throwback to an earlier age, resembling a Malakow tower, transported from the Ruhr coalfield and deposited on the North German Plain. It was decorated with a golden-horned ornamental brick ram, together with the inscription '1884', the firm's foundation year.

The tower, and the 600 metre-long façade of the NW&K wool warehouse, were the first buildings of note a rail traveller from Bremen would see upon arrival in Delmenhorst, and left one in little doubt of the Lahusen concern's imperial aspirations. The possibility of building on such an imposing scale was not an option open to Gustav Gericke and the management of the Anker linoleum company, as they considered the construction of two new oxydisation buildings, a drying hall and a large storage shed. The function of the required buildings dictated more modest, largely window-less structures, which would not easily lend themselves to an eye-catching architectural treatment. Gericke, who had become aware of Heinz Stoffregen's abilities through the Bahnhofstraße and town hall competitions, saw, however, that an impact could still be made by selecting an architect who emphasised quality rather than quantity, modernity rather than monumentality. Despite his heavy workload, Stoffregen accepted the challenge.

The oxydisation buildings, built in the course of 1910, were orthogonal brick structures of remarkable simplicity, with small square windows and low, barely visible pitched roofs. Their sober functionality was enlivened by the architect's highly-individual diamond window frames, and the suggestion of classical pediments above the white-painted doorways. Although this was perhaps the least successful feature of the design, it was, as Aschenbeck notes, largely irrelevant to the overall visual impression.[55]

---

54. The NW&K buildings are described in S. Auffarth, 'Die Nordwolle'.
55. N. Aschenbeck, 'Romantische Sachlichkeit', p.26.

Figure 46 Anker linoleum oxydisation buildings, Delmenhorst 1910
Arch. H. Stoffregen. From Werkbund Yearbook, 1913

The two oxydisation buildings, linked by a series of tanks and pumps for linseed oil, were illustrated in the 1913 Werkbund Yearbook, and featured in *Der Industriebau*, as was the drying hall, which was built at the same time.

The latter actually consisted of two parallel halls, with a minimum of fenestration and large, arched doorways. It was here that the fresh strips of linoleum were hung up to dry, with the help of a sophisticated central heating system. In order to provide a space without internal supports or partitions Stoffregen stabilised the main hall, which was over forty metres long and eleven metres high, with a series of external brick piers. Meanwhile the storage shed, where the finished rolls of linoleum were to be kept before distribution, was built in 1911. It was over fifty metres long, and nearly thirty metres wide, but required only a low roof. The small, square windows, arranged rhythmically along its length, featured the same characteristic diamond design used in the oxydisation buildings.

Writing in *Der Industriebau*, Stoffregen explained the thinking behind his Anker buildings:

> The main effort in the construction of these buildings was aimed at practicality and functionality, and it is for this reason that there are obvious differences in character between the individual buildings. Until now it has been possible to mistake an oxydisation building for a drying hall or a place of manufacture, and vice versa, due to the division of every façade into pillars and windows. This is done in a way which suggests the existence of internal floors, even when wide open spaces actually rise right up to the roof.[56]

Stoffregen claimed the Anker buildings proved that it was possible to use bricks and roofing-felt simply and aesthetically, without recourse to historical devices, and that in this way a 'genuine monumentality' could be achieved, at no extra cost to the client.

It did not take the German Museum for Art in Trade and Commerce long to hear about Stoffregen's work for the linoleum industry. On 7 April 1911, the museum wrote to Anker, 'we have been informed by the DWB that you have recently put up some very fine factory buildings. Could you send us some good illustrations for our exhibition of model industrial buildings, which will be shown in various towns at home and abroad?'[57] Anker's Gustav Gericke was, of course, happy to oblige. The critical reaction was equally positive, with A. Goetze of *Der Profanbau* writing in 1914:

56. H. Stoffregen, 'Die neuen Fabrikbauten der Delmenhorster Linoleumfabrik Ankermarke', in *Der Industriebau*, vol.3 (1912), p.2.

57. K.E.O. Archiv A/351 p.17. (7 April 1911).

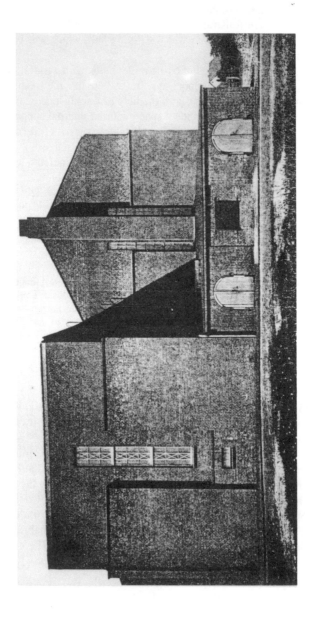

Figure 47 Anker linoleum drying halls, Delmenhorst 1910
Arch. H. Stoffregen. From Werkbund Yearbook, 1913

One may assert that they have already become exemplary . . . One feels here in the most concentrated way the language of a modern spirit, powerfully thrusting itself towards the New . . . Whoever sees these simple cubic forms, which make an impact through the careful distribution of masses, and have nothing more to do with the utilitarian air of earlier dreary industrial buildings, whoever recognises the effort to achieve harmony and beauty through the incredibly seductive design of the doors and windows, will grasp that within these walls the bleak spirit of hard toil and pauperisation no longer rules. Instead, an architect has succeeded, in keeping with the character of his client, to bring something of the dignity of labour into this factory.[58]

Adolf Behne, in his 1913 article 'Romanticists, Expressionists and Logicists in Modern Industrial Architecture', wrote of the same buildings: 'Here . . . pathos is combined with a tendency for the tragic, so that one can almost sense the shadows of Agamemnon and Aegisthus!'[59]

In addition to his work for the Anker-Marke, Stoffregen was employed as a consultant designer by the short-lived Delmenhorst automobile factory Carl Tönjes AG. One of his designs, for the inside of a limousine, was illustrated in the 1914 DWB Yearbook. In the previous edition of the yearbook Stoffregen had been one of the architects mentioned by Walter Gropius in his seminal essay 'The Development of Modern Industrial Architecture', where the Anker buildings were cited in the same breath as Behrens's work for the AEG, Wagner's Kaffee Hag complex, and Poelzig's chemical factory in Luban. It is somewhat surprising then, that his name does not feature more prominently in architectural histories of the period.

Apart from Aschenbeck's unpublished essay, an exhibition catalogue and a short entry in the *Bremische Biographie*, nothing has been written on the architect since his premature death at Bad Tölz in 1929.[60] This is in part a result of Stoffregen's own reluctance to express his views on architecture in print; whilst Gropius, Muthesius, Behrens and Poelzig sometimes seemed to spend as long at the typewriter as they did at the drawing board, Stoffregen's five short pieces for *Der Industriebau* were the sum total of his literary output. It has to be admitted too, however, that he probably did not build enough outside the Bremen-Delmenhorst area to achieve wider recognition.

Stoffregen was particularly ill-fated in the immediate pre-war years, when he appeared close to the all-important breakthrough on several

58. Quoted by N. Aschenbeck, 'Romantische Sachlichkeit', p.27.

59. A. Behne, 'Romantiker, Pathetiker und Logiker im modernen Industriebau', in *Preuß. Jahrbücher*, vol.154 (1913), p.174.

60. *Bremische Biographie 1912–1962*, p.507. Entry on Stoffregen by H. Fitger. An exhibition of Stoffregen's work was held in Delmenhorst in 1990, with a catalogue compiled by Nils Aschenbeck: *Heinz Stoffregen, 1879–1929. Architektur zwischen Tradition und Avantgarde*, Brunswick & Wiesbaden, 1990.

occasions, only to have his hopes dashed by circumstances beyond his control. His designs for a bank in Kassel (1907) and a hydro-electric power scheme on the Weser near Bremen (1908), were both second-prize winners in competitions. When he did pick up the first prize, in competitions for a housing development in Bremen, sponsored by the Association for Social Reform (1912), and for a 225 metre-long exhibition hall, required in Berlin by the Association of German Motor Vehicle Manufacturers (1914), he was not entrusted with the final commission. Some consolation came in the form of a machine hall for the Norddeutsche Seekabelwerke in Nordenham, built in 1912. His exhibition pavilion for the Werdandibund[61] at the Baltic Fair in Malmö was also built, only to be closed by the outbreak of war.

During the early war years Stoffregen became involved in the reconstruction of damaged East Prussian towns, but upon the cessation of hostilities he found it difficult to pick up the threads of his career. In the very different architectural conditions of the 1920s he struggled to find rewarding commissions, although he continued to design both buildings and patterns for the Delmenhorst linoleum industry. A large drying hall for the Hansa works, built in 1925 was his last major industrial project. He worked on a number of housing developments in Bremen, but was now neglected by the fashionable magazines, and a growing sense of bitterness may have contributed to his decision to sign the 1928 manifesto of Der Block, the nationalist, anti-Bauhaus group of architects, whose members included the *Werkbündler* Bonatz, Bestelmeyer and Schultze-Naumburg. He died, however, before the polarisation of professional and political life had reached its most harrowing phase.

In the first decade of the twentieth century Delmenhorst was fortunate to benefit from the chance association of three individuals, who came from very different backgrounds but shared a similarly strong commitment to improve the urban environment. The banner around which the politician, the industrialist and the architect were able to unite was that of the Werkbund, whose reformist ethos was allowed to blossom, albeit briefly, in this unassuming town, as it made its painful but rewarding transition to modernity. Although Stoffregen's Anker factory halls have long since

---

61. The Werdandibund was a cultural pressure group with *völkisch* leanings, involving many members of both the DWB and the Heimatschutz movement. It was led by the academic Friedrich Seeßelberg (1861–1956), and founder members included E. Högg, F. Schumacher, B. Möhring and H. Vogeler. See J. Frecot, 'Der Werdandibund', in B. Bergius, J. Frecot, D. Radicke (eds), *Architektur, Stadt und Politik*, Lahn-Gießen, 1979, p.37.

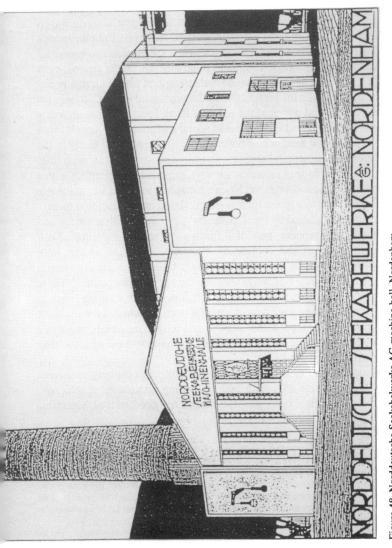

Figure 48 Norddeutsche Seekabelwerke AG machine hall, Nordenham
Arch. H. Stoffregen 1912. From *Der Industriebau*, vol. 3 (1912)

disappeared, sacrificed in the name of rationalisation,[62] the municipal buildings remain. They are not only a memorial to a fascinating chapter in the town's history, but a perfect illustration of the Werkbund ideal in action.

In a wider sense, the examples of Koch in Delmenhorst, Cuno in Hagen and Beutinger in Heilbronn, can perhaps shed some new light on an area of Wilhelmine life often overlooked by historians. Research into municipal politics in Germany's regions remains relatively thin on the ground, even though it is widely accepted that the real strength of liberal Germany can only be gauged from the perspective of the provincial town. Certainly for left liberals, denied power at the national level, local government was a valuable testing ground for theories of social and political reform.[63] From the instances cited here, it also appears to have been a vital factor in the promotion of architectural regeneration too. Industrial towns, with little architectural heritage or historical identity, provided the reformers with a particularly fertile soil, or, to use Koch's metaphor, a particularly malleable wax, with which to express their political vision in architectonic form.

The key role played by local 'notables' like Gericke, Bruckmann and Osthaus in this process, may also force us to reconsider some of our assumptions about the decline of *Honoratiorenpolitik* in the later Wilhelmine years, for it is clear that such figures remained powerful promoters of progressive change well into the age of 'mass politics'. These were respected pillars of the local establishment, with a strong sense of regional loyalty, who were nevertheless far from parochial in their outlook and commitments. Indeed, they contributed fully to the development of a liberal political culture which was rather more animated and dynamic than is sometimes suggested.

It must be remembered, however, that there was nothing inevitable about the transition of young and expanding communities into self-respecting municipal boroughs. Delmenhorst's good fortune contrasted

---

62. In 1926 the Delmenhorst linoleum companies became part of the Deutsche Linoleum-Werke AG (DLW), whose headquarters were established at Bietigheim in Württemberg. The over-capacity and duplication of facilties in the Delmenhorst factories inevitably led to a number of changes in the organisation of production, particularly after damage by allied bombers in World War Two. Unfortunately the archival records of the Delmenhorst companies were lost with the demolition of the former DLW administrative building in the town during the 1970s.

63. Other left liberal mayors to head reformist municipal administrations included Liebetrau (Gotha), Schwunder (Strasbourg), Dominicus (Schöneberg), and Pohlmann (Kattowitz). For further details see A. Thompson, 'Left Liberals in German State and Society', PhD thesis, Birkbeck College, London, 1989, p.151. Thompson writes: 'At its best, in theory and practice, left liberal municipal government was one of the few areas where Wilhelmine left liberalism had genuine claims to political glory. Like other areas of left liberal politics, however, this sphere was subject to wide regional variations.' (p.152).

sharply with the experience of other industrial settlements, such as Borbeck in the Ruhr, which failed to achieve either the administrative status or architectural character of a town, despite boasting a population of some 77,000 by 1915. It was not even able to retain the title of 'Prussia's largest village', losing that particular distinction to nearby Hamborn, whose population passed the 100,000 mark before it was granted a municipal charter in 1910. As Lutz Niethammer describes in his 1979 book on Borbeck, the village was frustrated in its development by the political and commercial calculations of conservative district councillors and the *Regierungspräsident* in Düsseldorf, whose machinations drove the *Communalbaumeister* of Borbeck, Johann Heinrich Voßkühler (1852–1914), to despair, disgrace and eventual death.[64]

Voßkühler, who apart from the mayor was the district's only senior administrative official, saw many treasured schemes for public parks and wide urban avenues fall victim of a council dominated by large landowners and the representatives of heavy industry, who had earmarked much of the district for the development of coal mining instead. Borbeck remained an 'industrial village' until it was swallowed up by Essen in 1915. As Niethammer notes:

> large industrial rural communities are a characteristic variant of urbanisation in Imperial Germany. They indicate that the development of bourgeois society did not happen with all factors marching in step down a one-way street called 'modernisation', but rather against a mesh of power interests, which could bring it to a standstill or divert it, but also steer it to sudden breakthroughs.[65]

64. L. Niethammer, *Umständliche Erläuterung der seelischen Störung eines Communalbaumeisters..*, Frankfurt, 1979.

65. L. Niethammer, *ibid*, p.9. Many other Ruhr communities failed to develop a true urban character or municipal identity in this way. See for instance Heinz Reif's 'Kind der Eisenbahn. Die Emscherstadt Oberhausen vor 1914', in L. Niethammer (ed.), *Die Menschen machen ihre Geschichte..*, Berlin 1984.

Epilogue

The indelible impression left on Wilhelmine society by the movements for architectural reform can perhaps best be illustrated by two examples drawn from the darkest days of World War One. The first concerns the reconstruction of East Prussian towns and villages destroyed in the first months of fighting, the second the expansion of Germany's armaments industries under the Hindenburg Programme of 1916–17. In both cases it is clear that the 'alternative' architectural styles and values of the 1900s, fought for with such vigour by *Heimatschützer* and *Werkbündler* throughout the previous decade, had become so well established by the war years that they no longer raised eyebrows in such bastions of conservatism as the Prussian civil service or the boardrooms of the Ruhr.

The Prussian Ministry of the Interior received many offers of help and advice on the reconstruction of war-damaged East Prussian communities in the winter of 1914–15, but it ultimately entrusted almost the entire rebuilding programme to teams of architects and planners nominated by the Werkbund and the Bund Heimatschutz, whose submissions to the authorities had stressed the need for the shattered communities to be rebuilt in a style which was both modern and functional, yet respectful of the region's architectural traditions.[1] Thus Delmenhorst's Heinz Stoffregen was joined in East Prussia by many other architects featured in earlier chapters, whilst another prominent reformer, Carl Rehorst, was taken on by the German forces of occupation in Belgium as special advisor on matters of reconstruction there.

The second example dates from late August 1916, when Germany's Supreme Military Command took a far-reaching decision to expand the output of the nation's factories to unprecedented levels; weapons manufacture was to be doubled and an even greater increase was proposed for the output of munitions. The Hindenburg Programme was designed to push German industry to its very limits, to exploit the available raw materials and labour force to the full, and to drive the war effort toward a

---

1. For the reconstruction in East Prussia see *Deutsche Bauzeitung*, vol. 48 (1914), p.771 and p.800. Also *Der Kunstwart*, vol. 28, no.4 (1914), p.146, and vol. 28, no.9 (1914), p.91.

spectacularly successful conclusion. New workshops were to be built for the production of powerful guns and shells, and the reservoir of female labour was to be tapped to previously unknown depths. Extra manpower was even to be drafted in from prisoner of war and detention camps, leaving thousands of foreign citizens with no choice but to toil for Germany's war machine.

The expansion was concentrated at existing centres of armaments production, such as the Krupp factories in Essen, where building work began in October 1916 on land to the north of the giant cast steel factory. Despite serious shortages of materials and construction workers, the new workshops had to be erected on a vast scale and in record time. Between 1916 and 1917 numerous halls were built for the production of shells, electrical components, gun-carriages and artillery pieces. The *Geschoßdreherei VII* alone measured over 470 metres in length and covered an area of 56,000 square metres.[2] As with previous factories for Krupp, the company's internal building and technical engineering departments were responsible for the entire planning and construction process, with no individual architect receiving credit for particular design features.

In view of the conditions under which the work was carried out, one might reasonably assume that the aesthetic quality of the new factories was of no great importance to the Krupp management. In fact, however, no fewer than six of the buildings constructed by the company under the Hindenburg Programme were given a careful architectural treatment. The official record of the Krupp *Baubüro* notes how a 'special effort' was made to ensure that although 'the strictest sobriety was safeguarded', an 'aesthetically pleasing external appearance' was given to workshops such as the *Kanonenwerkstätte IV/V*, the *Glühhaus III*, *Geschoßdreherei VII*, the *Elektrizitätswerk V* and the *Lafettenwerkstatt VIII*.[3]

A particular effort was made to give those façades which faced onto major traffic arteries an appearance 'in keeping with the importance of the works'.[4] The *Geschoßdreherei VII* for instance, which ran for over a quarter of a mile alongside the Kruppstraße, was a flat-roofed three storey brick-clad structure, with a sensitively proportioned façade in which the monotonous horizontal emphasis was broken up by the rhythmic use of vertical window panels. The offices of the Kanonenwerkstatt IV, on the Husmannstraße, were similarly characterised by an imaginative use of

2. HA Krupp WA VII f.1101 kd. 87 (Hindenburgprogramm).
3. HA Krupp WA VII f.1101 kd. 71 (Baubüro); WA VII f.1116 kd. 87 (Hindenburg-programm); WA VII f. 1098 kd.68. (Hindenburgprogramm).
4. HA Krupp WA VII f.1101 kd. 87, p.13 (Hindenburgprogramm).

fenestration to achieve a distinguished visual effect. Wartime shortages may have prompted the use of simple materials and standardised components, but it is clear that the buildings also reflected changing attitudes in the building department and the boardroom to questions of architectural expression.

All traces of heavy industry's previous predilection for historicist ornamentation had gone, to be replaced by the dignified and sober simplicity much favoured by Werkbund architects for buildings of industrial production. The buildings displayed a new-found confidence and awareness of heavy industry's vital role in the fortunes of the nation, and a tacit acknowledgement that the architectural forms promoted by the 'new' industrial faction were a more appropriate model for the future than those of the Imperial state. Other heavy industrial concerns joined the Krupp AG in this move towards architectural modernity at the end of World War One; a process which reflected both the general blurring of distinctions between the pre-war industrial factions and the gradual adoption of more 'flexible' forms of management by the giants of heavy industry.

If the architectural styles promoted by the reformers of the 1900s had become widely accepted by the war years, their popularity with the creative vanguard of the architectural profession was to prove predictably short-lived. In the radicalised cultural climate of the immediate post-war period, much of the Werkbund's industrial architecture suddenly seemed tired and pretentious, that of the *Heimatschützer* dated and irrelevant. More than one architect was heard to dismiss his entire pre-war *oeuvre*, whilst the younger generation of architects instead placed their faith in new manifestos and organisations, such as the 'Novembergruppe' or the 'Arbeitsrat für Kunst'.

Even so, many of the architectural virtues proclaimed by the Wilhelmine reformers – sobriety, honesty, simplicity – lived on, to be propagated with renewed vigour by the activists of the 1920s, and German industry continued to offer commissions to the likes of Behrens, Bonatz, Muthesius and Poelzig, as well as younger practitioners like Mendelsohn and Fahrenkamp. More importantly, the 'quality workplace' remained a preoccupation of the DWB throughout the Weimar years: indeed, with the increasing rationalisation and 'Americanisation' of German industry, it was to gain an even higher profile in the movement, as the lively Werkbund conference debates of the 1920s showed.

At the same time, the success – and relative popularity – of modern styles in architecture and design in Weimar Germany had much to do with the foundations laid by the pre-war Werkbund, whose efforts to 'educate' producers and consumers had not been without effect. With hindsight one can see that for all their pretentious and self-important slogans, their patronising concern for the 'social question' and their dubious nationalism, the Wilhelmine reformers had made a valuable and lasting contribution to German life. The establishment of the 'Normenausschuß der deutschen Industrie' in 1917, for instance, the Institute of Industrial Standards, whose 'DIN' codes were to play an integral part in the rationalisation of industrial production and building in Germany after 1918, owed much to *Werkbündler* such as Behrens and Muthesius. Muthesius had earlier been responsible for a thorough reform of the nation's art and craft colleges, whilst another member of the DWB, Peter Jessen, had performed a similar role in the museums service. The post of *Reichskunstwart*, established in the Weimar Republic as a sort of ombudsman for artistic affairs, to oversee all aspects of design and architecture in the public realm, was a further product of Werkbund agitation.

In a more general sense, the DWB's campaign to promote 'quality' in German manufacturing was a crucial factor in the long-term transformation of the nation's reputation, from a producer of 'cheap and nasty' surrogates to a respected exporter of first-class goods. It was the Werkbund, its designers and its member companies, which was largely responsible for turning the phrase 'Made in Germany' from an insult to a compliment. Whatever the experience of individual companies with the export of 'quality' goods – and there were no doubt many which continued to do very well from the export of *Schundwaren* – the public perception of German products changed fundamentally between the fall of Bismarck and the First World War.

The industrial buildings designed by DWB architects before 1918 had an impact on German society out of all proportion to their modest numbers and mundane functions. Their importance to an architectural profession looking to free itself from the shackles of academic historicism has long been recognised, but their wider significance as an expression of economic, political and cultural change in Wilhelmine Germany should not be underestimated either. The desire of a powerful section of German industry to match the modernity of its business operations with equally advanced forms of corporate architecture, product design, marketing and labour relations, reverberated throughout German society before World War One.

The Naumannite clique, the driving force behind the early DWB and the most vital link between the cultural, political and economic facets of the organisation, experienced a difficult passage into the post-Imperial age. In November 1918, as the Werkbund's young guns flirted with radical politics and radical art, the more established *Werkbündler* formed up under the banner of Walther Rathenau's Demokratische Volksbund. The signatures of Naumann, Heuss, Jäckh, Kerschensteiner, Bosch, Behrens, Muthesius and Bruno Paul were all to be found on a declaration supporting the proposed new party,[5] which hoped to win over large sections of 'reasonable' middle class opinion with a rather vague programme of centrist reform. When it became clear, however, that the Volksbund could represent no more than a transitional solution, the Werkbund leadership moved en bloc to participate in the foundation of the left liberal DDP, which had the backing of influential sections of the Berlin press.[6]

In July 1919 Naumann, who along with his DWB colleague Erich Koch-Weser had played an important part in drafting the Constitution for the Weimar Republic, was elected Chairman of the DDP, but within a month he was dead, the victim of a stroke. The Naumannites continued to play a dominant role in the DDP, though the party's electoral fortunes were to decline rapidly during the 1920s. In one sense, however, the Naumannites had the last laugh, for on 13 September 1949 Theodor Heuss – Naumann's most loyal follower and one time Executive Secretary of the Werkbund – was elected to be the first President of the Federal Republic of Germany.

There was much for the old *Werkbündler* to applaud in the democratic social-market economy which developed in West Germany under his presidency, with its quality manufacturing industries and harmonious labour relations, its well-planned cities and well-stocked shops. American capitalism, whose employee welfare schemes and huge industrial plants had so intrigued the Naumannites, was once more on the agenda, a source of inspiration and investment. On the fiftieth anniversary of the DWB's foundation Heuss was to write an essay in which he described the organisation as 'one of the greatest and most productive achievements of recent German history'.[7]

It was an exaggerated claim, no doubt, but understandable in view of the organisation's inexplicable and undeserved obscurity; an obscurity made all the more surprising given the fledgling Federal Republic's usual eagerness to establish lines of continuity with any earlier endeavour of a liberal or progressive nature. Significantly this continuity did not escape

5. Published in *Deutsche Stimmen*, vol. 30, no.47 (24 Nov. 1918). A few years later many of the same names gave their support to the 'Society for the Renewal of Economic Morality and Responsibility' ('Bund der Erneuerung'), founded in July 1920 by the *Werkbündler* Karl Scheffler. At one stage it was actually intended to fuse the new society with the DWB, which had published Scheffler's 'manifesto' entitled *Sittliche Diktatur. Ein Aufruf an alle Deutschen*, Berlin, 1920, but interest soon waned.

6. On the DDP see R. Opitz, *Ideologie und Praxis des deutschen Sozialliberalismus*, Cologne, 1973; L. Albertin, *Liberalismus und Demokratie*, Düsseldorf, 1972; K. Wegner, 'Linksliberalismus im wilhelminischen Deutschland und in der Weimarer Republik', in *Geschichte und Gesellschaft*, vol. 4 (1978).

7. T. Heuss, 'Notizen und Exkurse zur Geschichte des Deutschen Werkbundes', in H. Eckstein (ed.), *50 Jahre Deutscher Werkbund*, Frankfurt, 1958.

the notice of East Germans writing on the DWB, such as Günter Pollak, who noted in a 1971 thesis:

> The German Werkbund was not only an expression of its age, that is to say the period 1907–1919 ... for within it at this time the leading group were developing socio-political foundations which were to have their specific continuation in the Federal Republic ... The old Naumannite thesis of an epoch of 'Freedom and Technology' can be found once more in the current political climate of the FRG, as a view of the industrial society within the 'free' community of European states, in which the FRG would like to take a dominant position.[8]

In retrospect, neither the Bund Heimatschutz nor the Werkbund was able to do much more than scratch at the surface of the deep seated problems caused by industrialisation; the troubled relationships between capital and labour, the built environment and the natural world, remained largely unresolved. Despite this, however, the faith of the Wilhelmine reformers in their historical mission was not easily shaken. The belief that the modern age needed cultural legitimation, that a society based on industry and commerce could no longer rely on means of expression developed by the aristocracy, proved a strong source of motivation, as the buildings documented here testify.

---

8. G. Pollak, 'Die gesellschafts- und kulturpolitische Funktion des Deutschen Werkbundes', PhD thesis, Weimar, 1971, pp.257–261.

Bibliography

I. Archival Sources
(For full details of files used see footnotes)

Municipal and State Archives:

Bundesarchiv Koblenz (Bundesarchiv)
— *Nachlaß* Koch-Weser (NL12 Koch-Weser/125)
Zentrale Staatsarchiv Potsdam (ZStA Potsdam)
— *Nachlaß* Naumann (90 Na 3)
Staatsarchiv Bremen (StA Bremen)
— *Nachlaß* Stoffregen (7,137)
Staatsarchiv Dresden (StA Dresden)
— files on Heimatschutz (MdI 17518, 17522–17531); transcripts of Saxon
  parliamentary sessions etc.
Staatsarchiv Hamburg (StA Hamburg)
— files on Heimatschutz (A507/13); town planning etc. Good collection
  of local periodicals
Stadtarchiv Alfeld (SA Alfeld)
Stadtarchiv Delmenhorst (SA Delmenhorst)
— files on linoleum companies; town hall project (XIX 13.652); transcripts
  of council meetings etc. NB copies of *Delmenhorster Kreisblatt* on
  microfilm at newspaper offices in Delmenhorst
Stadtarchiv Heilbronn (SA Heilbronn)
— personal files on Beutinger (P28/1–2); Bruckmann (P47–1/2); etc.

Company Archives:

H. Bahlsens Keksfabrik KG, Hanover (Bahlsen-Archiv)
Bayer AG, Leverkusen (Bayer-Archiv)
Fagus-GreCon Greten GmbH, Alfeld (Fagus-Archiv)
Fried. Krupp GmbH, Essen (HA Krupp)
Mannesmann AG, Düsseldorf (Mannesmann-Archiv)
Thyssen AG, Duisburg (Thyssen-Archiv)

Other Archives:

Bergbau-Archiv, Bochum (BBA)
— files on individual coal mines
Karl Ernst Osthaus-Archiv, Hagen (K.E.O. Archiv)
— files on Werkbund (DWB1/1-331); German Museum for Art in Trade
   and Commerce (DM/8-33); correspondence Osthaus-Gericke (A/351)
   and much more
Werkbund-Archiv, Berlin (DWB-Archiv)
— Werkbund annual reports, yearbooks etc., together with examples of
   DWB design (as part of the *Museum der Alltagskultur des 20.
   Jahrhunderts*)

II. Newspapers and Periodicals Examined Systematically

Alfelder Kreiszeitung, 1910–1911
Delmenhorster Kreisblatt, 1905–1914
Deutsche Bauzeitung, 1907–1916
Deutsche Kunst und Dekoration, 1906–1917
Frankfurter Zeitung, 1909–1914
Glückauf, 1905–1922
Hamburger, Der, 1910–1912
Hamburgische Zeitschrift für Heimatkultur, 1910–1920
Hamburgische Zeitschrift für Wohnungskultur, 1908–1909
Heimatschutz, 1905–1914
Hilfe, Die, 1900–1914
Industriebau, Der, 1910–1922
Kölnische Zeitung, 1913–1914
Kunstgewerbeblatt, 1904–1916
Kunstwart, Der 1901–1917
Mitteilungen des Rhein. Vereins für Denkmalpflege u. Heimatschutz, 1907–
   1914
Rheinlande, Die, 1900–1915
Sozialistische Monatshefte, 1908–1916

III. Werkbund Publications

Yearbooks:

1912   *Die Durchgeistigung der deutschen Arbeit*, Jena, 1912
1913   *Die Kunst in Industrie und Handel*, Jena, 1913
1914   *Der Verkehr*, Jena, 1914
1915   *Deutsche Form im Kriegsjahr*, Jena, 1915

1916–17   *Kriegergräber im Felde und daheim*, Munich, 1917

Conference Reports:

1908   *Die Veredelung der gewerblichen Arbeit im Zusammenwirken von Kunst, Industrie und Handwerk. Verhandlungen des Deutschen Werkbundes zu München am 11. und 12. Juli 1908*

1909   *II. Jahresversammlung zu Frankfurt am Main in der Akademie für Sozialwissenschaften vom 30. Sept. bis 2. Okt. 1909*

1910   *Die Durchgeistigung der deutschen Arbeit. Ein Bericht vom Deutschen Werkbund. Verhandlungsbericht der III. Jahresversammlung vom 10. – 12. Juni 1910 zu Berlin*

1914   *Der Werkbundgedanke in den germanischen Ländern (VII. Jahresversammlung Köln 2. – 6. Juni 1914)*

Annual Reports:

1908–09   *I. Jahresbericht* – Wolf Dohrn (ed.)
1909–10   *II. Jahresbericht* – Wolf Dohrn (ed.)
1910–11   *III. Jahresbericht* – Alfons Paquet (ed.)
1911–12   *IV. Jahresbericht* – Alfons Paquet (ed.)
1913–14   *VI. Jahresbericht* – Ernst Jäckh (ed.)

IV. Other Contemporary Sources

Avenarius, Ferdinand, 'Über Ausdruckskultur', *Dürerbund Flugschriften*, no. 67, Munich, 1910
Behne, Adolf, 'Die ästhetischen Theorien der modernen Baukunst', in *Preuß. Jahrbücher*, no. 153, (1913)
— 'Romantiker, Pathetiker und Logiker im modernen Industriebau', in *Preuß. Jahrbücher*, no. 154, (1914)
— 'Heutige Industriebauten', in *Velhagen und Klasings Monatshefte*, vol. 28 (1914)
— 'Kritik des Werkbundes', in *Die Tat*, vol. 9 (1917)
— *Der modern Zweckbau*, Munich, 1926
Beutinger, Emil, 'Die künstlerische Gestaltung der Industriebauten', *Dürerbund Flugschriften*, no. 154, Munich, 1916
Bodenbender, H., *Linoleum-Handbuch. Ein praktischer Führer für Industrie und Handel*, Berlin, 1931
Borst, Hugo, 'Das sogenannte Taylor-System vom Standpunkt des Organisators aus betrachtet. Vortrag gehalten am 15. Januar 1914', Stuttgart, 1914
— Mechanisierte Industriearbeit, muß sie im Gegensatz zu freier Arbeit

Mensch und Kultur gefährden?', in *Das Problem der Industriearbeit* (with Willy Hellpach), Berlin, 1925

— *Wie ich Sammler wurde. Erinnerungen und Bekenntnisse*, Stuttgart, 1941

Bredt, F.W., 'Die neue Gesetzgebung auf dem Gebiete der Denkmalpflege und des Heimatschutzes', *Dürerbund Flugschriften*, no. 53, Munich, 1909

Bröcker, Paul, *Über Hamburgs neue Architektur*, Hamburg, 1908

— *Hamburg in Not. Ein eiliger Hilferuf und ein Vorschlag zur Rettung der vaterstädtischen Baukultur*, Hamburg, 1908

— *Die Architektur des Hamburgischen Geschäftshaus. Ein zeitgemäßes Wort für die Ausbildung der Mönckebergstraße*, Hamburg, 1910

— *Wie gestaltet man landwirtschaftliche Nutzbauten zugleich ästhetisch und praktisch?*, Hamburg, 1910

— 'Der Heimatschutzgedanke und die Urbarmachung der Oedländereien durch Kriegsgefangene', *Dürerbund Flugschriften*, no. 136, Munich, 1915

— *Wertgutgedanken. Die Wertgutgestaltung als Problem der Ästhetik, der Wirtschaft und des Staates*, Hamburg, 1919

— *Was ist Klassenkampf?*, Hamburg, 1919

— *Die Arbeitnehmerbewegung. Eine Darstellung ihrer geistigen Entwicklung und kulturellen Macht*, Hamburg, 1919

— *Vom Christlich-Sozialen Gedanken zur Deutschnationalen Arbeitnehmerbewegung*, Hamburg, 1921

Bruckmann, Peter, 'Deutscher Werkbund und Industrie. Vortrag, gehalten auf der 6. Generalversammlung des Verbandes Württ. Industrieller zu Heilbronn a. N. am 18. Januar 1914', Stuttgart, 1914

Dürks, Erich, 'Die deutsche Linoleum-Industrie, unter besonderer Berücksichtigung der Fabriken in Delmenhorst i.O.', PhD thesis, Heidelberg University, 1919

Erlwein, Hans, 'Einfache städtische Nutzbauten in Dresden von Hans Erlwein', *Dürerbund Flugschriften*, no. 107, Munich, 1913

Fischer, Johannes, *Als Arbeiter auf der Weltausstellung*, Munich, 1911

Ford, Henry, *Mein Leben und Werk*, Leipzig, 1925

Franz, W., 'Industriebauten', in *Städtebauliche Vorträge*, vol. 7 (1914)

Freese, Heinrich, *Die konstitutionelle Fabrik*, Jena, 1909

— *Die Bodenreform, ihre Vergangenheit und ihre Zukunft*, Berlin, 1918

Fritsch, Theodor, *Die Stadt der Zukunft*, Leipzig, 1896

Fürst, Artur, *Emil Rathenau. Der Mann und sein Werk*, Berlin, 1915

Göhre, Paul, *Das Warenhaus*, Frankfurt, 1907

Gropius, Walter, 'Faltblatt zur Wanderausstellung 18 des Deutschen Museums für Kunst in Handel und Gewerbe', 1911

Hartnauer, Richard, *Kunst in Leverkusen. Zum fünfzigsten Jahrestag des*

Eintritts von Dr. Carl Duisberg bei den Farbefabriken vorm. Friedr. Bayer & Co. am 29. September 1933. Plastiken, Bauten, Gartenkunst

Haupt, Albrecht, *Der deutsche Backsteinbau der Gegenwart und seine Lage. Auch eine Frage des Heimatschutzes*, Leipzig, 1910

Hellpach, Willy, 'Die Erziehung der Arbeit', in *Das Problem der Industriearbeit* (with Hugo Borst), Berlin, 1925

Henrici, Karl, 'Über die Pflege des Heimatlichen im ländlichen und städtischen Bauwesen *Dürerbund Flugschriften*, no. 16, Munich, 1906

Heuss, Theodor, 'Gewerbekunst und Volkswirtschaft', in *Preuß. Jahrbücher*, 141 (1910)

Hoeber, Fritz, *Peter Behrens*, Munich, 1913

Högg, Emil, 'Heimatschutz, Baukunst und Industrie', *Dürerbund Flugschriften*, no. 86, Munich, 1911

Jäckh, Ernst, 'Werkbund und Mitteleuropa. Vortrag auf der Jahresversammlung des Deutschen Werkbundes in Bamberg. Gehalten am 14. Juli 1916', Weimar, 1916/17

— 'Mitteleuropa als Organismus', in *Deutsche Politik*, no. 25 (1916)

Kampffmeyer, Hans, *Die Gartenstadtbewegung*, Leipzig & Berlin, 1913

Kohlmann, Curt, 'Das Taylor-System', in *Velhagen und Klasings Monatshefte*, vol. 28 (1914)

Krupp, 'Festschrift zur Jahrhundertfeier', Essen, 1912

Levenstein, Adolf, *Arbeiter-Philosophen und -Dichter*, Berlin, 1909

— *Die Arbeiterfrage*, Munich, 1912

Lichtwark, Alfred, *Hamburg-Niedersachsen*, Dresden, 1897

Lüthgen, G. Eugen (ed.), *Jahrbuch 1913 der Vereinigung für Kunst in Handel und Gewerbe Cöln*, Bonn, 1913

Malkowsky, Georg, *Die Kunst im Dienste der Staats-Idee. Hohenzollerische Kunstpolitik vom Großen Kurfürsten bis auf Wilhelm II*, Berlin, 1912

Mannesmann, 'Zur Erinnerung an die Einweihung des Verwaltungsgebäudes der Mannesmannröhrenwerke in Düsseldorf, am 10. Dezember 1912', Düsseldorf, 1913

Meißner, Else, 'Das Verhältnis des Künstlers zum Unternehmer im Bau- und Kunstgewerbe', *Staats- und sozialwissenschaftliche Forschungen*, no. 185, Munich & Leipzig, 1915

Moeller van den Bruck, Arthur, *Der Preußische Stil*, Munich, 1916

Most, Otto (ed.), *Die deutsche Stadt und ihre Verwaltung*, Berlin & Leipzig, 1912

Müller-Wulckow, Walter, *Bauten der Arbeit und des Verkehrs aus deutscher Gegenwart*, Königstein im Taunus & Leipzig, 1925/29

Münsterberg, Hugo, *Psychologie und Wirtschaftsleben. Ein Beitrag zur angewandten Experimental-Psychologie*, Leipzig, 1913

Muthesius, Hermann, *Stilarchitektur und Baukunst*, Mülheim, 1902

Bibliography

— *Kultur und Kunst*, Leipzig & Jena, 1904
— *Kunstgewerbe und Architektur*, Jena, 1907
— 'Wo stehen wir? Vortrag auf der IV. DWB Jahresversammlung Dresden 1911'
— 'Die Zukunft der deutschen Form', in *Der Deutsche Krieg*, no. 50 (1915)
— 'Der Deutsche nach dem Kriege', in *Weltkultur und Weltpolitik – Deutsche Folge*, no. 4 (1915)
— 'Der Werkbundgedanke. Seine Grundlagen', in *Deutsche Politik*, Weimar, 1916
— *Handarbeit und Massenerzeugnis*, Berlin, 1917
Naumann, Friedrich, 'Demokratie und Kaisertum', 1900
— 'Düsseldorfer Industrie-Ausstellung', 1902
— 'Die Kunst im Zeitalter der Maschine', 1904
— 'Kunst und Industrie', 1906
— 'Neudeutsche Wirtschaftspolitik', 1906
— 'Deutsche Gewerbekunst. Eine Arbeit über die Organisation des Deutschen Werkbundes', 1908
— 'Die Veredelung der gewerblichen Arbeit', 1908
— 'Der ästhetische Mensch und die Politik', 1908
— 'Der Industriestaat', 1909
— 'Form und Farbe', 1909
— 'Der deutsche Stil', c.1913
— 'Mitteleuropa', 1915
Neidlich, Joachim, *Deutscher Heimatschutz als Erziehung zu deutscher Kultur*, Leipzig, 1920
Pantzer, Robert, *Zur Frage der Qualitätsverfeinerung oder Entfeinerung unseres Exports*, Berlin, 1912
Pechmann, Günther Freiherr von, *Die Qualitätsarbeit. Ein Handbuch für Industrielle, Kaufleute und Gewerbepolitiker*, Frankfurt, 1924
Pudor, Heinrich, *Deutsche Qualitätsarbeit*, Gautzsch bei Leipzig, 1910
Rathenau, Walther, *Reflexionen*, Leipzig, 1912
— *Kunstphilosophie und Ästhetik*, Munich, 1923
Rauecker, Bruno, 'Nochmals zur Kritik des Werkbundes', in *Die Tat*, vol. 9 (1917)
Rehorst, Carl, 'Alte Städtebilder und moderner Verkehr', *Dürerbund Flugschriften*, no. 38, Munich, 1908
Riezler, Walter, 'Die Kulturarbeit des Deutschen Werkbundes', in *Weltkultur und Weltpolitik*, no. 7, Munich, 1916
Rohrbach, Paul, 'Warum es der Deutsche Krieg ist', Stuttgart & Berlin, 1914
Sarason, D. (ed.), *Das Jahr 1913. Ein Gesamtbild der Kulturentwicklung*, Leipzig & Berlin, 1913

Scheffler, Karl, *Die Architektur der Großstadt*, Berlin, 1913

— *Sittliche Diktatur*, Berlin, 1920

Schultze-Naumburg, Paul, *Die Entstellung unseres Landes*, 3rd ed., Munich, 1908

— 'Aufgaben des Heimatschutzes', *Dürerbund Flugschriften*, no. 39, Munich, 1908

— *Vom verstehen und geniessen der Landschaft*, Rudolstadt, 1924

Schumacher, Fritz, *Kulturpolitik*, Jena, 1920

Schwindrazheim, Oskar, *Von alter zu neuer Heimatkunst*, Hamburg, 1908

Seeßelberg, Friedrich, *Volk und Kunst*, Berlin, 1907

— *Das flache Dach im Heimatbild*, Berlin, 1914

Seidel, Paul, *Der Kaiser und die Kunst*, Berlin, 1907

Sternaux, Ludwig, 'Die Deutsche Werkbund-Ausstellung Cöln 1914', in *Velhagen und Klasings Monatshefte*, vol. 28 (1914)

Verbeek, Hans, 'Die Hochbautätigkeit in der Alt- und Neustadt von 1888–1918', in *Köln, bauliche Entwicklung 1888–1927*, Berlin, 1927

Vetter, Adolf, 'Die staatsbürgerliche Bedeutung der Qualitätsarbeit', *Dürerbund Flugschriften*, no. 87, Munich, 1911

Waentig, Heinrich, *Wirtschaft und Kunst. Eine Untersuchung über Geschichte und Theorie der modernen Kunstgewerbebewegung*, Jena, 1909

Weigand, Karl, *50 Jahre Continental. Gedenkbuch zum 50-jährigen Bestehen der Continental Caoutchouc und Gutta-Percha Compagnie, Hannover 1871–1921*, Hanover, 1921

Zörner, Richard (ed.), 'Denkschrift zum 25-jährigen Bestehen des Deutschen Stahlbau-Verbandes 1904–1929', Essen, 1929

V. Secondary Sources

Ackermann, Kurt, *Industriebau*, Stuttgart, 1984

Albertin, Lothar, *Liberalismus und Demokratie am Anfang der Weimarer Republik. Eine vergleichende Analyse der DDP und der DVP*, Düsseldorf, 1972

Allmendinger, Claus-Michael, *Struktur, Aufgabe und Bedeutung der Stiftungen von Robert Bosch und seiner Firma*, Stuttgart, 1977

Anderson, Stanford, 'Peter Behrens and the new architecture of Germany; 1900–1917', PhD thesis, Columbia University, 1968

Andresen, Hans-Günther, 'Heimatschutzarchitektur in Lübeck – ein vergessener Versuch des angemessenen Umgangs mit einem Stadtdenkmal', in M. Brix (ed.), *Lübeck. Die Altstadt als Denkmal*, Munich, 1975

— *Bauen in Backstein. Schleswig-Holsteinische Heimatschutz-Architektur*, Heide in Holstein, 1989

Applegate, Celia, *A Nation of Provincials: The German Idea of Heimat*, Berkeley, 1990

Aschenbeck, Nils, 'Heinz Stoffregen 1879–1929; Romantische Sachlichkeit. Dokumentation und Bewertung des Werks und der architektur-historischen Bedeutung des Bremer Architekten Heinz Stoffregen', unpublished manuscript, Bremen, 1986

Auffarth, Sid & Stracke, Ferdinand, *Die Nordwolle. Neues Leben für ein Industriedenkmal*, Delmenhorster Schriften no. 10, 1982

Bahlsens Keksfabrik 1889–1939, Frankfurt, 1939

Bahlsens Keksfabrik 1889–1964, Hanover, 1964

Banham, Reyner, *Theory and Design in the first machine age*, London, 1960

— *The Architecture of the well-tempered environment*, Chicago, 1969

— *A Concrete Atlantis. US industrial building and European modern architecture*, Cambridge Mass., 1986

Barner, Wilhelm, *Carl Benscheidt d.Ä. 1858–1947*, Hildesheim, 1947

Becher, Bernd & Hilla, *Die Architektur der Förder- und Wassertürme*, Munich, 1971

Becher, Bernd & Conrad, Hans-Günther & Neumann, Eberhard
— *Zeche Zollern II. Aufbruch zur modernen Industriearchitektur und Technik*, Munich, 1977

Bendix, Reinhard, *Work and Authority in Industry. Ideologies of Management in the course of Industrialization*, New York, 1960

Benjamin, Walter, *Das Kunstwerk im Zeitalter seiner technischen Reproduzierbarkeit*, Frankfurt, 1970

Bergius, Burkhard & Frecot, Julius & Radicke, Dieter (eds.), *Architektur, Stadt und Politik. Festschrift für J. Posener*, Lahn-Gießen, 1979

Bergmann, Klaus, *Agrarromantik und Großstadtfeindschaft*, Meisenheim am Glan, 1970

Biecker, Johannes & Buschmann, Walter (eds), *Bergbauarchitektur*, Bochum, 1986

Blackbourn, David, *Popularists and Patricians. Essays in modern German History*, London, 1987

Blackbourn, David & Eley, Geoff, *The Peculiarities of German History*, Oxford, 1984

Boberg, Jochen & Fichter, Tilmann & Gillen, Eckhard (eds.), *Exerzierfeld der Moderne. Industriekultur in Berlin im 19. Jahrhundert*, Munich, 1984

— *Die Metropole. Industriekultur in Berlin im 20. Jahrhundert*, Munich, 1985

Bodenhausen, Eberhard von, *Ein Leben für Kunst und Wirtschaft*, 1955

Böllhof, Florian & Bostram, Jörg & Hey, Bernd (eds.), *Industriearchitektur in Bielefeld. Geschichte und Fotografie*, Bielefeld, 1987

Bollerey, Franziska & Hartmann, Kristiana, 'Bruno Taut und die Tempel der Industrie', in *Archithese*, no. 4 (1980)

Bohle-Heintzenberg, Sabine, 'Architektur der Berliner Hoch- und Untergrundbahn', PhD thesis, Berlin University, 1978

Bonatz, Paul, *Leben und Bauen*, Stuttgart, 1950

Bonham, Gary, 'Bureaucratic Modernizers and traditional constraints; higher officials and the landed nobility in Wilhelmine Germany', PhD thesis, University of California, 1985

Bott, Gerhard (ed.), *Vom Morris zum Bauhaus*, Hanau, 1977

— *Leben und Arbeiten im Industriezeitalter*, Nuremberg, 1985

Boyd-Whyte, Iain, *Bruno Taut and the architecture of Activism*, Cambridge, 1982

Braun, Rudolf, 'Die Fabrik als Lebensform', in R. von Dülmen & N. Schindler (eds.), *Volkskultur. Zur Wiederentdeckung des vergessenen Alltags*, Frankfurt, 1984

Bremische Biographie 1912–1962, Bremen, 1962

Brepohl, Wilhelm, *Industrievolk im Wandel von der agraren zur industriellen Daseinsform dargestellt am Ruhrgebiet*, Tübingen, 1957

Brix, Michael & Steinhauser, Monika, 'Geschichte im Dienste der Baukunst. Zur historischen Architektur-Diskussion in Deutschland', in M. Brix & M. Steinhauser (eds.), *Geschichte allein ist zeitgemäß*, Lahn-Gießen, 1978

Broadbent, Geoffrey & Bent, R. & Jencks, Charles (eds.), *Signs, Symbols and Architecture*, Chichester, 1980

Brockmann, H.A.N., *The British Architect in History 1841–1940*, London, 1975

Buddensieg, Tilmann (ed.), *Die nützlichen Künste. Gestaltende Technik und bildende Kunst seit der industriellen Revolution*, Berlin, 1981

— *Villa Hügel. Das Wohnhaus Krupp in Essen*, Berlin, 1984

Buddensieg, Tilmann (with Rogge, Henning), *Industriekultur. Peter Behrens and the AEG 1907–1914*, Cambridge Mass., 1984

Bullen, R.J. & Pogge von Strandmann, H. & Polonsky, A. (eds.), *Ideas into politics. Aspects of European History*, London, 1984

Bullock, Nicholas & Read, James, *The movement for Housing Reform in Germany and France 1840–1914*, Cambridge, 1985

Burckhardt, Lucius (ed.), *The Werkbund. Studies in the History and Ideology of the Deutscher Werkbund*, London, 1986

Buschmann, Walter (ed.), *Eisen und Stahl*, Essen, 1989

Campbell, Joan, *The German Werkbund; the politics of reform in the applied arts*, Princeton, 1978

— *Joy in Work, German Work. The National Debate 1800–1945*, Princeton, 1989

Clark, Vincent, 'A Social History of German architects', PhD thesis,

University of California, 1983

Collins, George & Christine, *Camillo Sitte and the birth of modern city planning*, New York, 1965

Conrads, Ulrich (ed.), *Programme und Manifeste zur Architektur des 20. Jahrhunderts*, 1964

Continental, *Continental. Ein Jahrhundert Fortschritt und Leistung 1871– 1971*, Hanover, 1971

Conze, Werner, 'Friedrich Naumann. Grundlagen und Ansatz seiner Politik in der nationalsozialen Zeit', in W. Hubatsch (ed.), *Schicksalswege deutscher Vergangenheit. Festschrift für S. Kaehler*, Düsseldorf, 1950

Conze, Werner (ed.), *Arbeiter im Industrialisierungsprozess*, Stuttgart, 1979

Conze, Werner & Kocka, Jürgen (eds.), *Bildungsbürgertum im 19. Jahrhundert*, Stuttgart, 1985

Cremers, Paul, *Peter Behrens. Sein Werk von 1909 bis zur Gegenwart*, Essen, 1928

Crew, David, *Town in the Ruhr; A social history of Bochum*, New York, 1979

— 'Definitions of Modernity: social mobility in a German town, 1880– 1901', in *Journal of Social History*, vol. 1 (1973)

Croon, Helmut & Hofmann, Wolfgang & Unruh, Georg C. von (eds.), *Kommunale Selbstverwaltung im Zeitalter der Industrialisierung*, Stuttgart, Berlin, Cologne, Mainz, 1971

Dahrendorf, Ralf, *Industrie- und Betriebssoziologie*, Berlin, 1956

— *Society and Democracy in Germany*, New York, 1969

Dellheim, Charles, 'The creation of a company culture. Cadbury's 1861– 1931', in *American Historical Review*, vol. 92 (1987)

Diederichs, Eugen, *Leben und Werk. Ausgewählte Briefe und Aufzeichnungen*, Jena, 1936

Dillschneider, Karl, *Das Delmenhorster Rathaus*, Delmenhorster Schriften no. 5, 1972

— *Denkmalwerte Bauten in Delmenhorst*, Delmenhorster Schriften no. 8, 1977

Drebusch, Günter, *Industriearchitektur*, Munich, 1976

Drury, Jolyon, *Factories. Planning, Design and Modernisation*, London, 1981

Düding, Dieter, *Der Nationalsoziale Verein 1896–1903. Der gescheiterte Versuch einer politischen Synthese von Nationalismus, Sozialismus und Liberalismus*, Munich, 1972

Düwell, Kurt & Köllmann, Wolfgang, *Rheinland-Westfalen im Industriezeitalter*, Wuppertal, 1984

Eckstein, Hans, *50 Jahre Deutscher Werkbund*, Frankfurt, 1958

Eley, Geoff, *Reshaping the German Right*, New Haven & London, 1980

— *From Unification to Nazism. Reinterpreting the German past*, London, 1986

— 'Putting German liberalism into context: Liberalism, Europe, and the bourgeoisie, 1840–1918', CSST Working Papers, University of Michigan, Ann Arbor, 1990

Elm, Ludwig, *Zwischen Fortschritt und Reaktion. Geschichte der Parteien der liberalen Bourgeoisie in Deutschland 1893–1918*, Berlin, 1968

Engel, Frauke, 'Zwei frühe Bauten Karl Siebrechts für die Keksfabrik Bahlsen', M.A. thesis, Göttingen University, 1987

Evans, Richard J., *Death in Hamburg. Society and Politics in the Cholera Years*, Oxford, 1987

— *Rethinking German History. Nineteenth Century Germany and the Origins of the Third Reich*, London, 1987

Evans, Richard J. (ed.), *Society and Politics in Wilhelmine Germany*, London, 1978

— *The German Working Class 1888–1933*, London, 1982

Feldenkirchen, Wilfried, *Die Eisen und Stahlindustrie des Ruhrgebiets 1879–1914*, Wiesbaden, 1982

Feldman, Gerald D., 'The Collapse of the Steel Works Association 1912–19. A case study in the operation of German Collectivist Capitalism', in H.-U. Wehler (ed.), *Sozialgeschichte Heute. Festschrift für H. Rosenberg*, Göttingen, 1974

— 'The large firm in the German industrial system. The MAN 1900–25', in D. Stegmann, B.-J. Wendt, P.-C. Witt (eds.), *Industrielle Gesellschaft und politisches System. Festschrift für F. Fisher*, Bonn, 1978

Fisher, Wolfram, *Wirtschaft und Gesellschaft im Zeitalter der Industrialisierung*, Göttingen, 1972

Fletcher, Roger, *Revisionism and Empire. Socialist Imperialism in Germany 1897–1914*, London, 1984

Flohr, Bernd, *Arbeiter nach Maß. Die Disziplinierung der Fabrikarbeiterschaft während der Industrialisierung Deutschlands im Spiegel von Arbeitsordnungen*, New York, 1981

Flora, P., *Modernisierungsforschung. Zur empirischen Analyse der gesellschaftlichen Entwicklung*, Opladen, 1974

Föhl, Axel, *Technische Denkmale im Rheinland*, Landeskonservator Rheinland, Arbeitsheft no. 20, Cologne, 1976

— *Hessen. Denkmäler der Industrie und Technik*, Berlin, 1986

Föhl, Axel & Hamm, Manfred, *Sterbende Zechen*, Berlin, 1983

— *Bahnhöfe*, Berlin, 1984

— *Industriegeschichte des Wassers*, Düsseldorf, 1987

— *Industriegeschichte des Textils*, Düsseldorf, 1988

— *Industriegeschichte des Eisens*, Düsseldorf, 1989

— *Industriegeschichte des Elektrizität*, Düsseldorf, 1989

Fox, Alan, 'The politics of the workplace', in *Architectural Review*, Oct. 1979

Frampton, Kenneth, *Modern Architecture. A Critical History*, London, 1985

Friemert, Chup, 'Der Deutsche Werkbund als Agentur der Warenästhetik in der Aufstiegsphase des deutschen Imperialismus', in W. Haug (ed.), *Warenästhetik; Beiträge zur Diskussion*, Frankfurt, 1975

Friedrichs, Hans, 'Die bauliche Gestaltung der deutschen Eisenhütten-anlagen seit Beginn des 19. Jahrhunderts', in *Stahl und Eisen*, vol. 80 (1960)

Führ, Eduard, *Worin noch niemand war; Heimat. Eine Auseinandersetzung mit einem strapazierten Begriff*, Wiesbaden & Berlin, 1985

Funk, Anna-Christa, *Karl-Ernst Osthaus gegen Hermann Muthesius. Der Werkbund-Streit 1914 im Spiegel der im Karl Ernst Osthaus Archiv erhaltenen Briefe*, Hagen, 1978

Gall, Lothar, *Liberalismus*, Cologne, 1976

Gebhardt, Gerhard, *Wegweiser durch die westdeutschen Industrieviere*, Essen, 1961

— *Ruhrbergbau. Geschichte, Aufbau und Verflechtung seiner Gesellschaften und Organisationen*, Essen, 1957

Giedion, Siegfried, *Mechanization takes command; a contribution to anonymous history*, Oxford, 1948

— *Walter Gropius. Work and Teamwork*, New York, 1954

— *Space, Time and Architecture*, 8th ed., Cambridge Mass., 1967

Glaser, Hermann, *Maschinenwelt und Alltagsleben. Industriekultur in Deutschland vom Biedermeier bis zur Weimarer Republik*, Munich, 1981

Glaser, Hermann & Ruppert, W. & Neudecker, N., *Industriekultur-Nürnberg. Eine deutsche Stadt im Maschinenzeitalter*, Munich, 1980

Golücke, Dieter (ed.), *Bernhard Hoetger*, Worpswede, 1984

Grebing, Helga, *The History of the German Labour Movement*, London, 1969

Groh, Dieter, 'Intensification of work and industrial conflict in Germany 1896–1914', in *Politics and Society*, vol.8 (1978)

Grote, Ludwig (ed.), *Die deutsche Stadt im 19. Jahrhundert*, Munich, 1974

Grube, Oswald, *Industrial buildings and factories*, London, 1971

Grubert, Beate, 'Hermann Bahlsen und das Projekt der TET-Stadt', unpublished manuscript, Hanover, 1988

Grundig, Edgar, 'Geschichte der Stadt Delmenhorst', unpublished manuscript, Delmenhorst, 1960

Gubler, Hans Martin, 'Industriearchäologie', in *Archithese*, no. 5 (1980)

Günter, Roland, 'Zu einer Geschichte der technischen Architektur im Rheinland', in *Die Kunstgeschichte und Denkmalpflege des*

Rheinlandes, Beiheft no. 16, Düsseldorf, 1970
— 'Krupp in Essen', in M. Warnke (ed.), *Das Kunstwerk zwischen Wissenschaft un Weltanschauung*, Gütersloh, 1970
— *Die Denkmale des Rheinlandes Band 22 – Oberhausen*, Düsseldorf, 1975
Haase, Egon, 'Die Ideologiefunktion des ästhetischen Produkt- und Umweltgestaltung, dargestellt an der Arbeit und Wirkung des Deutschen Werkbundes', PhD thesis, East Berlin, Humboldt University, 1970
Haber, Samuel, *Efficiency and uplift. Scientific management in the progressive era, 1890–1920*, Chicago, 1964
Hamel, Iris, *Völkischer Verband und nationale Gewerkschaft. Der Deutschnationale Handlungsgehilfen-Verband 1893–1933*, Frankfurt, 1967
Hamm, Manfred, *Berlin. Denkmäler einer Industrielandschaft*, Berlin, 1978
Hartmann, G. von & Fischer, Wend (eds.), *Zwischen Kunst und Industrie: Der Deutsche Werkbund*, Munich, 1975
Hartmann, Kristiana, *Die deutsche Gartenstadtbewegung*, Munich, 1976
Harvie, Martin (ed.), *Industrialisation and culture 1830–1914*, London, 1970
Heckart, Beverly, *From Bassermann to Bebel. The Grand Bloc's quest for reform in the Kaiserreich 1900–1914*, Yale, 1974
Helfenstein, Heinrich, 'Industriebauten: Geräte und Fetische', in *Archithese*, no. 5 (1980)
Henning, Friedrich-Wilhelm, *Die Industralisierung in Deutschland 1800–1914*, Paderborn, 1984
Henning, Hansjoachim, *Das westdeutsche Bürgertum in der Epoch der Hochindustrialisierung 1880–1914*, Wiesbaden, 1972
— 'Soziale Verflechtungen der Unternehmer in Westfalen 1860–1914', in *Tradition*, vol. 23 (1978)
Hermand, Jost & Hamann, Richard, *Stilkunst um 1900*, East Berlin, 1967
Hermann, Wilhelm & Gertrude, *Die alten Zechen an der Ruhr*, Königstein, 1981
Herzogenrath, Wulf & Teuber, Dirk & Thiekötter, Angelika (eds.), *Der westdeutsche Impuls 1900–1914. Die DWB Ausstellung Cöln 1914*, Cologne, 1984
Heskett, John, *Industrial Design*, London, 1980
— *Design in Germany 1870–1918*, London, 1986
Heuss, Theodor, *Friedrich Naumann. Der Mann, Das Werk, Die Zeit*, Berlin, 1937
— *Robert Bosch: Leben und Leistung*, Stuttgart, 1946
— *Hans Poelzig. Das Lebensbild eines deutschen Baumeisters. Bauten*

und Entwürfe, Tübingen, 1948
— *Was ist Qualität? Zur Geschichte und zur Aufgabe des Deutschen Werkbundes*, Tübingen & Stuttgart, 1951
— *Erinnerungen 1905–1933*, Tübingen, 1963
— *Lust der Augen. Stilles Gespräch mit beredtem Bildwerk*, Tübingen, 1960
— *Bilder meines Lebens*, Tübingen, 1964
Hesse-Frielinghaus, Herta (ed.), *Karl Ernst Osthaus. Leben und Werk*, Recklinghausen, 1971
— *Briefwechsel Le Corbusier-Karl Ernst Osthaus*, Hagen, 1977
— *Hagener Architektur 1900–1914*, Recklinghausen, 1987
Hildebrand, Grant, *Designing for industry: the architecture of Albert Kahn*, Cambridge Mass., 1974
Hillebrecht, Rudolf & Venzmer, Wolfgang (eds.), *Hermann Bahlsen*, Hanover, 1969
Hirsch, Felix, *Stresemann. Ein Lebensbild*, Göttingen, 1978
Hoesch, *80 Jahre Eisen und Stahlwerke Hoesch*, Dortmund, 1951
— *100 Jahre Hoesch 1872–1972*, Dortmund, 1972
Hofmann, Wolfgang, *Zwischen Rathaus und Reichskanzlei. Die Oberbürgermeister in der Kommunal- und Staatspolitik des Deutschen Reichs 1890–1933*, Stuttgart, 1974
Hoffmann, Ot (ed.), *Der Deutsche Werkbund – 1907, 1947, 1987*, Frankfurt, 1987
Holme, C.G., *Industrial Architecture*, London, 1935
Homburg, Heidrun, 'Anfänge des Taylorsystems in Deutschland vor dem ersten Weltkrieg', in *Geschichte und Gesellschaft*, vol. 4 (1978)
Hounshell, David, *From the American System to Mass Production 1880–1932. The development of manufacturing technology in the United States*, Baltimore & London, 1984
Hubrich, Hans-Joachim, *Hermann Muthesius. Die Schriften zu Architektur, Kunstgewerbe, Industrie in der 'Neuen Bewegung'*, Berlin, 1981
Hudson, Kenneth, *Industrial Archaeology. An Introduction*, Newton Abbott, 1963
— *Exploring our industrial past*, London, 1975
— *World Industrial Archaeology*, Cambridge, 1979
Hunt, James C., *The People's Party in Württemberg and Southern Germany*, Stuttgart, 1975
Hüter, Karl-Heinz, *Architektur in Berlin*, Dresden, 1987
Isaacs, Reginald, *Walter Gropius. Der Mensch und sein Werk*, Berlin, 1983
Ivers, Holger, 'Erich Koch-Weser's politische Tätigkeit als Bürgermeister von Delmenhorst', unpublished manuscript, Oldenburg, 1985
Jäckh, Ernst, *Der goldene Pflug. Lebensernte eines Weltbürgers*, Stuttgart, 1954

Jaeger, Hans, *Unternehmer in der deutschen Politik 1890–1918*, Bonn, 1967

Jarausch, Konrad & Jones, Larry Eugene (eds.), *In Search of Liberal Germany*, New York, 1990

⌖ Jencks, Charles, *Modern movements in architecture*, Harmondsworth, 1973

Joll, James, *Three intellectuals in politics; Blum, Rathenau and Marinetti*, London, 1960

Jones, Edgar, *Industrial Architecture in Britain 1750–1939*, London, 1985

Joyce, Patrick, *Work, Society and Politics. The culture of the factory in later Victorian England*, Brighton, 1980

Junghanns, Kurt, *Der Deutsche Werkbund. Das erste Jahrzehnt*, East Berlin, 1982

— *Bruno Taut 1880–1938*, East Berlin, 1970

Kadatz, Hans-Joachim, *Peter Behrens. Architekt – Maler – Grafiker und Formgestalter*, Leipzig, 1977

Kaelble, Hartmut, *Industrielle Interessenpolitik in der wilhelminischen Gesellschaft: Centralverband Deutscher Industrieller 1895–1914*, Berlin, 1967

Kaelble, Hartmut (ed.), *Probleme der Modernisierung in Deutschland*, Opladen, 1978

Kallen, Peter, *Unter dem Banner der Sachlichkeit. Studien zum Verhältnis von Kunst und Industrie am Beginn des 20. Jahrhunderts*, Cologne, 1987

Kern, Stephen, *The Culture of Time and Space*, London, 1983

Kessler, Hansi (ed.), *Hermann Bahlsen*, Hanover, 1969

King, Anthony (ed.), *Buildings and Society. Essays on the Social Development of the Built Environment*, London, 1980

Klingender, Francis, *Art and the Industrial Revolution*, London, 1947

Knauss, Hans, *Zweckbau-Architektur zwischen Repräsentation und Nutzen. Konzeption und Ästhetik ausgewählter Zweckbauten in der Zeit von ca. 1850–1930 in Bayern*, Munich, 1983

Knobel, Lance, *The Faber guide to twentieth century architecture in Britain and northern Europe*, London, 1985

Koch, Heinrich, *75 Jahre Mannesmann, Geschichte einer Erfindung und eines Unternehmen*, Düsseldorf, 1965

Kocka, Jürgen, *Unternehmensverwaltung und Angestelltenschaft am Beispiel Siemens 1847–1914. Zum Verhältnis von Kapitalismus und Burokratie in der deutschen Industrialisierung*, Stuttgart, 1969

— *Unternehmer in der deutschen Industrialisierung*, Göttingen, 1975

Kocka, Jürgen (ed.), *Bürger und Bürgerlichkeit im 19. Jahrhundert*, Göttingen, 1987

— *Bürgertum im 19. Jahrhundert. Deutschland im europäischen Vergleich*,

3 vols., Göttingen, 1988

Kofler, Leo, *Der asketische Eros, Industriekultur und Ideologie*, Vienna, 1967

Köln. Bauliche Entwicklung 1888–1927, Berlin, 1927

Korzus, B. (ed.), *Fabrik im Ornament. Ansichten auf Firmenbriefköpfen des 19. Jahrhunderts*, Münster, 1980

Koschwitz, Carl, 'Die Hochbauten auf den Steinkohlenzechen des Ruhrgebiets', PhD thesis, Berlin TH, 1928

Krabbe, Wolfgang, *Studien zur deutschen Lebensreform-Bewegung. Ein Beitrag zur Sozialgeschichte der Jahrhundertwende*, Münster, 1972

Kranz–Michaelis, Charlotte, *Rathäuser im deutschen Kaiserreich 1871– 1918*, Munich, 1976

Kratzsch, Gerhard, *Kunstwart und Dürerbund: Ein Beitrag zur Geschichte der Gebildeten im Zeitalter des Imperialismus*, Göttingen, 1969

Landes, David, *The Unbound Prometheus*, Cambridge, 1969

Lane, Barbara Miller, *Architecture and politics in Germany, 1918–1945*, Cambridge Mass., 1968

Langewiesche, Dieter, *Liberalismus in Deutschland*, Frankfurt, 1988

Latham, Ian, *Joseph Maria Olbrich*, London, 1980

Lawrence, D.H., *Women in Love*, Harmondsworth 1986 (first publ. 1921)

Lebovics, H., '"Agrarians" versus "Industrializers". Social conservative resistance to industrialism and capitalism in late nineteenth century Germany', in *International Review of Social History*, vol.12 (1967)

Lees, Andrew, 'Debates about the big city in Germany, 1890–1914', in *Societas*, 1975

— 'Critics of urban society in Germany 1854–1914', in *Journal of the History of Ideas*, vol.40 (1979)

Lidtke, Vernon, *The alternative culture*, Oxford, 1985

Lindern, Georg von, *Kleine Chronik der Stadt Delmenhorst*, Oldenburg, 1971

Loewe, *Ludw. Loewe & Co. AG Berlin, 1869–1929*, Berlin, 1930

Lübbing, Hermann, *Delmenhorsts Aufstieg zur Industriestadt*, Delmenhorster Schriften no. 1, Delmenhorst, 1971

Lucas, Adolf, *Erinnerungen aus meinem Leben*, Opladen, 1959

Mai, Ekkehard & Waetzold, Stephan (eds.), *Kunstverwaltung, Bau- und Denkmalpolitik im Kaiserreich*, Berlin, 1980

Mai, Ekkehard & Pohl, Hans & Waetzold, Stephan (eds.), *Kunstpolitik und Kunstförderung im Kaiserreich*, Berlin, 1981

Mai, Ekkehard & Paul, Jürgen & Waetzold, Stephan (eds.), *Das Rathaus im Kaiserreich. Kunstpolitische Aspekte einer Bauaufgabe des 19. Jahrhunderts*, Berlin, 1982

Maier, Charles, 'Between Taylorism and technocracy: European ideologies and the vision of industrial productivity in the 1920s', in *Journal of*

Contemporary History, vol. 5 (1970)
— 'The factory as society. Ideologies of industrial management', in R. Bullen, H. Pogge von Strandmann, A. Polonsky (eds.), Ideas into Politics. Aspects of European History, London, 1984

Maschke, Erich, Es entsteht ein Konzern: Paul Reusch und die GHH, Tübingen, 1969

Matschoss, Conrad & Schlesinger, Georg, Die Geschichte der Ludw. Loewe & Co. AG Berlin: 60 Jahre Edelarbeit, 1869–1929, Berlin, 1930

Matschoss, Conrad, Robert Bosch und sein Werk, 1931

Matz, Reinhard, Industriefotografie aus Firmenarchiven des Ruhrgebiets, Essen, 1987

McLeod, Mary, 'Architecture or Revolution: Taylorism, Technocracy, and Social Change', in Art Journal, Summer 1983

Mehrtens, Jürgen (ed.), Alt Delmenhorst, Delmenhorst, 1981

Meyer, Henry Cord, Mitteleuropa in thought and action, 1815–1945, The Hague, 1955

Mielke, Siegfried, Der Hansa-Bund für Gewerbe, Handel und Industrie. Der gescheiterte Versuch einer antifeudalen Sammlungspolitik, Göttingen, 1976

Mommsen, Wilhelm (ed.), Deutsche Parteiprogramme, Munich, 1960

Mulert, Jürgen, 'Erfolgsbeteiligung und Vermögensbildung der Arbeitnehmer bei der Firma Robert Bosch zwischen 1886 und 1945', in Tradition, vo. 30 (1985)

Müller, Johann Heinrich (ed.), Der westdeutsche Impuls 1900–1914. Die Folkwang-Idee des Karl Ernst Osthaus, Hagen, 1984

Müller, Sebastian, Kunst und Industrie. Ideologie und Organisation des Funktionalismus in der Architektur, Munich, 1974

Moses, John, Trade Unionism in Germany from Bismarck to Hitler 1869–1933, London, 1982

Murken, Axel Hinrich, Die neuen Bade- und Kuranlagen in Bad Nauheim zu Beginn des 20. Jahrhunderts, Göttingen, 1987

Muthesius, Stefan, Das englische Vorbild, Munich, 1974

— 'The origins of the German conservation movement', in R. Kain (ed.), Planning for Conservation, London, 1981

Naumann, Friedrich, Werke, 6 vols., Cologne, 1964–69

Nelson, Daniel, Managers and Workers. Origins of the new factory system in the United States 1880–1920, Wisconsin, 1975

Nerdinger, Winfried, 'Theodor Fischer', in Architectural Review, November 1986

Niethammer, Lutz, Umständliche Erläuterung der seelischen Störung eines Communalbaumeisters in Preußens größtem Industriedorf, oder, die Unfähigkeit zur Stadtentwicklung, Frankfurt, 1979

— Die Menschen machen ihre Geschichte nicht aus freien Stücken, aber

Bibliography

sie machen sie selbst. Einladung zu einer Geschichte des Volkes in NRW, Berlin & Bonn, 1984

Nipperdey, Thomas, 'Interessenverbände und Parteien in Deutschland vor dem ersten Weltkrieg', in *Politische Vierteljahresschrift,* vol. 1 (1960–61)

— *Gesellschaft – Kultur – Theorie,* Göttingen, 1976

— *Wie modern war das Kaiserreich? Das Beispiel der Schule,* Opladen, 1986

— *Wie das Bürgertum die Moderne fand,* Berlin, 1988

Nussbaum, Helga, *Unternehmer gegen Monopole. Über Struktur und Aktionen anti-monopolistischer bürgerlicher Gruppen zu Beginn des 20. Jahrhunderts,* East Berlin, 1966

Nye, David, *Image Worlds. Corporate Identities at General Electric, 1890–1930,* Cambridge Mass., 1985

Ogden, Christine, *Buildings for Industry,* Reading, 1979

Opitz, Reinhard, *Der deutsche Sozialliberalismus, 1917–33,* Cologne, 1973

Otto, Christian, 'Modern Environment and Historical Continuity: The Heimatschutz Discourse in Germany', in *Art Journal,* Summer 1983

Paret, Peter, *The Berlin Secession: modernism and its enemies in Imperial Germany,* Cambridge Mass., 1980

Paul, Jacques, 'German neo-classicism and the modern movement', in *Architectural Review,* Sept. 1972

Paulinyi, Akos, *Industriearchaeologie. Neue Aspekte der Wirtschafts- und Technikgeschichte,* Dortmund, 1975

Pehnt, Wolfgang, *Expressionist architecture,* London, 1973

Peters, Lon LeRoy, 'Co-operative competition in German coal and steel 1893–1914', PhD thesis, Yale University, 1981

Petsch, Joachim, *Architektur und Gesellschaft. Zur Geschichte der deutschen Architektur im 19. und 20. Jahrhundert,* Cologne, 1977

Pevsner, Nikolaus, *Pioneers of Modern Design,* New York, 1949

— *The Sources of Modern Architecture and Design,* London, 1968

Piccinato, Giorgio, *Städtebau in Deutschland 1871–1914,* Brunswick, 1983

Plagemann, Volker (ed.), *Industriekultur in Hamburg,* Munich, 1984

Pollak, Günter, 'Die ideologische, wirtschaftliche, und gesellschaftspolitische Funktion des Deutschen Werkbundes 1907–1919', PhD thesis, Weimar Hochschule für Architektur, 1971

Pommer, Richard, 'The flat roof: a modernist controversy in Germany', in *Art Journal,* Summer 1983

Posener, Julius, 'Poelzig', in *Architectural Review,* June 1963

— *Anfänge des Funktionalismus,* Berlin, 1964

— *From Schinkel to the Bauhaus. Five lectures on the growth of modern*

German architecture, London, 1972
— *Hans Poelzig. Gesammelte Schriften und Werke*, Berlin, 1970
— *Berlin. Auf dem Wege zu einer neuen Architektur. Das Zeitalter Wilhelms II*, Munich, 1979
Rathenau, Walther, *Walther Rathenau, industrialist, banker, intellectual and politician. Notes and diaries 1907–1922*, H. Pogge v. Strandmann (ed.), Oxford, 1985
Rauschnabel, Kurt, *Stadtgestalt durch Staatsgewalt? Das Hamburger Baupflegegesetz von 1912*, Hamburg, 1984
Rosner, Rolf, 'Fritz Schumacher's Hamburg', in *Architectural Review*, March 1980
Reulecke, Jürgen (ed.), *Die deutsche Stadt im Industriezeitalter*, Wuppertal, 1978
— *Arbeiterbewegung an Rhein und Ruhr*, Wuppertal, 1974
Reulecke, Jürgen & Weber, Wolfgang (eds.), *Fabrik, Familie, Feierabend. Beiträge zur Geschichte des Alltags im Industriezeitalter*, Wuppertal, 1978
Ribbe, Wolfgang & Schäche, Wolfgang (eds.), *Die Siemensstadt, Geschichte und Architektur eines Industriestandortes*, Berlin, 1985
Richards, J.M., *The functional tradition in early industrial buildings*, London, 1958
Ritter, Gerhard A. & Niehuss, M., *Wahlgeschichtliches Arbeitsbuch*, Munich, 1980
Rödel, Volker, *Fabrikarchitektur in Frankfurt am Main 1774–1924*, Frankfurt, 1984
Rogge, Henning, *Fabrikwelt um die Jahrhundertwende am Beispiel der AEG Maschinenfabrik in Berlin-Wedding*, Cologne, 1983
Rohe, Karl, *Vom Revier zum Ruhrgebiet*, Essen, 1986
Roselius, Hildegard, *Ludwig Roselius und sein kulturelles Werk*, Bremen, 1954
Rossbacher, Karlheinz, *Heimatkunstbewegung und Heimatsroman*, Stuttgart, 1975
Ruckdeschel, Wilhelm & Luther, Klaus, *Technische Denkmale in Augsburg. Eine Führung durch die Stadt*, Augsburg, 1984
Ruppert, Wolfgang, *Die Fabrik. Geschichte von Arbeit und Industrialisierung in Deutschland*, Munich, 1983
Rüschemeyer, Dietrich, 'Modernisierung und die Gebildeten im kaiserlichen Deutschland', in Peter C. Ludz (ed.), *Soziologie und Sozialgeschichte*, Opladen, 1972
Saebens, Hans (ed.), *Delmenhorst. Werden einer Wirtschaftsstadt*, Delmenhorst, 1953
Saul, Klaus, *Staat, Industrie, Arbeiterbewegung im Kaiserreich. Zur Innen- und Sozialpolitik des wilhelminischen Deutschlands, 1903–1914*,

Düsseldorf, 1974

Scheffler, Karl, *Die fetten und die mageren Jahre. Ein Arbeits- und Lebensbericht*, Leipzig & Munich, 1946

Schiefler, Gustav, *Eine Hamburgische Kulturgeschichte 1890–1920*, Hamburg, 1985

Schirren, Matthias (ed.), *Hans Poelzig. Die Pläne und Zeichnungen aus dem ehemaligen Verkehrs- und Baumuseum in Berlin*, Berlin, 1989

Schivelbusch, Wolfgang, *The Railway Journey: The industrialisation of time and space in the nineteenth century*, Leamington Spa, 1986

Schleper, Thomas, 'Kunstwissenschaft und Fabrikbau. Über den Beitrag der "visuellen Sozialgeschichte" zur Industriekulturforschung', PhD thesis, Osnabrück University, 1987

Schmidt, Gustav, 'Parlamentarisierung oder "Präventive Konterrevolution"? Die deutsche Innenpolitik im Spannungsfeld konservativer Sammlungsbewegungen und latenter Reformbestrebungen (1907–1914)', in G.A. Ritter (ed.), *Gesellschaft, Parlament und Regierung*, Düsseldorf, 1974

Schmitt, Otto, 'Fabrikbau' in *Reallexikon zur deutschen Kunstgeschichte*, vol. 6, Munich, 1973

Schomerus, Heilwig, *Die Arbeiter der Maschinenfabrik Esslingen; Forschungen zur Lage der Arbeiterschaft im 19. Jahrhundert*, Stuttgart, 1977

Schorske, Carl, *Fin-de-Siecle Vienna*, New York, 1981

Schumacher, Fritz, *Stufen des Lebens. Erinnerungen eines Baumeisters*, Stuttgart & Berlin, 1935

— *Selbstgespräche. Erinnerungen und Betrachtungen*, Hamburg, 1949

Schumacher, Martin, 'Zweckbau und Industrieschloss. Fabrikbauten der rheinisch-westfälischen Textilindustrie vor der Gründungszeit', in *Tradition*, vol. 15 (1970)

Schwarz, Felix & Gloor, Frank (ed.), *Die Form. Stimme des Deutschen Werkbundes 1925–1934*, Gütersloh, 1969

Selle, Gert, *Design-Geschichte in Deutschland. Produktkultur als Entwurf und Erfahrung*, Cologne, 1987

Service, Alastair, *Edwardian Architecture*, London, 1977

Shanahan, W.O., 'Friedrich Naumann. A mirror of Wilhelmine Germany', in *Review of Politics*, vol. 13 (1951)

Sheehan, James, *The career of Lujo Brentano. A study of Liberalism and social reform in Imperial Germany*, Chicago & London, 1966

— *German Liberalism in the nineteenth century*, Chicago & London, 1978

— 'Deutscher Liberalismus im postliberalen Zeitalter 1890–1914', in *Geschichte und Gesellschaft*, vol. 4 (1978)

Sieferle, Rolf Peter, *Fortschrittsfeinde?*, Munich, 1984

Siegrist, Hannes (ed.), *Bürgerliche Berufe. Beiträge zur Sozialgeschichte* der Professionen, freien Berufe und Akademiker im internationalen Vergleich, Göttingen, 1988

Siepmann, Eckhard (ed.), Kunst und Alltag um 1900, Lahn-Gießen, 1978

Siepmann, Eckhard & Thiekötter, Angelika (eds.), Packeis und Preßglas. Von der Kunstgewerbebewegung zum Deutschen Werkbund, Lahn-Gießen, 1987

Simon, Klaus, Die württembergischen Demokraten. Ihre Stellung und Arbeit im Parteien- und Verfassungssystem in Württemberg und im Deutschen Reich, 1890–1920, Stuttgart, 1969

Slotta, Rainer, Einführung in die Industriearchaeologie, Munich, 1982

— Technische Denkmäler in der BRD, (5 vols.), Bochum, 1975–

Spencer, Elaine Glovka, 'Businessmen, bureaucrats and social control in the Ruhr, 1896–1914', in H.-U. Wehler (ed.), Sozialgeschichte Heute. Festschrift für H. Rosenberg, Göttingen, 1974

— 'Ruhr coal industrialists before 1914', in Journal of Modern History, vol. 48 (1976)

Spille, Rolf, Delmenhorst in alten Ansichten, Zaltbommel (NL), 1987

Staisch, Erich, Eisenbahnen rollen durch das "Tor zur Welt", Hamburg, 1956

— Hauptbahnhof Hamburg, Hamburg, 1981

Stark, Gary, Entrepreneurs of Ideology. Neoconservative Publishers in Germany, 1890–1933, Chapel Hill, 1981

Stegmann, Dirk, Die Erben Bismarcks, Cologne, 1970

— 'Linksliberale Bankiers, Kaufleute und Industrielle 1890–1900', in Tradition, vol. 21 (1976)

Stern, Fritz, The Politics of Cultural Despair. A Study in the Rise of the Germanic Ideology, Berkeley, 1963

Stolle, Uta, Arbeiterpolitik im Betrieb. Frauen und Männer, Reformisten und Radikale, Fach- und Massenarbeiter bei Bayer, BASF, Bosch und in Solingen 1900–1933, Frankfurt, 1980

Strandmann, Hartmut Pogge von, 'Widersprüche im Modernisierungsprozeß Deutschlands. Der Kampf der verarbeitenden Industrie gegen die Schwerindustrie', in D. Stegmann, B.-J. Wendt, P.-C. Witt (eds.), Industrielle Gesellschaft und politisches System, Bonn, 1978

— Unternehmenspolitik und Unternehmensführung. Der Dialog zwischen Aufsichtsrat und Vorstand bei Mannesmann, 1900–1919, Düsseldorf, 1978

— 'Rathenau, die Gebrüder Mannesmann und die Vorgeschichte der zweiten Marokkokrise', in I. Geiss & B.-J. Wendt (eds.), Deutschland in der Weltpolitik des 19. und 20. Jahrhunderts, Düsseldorf, 1973

Sturm, Hermann, Fabrikarchitektur, Villa, Arbeitersiedlung, Munich, 1977

Suhrbier, Hartwig, 'Der Putt als Kunst. Industriebauten unter Denkmalschutz', unpublished manuscript, 1971

Bibliography

— 'Maschinenhalle und Mietskaserne. Industriekultur und Arbeitsalltag', unpublished manuscript, 1981

— '15 Jahre Denkmalschutz für Bauten der Industrie', unpublished manuscript, 1985

Tafuri, Manfredo, *Architecture and Utopia: Design and Capitalist Development*, Cambridge Mass., 1976

Tann, Jennifer, *The Development of the Factory*, London, 1970

Tenfelde, Klaus, 'Schwierigkeiten mit dem Alltag', in *Geschichte und Gesellschaft*, vol. 10 (1984)

Tenfelde, K. & Volkmann, H., *Streik. Zur Geschichte des Arbeitskampfes in Deutschland während der Industrialisierung*, Munich, 1981

Teuteberg, H.J., *Die Geschichte der industriellen Mitbestimmung in Deutschland*, Tübingen, 1961

Theiner, Peter, *Sozialer Liberalismus und deutsche Weltpolitik. Friedrich Naumann im wilhelminischen Deutschland*, Baden Baden, 1983

Theodor, Gertrud, *Friedrich Naumann oder der Prophet des Profits*, East Berlin, 1957

Thiersch, Heinz (ed.), *Wir fingen einfach an. Arbeiten und Aufsätze von Freunden und Schülern um Richard Riemerschmid zu dessen 85. Geburtstag*, Munich, 1953

Thompson, Alastair, 'Left Liberals in German State and Society', PhD thesis, London Birkbeck College, 1989

Tilly, Richard, 'The growth of large-scale enterprise in Germany since the middle of the nineteenth century', in H. Daems & H. van der Wee (eds.), *The Rise of Managerial Capitalism*, The Hague, 1974

Timm, Albrecht, *Technische Denkmäler im Blickfeld des Historikers*, Landeskonservator Rheinland Arbeitsheft no. 7, Cologne, 1973

Tipps, Dean, 'Modernization theory and the comparative study of societies: a critical perspective', in *Comparative Studies in Society and History*, vol. 15 (1973)

Trier, Eduard & Weyres, Willy, *Kunst des 19. Jahrhunderts im Rheinland*, (5 vols.), Düsseldorf, 1980

Treue, Wilhelm, *Die Feuer verlöschen nie. August Thyssen Hütte 1890–1926*, Düsseldorf, 1966

Ullmann, Hans-Peter, *Der Bund der Industriellen. Organisation, Einfluß und Politik klein- und mittelbetrieblicher Industrieller im Deutschen Kaiserreich 1895–1914*, Göttingen, 1976

Unruh, Georg Christoph von, *Der Landrat. Mittler zwischen Staatsverwaltung und kommunaler Selbstverwaltung*, Cologne, 1966

Väth-Hinz, Henriette, *Odol. Reklame-Kunst um 1900*, Lahn-Gießen, 1985

Volkov, Schulamit, *The rise of popular anti-modernism in Germany; the urban master artisans, 1873–1896*, Princeton, 1978

Vondung, Klaus (ed.), *Das wilhelminische Bildungsbürgertum; zur*

Sozialgeschichte seiner Ideen, Göttingen, 1976

Vorsteher, Dieter, *Borsig. Eisengießerei und Maschinenbauanstalt zu Berlin*, Berlin, 1983

Wangerin, Gerda & Weiss, Gerhard, *Heinrich Tessenow: Ein Baumeister 1876–1950*, Essen, 1976

Warnke, Martin (ed.), *Politische Architektur in Europa vom Mittelalter bis heute – Repräsentation und Gemeinschaft*, Cologne, 1984

Weber, Helmut, *Walter Gropius und das Faguswerk*, Munich, 1961

Weber, Wolfhard, 'Von der "Industriearchaeologie" über das "Industrielle Erbe" zur "Industriekultur". Überlegungen zum Thema einer handlungsorientierten Technikhistorie', in U.Troitsch & G. Wohlauf (eds.), *Technikgeschichte. Historische Beiträge und neuere Ansätze*, Frankfurt, 1980

Wegner, Konstanze, *Theodor Barth und die Freisinnige Vereinigung*, Tübingen, 1969

— 'Linksliberalismus im wilhelminischen Deutschland und in der Weimarer Republik', in *Geschichte und Gesellschaft*, vol. 4 (1978)

Wehler, Hans-Ulrich, *Das deutsche Kaiserreich, 1871–1918*, Göttingen, 1973

— *Modernisierungstheorie und Geschichte*, Göttingen, 1975

Westphal, Carl, *Fritz Höger, der niederdeutsche Backstein-Baumeister*, Wolfshagen, 1938

Wenger, Fritz, 'Wandlungen architektonischer Vorstellungen, dargestellt an Düsseldorfer Bauten des Gewerbes und der Wirtschaft aus dem ersten Jahrzehnt des 20. Jahrhunderts', PhD thesis, Hanover TH, 1967

White, Dan, *The Splintered Party. National Liberalism in Hessen and the Reich, 1867–1918*, Cambridge Mass., 1976

Whittock, Arnold, *Eric Mendelsohn*, London, 1956

Wilhelm, Karin, *Walter Gropius, Industriearchitekt*, Brunswick & Wiesbaden, 1983

Willett, John, *The New Sobriety. Art and politics in the Weimar period, 1917–1933*, London, 1978

Windsor, Alan, *Peter Behrens. Architect and designer*, London, 1981

Winter, John, *Industrial architecture. A survey of factory building*, London, 1970

INDEX

Index

Index

Index